GLOBALIZED AUTHORITARIANISM

GLOBALIZATION AND COMMUNITY

Susan E. Clarke, Series Editor
Dennis R. Judd, Founding Editor

(continued on page 325)

GLOBALIZED AUTHORITARIANISM

Megaprojects, Slums, and Class Relations in Urban Morocco

Koenraad Bogaert

GLOBALIZATION AND COMMUNITY, VOLUME 27

UNIVERSITY OF MINNESOTA PRESS

MINNEAPOLIS • LONDON

Portions of chapters 4, 5, and 6 were published in earlier forms as "The Problem of Slums: Shifting Methods of Neoliberal Urban Government in Morocco," *Development and Change* 42, no. 3 (2011): 709–31; "Cities without Slums in Morocco? New Modalities of Urban Government and the Bidonville as a Neoliberal Assemblage," in *Locating the Right to the City in the Global South*, edited by Tony Roshan Samara, Shenjing He, and Guo Chen (New York: Routledge, 2013), 41–59; and "New State Space Formation in Morocco: The Example of the Bouregreg Valley," *Urban Studies* 49, no. 2 (2012): 255–70.

Published by the University of Minnesota Press
111 Third Avenue South, Suite 290
Minneapolis, MN 55401-2520
http://www.upress.umn.edu

The University of Minnesota is an equal-opportunity educator and employer.

Names: Bogaert, Koenraad, author.
Title: Globalized authoritarianism : megaprojects, slums, and class relations in urban Morocco / Koenraad Bogaert.
Description: Minneapolis : University of Minnesota Press, 2018. |
Series: Globalization and community ; 27 |
Includes bibliographical references and index.
Identifiers: LCCN 2017042821 | ISBN 978-1-5179-0081-6 (pb) | ISBN 978-1-5179-0080-9 (hc)
Subjects: LCSH: Morocco–Economic conditions–21st century. |
Public works–Morocco. | Slums–Morocco. | Social classes–Morocco. |
Authoritarianism–Morocco. | BISAC: SOCIAL SCIENCE / Sociology / Urban. |
POLITICAL SCIENCE / Globalization.
Classification: LCC HC810 .B64 2018 | DDC 338.964–dc23
LC record available at https://lccn.loc.gov/2017042821

TO ARIANA, SIMON, AND BRUNO

CONTENTS

ABBREVIATIONS

AAVB Agence pour l'Aménagement de la Vallée du Bouregreg (Agency for the Development of the Bouregreg Valley, or the Bouregreg Agency)

ADS Agence de Développement Social (Social Development Agency)

AFD Agence Française de Développement (French Development Agency)

ANHI Agence Nationale pour l'Habitat Insalubre (National Agency for Degraded Housing)

AS *accompagnement social* (social accompaniment)

AUC Agence Urbaine de Casablanca (Urban Agency of Casablanca)

CAS *cellule d'accompagnement sociale* (social accompaniment team)

CDG Caisse de Dépôt et de Gestion (Deposit and Management Fund)

CDT Confédération Démocratique du Travaille (Democratic Workers' Confederation)

CERF Centre d'Etude, de Recherche et de Formation (Research, Formation and Study Center)

CGEM Confédération Générale des Entreprises du Maroc (General Confederation of Moroccan Enterprises)

DGCL Direction Générale des Communautés Locales (General Direction of the Local Communities)

EU	European Union
FDI	foreign direct investment
FMDT	Fonds Marocain de Développement Touristique (Moroccan Fund for Tourism Development)
FOGARIM	Fonds de garantie des prêts au logement en faveur des populations á revenus modestes et/ou non réguliers (Housing loan guarantee fund for moderate or non-regular income populations)
FSH	Fonds Solidarité de l'Habitat (Solidarity Fund for Housing)
GCC	Gulf Cooperation Council
GDP	gross domestic product
HC	*habitats clandestins* (clandestine housing)
IMF	International Monetary Fund
INDH	Initiative Nationale pour le Développement Humain (National Initiative for Human Development)
ISI	import-substituting industrialization
MATEUH	Ministère de l'Aménagement du Territoire, de l'Environnement, de l'Urbanisme et de l'Habitat (Ministry for National Planning, Environment, Urbanism and Housing)
MDG	Millennium Development Goals
MENA	Middle East and North Africa
MET	Ministère de l'Equipement et des Transports (Ministry of Infrastructure and Transport)
MHUAE	Ministère Délégué Chargé de l'Habitat, de l'Urbanisme et de l'Aménagement de l'Espace (Ministry of Housing, Urbanism and Spatial Planning)
MOS	*maîtrise d'ouvrage social* (social management)
MUHTE	Ministère de l'Urbanisme, de l'Habitat, du Tourisme et de l'Environnement (Ministry of Urbanism, Housing, Tourism and Environment)
NGO	nongovernmental organization
OBG	Oxford Business Group

OCP	Office Chérifien des Phosphates (Sharifian Office of Phosphates)
ONA	Omnium Nord Africain
PAG	Parti d'Aménagement Global (Global Development Plan)
PAS	Plan d'Aménagement Spécial (Special Development Plan)
PJD	Parti de la justice et du développement (Justice and Development Party)
PPP	public–private partnership
PPS	Parti du Progrès et du Socialisme (Party of Progress and Socialism)
SAP	structural adjustment program
SDAU	*schéma directeur d'aménagement urbain* (urban master plan)
SNI	Société Nationale d'Investissement (National Investment Company)
SPV	special purpose vehicle
STRS	Société du Tramway de Rabat-Salé (Rabat-Salé Tramway Company)
TMSA	Tanger Med Special Authority
UNFP	Union Nationale des Forces Populaires (National Union of Popular Forces)
USAID	United States Agency for International Development
USFP	Union Socialiste des Forces Populaires (Socialist Union of Popular Forces)
VAT	value-added tax
VSB	Villes Sans Bidonvilles (Cities Without Slums)
WTO-TRIPS	World Trade Organization Agreement on Trade-Related Aspects of Intellectual Property Rights

PREFACE AND
ACKNOWLEDGMENTS

BACK IN 2007, when I first arrived in Rabat, the plan was to study processes of democratization in both Egypt and Morocco. What's more, the case of Morocco was actually more of a second option, a comparative by-product of the real case I wanted to explore: Egypt.

However, parliamentary elections took place in Morocco in the first year of this research and my colleague Sami Zemni convinced me to go. I could postpone Egypt for a later date. "Rabat will be a soft landing compared to Cairo," he told me. The rest is history. In the concurrence of circumstances that followed, I actually never made it to Egypt.

During my first weeks in the field, it struck me that very few people went to vote, especially in the cities. Even those young campaigners I met during the days before the elections informed me later that they didn't vote: "It wouldn't change anything anyway." They were just campaigning for the money.

A lot was changing at that time, but it did not seem to have anything to do with the formal democratic process. The deepwater port of Tanger Med became operational that year. It was the flagship project of a young monarch willing to open his country to the rest of the world. The port complex had to become a crucial nodal point in global maritime business and the most important hub of containerized trade in Africa. Other new urban megaprojects in tourism, real estate, and business around the country were announced constantly in the local press. Besides these sorts of spectacles, people seemed captivated by another promising feature of modern Moroccan policy: nationwide poverty alleviation programs such as Villes Sans Bidonvilles (VSB, Cities Without Slums) and the Initiative Nationale pour le Développement Humain (INDH, National Initiative for Human Development). Others were much less enthusiastic about these reform plans and contested, for example, the privatization of water and electricity with sit-ins, marches, and other actions.

My attention was increasingly drawn to these very visible and—at first sight—seemingly unrelated events and changes at the urban scale. It was through a sense of discomfort and unease, triggered by the contradictions of what I observed in the field during those first weeks and months, that I discovered one of my main case studies. I remember passing a billboard of the Bouregreg project together with Sami after being in Rabat only a few days. Although the valley of the Bouregreg River, located between the cities of Rabat and Salé, was still an empty place at that time, the billboard forecasted the most radical change the city of Rabat would see since the days of the French protectorate. We immediately decided that we had to talk to one of the people working for the Bouregreg state agency. Not much later, we walked into one of the buildings of the agency, hoping for the best, asking the guard if we could talk to somebody, anybody.

The resulting interview convinced me to dig deeper into the case of the Bouregreg Valley and its megaproject. It also fed a creeping existential crisis I experienced as a political scientist. Here I was, trying to understand political change, and instead of looking at elections, the dynamics between political parties, the recommendations of international donors, the increasing popularity of the Islamist Parti de la justice et du développement (PJD, Justice and Development Party), and the efforts of the makhzan (the inner circle of power in Morocco) to control the political realm, I wanted to focus on the changes at the urban scale, the megaprojects, the slum upgrading program, the protests against the degrading public services, and the rising cost of living in the city. I was not finding suitable answers in the political science literature on Morocco. At the same time, however, I was not trained to be a geographer, an economist, or an anthropologist.

The advantage of writing a preface at the end of a book project is that by then it all seems relatively logical, structured, and coherent. The stress about "what the hell am I doing?" seems long gone. The recollections of the concrete details, doubts, and frustrations of my everyday life in the field now seem futile. However, when I think back on those first years, I do recognize how much my fieldwork has been a real struggle at certain moments, and often a chaotic one too. My brother is a film director, and he always tells me that before you can even think about starting to shoot a film, every new project needs a well-developed shooting script in which every step is carefully worked out and calculated. I did not have such a shooting script. And if I did have something of a plan, it was quickly messed up by the observations and attractions I experienced in the field. Hence, I improvised a lot.

The rather eclectic search for new entry points—since neither the elections nor the "Arab regime" were one of them—pushed me, especially in the beginning, in all kinds of directions, of which eventually only a few made it into this book. The more directions I took, the more complicated the general picture became. It was often frustrating at the time. Now I know I did the right thing. Today, I am still not sure whether my existential crisis is completely solved. Yet in the end—luckily maybe— I did not try to become someone else. I am still a political scientist, and my main focus was to understand politics and political change. Nevertheless, my analyses in this book identify more with the process of understanding itself than with the laws and boundaries of the imperative questions posed by a specific discipline. In other words, I did not want my research questions and problems to be "disciplined."

Most of my story draws on fieldwork in Rabat and Casablanca. Yet the political story of this book cannot be confined to these two localities, or to the Moroccan national context, for that matter. It involves global investment strategies, international donor concerns, "starchitectural" designs, and seemingly universal rationalities and practices. I was interested in the global connections that made these places into what they are today and I wanted to understand how these complex processes of placemaking inform our notion of politics in the region. In other words, I wanted to explain how local politics in the region have become, in many ways, a global enterprise.

This is not a book about the physical transformation of the Moroccan city. The changes I observed were, in the first place, *social*. A new skyscraper, apartment, road, or marina are the visible materializations of social connections and particular power relations that determine, to a large extent, the lives of all urban and even nonurban citizens. Understanding the impact of these relations and connections within the context of our global situation was my main concern. In fact, I am convinced that it should concern all engaged scholars dealing with politics in the region.

I need to thank a lot of people who have made the (often lonely) process of both my research and later the writing of this book much easier. First, I thank my editors at the University of Minnesota Press. I am particularly grateful to Susan Clarke, who did an amazing job, challenging and pushing me to a higher level; and to Pieter Martin, for his professional guidance and encouragements during the writing process. It was a comfort to feel their confidence.

I would also like to thank my colleagues Sami Zemni and Chris Parker for their support, advice, and friendship at the Middle East and North Africa Research Group (MENARG). Team MENARG is an inspiring and wonderful research environment and I thank all my colleagues from over the years for their friendship and collegiality.

Further, I would like to express my gratitude to the many people who helped me along the way. I thank Fadma Ait Mouss, Nida Alahmad, Ray Bush, Myriam Catusse, Ipsita Chatterjee, Loes Debuysere, Brecht De Smet, Marion Dixon, Ruddy Doom, Soraya El Kahlaoui, Adam Hanieh, Omar Jabary Salamanca, Sylvie Janssens, Ahmed Kanna, Marieke Krijnen, Khalid Madhi, Paola Rivetti, Steven Schoofs, Cristiana Strava, Robin Thiers, Dorien Vanden Boer, and Sigrid Vertommen for their insightful comments on earlier versions of this project.

My fieldwork has been a fascinating experience, and I also have to thank many people whom I met during my time in Morocco. There were too many to name them all, but I would especially like to thank my roommate in Rabat, Montserrat Emperador Badimon, my philosopher friend Alejandro Muchada, Chafik el Younoussi, Mounaime Oubai, Abdellatif Zeroual, Aziz el Yaakoubi, Olivier Toutain, Béatrice Allain-El Mansouri, Ellen Van Bovenkamp, Anja Hoffman, Mimoun Rahmani, Hicham Mouloudi, Charaf Britel, Cynthia Plette, Souad Guennoun, Jacopo Granci, and Ward Vloeberghs.

I also express my gratitude to Béatrice Platet for the map of the Bouregreg project and Soumia El Majdoub for the photographs. Finally, I thank friends and family for being there for me, especially my beautiful wife, Ariana. She is my biggest support and my most critical sounding board. I admire her intelligence and empathy.

MOROCCO'S URBAN REVOLUTION

On September 15, 2013, in the morning, while entering the station of Casa-Port, I saw the new high-rises of Casablanca Marina out my window. Although still under construction, they already transformed Casablanca's skyline radically. Casablanca Marina is situated just in front of the old medina between the harbor and the impressive Mosque Hassan II. The medina, the old city that predates the French protectorate, with its robust stone walls, narrow streets, and numerous small shops, will be hidden from now on behind a new city panorama of concrete and glass.

A new beachfront reaches out to the Atlantic Ocean and to the rest of the world. It will consist of yachting marinas, luxury hotels, shops and residences, offices, a conference center, and even a grand aquarium. Launched in 2006 by King Mohammed VI, Casablanca Marina holds out a vision of a "modern" city, a "globalized" city, one where businesses can thrive and tourists can enjoy the sights. A place of living, leisure, and business: those are the three keywords by which the marina marketeers describe Casablanca's message to the world.

The project's skyscrapers symbolize the new Morocco, a country led, since 1999, by a benevolent monarch. Young, modern, and popular, Mohammed VI contrasted sharply with the authoritarian and repressive image of his father, Hassan II. He seemed the right man at the right time, ready to steer his country into the twenty-first century. With Mohammed VI at the helm, Morocco promotes itself as a haven of political stability in the midst of a turbulent region (Nsehe 2013).

But alongside the same train tracks, just before entering Casa-Port, I passed another prominent feature of modern cities in the Global South: the slums or bidonvilles (oilcan cities), as they are called in Morocco. Small shacks, usually with a satellite dish and sheets of corrugated iron as a roof, are built only a few meters away from the track. The roofs have stones on top so they will not be blown off by the wind.

Carefully hidden behind walls, so the traveler cannot be too disturbed by their sight, these pockets of poverty are not just an urban or a social problem. They are also subject to a particular political concern. In this age of globalization, financialization, and global communication, the aesthetic qualities of urban centers are essential to contemporary economic growth strategies. Land and property interests have become a vital mechanism in the commodification of urban space and property capital has become a central motor of urban "regeneration" (Massey 2010, 91).

Consequently, the *image* of a city like Casablanca becomes a crucial asset and city marketing is the tool to optimize and develop that asset. Slums, obviously, do not fit the particular picture of modernity advertised by Casablanca Marina. They are a burden, both physically, as they often occupy valuable land, and symbolically, as they disturb a city's sight and attractiveness to the outside world (to investors).

That day in Casablanca I met with Souad, an architect and long-time political activist.[1] Over the past few years, she has been active in the 20 February movement, the social protest movement that emerged in the wake of the 2011 Arab uprisings. As we were walking through the old medina toward the construction site of the marina project, she explained that the rocky shore in front of the medina used to be a place of social encounter. It was a place where people went fishing and afterward they would drink tea in one of the cafés of the medina. Nowadays, these encounters belong to the past with the enclosure of the seashore. The construction site was now closed off with an iron fence covered with billboards promising a different future.

Souad turned my attention to the urban life, the public space, however modest it might have been, that had to make room for Casablanca Marina. She wanted to tell me another story, one that contrasted with that of the urban developers and designers of such megaprojects who usually ignore these kinds of encounters, or at best consider them unproductive.

In the developer's view, the marina occupied a degraded or even desolate space, where there was little or no development before, little or no life. After the independence, the story then usually goes, Moroccan cities had turned their back to the Atlantic Ocean, and now the time had come to remedy this historic mistake. Urban spectacles such as

Casablanca Marina will put Morocco's cities back on the world map: a metaphor that has to be taken quite literally. The promotional video of Casablanca Marina starts with a picture of the globe where, one after the other, Dubai, London, New York, and Casablanca appear as flashes of light, accompanied by the melodramatic tunes of the soundtrack of the movie *The Rock*.[2] Thanks to the new megaproject, Casablanca is going to be among the great cities of the globe.

Casablanca Marina also promises a better world for local residents. If the project manages to "bring in" globalization, it will generate growth, create employment, and bring about development. The benefits of these projects are imagined to trickle down and flow outward to the rest of the city and even the wider country.

Of course, the urban developer's story represents a particular kind of development, a particular kind of urbanism. Casablanca Marina reflects a hegemonic and deeply political project, one that resembles many other urban megaprojects around the globe. Yet it is rarely presented as such. On the contrary, the developer's story transforms the political reproduction of urban space into a mere technocratic problem of economic growth and urban modernization. This is precisely why Souad took me to this place. She wanted to draw my attention to an important political issue and she regretted that her fellow activists missed the importance of this issue. "While the 20 February movement was debating abstract things like democracy, capital took over the city," she said with a sigh while we were looking over the construction site.

The Neoliberal Turn and Its Relation to Crisis, the City, and Struggle

What happens when capital takes over a city? More concretely, what might it mean for the ways we understand political change, power, and agency in a country such as Morocco, or the region more broadly? And if we relate very specific urban developments to politics more generally, how might such a maneuver challenge the dominant paradigms that inform our understanding of politics in the region today?

This book explores political change through the lens of the city. My approach links more abstract questions of government, globalization, and neoliberalism with concrete changes in the city and urban projects such as Casablanca Marina. It is about the exchanges and connections that are made through the reproduction of urban space and what they reveal about the power that materializes in the creation of new spatial realities.

The transformation of the Moroccan city tells a broader story about the transformation of politics, the state, and the economy and how it all connects within a context of increasing globalization and neoliberal reform. Like Souad, I consider political change to be intimately related to place and placemaking. I explore how urban projects such as Casablanca Marina reveal political practices and agency that materialize the interrelation between globalization and countries such as Morocco, or between *global* capitalism and *local* places such as Casablanca.

The project of Casablanca Marina is not an isolated case. The whole coastline has been or is in the process of being reshaped by other projects, such as Morocco Mall, Anfaplace Living Resort, and Wessal Casablanca Port. Likewise, these restructurings are not limited to the coastline itself. Another flagship project, the Casablanca Finance City, aims to create a whole new city center in the district of Anfa, transforming this area into a new financial hub for the wider French-speaking African region.

And Casablanca is not an exception in Morocco. In 2009 the weekly magazine *TelQuel* referred to an "urban revolution" that fully erupted in the middle of the first decade of the twenty-first century following the launch of megaprojects such as the Bouregreg project, Tanger Med, and Tanger City Center. These projects are reshaping other major coastal cities like Rabat and Tangier (Ghannam and Aït Akdim 2009).

This book understands the political dimension of this urban revolution in two ways: as a class project and as a governmental problem. First, urban projects such as Casablanca Marina turn the city itself into a place of extraction and roll out the necessary infrastructure to extract surplus value and profit. Second, this reshaping of the city according to class interests impacts the conditions of people already living in the city. The tensions between the interests of ordinary citizens and the class interests of those in power have to be solved, stabilized, and governed. As such, Morocco's urban revolution should also be analyzed within the history of what Michel Foucault called "biopolitics": the technologies and mechanisms through which the (urban) population became the object of a political strategy of power (Collier 2011; Foucault 2007, 2008). The city, in other words, was central not only in terms of the increasing commodification of urban land as a means to extract profits and generate growth but also as a laboratory for the development of new modalities of government, social control, and political domination. The origins of this so-called urban revolution can be traced back to the early 1980s. At the time, numerous countries in the Global South faced severe deficit crises and were forced to adopt structural adjustment programs. These programs, together with subsequent neoliberal reforms, marked a political and economic turning point. The implementation of a structural adjustment program (SAP) in Morocco in 1983 can be considered a watershed from which the current transformations are to be explained.

Previously, urban politics were not very central and dominant in postindependence Morocco.[3] Up until the end of the 1970s there was no coherent political vision on urbanization and city planning at the national level (Kaioua 1996, 615; see also Abouhani 1995a; Cattedra 2001; Naciri 1989; Rachik 2002). The structural conditions at the beginning of the 1980s, however, marked the end of this neglect, and the city became the main object and instrument for the reinvention of Morocco's political economy. This turn can be inscribed into a more global shift that has been transforming societies around the world since the 1980s. Worldwide, the city played a crucial role in the construction of neoliberal globalization and hegemony (Hackworth 2007; Harvey 1989b; Lefebvre 2003; Massey 2010; Sassen 1991).

Social struggle was at the heart of this global turn. One cannot fully understand the relation between neoliberalism and urbanism without taking into account their relation to resistance and violence. Although the rise of a neoliberal age is generally ascribed to the politics of iconic figures such as Margaret Thatcher and Ronald Reagan, Doreen Massey (2010) stresses that in the early 1980s this future was still open, full of conflict, and uncertain. Neoliberalism did not only emerge as a response to a structural crisis of Fordism; it was also substantially shaped by contestation itself (Peck and Tickell 2007). In other words, the construction of a neoliberal order did not happen without a fight. Both Thatcher and Reagan faced serious opposition, not in the least from the labor movement.

More important, while these two neoliberal icons eventually succeeded in rolling back the old social order of Fordism-Keynesianism in their respective countries, the establishment and, even more so, the consolidation of a new order was actually the work of the political forces that followed these imagined pioneers. The so-called Third Way represented by politicians such as Tony Blair and Bill Clinton entailed not only a correction to first generation neoliberal policies but also a response to the threat of more radical politics coming from within the working classes, the labor unions, and the social movements. In the case of England and the city of London, New Labour played a crucial role in strengthening and consolidating a neoliberal social order by resolving—temporarily, as it has become very clear by now—the conflicting interests that arose out of early neoliberal reform (Massey 2010). Consequently, the 1980s were still part of a critical period in the UK and the United States, because if the struggle had ended otherwise, the contemporary social order and global city might have been reinvented on other terms (Massey 2010, 80).

A similar argument can be made with regard to the Global South.[4] The Third World debt crisis of the 1980s opened up space for politics of "structural adjustment," imposed by international donor institutions such as the World Bank and the International Monetary Fund (IMF) and underpinned ideologically by the Washington Consensus. These politics succeeded in undermining, to a large extent, the then prevalent social order of state developmentalism that had emerged out of Third World anticolonial and nationalist struggles.[5]

Also in the Global South, structural adjustment did not take place without a fight. Social struggle was at the heart of these restructurings, and the political future in those days was equally very open, uncertain, and undecided. From the late 1970s onward, we saw the emergence of "new waves" of protest in many African countries and in the rest of the Global South, due to the fundamental restructuring of class and state–society relations by neoliberal reform (Seddon and Zeilig 2005; see also Branch and Mampilly 2015). Since the very beginning of the Third World debt crisis, political–economic programs of "free-market reform" coincided with socioeconomic protests. Urban mass protests and riots were among the first expressions of popular discontent with the new neoliberal policies (Bayat 2002).

In *Free Markets and Food Riots*, John Walton and David Seddon argue that despite the particular contexts in which urban mass protests took place, these waves must be seen as "a more general social and political response to the systematic undermining of previous economic and social structures and of an earlier moral order" (1994, 3).

I start from this transformative moment and explore how a neoliberal order was constructed and consolidated in Morocco. The "IMF riots" of 1981 in Casablanca marked the beginning of a turbulent period of political and economic change. It gave rise to new forms of government, new forms of control and domination, and new forms of popular revolt (on this last point, see Bogaert 2015c). The critical task, therefore, is to understand not only the context in which neoliberal reform became possible but also the continuous process of change generated by new contradictions and conflicts that arise out of that reform, forcing neoliberal projects to be reinvented constantly.

In the same vein as Massey's analysis of the UK, neoliberal projects in Morocco were not only a response to a suffocating debt crisis; they were also shaped by social struggle and responded directly to "threats" coming from within the subaltern classes and poor urban neighborhoods. In other words, neoliberalism in Morocco was profoundly shaped by the ways in which interests of capital converged with security concerns and the problem of the "riotous city." Within this convergence, the city was brought to the forefront of the construction of a new social order both as a privileged space for capital accumulation as well as a space for the construction of new modalities of authoritarian government and control.

Two additional points highlight the need to integrate this latter aspect into our understanding of the impact of neoliberal projects in a country such as Morocco. First, state developmentalism displayed an urban bias (Walton 1998). State investments in education and the public sector went disproportionally to major cities and, as a result, many of these cities, in Morocco as elsewhere in the region, attracted a lot of migrants from the countryside. The rollback of the developmental state did not stop this disproportionate demographic growth of cities, and further "urbanization without economic growth" increased pressure on political stability (M. Davis 2006b, 11–19).

Second, the protests against early neoliberal restructuring were largely concentrated in Morocco's major cities. Therefore, the control over the Moroccan city, and especially Casablanca, came to be seen as a political "urgency" where spaces of "high risk"—that is, the slum areas and the working-class neighborhoods—needed to be stabilized and supervised (Rachik 1995, 2002). Otherwise, there would be no viable economic project for the Moroccan city.

After 1981, the marginalized urban areas—the slums, the informal housing quarters, and the working-class areas—became a primary focus within a master plan for the restructuring and securitization of Casablanca. Urban planning and administrative division were the two core components of this project of urban control. Following the disturbances of 1984 and 1990, other major cities were also subjected to similar projects.

A Moroccan Exception?

With the accession to the throne of Mohammed VI in 1999, urban politics in Morocco took a new turn. Generally, the Moroccan political system is considered a more moderate system compared to some of the other authoritarian regimes in the region. From the very beginning, Mohammed VI seemed to break with his father's openly repressive way of rule and willingly presented himself as a model reformer dedicated to economic and political liberalization. In his speeches, he repeatedly stressed the importance of good governance, human rights, poverty alleviation, economic development, and citizen participation. This sudden change in style, contrasted with the more repressive image of his father, Hassan II, even earned Mohammed VI the reputation of "king of the poor" in the mainstream press.[6]

The optimism of a "Moroccan exception" took a setback after the suicide bombings in Casablanca in May 2003. First, the authorities immediately responded with repressive measures in order to deal with the political crisis. Second, since all the suicide bombers came from Sidi Moumen, a famous slum area in the eastern periphery of Casablanca, it strengthened the idea that the country's neglect of its urban poor and the problem of slums were a breeding ground for jihadism and domestic terrorism.

The monarchy responded immediately and decisively to this political crisis, pushing Morocco's urban politics into a new direction after the events of 2003. The new king's reign marked itself not only by spectacular economic growth strategies involving land and property capital (e.g., the Casablanca Marina project) but also by new and very ambitious state-promoted social development initiatives and poverty alleviation programs. The urban restructurings of the 1980s, mainly concerned with getting the riotous cities back under control, were complemented with more "inclusive" modalities of government in order to cope with the urban and social crisis exacerbated by structural adjustment. This appeared to be vital in the preservation and reconstitution of this image of a Moroccan exception.

Many believed that social initiatives such as the Cities Without Slums (VSB) program and the National Initiative for Human Development (INDH), launched in the immediate aftermath of the bombings, testified that there was still evidence of a genuine process of political liberalization. Those programs were underpinned by the ideals of good governance, participatory development, and social innovation. Furthermore, these initiatives created the expectation that the young king was serious about tackling the growing social inequality in the country (Navez-Bouchanine 2009; for a more generalized argument, see El Hachimi 2015; Malka and Alterman 2006; Storm 2007).

Moreover, the launch of several urban megaprojects in Casablanca, Rabat, Tangier, and elsewhere reconfirmed, in the eyes of many within the national and international press, Morocco's commitment to market-oriented growth, the promotion of tourism, and state-of-the-art urbanism. The country wanted to show the world that it would not be driven off course under threat of international terrorism. These megaprojects presented the visual spectacles of an open, globalized, and market-friendly Morocco. Both slum upgrading projects and real estate megaprojects seemed to fit within a comprehensive and inclusive strategy of economic growth and urban development.

The central arguments of this book contradict this popular mythification of the Moroccan exception. I argue that the reforms and projects implemented in Morocco over the past few decades should not be understood as some kind of gradual democratization or liberalization but rather as examples of how authoritarian government converges with increasing globalization and transforms through its interaction with a rationale of economic liberalization.

There is a political symbiosis between both urban megaprojects and social initiatives such as VSB and INDH. While the first are directly concerned with the opening up of local places to global market penetration and foreign investment, the second invest directly in the transformation of urban life itself. Social initiatives such as VSB and INDH seek to adapt urban life, especially the lives of the urban poor who have a historical record of social protest and urban violence, to the new conditions brought forth by neoliberal globalization. They implicate not so much a return to developmentalist policies but rather the development of new kinds of social welfare mechanisms with new techniques of market expansion and commercialization and new forms of control and domination. These latter examples show that neoliberal projects are not necessarily "anti-social" but fundamentally reconfigure the social question and the question of government. In other words, neoliberal projects actively deal with the issue of poverty and social inequality, but from a radically different rationale and within the context of a changed balance of (class) power.

The Urban as an Entry Point

The city helps to unsettle and question some of the dominant narratives on politics in the Arab region. It is an entry point through which we can develop new ways of understanding power, agency, and struggle.

One cannot fully understand the dynamics of contemporary globalization without putting it into the context of its urban condition and vice versa. Moreover, given that most urban expansion happens outside the Western world, the global urban condition is shaped in many ways by the urban spaces in the Global South (Chatterjee 2014). Cities are sites par excellence to study political change because they do not just provide the necessary infrastructure to reorganize and restructure global capitalism; they also function as laboratories for new modalities of government.

One may argue that, historically, the capitalist city has always played this double role. However, the contemporary interrelation between urbanization and globalization has changed in fundamental ways. The French philosopher Henri Lefebvre realized this already in the early 1970s. In *The Urban Revolution*, he analyzed the political and social dynamics of ever-increasing urbanization. According to Lefebvre, the urbanization of society was a historical process that reflected a transformation from an agrarian to an industrial to, finally, an "urban society" in which all other spaces (natural space, rural space, etc.) would be penetrated and dominated by urban forms. He linked this evolution to a historical shift in the territorial form of the city, that is, the transformation of the original polis (the political city) to a merchant city, then to an industrial city, and finally to the contemporary neoliberal city—what Lefebvre, at the time of writing, termed a "critical phase" (2003, 16).

In this evolution toward an urban society, Lefebvre envisioned not so much the emergence of global cities such as New York, London, or Shanghai but more the actual globalization of the *urban fabric*, which is a much broader conceptualization of urban space. "This expression," he states, "does not narrowly define the built world of cities but all manifestations of the dominance of the city over the country. In this sense, a vacation home, a supermarket in the countryside are all part of the urban fabric" (2003, 3–4).

As such, he was convinced that we needed new methodological and theoretical tools to grasp the urban phenomenon. To Lefebvre, our urban society was not only a product of capitalist relations but at the same time also a producer of new conditions and relations within capitalist organization. He knew that the modern city was "not the passive place of production or the concentration of capitals, but that of the *urban* intervening as such in production (in the *means* of production)" (Lefebvre 1996, 109–10). Those forces that shape the city are eventually also shaped by urban space itself. Lefebvre was one of the first spatial theorists who pointed out the essentially dialectic character of the relationship between spatial and social structures (Soja 1980).

Besides Lefebvre, another French philosopher, Michel Foucault, has been crucial to my understanding of Morocco's "urban revolution" and its relation to political change. Foucault's (2007) intellectual project on biopolitics sought to understand within the history of modernity and modern thinking a fundamental shift in governmental reason, one that understood individuals and collectivities no longer as legal subjects at the mercy of a sovereign or sovereign power but as living human beings that needed to be governed.

The rise to power of cities and their urban mercantile elite—the bourgeoisie—at the cost of the landed aristocracy and feudal lords in Europe was at the heart of this shift. It made sure that problems related to increasing urbanization and a growing urban population (epidemics, food scarcity, and revolt) became the governmental priorities with which the new powers had to grapple. Moreover, these were the kinds of problems that could not be readily managed within the framework of sovereignty and the technologies of power defined by feudalism. Thus, a new system of power emerged, generating new technologies of government that were linked to what Foucault called the "problem of the town" and the emergence of "the population" as a new political subject (Foucault 2007, 63–79; see also Collier 2011, 16–19, 42).

A Foucauldian perspective on urban politics in Morocco complements the Marxist approach I am developing in this book. The first focuses not so much on the *institutions* of power—"the great instruments of the state"—and the interests and (class) agency behind it but rather on the governmental *techniques* necessary for the "insertion of bodies" into the new urban order and the "adjustment of the phenomena of population" to the neoliberal restructuring of the city (Foucault 1990, 141). Foucault wanted to point our attention to the fact that projects of capital accumulation and—in our case—neoliberal reform could not exist outside the central problem of modern society: how to govern human beings? As such, neoliberalism should thus also be analyzed as a "contemporary form through which life and population are being raised as problems of government" (Collier 2011, 125).

Starting from both Lefebvre and Foucault, one could argue that the area study of the Arab region needs new methodological and theoretical tools to understand the deeper urban structures and urban agency behind current dynamics of political change and changing modalities of authoritarian government. This has been highlighted both by the challenges the neoliberal order faces today in the aftermath of the global economic crisis and by the unprecedented scale of mass uprisings and popular contestation we have seen in the region since 2011.

I do not necessarily want to reject current mainstream analyses but critically engage with them by trying to bridge the existing gap between, on the one hand, Middle East urban studies and, on the other hand, the wider field of political science on the region dealing with questions of power, state, government, and globalization.

Neoliberalism and Its Place

Studying urban politics in Morocco in relation to the issue of neoliberalism raises two important concerns. First, what do we really mean when we talk about neoliberalism and how do we understand it in the context of Morocco? Second, where does it come from?

With regard to the first concern, it is important to stress that precisely because a new neoliberal social order emerges out of concrete struggles, it cannot just be reduced to some pure theoretical abstraction disconnected from locality. Nevertheless, we should still try to understand the concrete outcomes of conflicting interests in relation to more general and global shifts.

Scholars who take into account the issue of neoliberalism risk to make the mistake of comparing the specific contexts of their fields of study with some kind of ideal type, one of what neoliberalism is supposed to represent or what a neoliberal state is supposed to look like. As a result, for example, distinctions are made between "authoritarian neoliberalism" and "healthy neoliberalism" (Dahi and Munif 2012, 328) or references are made to some kind of converging system or state that is "simultaneously more liberal and more autocratic, characterized not as *a fully neoliberal state*, but as a state marked—quite literally and physically—by neoliberal exceptions" (Schwedler 2012, 269, emphasis added).

But where does such a fully neoliberal state exist in the real world? Or, what would we define as "healthy neoliberalism" and where can we then find an example of it? Samir Amin has reminded us that conceptions of pure forms of capitalism or "pure economics" reflect only a theory of imaginary capitalism that does not really answer to its actual existing forms (2003, 16). Any assumed universal law or global logic of capitalism will always have to touch the ground somewhere before it can materialize. The question is what happens when logic collides with particular practices, interests, and conflicts in different places? How does place then contribute to the significance and validity of so-called global logics? Without giving a comprehensive answer here, it is clear that studying change in relation to these ideal type conceptions gets off to a quite uncomfortable start.

In this book I argue that the *economic* reforms in Morocco of the last four decades are at the same time evidence of a fundamental *political* transformation. Yet this transformation cannot be understood in terms of mainstream assumptions linking economic liberalization and free-market reform to democratization. These assumptions are too often presented as "global logics" independent from "local place." But it cannot be understood as just an incomplete or imperfect implementation of economic reform either, or as a form of crony capitalism, in the course of which a small minority of domestic corrupt elites, close to the monarchy, skim off all the capital surpluses.

The concept of "crony capitalism" implicitly suggests that capitalism in authoritarian political systems is somehow disconnected from capitalism in the so-called democratic world. Capitalism obviously evokes imaginations of the global, yet crony capitalism always seems to refer to a particular local and, above all, deviant imitation. Consequently, it risks to erect simplistic conceptual boundaries between the realm of economics and the realm of politics. By interpreting globalization through the mechanism of "cronyism," one can easily come to the conclusion that certain problems related to increasing globalization (limited economic growth, unemployment, social inequality) are "political rather than economic" (Chekir and Diwan 2014, 207). In other words, they are mainly considered as local problems, despite the obvious observation that many countries around the globe face exactly *the same* problems at *the same* time. These kinds of explanations neglect, first of all, the deeply relational geography of global capitalism, and secondly, a more radical process of political change.

This brings us to our second concern about the study of urban transformation in Morocco. If the contemporary city has been radically reshaped in the context of a global neoliberal turn, two important interrelated questions emerge: By whom? And from where? Put differently, the question of *who* makes our contemporary globalization is intimately linked to the question of *where* it is made.

Massey forcefully addressed these questions. There lies a problem, she argues, in the way imaginations of the local and the global are often counterposed to each other. The local is usually associated with authenticity, everyday life, cultural particularity, tradition, and so on, while the global then refers to an abstract dimension of space, the space of logics and laws situated somehow above the local (Massey 2010, 165).

This counterposition usually implies a particular kind of spatial mapping and hierarchy. With regard to the impact of globalization, the local will be seen either as a passive place that adapts to the imperatives of global forces or as a recalcitrant place that adopts imperfectly. In either case, globalization is still imagined as coming from somewhere else. And because of this, globalization becomes in a way intangible or even otherworldly from the perspective of a local place. Clement Henry and Robert Springborg, for example, argue that "globalization, today's equivalent to yesterday's imperialism, at least in many of its impacts on non-Western economies, is the primary *external thesis* against which MENA [Middle East and North Africa] countries are reacting" (2001, 223, emphasis added).

This constructed counterposition between the local (the internal, the realm of politics) and the global (the external, the realm of economics) also informs ideal type imaginations of neoliberalism. Neoliberalism then becomes this kind of "one size fits all" model that can either be adopted or resisted (i.e., adopted imperfectly).

Yet the local is not just a product of the global, nor does it just try to resist the global. The local is an agent in globalization. The production of contemporary global capitalism is the result of the *localization* of wider political interests and projects that involve local, regional, national, and global actors who are assembled through and within new political configurations (Massey 2005; M. P. Smith 1998). To come back to our example of Casablanca Marina, such a project does not just "bring in" globalization; it produces it. And it provides a model for future projects elsewhere. Globalization is thus made *in* places (Massey 2010).

Urban Projects and the Reconceptualization of Neoliberalism

This book offers a different perspective on the phenomenon of neoliberalism: to put it in the words of Stephen Collier, this perspective takes neoliberalism as part of the *"problem* of inquiry rather than its premise" (2011, 12). It acknowledges the fact that there are global "neoliberal" shifts in thinking about capitalism, the economy, and the role of politics since the early 1980s. Yet, at the same time, these shifts cannot be understood properly on their own. We have to relate them to place and place-making projects and grasp the ways in which these projects are actually the starting points of global shifts.

By paying attention to the complexity of placemaking and urban politics, I argue that neoliberalism can be best understood as *a set of projects.*[7] If we rely on predefined or ideal type notions of neoliberalism, as a ready-made system to be applied in different settings, we risk disguising or even erasing the very practices, interrelations, and global connections that lie at the basis of its emergence "in place." In contrast, the concept of "project" allows us to direct the focus on what Anna Tsing calls the "sticky materiality of practical encounter" (2005, 1) and helps us understand how these encounters are not so much *the result* of an unstoppable global logic (globalization as a quasi-law of nature) but rather how they are implicated in the *production* of a seemingly global logic. The conceptualization of neoliberalism or neoliberal globalization as a set of projects is committed to the idea that "the global" is always grounded, that the relation between globalization and placemaking is deeply political and often contested, that globalization is not something external but integral to political change itself.

Obviously, neoliberal projects fundamentally restructure the economy, but they are also projects of societal and governmental transformation. One of the central arguments of the book is that neoliberal projects in Morocco have reflected a profound shift from some form of state developmentalism toward market-oriented modalities of *government.*[8]

As a result, authoritarianism in Morocco has been transformed by the ways in which the interests of ruling domestic elites and (global) economic elites increasingly intertwine. This gives rise to new arrangements where "market requirements" define and justify the (authoritarian) mode of government. Consequently, the making of a new political world in Morocco, and the Arab region more generally, has been determined not only by "the regime" or by domestic state–society relations but also, and increasingly, by interests and interventions related to global capitalism. In other words, authoritarian government in Morocco has become, in many ways, a more globalized affair.

To understand this intertwinement, I look at particular urban projects as sites of global connection and as sites where new political practices and institutions are developed. I am interested in how these projects connect global capital with local interests, how the market enters the political sphere and impacts desires to reshape the city as a neoliberal class project, and, finally, how these urban projects match global (humanitarian) goals like poverty alleviation and the right to housing, but with the aim to control and transform urban life. The power relations articulated through this kind of (re)production of urban space comprise a wide range of actors, with quite different objectives and agendas, who are not necessarily all physically present in the city despite the fact that they are involved in the reshaping of urban living space.

Megaprojects and Slum Upgrading: Two Different Kinds of Neoliberal Projects

Two of the most visible manifestations of Morocco's contemporary urban politics are brought together in this book: urban megaprojects and slum upgrading projects. I situate these two kinds of urban projects within a broader historical context of political change. My field research was primarily based in Casablanca and Rabat.

On the one hand, I explore the urban politics invested in a high-end urban development scheme in the valley of the Bouregreg River between the twin cities of Rabat and Salé. The Bouregreg project is exemplary of Morocco's urban revolution. It is one of the flagship megaprojects of the country. It transforms the cityscape with luxury residential units, marinas, new shopping facilities, five-star hotels, and a grand theater as the new top landmark of Rabat. The project is a salient example of how the contemporary city is perceived as the primary motor for economic growth and how cityscapes are redesigned and restructured to satisfy the desires and interests of (global) capital. Furthermore, the project gave rise to a new institutional model of state power specifically developed to serve those desires and interests: the Agence pour l'Aménagement de la Vallée du Bouregreg (AAVB, Agency for the Development of the Bouregreg Valley).

On the other hand, I examine the changing methods, techniques, and rationalities implicated in the government of slums. Here, I point to an important shift in the ways in which slums were governed between the 1980s and the beginning of the twenty-first century. The highly disruptive moment of structural adjustment in the early 1980s forced Moroccan authorities to revert to repressive methods of power to take back control over the urban territory and restore order in the riotous city. Casablanca stands as the paradigmatic example. Besides the military repression of the riots of 1981, the authorities also increased administrative and political control over the city by elaborating a new master plan, by dividing the territory of Casablanca into different administrative zones, and by making these new spatial interventions visible through state architecture and large-scale renovation projects.

These methods of urban planning and control served to fill in a governmental vacuum created by structural adjustment. From a Foucauldian perspective, one could say that the more repressive methods of urban territorial control temporarily replaced the loss of ability to "govern" the urban (slum) population through the typical technologies of state developmentalism and its social compromise (food subsidies, public employment, and education).

This focus on urban *territorial* control in the 1980s gradually shifted again with the development of a new neoliberal order and new techniques of power invested in the government of slums and its *population*. Especially after the suicide bombings of 2003, we saw increased efforts to "govern" the individual slum dweller and the slum population as a whole in order to assure their inclusion into the formal market society.

While the methods of urban control in the 1980s still represented an open struggle, one that coincided with the rollback of the old developmentalist order, the new governmental methods of the early twenty-first century give us more insight into the particular ways a neoliberal social order has been constructed, expanded, and consolidated in Morocco, or at least how it has been attempted. The VSB program shows how slum dwellers are being required to participate in the making of a specific political world in which the ability to claim political rights and articulate social justice are circumscribed not only by "the Arab regime" but also by the sanctions and incentives of "the freemarket" (Parker and Debruyne 2012).

Taking into account these innovations in government and urban projects, it becomes clear that neoliberalism itself is not some social order or political rationality immune to change itself. By understanding how globalization is produced in different places, we can explore the transformative and contingent character of neoliberal government and neoliberal governmentality. In the case of Morocco, the crises of the 1980s, the social impact of structural adjustment, and the protests against austerity (i.e., the problem of the riotous city) are some of the dynamics that have set in motion the development of new critical reflections on government, new forms of state intervention, and new ways of market support. National programs such as Cities Without Slums were deliberate attempts to resolve the social tensions exacerbated by the early neoliberal reforms of the 1980s.

Consequently, what one associates with neoliberalism today is not the same anymore with what one associated with neoliberalism in the era of structural adjustment (see Collier 2011, 161). Nevertheless, what makes it *neo*liberal in the end is its break from developmentalism or Fordism, its changed balance of class power, and its inspiration and legitimation found in particular traditions of political thinking that have become "common sense."

Neoliberal Projects, Class, and State

To conclude this conceptual discussion on the link between political change, urban projects, and contemporary globalization, let me briefly address two concerns with regard to the nature of the agency and practices involved in the reproduction of urban space in Morocco.

First, neoliberal urban projects should be understood as class projects. I use a particular notion of class. I understand class not so much as a defined group of people with a set of fixed characteristics (e.g., ownership over the means of production) but as a concept that clarifies the political nature of certain practices and social relations. Within the context of neoliberal urban projects, class denotes the practices and relations of capital accumulation and surplus-value appropriation that are involved in the reproduction, exploitation, and dispossession of urban space. In other words, I am interested not in an all-encompassing definition of class as an actual social group but rather in the *nature* of production, exploitation, and dispossession itself.

The new emerging landscape of Casablanca, described above, may project, at first sight, a modern and welcoming image of Moroccan society with which the international tourist, the private sector, the contemporary technocrat, or the world of global finance can easily identify. Yet underneath this appearance of modernity, openness, and liberalism hides a class project of authoritarian transformation. The important question is not whether those who remodel the city can be described as a class but rather whether their practices and strategies can be understood as *class practices* or *class strategies*.

Second, the Moroccan state, in various degrees, plays a crucial role in these class projects. After all, it requires state intervention and statecraft to impose the logic of the market (Block 2001). Moreover, to the extent that global class actors are involved in local politics, these actors do not so much negatively affect state authority but are drawn within reach and become active players on the field of the state (Allen 2011b; Allen and Cochrane 2010; Panitch 1998). In this sense, state power was not necessarily undermined by economic liberalization but rather re-institutionalized, reassembled, and redeployed. Power and authority are not so much slipping away from local authorities but are subject to re-negotiation within what John Allen and Allan Cochrane call new assemblages of state power.

The Bouregreg Agency (AAVB), for example, is such a new assemblage. These kinds of assemblages contradict the image of a coherent and unitary state entity. By tracing different connections of authority, negotiation, and engagement, and the ways in which they crisscross one another through various distinct spatial configurations of power, neoliberal reform gave way to new forms of government and new state forms that manifest themselves differently across space (Allen and Cochrane 2010). Therefore, we should not make the mistake of seeing the state—just as the city—as an actor in itself but focus instead on the many different actors that use state power to pursue their goals and interests.

The Structure of the Book

This book is divided into three parts and six chapters. Each part tackles a different aspect of neoliberal projects. The first part further elaborates on the relation between global capitalism and local places through this concept of neoliberal projects. The second part looks at the changing (state) institutions of power and the class nature of the agency behind them. Finally, the last part explores new techniques of neoliberal government, the creation of new subjectivities (the good citizen, the responsible citizen, and the individual entrepreneur) and the space of habitation—more concretely the urban slums—as a key arena for the reproduction of neoliberal power.

The first part of the book brings in globalization as a phenomenon that not only impacts the political economy of a country like Morocco but is coproduced through the Moroccan political system itself. Chapter 1 situates my approach on urban projects within the broader debate on Arab politics.[9] The city as lens challenges perspectives that consider the nation-state or the "Arab regime" as the privileged domain of politics. It also challenges the way political change is often framed within a conceptual dichotomy between democratic *transition* and authoritarian *persistence* (which implies a nontransition). These two conceptions dominated the research on Arab politics over the past decades (Heydemann and Leenders 2011; Valbjørn 2012; Valbjørn and Bank 2010). This particular dichotomy suggests a linear understanding of political change, one that measures the possibilities of change against a presumed universal model of democratization. Moreover, this understanding of change usually seeks to explain "failure" or "stagnation" in pathologies that are internal to Arab societies or Arab regimes, thereby ignoring or minimizing important dynamics of globalization (Branch and Mampilly 2015, 42, 65; see also Parker 2009).

With the concept of "projects" I wish to bring in new power relations, global connections, and struggles that explain the nature of political change since the neoliberal turn in the 1980s. It helps us to distinguish current relations of power and methods of government from past struggles, rationalities, and forms of authoritarianism.

Chapter 2 deals with the broader history of neoliberal reform and its urban condition in Morocco, a history that started with the turbulent 1980s of structural adjustment, accumulation by dispossession, and urban mass riots. However, neoliberal urban projects changed significantly over time. The projects of creative destruction in the 1980s reflected capital's need to create an (urban) landscape to accommodate its own interests and requirements at one point in time, only to revolutionize it at a later point in time in order to maintain the rate of growth, expand the possibilities for further accumulation, and protect this process from possible threats (Harvey 2010b, 86).

Consequently, the second chapter describes not only a transition to a neoliberal order but also a transition within this order, one from a period of open struggle in the 1980s to a more creative and constructive period of consolidation in the first decade of the twenty-first century. Over the past fifteen years, neoliberal projects were characterized by an attempt to address the limits of structural adjustment and its social consequences. From a neoliberal viewpoint, the structural adjustments of the 1980s were not only unable to combat poverty and social exclusion; they also compromised the further development of the neoliberal order itself.

The second part of the book looks at the relation between the state, those who have access to state power, and neoliberal projects. The state as an institutional apparatus of power has played a vital role in Morocco's urban politics. Yet we need to rethink the state in relation to the global situation, space, and the practices through which both state and nonstate actors, public and private, global and local are connected and intertwined.

Chapter 3 tries to make sense of these practices by looking at the nature of the agency behind the transformation of the Moroccan city. It addresses the relation between neoliberal projects and the concept of class. Neoliberal projects articulate the coming together of particular relations and practices that make surplus extraction, enclosure, and dispossession possible. Class as a concept makes those relations and practices not only legible but also explicitly political.[10]

Chapter 4 looks at a particular example of neoliberal statecraft: the Bouregreg project. By studying this relation between statecraft and neoliberal projects, it becomes clear that the state itself turns out to be a complex of various institutional and governmental arrangements across space. These different arrangements serve different kinds of neoliberal projects. By drawing on the case of the Bouregreg project, I show the class agency implicated in the creation of a *new state space* and consider what it reveals about some of the dynamics of politics and placemaking that have often been elided in the literature on Arab politics.

The third part of the book looks at the impact of struggle, urban violence, and political instability on the reconfiguration of neoliberal projects and authoritarian government. While the Bouregreg project represents the ambitions, desires, and interests of the ruling elite and the wealthy, their utopian vision for the Moroccan city is only one side of the picture. The political analysis of three decades of neoliberal urban projects in Morocco cannot be reduced to urban spectacles and a changing state spatiality alone. Neoliberal projects involve not only a reengineering of the state but also the reengineering—if you like—of the urban citizen.

Urban spectacles like the Bouregreg project do not take place in a social vacuum. Unfortunately, one might say from the developers' viewpoint, one rarely gets an opportunity to design a city from scratch, to start with a clean slate. Already existing urban life, its movement, its connections, and its own interests and desires can pose considerable problems and threats from the point of view of those in power. In other words, those with the power to design and implement neoliberal projects are at the same time confronted with the city and its population as a problem of government.

Two moments of urban violence, which involved slum dwellers, had a big impact on the ways in which ruling power in Morocco dealt with the city and its population as a governmental problem. The "IMF riots" of 1981 and the suicide bombings of May 16, 2003, both occurring in Casablanca, shook the political system to its foundations. Slum dwellers were seen as the primary agents in these events, and after each crisis, the slums became a primary political concern for the preservation of stability and the securitization of the city. Moreover, as these events took place in the economic capital of the country, the city of Casablanca became a *"ville laboratoire,"* a test case and model for other Moroccan cities (Catusse, Cattedra, and Janati 2005).

Within this context, the construction and consolidation of a neoliberal order in Morocco also depended on new methods of power and techniques of government integrating the "dangerous classes" and urban informality into a general project of remaking urban society. The last two chapters deal with these new methods of power and "the problem of slums." The main argument is that we can distinguish an important shift in the ways in which the city and the slums more particularly are governed over the last three decades. This shift also reflects the broader shift within the neoliberal order itself.

Chapter 5 discusses the reinvention of social policy in Morocco in the beginning of the twenty-first century responding to the social consequences of structural adjustment. This implied not so much a return to some form of welfarism or developmentalism, nor a compensation for neoliberal reform or a form of "inclusive growth"—even though it is often presented as such. To the contrary, it represented the attempt to make the neoliberal order more stable, secure, and embedded. As such, a neoliberal governmentality does not ignore the social question but approaches it from a radically different point of view.

Moreover, I contrast these new methods of urban government and control with the repressive methods of repression and urban territorial control used during the era of structural adjustment and the early days of neoliberal reform. The repression of the 1980s was meant to fill in the vacuum created by the undermining of the developmentalist order and the rollback of developmentalist techniques of government.

Chapter 6 focuses more specifically on the problem of slums after the suicide bombings of 2003. While the repressive methods of urban control in the 1980s targeted above all the physical environment through which people move (the urban *territory*) and dealt with individuals as a set of legal subordinated subjects within that territory, the technologies of security developed after the events of 2003 intervened foremost at the level of the individual slum dweller and targeted the slums as a *population*. This particular shift will be conceptualized with Mariana Valverde's distinction between *"sovereign city planning"* and *"cities of security."* While sovereign city planning in the 1980s relied predominantly on techniques that capitalize the urban territory in order to incite loyalty to a sovereign (the Moroccan king), the methods of security in the beginning of the twenty-first century involved specific techniques that were more concerned with the management (or administration) of urban life—the lives of slum dwellers, in this case—and the future risks related to that life (Valverde 2007).

Finally, there is an additional point to be made here. The governmental methods that were developed within the framework of the VSB program were crucial to the expansion and reconfiguration of capitalism in Morocco. Therefore, besides institutional reform and class agency, neoliberal projects should also be understood by the ways in which they insert people and (informal) capital into an expanding "market-based ecosystem." In this sense, poverty alleviation programs and strategies to prevent radicalization and extremism were intended not only to enhance social and political control over the slums but also to maximize profit. The reinvention of social policy in Morocco was thus equally inspired by the exploration of new frontiers of capital accumulation and the exploitation of what Ananya Roy (2010) calls "poverty capital."

A Note on Method and Approach

Allow me to end this Introduction with a few comments about method and approach. The goal of the book is not only to understand political change in Morocco in relation to neoliberal globalization but to question this phenomenon of neoliberalism itself. Yet instead of dismissing the concept of neoliberalism altogether, my aim is to explore how a particular understanding of it, that is, as a set of (class) projects, informs our understanding of globalization as a deeply political phenomenon inherently linked to locality and placemaking.

My fieldwork helped me to reveal the forces, strategies, and rationalities that shape our political world. It was a starting point to problematize (my own) preconceived notions of power, politics, and globalization in the Global South. Interviews, informal talks, observation, walking the city, just hanging around particular sites and places, and following my instincts were some of the methods to discover "research problems."[11] When I started this study in 2007, I did not have a clear research plan in advance. It took shape in the course of my fieldwork.

As such, this research was first of all "problem-driven" rather than "method-driven," which, as Diane Singerman and Paul Amar argue, "builds on an incremental approach to knowledge and addresses political realities in useful ways, rather than exploring theory and generating method games that dismiss social, policy, and justice implications and commitments" (2006b, 28). I prioritized "understanding" over the laws and boundaries of the imperative questions posed by a specific discipline. Thinking outside the framework of a single discipline means adopting one's conceptual tools and methodological strategies to the challenges of understanding a particular social phenomenon rather than fitting this phenomenon within the requirements of a traditional disciplinary division of labor (Brenner 2004).

The work of many critical thinkers has informed this work. Two—at first sight—noncomplementary critical traditions have strongly influenced my own ideas on power. First, I draw extensively on the work of Marxist or radical (urban) scholars of the post-1968 period such as Henri Lefebvre and David Harvey. Second, my work also relies on the insights of Michel Foucault and Foucauldian studies on governmentality.

Marxist and Foucauldian analyses have long been considered as conflicting (Marsden 1999). One of the main differences between these two traditions lies in their conception of power. While Marxist inquiries have always been concerned with the question of where power was situated, explaining the (class) relations of who dominated whom, Foucault and scholars on "neoliberal governmentality" were more concerned with another kind of—some would say more empirical—question: how is power exercised? (Rose-Redwood 2006). The latter approach focuses on the kinds of technologies that are deployed without necessarily trying to pinpoint the sources of power.

Precisely because of their very different ontological and epistemological positions, both traditions should be seen as complementary (Lemke 2002). On the one hand, Marxist critiques on neoliberalism have pointed out how and why class agency has been involved in the spreading of neoliberal projects all around the world. On the other hand, governmentality studies inform us how that very project is underpinned and directed by rationalities that intervene at the level of the individual, that is, the government of the body (biopolitics). They remind us, Thomas Lemke argues, that political economy relies on a political anatomy of the body. And within a neoliberal governmentality, not only the individual body but also collective bodies, institutions (the public administration), corporations, and states have to be made "efficient," "flexible," and "autonomous" (Lemke 2002, 60). The concept of governmentality helps us to understand how neoliberalism incorporates not only a class-dominated political program but a whole new understanding of human nature and social existence that has penetrated and influenced our image of society (Read 2009).

Both critical traditions help us link two critical, contemporary, and inherently connected urban dilemmas from the viewpoint of power: on the one hand, the dilemma of how to reshape the city in order to serve power's interest—that is, the city as a class project; and on the other hand, the dilemma of how to deal with the population residing in those cities who might suffer from this class project and resist it—that is, the city as a governmental problem. The case of the Bouregreg project as a new form of neoliberal statecraft fits within this first dilemma. The slum upgrading strategies of VSB aiming to create new self-sustaining and entrepreneurial subjectivities are evidence of the second one.

I conclude with two final notes on the location of my case studies. First, a focus on cases in the Global South highlights different aspects of neoliberal projects: the importance of land reform and the control over natural resources, the specific restructurings of state power based on postcolonial legacies, the central role of the military in some countries, the way in which informal urban areas (e.g., the slums) are integrated in neoliberal projects, and, finally, the sometimes overtly violent and repressive means by which some of these projects are implemented (Connell and Dados 2014). Of course, I cannot integrate all these different aspects in this study. My focus will be explicitly on urban transformation.

Second, the point is not to understand how neoliberal forces impacted a country or city "from the South," as if these forces somehow conquered these places. The implicit idea that often precedes such assumptions is that this conquest is happening from the Global North. In contrast, I want to make a different point. Cities in the Global South can also be starting points in world-making projects. Margit Mayer and Jenny Künkel (2011, 13) argue, for example, that neoliberal experiments in the South have served as testing grounds for antipoverty policies in urban settings in the North (e.g., microcredits). Ahmed Kanna (2012, 93) stresses that while Southern megacities such as Shanghai, Bombay, and Dubai borrow "from the architectural and aestheticism of high modernism and postmodernism, cities in the deindustrializing North in turn borrow from the apparently unrestrained, future-oriented spirit of cities in the Global South." A reflection on urban transformation and the making of neoliberal globalization in places of the Global South, in countries such as Morocco, thus also helps us to liberate the study of neoliberalism from its Western focus, and sometimes Eurocentric bias (Connell and Dados 2014).

Contemporary neoliberal globalization is the result of a set of variegated political projects that assemble the interests of local and global class forces and contrasts with the interests of the majority of the world population. My explorations and case studies reveal some of the essential dynamics behind these political projects in Morocco. This book contributes to a more critical reflection about current political change in the Arab world, one that does not revert to normative questions about whether there is or there is not a democratic transition (toward our model of liberal democracy) and does not ignore the analogies with—to some extent—similar transformations in "democratic societies" in the world. This last element opens up a whole new space for comparison and liberates politics in the region from their stigma of "Arab exceptionalism."

PART I

NEOLIBERALISM AS PROJECTS

1

CONSIDERING THE
GLOBAL SITUATION

Academic specialists on Arab politics, such as myself, have quite a
bit of rethinking to do. That is both intellectually exciting and
frightening. Explaining the stability of Arab authoritarians was an
important analytical task, but it led some of us to underestimate
the forces for change that were bubbling below, and at times
above, the surface of Arab politics.

—F. Gregory Gause, "Why Middle East Studies Missed
the Arab Spring"

How should social scientists analyze these changes? This
question is muddied by the fact that social science changes too.
"Global" practices challenge social scientists to internationalize
their venues, as North American and European scholars are
brought into discussion with scholars from the South. . . .
Globalization is a set of projects that require us to imagine space
and time in particular ways.

—Anna Tsing, "The Global Situation"

SCHOLARS on the Middle East and North Africa (MENA) region addressing the problem of democracy and political change have surprisingly, for
a region that has always been the middle point of geopolitical interests,
little to say about the global situation. Or, more precisely, they have little
to say about capitalist globalization and the place of the region therein.
I do not mean to suggest that there are no important contributions dealing with issues of neoliberalism or global capitalism. Yet when it comes
to the understanding of *politics* in the MENA region, they often stay
under the radar and are overshadowed by two dominant scholarly traditions, namely transitology and the so-called postdemocratization strand.

Over the past twenty-five years, the tendency to understand the dynamics of Arab politics in relation to a specific end stage, namely liberal

democracy, has been dominant. Political transformations were perceived as either a gradual evolution toward that end stage or evidence of authoritarian persistence and resilience in the face of that end stage. Yet it is precisely the framing of general research questions within this binary logic that obscures many of the actual dynamics and characteristics of contemporary political change in the region.

Of course, I do not stand alone with this critique. I build on a longer history of critical debates concerning the nature of Arab politics and their link with globalization (Amin 2003; Guazzone and Pioppi 2009a; T. Mitchell 2002, 2011; Singerman and Amar 2006a). However, two substantial issues have been largely neglected or misunderstood in many contemporary political accounts: the question of space and the role of the city. Despite important exceptions (Abu-Lughod 1980; Kanna 2011; Parker 2009; Singerman and Amar 2006a), the significance of these two issues remains largely unrecognized in the study of Arab political life (Harb 2017). By integrating the issue of space and the role of the city into a more general analysis of political change and by making sense of that change through the concept of (urban) *projects*, I want to understand complexity rather than direction (Tsing 2000).

Paradigms Lost? From an Aspatial to a Spatial Analysis of Political Change

In the area study of the Arab region, the question of the "regime" and its susceptibility or resilience to "democratic" transition has dominated research on politics over the past decades. Even before that, in the heyday of liberal modernization theory, questions of regime change and democratization were already at hand, albeit in a different context. The narrative of modernization theory has, since the late 1950s, provided a popular framework of analysis for Third World politics in Western social science (Guazzone and Pioppi 2009a). It revolved around the assumption that political trajectories in the rest of the world would eventually follow the trajectory of the core countries of Western modernity.

Contemporary narratives on the global situation have the same structuring characteristics. Just as in the old story of modernity, Massey (2005) argues, globalization implies a similar tale of "inevitability." Increasing globalization coincided with the idea that liberal democracy had become a global or universal model. From the 1990s onward, it was said, "democracy ceased being a mostly Western phenomenon and 'went global'" (Diamond 2010).

Yet the MENA region always seemed to be some kind of an outsider. Ever since the end of the Cold War and the controversy about the so-called end of history, scholars on Arab politics have wondered about the exceptional position of the region. Why did the region escape the "third wave of democratization" (Huntington 1993b)? Only a year before the 2011 uprisings, Larry Diamond asked, "Why are there no Arab democracies?"

> By the time the *Journal of Democracy* began publishing in 1990, there were 76 electoral democracies (accounting for slightly less than half the world's independent states). By 1995, that number had shot up to 117—three in every five states. By then, a critical mass of democracies existed in every major world region save one—the Middle East. Moreover, every one of the world's major cultural realms had become host to a significant democratic presence, albeit again with a single exception—the Arab world. Fifteen years later, this exception still stands. (Diamond 2010, 93)

The authoritarian persistence and resilience of Arab regimes was considered both symptomatic of and responsible for the crisis of social, political, and economic development in the region (Parker 2004). Indeed, as Christopher Parker (2004, 1) notes, the resilient nature of the Arab regime in the face of a prolonged crisis of political legitimacy "has come to constitute a, if not *the*, central theme in contemporary political sociology of the Middle East."[1]

The False Opposition between Transitology and Postdemocratization Studies

Despite this very broad range of explanations, the common preoccupation with democracy, authoritarianism, and transition can be divided into two, at first sight opposing, bodies of literature. During the 1990s, a branch of Middle East scholarship emerged that Morton Valbjørn and André Bank typified as a "democrazy." Scholars within this tradition all too willingly put themselves forward as "democracy-spotters" (Valbjørn and Bank 2010). This body of literature, also known as transitology, emerged in the wake of scholarship studying the third wave of democratization. Shaped by the experiences of Latin America and Eastern

Europe, transitology postulated the possibility of a linear transition from authoritarianism to liberal democracy, depending on the existence of structural preconditions, the rational choices of ruling elites, and, of course, a free market (Guazzone and Pioppi 2009a, 2).

The ambition for area specialists was to demonstrate that the Arab region was subject to the same global logics as elsewhere (Valbjørn and Bank 2010). Lise Storm, for example, argued that Latin America, contrary to the beliefs of many scholars at the time, succeeded in undergoing a transition to democracy. So why, she wondered, couldn't skeptics about the MENA region be wrong? In contrast, she argued that

> the development of democracy in the MENA cannot be categorically dismissed. Moreover, although these countries *are lagging far behind* the countries of most other regions, some democratic development has indeed taken place. Although it may seem to some scholars that the countries in this particular region are not moving towards democracy . . . , I maintain that just because the movement has been rather limited and slow it does not mean it should not be studied. (Storm 2007, 5, emphasis added)

The transition paradigm tells a linear story about the inevitability (and glorification) of the global logic—read Western logic—to which the Arab region is equally subjected; that is, if one is willing to look hard enough.

At the turn of the new millennium, transitologists have been met with growing criticism within the area study. Despite all democratization efforts and global logics, the region still remains "the least free region of the world" (Valbjørn and Bank 2010, 187). Indeed, some scholars proclaimed the "end of the transition paradigm" and thought it was time for the "democracy-promoting community" to realize that the label of "transitional countries" was no longer applicable to many countries in the world, not in the least to the Arab countries (Carothers 2002).

This critique gave rise to a second dominant branch of Middle East scholarship that tried to bring the area study into the "era of post-democratization" (Valbjørn and Bank 2010). This branch denounced the transitologist's perception of "political development within a pseudo-universalist, teleological and normative autocracy/democracy scheme" (2010, 187). The way out of this normative connotation was redirecting the focus from "something desirable but absent" (i.e., democracy) to a concern for "what in fact is going on" (188; some examples are Albrecht and Schlumberger 2004; Brownlee 2002; Brumberg 2002; Cavatorta 2005; Heydemann 2007; Kienle 2001; Maghraoui 2002; Volpi 2004). Postdemocratization, so it was said, spent more attention on the actual political developments.

> This critique derives from observations of how the Arab Middle East, after more than a decade of countless nominal reform initiatives, continues to be predominantly authoritarian. The natural answer from this perspective to the question of "what in fact is" will be "authoritarianism." Instead of posing questions about reasons for the "failure of democratization" (i.e. the absence of something desirable) we therefore should seek to get a better understanding of the "success of authoritarianism" (i.e. something actually present). This change of perspective has given rise in recent years to a major and fertile debate on Arab authoritarianism, its renewal, resilience, persistence, endurance, robustness, durability and sustenance. (Valbjørn and Bank 2010, 189)

Yet, if the seemingly more objective question of "what in fact is" is reduced to the seemingly simple answer "authoritarianism," more precisely an authoritarianism that "resists" or "persists," postdemocratization theories still seem to suggest implicitly that Arab political systems are resisting a certain end goal. The only difference is that they do not see gradual progress but utter failure. And this failure lies not so much with the democratic model, or with the promotion of it, but with the countries themselves.

The basic underlying question that informs both of these so-called opposing bodies of literature actually remains the same: what about the condition of (liberal) democracy in the Arab region? Of course, Valbjørn and Bank try to put forward as convincingly as possible that one has to make a distinction between "optimistic expectations (i.e. democratic transition) and the depressing reality (i.e. the persistence of authoritarianism)" (2010, 188). Still, what distinguishes these two traditions is not so much their epistemological foundations or normative positions but their degree of optimism.

As such, the apparent opposition between these two scholarly traditions is a false one. What unites them is much stronger than what divides them. In the postdemocratization literature, the question of authoritarianism, whether they like it or not, is still regarded as a residual category or phenomenon—as the absence of liberal democracy (Parker 2004). The postdemocratization standpoint has thus a similar linear and predestined view of political trajectories, maybe not in the sense that it focuses exclusively on "catching up" but more in the form of a narrative that implicitly suggests a distinction between "good democracy" (we) and "bad authoritarianism" (the depressing reality).

The widespread uprisings of 2011 created an opportunity to break away from these dominant perspectives and question some of the hegemonic narratives on Arab political life. Even among the most prominent advocates of the postdemocratization paradigm, doubts were raised about their approaches and methodologies. Did the dominant focus on the persistence of undemocratic rulers created a myth of authoritarian stability? And did this explain, as Gregory Gause (2011) tried to provoke his fellow scholars, why Middle East Studies missed the so-called Arab Spring?

In the end, however, the Arab uprisings did not really unsettle the dominant paradigms. To the contrary, they were largely reanimated. The dilemma whether the Arab world was (finally) experiencing its own genuine democratic transition reinvigorated the debates—yet again—between believers (Hamzawy 2011; Khanna 2011; Stepan and Linz 2013) and nonbelievers (Brown 2013; Masoud 2015; Springborg 2011).

Within postdemocratization theories, scholars assessed the impact of the uprisings. And as the Arab uprisings were repressed one by one, it permitted them to argue that their concepts and methods only needed an "upgrade" (Valbjørn 2012). Authoritarianism adapted to the renewal of mass politics, and instead of looking for a democratic transition, scholars needed to pay attention to transitions in authoritarianism and "authoritarian learning" (Heydemann 2013; Heydemann and Leenders 2011). In other cases, the uprisings provided new possibilities to apply the authoritarian resilience paradigm on a particular "regime type." Distinctions could now be made, for example, between an "Arab *Republics*' Spring" and monarchical durability, like in the case of Morocco (Yom and Gause 2012; see also Barari 2015).

We should ask ourselves whether this reinvigoration of the same old debate really adds something to our understanding of the political changes of the last four decades and the causes of the Arab uprisings. For Roger Owen, the political future of the Arab region after the uprisings remains limited to two options: either a transition to liberal democracy or a return to authoritarianism (2012, 189). But what if the Arab uprisings were part of a larger historical process that cannot simply be compressed into a temporal sequence of progression or stagnation toward a singular end goal? What if, by the very nature of struggle, continuous struggle, this process is open ended in much more fundamental ways? The fact that transitologists and postdemocratization scholars were looking for something particular (i.e., a democratic transition or authoritarian persistence) has perhaps blinded them to see what has actually been changing for years, even decades.

The obvious answer "authoritarianism" to the question of "what in fact is" is actually hardly illuminating. Processes of change become more visible when they are detached from any compulsory trajectory or predestination. Both the transition paradigm and the authoritarian persistence paradigm are blinded by the established "truths" of liberal democracy and liberal ideology. By proclaiming these truths as universal norms, they do not so much advance the understanding of political processes in the region as make political claims about their preferred global future. In doing so, important changes have remained outside the scope of their methodologies and concepts.

Toward a Spatial Approach on Politics and Change

According to scholars such as Doreen Massey and Anna Tsing, these kinds of narratives do not allow us to imagine other countries and political forces in the world to have their own specific trajectories, their own particular histories, and the potential for their own futures. From a transitologist's perspective, the research cases are not recognized as coeval others but rather as cases situated on a logical historical timeline, implying that those who are "lagging behind" are merely situated at an earlier stage. Allegedly, there is only one possible narrative on political change, only one story of progress.

The study of these countries that are lagging behind then comes down to a simple question, as for example the one Storm (2007, 163) poses in the case of Morocco: "Today, fifty years after independence, how far has Morocco come?" To provide such questions with a scientific claim, scholars often reduce complex questions of political change and democracy to quantifiable parameters that can then be measured and classified; for example, the level of transparency of elections, the level of press freedom, and so on.

Moreover, the assumed inevitability of global logics (i.e., contemporary globalization, liberal democracy) is often framed within a simplistic and naïve correlation between democratic transition and market liberalization. More astonishingly, these claims of inevitability are frequently accompanied by the a priori assumption that antihegemonic projects (e.g., communism or Islamism) are nondemocratic (Storm 2007, 184n1, 194n61; see also Diamond 2003; McFaul 2004).

Massey (2005) characterizes these kinds of normative perspectives as *aspatial* perspectives on politics. The cosmology of the one and only possible narrative obliterates the potential differences in political, social, and economic trajectories. She calls these a-spatial because spatial difference is compressed into a temporal sequence, because different "places" are interpreted as mere different stages in a single temporal development (2005, 68). Every country in the world is assumed to follow "the same ('our') path of development" (82). The French philosopher Michel de Certeau warned us that by privileging progress (i.e., time), the conditions of its own possibility (space itself) tend to be forgotten. Space then becomes the blind spot of both scientific and political technology (de Certeau 1984, 95).

The effect of such an aspatial narrative is very political. As Massey argues, "because space has been marshalled under the sign of time, these countries have no space—precisely—to tell different stories, to follow another path. They are dragooned into line behind those who designed the queue." Ironically, she adds—and this will be central in this book as well—their future is not only supposedly foretold; "even this is not true, for precisely their entanglement within the unequal relations of capitalist globalization ensures that they do not 'follow.' The future which is held out as inevitable is unlikely to be reached" (2005, 82). That kind of democracy and democracy promotion does not reflect universal values, as people like Larry Diamond and Michael McFaul would like us to believe, but answers to particular *projects* that reflect certain interests, ideologies, and relations of power.

The same critique can be also be applied to the postdemocratization literature. The scope for alternative political trajectories and futures remains very limited. Imaginations of what went "wrong" in the region after the uprisings (Masoud 2015), the "meaning of failure" (Brown 2013, 55), or the "depressing reality" (Valbjørn and Bank 2010, 188, 192) are inseparably related to the absence of liberal democracy as it exists in the West.

In contrast, the spatial view of people like Massey and other critical thinkers offers conceptual tools to transcend this false opposition between persistent authoritarianism and democratic transition. First, it offers an understanding of uneven development in the Arab region, not as a (temporary) problem of some regions, cities, or even populations that are "lagging behind" and need to "catch up"—in the sense that they are "developing" and we are "developed"—but rather as the produced result of political processes that cannot be disconnected or separated from the outside world, from a wider set of relations involved in the making of contemporary globalization.

Second, it implies abandoning "the search for a single global future." A spatial view looks at the very struggles, the (global) connections, and the various projects of placemaking that make processes of change in the end very dynamic and open ended (Tsing 2000). Especially since 2011, the political future of the region is radically open. What is at stake since then is much more than just explaining the disposal, survival, or authoritarian learning of regimes, kings, or presidents for life; it is the understanding of a much greater complexity of power.

The Regime versus Complexes of Power

The intrinsically interesting question posed by Valbjørn and Bank about "what in fact is going on" does not seem to break loose from an endogenous and regime-centered perspective on political change. Both transitologists and postdemocratization scholars view "the regime" as the key to understanding Arab political life.

In Morocco, the regime is often equated with the makhzan—derived from the Arab verb *khazana*, "to hide or preserve"—which can be translated in English as "magazine" (warehouse, depot) (Claisse 1987). It referred to the place where the sultan's taxes were stored in precolonial Morocco. The term "makhzan" became a synonym for the royal family, its entourage, and the apparatuses of the precolonial state. Today, the term is still commonly used and has become a sometimes vague and polymorphic concept to represent central power (i.e., the regime) in Morocco. The contemporary makhzan denotes the ruling clique around the royal family (the royal advisors, the ulama, the superior army officers, the leading families, and businessmen) (Claisse 1987).

The problem with the dominant narratives on political change in the Arab region is not so much that they are wrong about the authoritarian character of the political systems they study but that they erect a stereotype of the "Arab regime" that actually gets in the way of understanding the complexity of social forces that are manifesting themselves in the current political orders of the region (Parker 2006, 84). For example, a one-sided focus on the makhzan to understand the nature of Moroccan politics might nourish the false impression that nothing really changed in Morocco and that "the reality of power and politics . . . remains as it has been since the independence" (Entelis 2007, 23).

The regime is presented as something that can be studied and understood as a separate entity in itself. The absence of political change—that is, change seen as a democratic transition—can then be explained in terms of the regime's own unwillingness to change. In other words, the regime is the "possessor" of political power and has the ability to block change, or more precisely, the desired direction of change.

Moreover, the stereotype of "the regime as a black box that contains the institutional programming of a society" also informs the assumption that *the* regime controls *the* state (Parker 2006, 97). The state in the Arab world has often been depicted as a coherent entity. In this view, regime power emerges from an institutional core that exerts, via direct intervention, its hegemony over subordinated institutions, spaces, and scales. Arab states are then depicted as bounded entities, with their own internally generated authenticities, and defined by their difference from other geographical imaginations of space, which are obviously situated on the outside (Massey 2005).

Other social forces that can impact regime politics (U.S. support and Western imperialism, foreign investors, European Union [EU] democracy promotion policies, globalization itself) are often categorized as external dimensions, the international context, or exogenous factors (cf. Albrecht and Schlumberger 2004; Cavatorta 2004; 2005; Durac 2009; Henry and Springborg 2001). They do not change the fact that regime remains the key to understand change. Insofar as the dynamics of globalization are taken into account, they are considered to be subjected to endogenous political legacies of state building and regime consolidation (Parker 2009).

Unfortunately, such explanations fail to recognize the complex ways in which statist agency became enmeshed in the global situation, in its interrelation with capitalist agency and capital formation (Parker 2006). In other words, the power attributed to the regime does not necessarily clarify the workings of that power but makes it invisible and hides it behind the discursively constituted image of the unitary and homogenous Arab regime.

Consider, for example, the tension in the recent work of Roger Owen. On the one hand, Owen argues that Arab politics in the postcolonial period were above all "a matter of personality, of personal character, and of family relationships" (2012, 6). Political power was concentrated in the hands of a "president for life" or a monarch. The rulers, their families, and their allies formed the nucleus of the Arab regime. Yet, at the same time, these presidents and kings cannot do exactly what they want as socioeconomic and cultural forces also play an important role (11). However, despite Owen's concern with political economy, economic liberalization, and globalization throughout the book, these forces always remain situated outside the center of Arab politics and what he calls the "mirror state": a system that mirrors presidential beliefs and is dependent "on the institutionalized monopoly of all political activity in the hands of one long-serving president and his associated colleagues and cronies" (194).

If one wants to make sense of Arab politics, Owen argues, one should try to understand first of all the president for life or the king who monopolizes power and personifies the regime. With regard to the Arab uprisings, Owen stresses the importance of political economy, increasing globalization, and the deleterious effect of "poverty, unemployment, and inequality" (200). However, if one wants to understand the *political causes* of the uprisings, one should be looking first and foremost at authoritarian leaders and the regimes who failed to manage the social question and the transition to a successful market economy (200). For Owen, Shakespeare and Machiavelli provide the perfect metaphors for the absolute ruler and his obedient administration.

> Shakespeare is present in the human and family drama of it all: think of the Macbeths' ambitious drive for power, and of Lear's vanity and lack of imagination, making elaborate arrangements for the future rule of his kingdom only to disrupt them in his petulant old age. So too is Machiavelli with his advice that a ruler's counselors should tell him only what they think he wants to hear. (Owen 2012, 11)

Yet this focus on all-powerful kings and monarchical presidents conceals more than it clarifies. And here, Foucault might have been a better reference than Shakespeare or Machiavelli. A predominant focus on the so-called possessor of power does not really explain how the regime is actually situated within a much broader political context and how the dominant position of a small clique of powerful elites is articulated through a much wider set of social relations and apparatuses of rule. As Foucault (2003, 129) noted: "The [royal] administration allows the king to rule the country at will, and subject to no restrictions. And conversely, the administration rules the king thanks to the quality and nature of the knowledge it forces upon him."

"The administration" should be understood, in the broad sense, as the collection of apparatuses and mechanisms of government. Any individual ruler, any regime, is supported by an apparatus of government that has its own dynamics, its own powers, and its own interests. Moreover, as I argue, the contemporary "administrations" in the MENA region are not a purely domestic affair but incorporate many global connections. In fact, kings and presidents are entangled in—to stick with Foucault's way of phrasing—*globally connected administrations of government.* That does not necessarily mean that ruling elites are less powerful, let alone powerless, only that the structures and mechanisms of domination and exploitation in which they are engaged have origins and a reach far beyond national boundaries.

How then do we conceptualize governmental power? Again Foucault is helpful here. Power, according to Foucault, is not something that can be possessed but something that structures relationships. If we go back to the epigraph of this chapter by Gregory Gause, the solution lies not in the shift of focus from the authoritarian regime to "the forces for change that were bubbling below" but in trying to capture the relation between them. "One cannot, therefore, write either the history of kings or the history of peoples," Foucault argues; rather, "one can write the history of what constitutes those opposing terms" (2003, 168). It is within the relational character of power that change is situated. The regime is not a thing that possesses power but a constellation of social relations, global connections, and struggles that implies constant change, even though this change might not always be the desired one.

A spatial view thus requires a much more complex picture of power. This book proposes an alternative approach to think about (authoritarian) transformation and modalities of government in the Arab region. This approach does not start from the regime or any other conceptualization of power as entities in themselves but from the relations, practices, and global encounters that shape and, more important, constantly reshape these representations of power.

This more complex conception of political power—what Christopher Parker has called the "complexes of power" that constitute the dynamics of change—attempts to "recombine global and local, state and market, public and private, and 'traditional' and 'modern'" to unravel the diffuse, open, relational, and often contingent outcomes of political transformation behind the seemingly ubiquitous and stagnant authoritarian image of the "Arab regime" (2004, 7). The *continuity* of authoritarianism in a country such as Morocco should be understood through the practices and global encounters of various agents of transformation within *new* complexes of power that are involved, for example, in the reproduction of urban space.

This does not imply that we should just do away with structuring concepts and leave everything to our imagination of complexity, flow, and contingency. As I elaborate further in chapter 3, there are other concepts that manage to incorporate the global situation in a structuring logic. Class is one such concept. With this concept, I do not wish to erect a new type of power possessor. As mentioned, I do not use class to indicate a well-defined group (e.g., the capitalist class) that possesses power, wealth, the means of production, and so on. Instead, I use class to understand the nature of power *relations* and the complex multiplicity and heterogeneity of these relations in space. Class reproduces itself through space. It does not necessarily exist beforehand but arises out of the struggles over (urban) space. Class explains the particular process— a process of capital accumulation and capitalist expansion—that drives the production, exploitation, and dispossession of urban space today.

Projects of Globalization

So how do we relate new complexes of power to the global situation? How do we bring in the reality of neoliberalism? Most important, how do we grasp this reality, the making of contemporary globalization, as something political to the core?

It is strange in a way that on the one hand we have our mouths full of the interconnectedness, the mobility, the freedom, and the potential of contemporary globalization, a process that transforms our world into a "global village," while on the other hand, when it comes to studying issues such as poverty, inequality, oppression, exploitation, and authoritarianism, we hear much less of this globalizing jargon. Instead, we hear references to localities, particularities, and specificities, as if these phenomena are located somehow outside the global village. There is an obvious tension here. Economics are obviously global; politics, by contrast, much less.

Features and consequences such as global market integration and commercial exchanges, the improvement in means of transportation and communication, technological innovations, migration, new global health and ecological challenges, and the worldwide spread of certain values and norms all seem to suggest that different places around the world are becoming irreversibly and ever more connected. Yet the charisma of globalization lies in its portrayal as an almost natural process, usually with little reference to (local) agency. A truly *global* economy is often claimed to have emerged beyond the reach and control of local governments and nation-states. This picture has captured the imagination of many scholars, journalists, activists, and politicians, ever since the end of the Cold War.

While, in a sense, this assumption is not necessarily untrue, it is the inevitable and almost natural character of this process that is problematic. Globalization is not so much the result of a law of nature but is a project (Massey 2005, 5); or, more precisely, the convergence of a whole series of projects all over the world.

The Antipolitics of Good Governance

This imaginary boundary between global economics and local politics does not hinder political actors to promote intervention. To the contrary, references to the "global" constantly inform political discourse, policymaking, and scholarly analysis. Many stress the inevitability of reform, and more specifically the necessity of reorganizing national economic and political life to reflect the demands and incentives of the "global market." To give one example: in the 2007 trade and investment guide of the American Chambers of Commerce, Mustapha Mechahouri, the Moroccan minister of foreign trade at that time, addressed American investors in the following way:

> As economic actors and experts the users of this guide are certainly aware that the current intensive shift towards globalization is putting the economies of developing countries, such as Morocco, under increasing pressure and requires large scale reforms and structural adaptations. For this reason, the Kingdom of Morocco is now engaged in huge reforms, initiatives and restructuring programs to accelerate its integration into a broad free trade zone alongside Mediterranean countries, Arab countries, the United States of America, and other nations as part of the globalization process. (Amcham Morocco 2007, 6)

The association with inevitability and necessity reveals a depoliticized conception of reform. While contemporary globalization may be the *object* of policy, it is thought to have little to do with the *process* of policy-making itself (for a similar argument on culture and policy, see Kapoor 2008, 19). Social and economic policies responding to the dynamics of globalization are typically viewed as mere technocratic measures. Globalization itself is somehow seen as a place-less realm, beyond the scope of policy, as something that affects local or national policy and not the other way around (Massey 2005).[2] The policy question is thus: how to deal with this force of globalization? The answers are usually built around a general consensus on the virtues of liberal democracy, economic liberalization, and technocratic management and can be brought under one container concept: good governance.

The failure of Third World developmentalist projects, combined with the neoliberal turn in the West, left the door wide open for mainstream discourse and international organizations to claim that there was no alternative to neoliberal globalization, leading to the promotion of a particular project of globalization by the World Bank and other donor agencies, first through the Washington Consensus and then later through the discourse of good governance.

The concept of good governance served as a general guiding principle and "policy metaphor" for international donor institutions who expected adherence from recipient governments to put in place the reforms that satisfied the donor's requirements (Doornbos 2001, 2003). But more than that, it became a universal truth. According to the World Bank, good governance was not only a means to ensure growth and social improvement but also a "fundamental dimension of human development itself" (World Bank 2003, 15). It presented a set of objective principles informed by so-called universal values (i.e., Western values).

The seemingly consensual and universal undertone (also symbolized with the adjective "good") could be used to invite judgment on how a country, a region, a city, or an agency should be governed without actually presenting it as a *political* intervention (Doornbos 2001). In short, good governance was seen as a set of principles that could be applied to any country anywhere in the world, a simple manual to deal with the challenges and—even more so—the opportunities of globalization. Some go even so far to state that the *technical* aspect of good governance, more than its democratic quality, is the real universal condition for happiness (Ott 2009). As a result, there is an extensive body of literature on governance that takes contemporary globalization for granted and, subsequently, also "takes it for granted that the political and social cleavages between those who profit from globalization and those who do not can be bridged by 'modern' or 'good' governance" (Lemke 2007, 57). In the case of Morocco, the works of Ali Sedjari (2008) and Mostapha Fikri (2005) are salient examples.

Uneven development and poverty are mainly seen as technical problems related to inadequate market integration. The disconnection between good governance as a guiding principle, on the one hand, and the domestic affairs of individual states, on the other hand, serves the argument that poverty and underdevelopment are a result of people's inadequate integration, or even exclusion, from the benefits and opportunities of the free-market environment.[3] The World Bank, for example, acknowledges the "spatial disparities" in living standards in the MENA region. These disparities produce "lagging areas," caused for example by rural–urban disparities, whereby some areas are less integrated and have less access to services than others. In fact, Morocco is the area with the biggest rural–urban disparity in the whole MENA region (World Bank 2011, 6). To solve this problem, it is up to policymakers to let "the market determine the spatial distribution of economic activity" (11).

This governance narrative on globalization is exactly what Massey describes as an aspatial narrative. As long as inequality is considered in terms of temporal stages of progress and backwardness, alternative political stories will be disallowed and the political nature of the production of poverty within and through globalization will be obstructed from view (Massey 2005, 84). Relations of power, exploitation, and domination are totally absent from the good governance discourse and framework of analysis. And what is made invisible is also more difficult to contest. To paraphrase James Ferguson, the good governance perspective has an "anti-political effect." The seemingly neutral and technocratic discourse that underpins it does not allow the role of the promoter (e.g., the World Bank) to be formulated as a political one (Ferguson 2006).

Many have criticized this narrative, of course. According to Ray Bush, to give one example, the "poor are poor precisely because of their incorporation into the reality of the contemporary capitalist economies" (2004, 675). Poverty does not emerge from the poor man's exclusion but from his particular economic and political inclusion. This inclusion is characterized by such factors as exploitative labor regimes, a decline in employment due to privatization, the prioritization of investment in rent-seeking economic sectors (e.g., real estate) over redistribution, and the informalization of economic activities. As such, Bush wants to direct our focus to "the crucial issue of how poverty is *created* and *repro-duced*" (674).

Critical questions thus need to challenge this antipolitical narrative. Where does the need for greater market integration come from? Why is it proclaimed in virtually all poverty alleviation strategies? Who develops these strategies and discourses and whose interests do they actually serve? (Bush 2004, 686). Can we just assume that economic growth automatically leads to less poverty? How do we explain, for example, that despite the improved macroeconomic performances in the MENA region, due to the structural adjustments of the 1980s, global market integration coincided with a decline in purchasing power of the average citizen, increasing uneven development, and social inequality? (Bush 2004; see also El-Said and Harrigan 2014).

Neoliberalism as Political Projects

To formulate satisfying answers to the above questions, we need to bring politics back into these stories of economic, social, and technological transformation. We also need to converge these stories with our analyses of authoritarianism in the Arab region. The global situation cannot be separated from the political situation in the region. To understand globalization as a project is to understand the global encounter of networks of power, trade, and meaning within the context of placemaking and government (Tsing 2005, 3).

I propose the concept of "projects" to understand urban politics and placemaking in relation to globalization, neoliberalism, and capitalist reconfiguration. The specificity of neoliberal projects on the ground, in places like Rabat and Casablanca, reminds us of two things. First, the universal claims of neoliberalism—or the claim that neoliberalism is universal—does not mean that every place on earth is turning out to be the same. Second, different places and projects around the world contribute to the constitution of this idea of universality, to the idea of neoliberalism itself (Tsing 2005, 1–10). Instead of starting from a pre-defined, monolithic, and often intangible idea of neoliberalism (just like globalization itself), the concept of projects allows us to focus on the actual practices and connections that are constitutive of that idea (I draw here on Hughes Rinker 2014).

There are three concrete reasons why the concept of projects or neoliberal projects serves to understand political change in the Arab region. First, as Anna Tsing notes, "to identify projects is to maintain a commitment to localization, even of the biggest world-making dreams and schemes" (2000, 347). Neoliberalism as a set of projects is the attempt to translate ideologies, paradigms, economic principles, and even religious-like features attributed to neoliberalism into concrete and material articulations on the ground. This also means, as Cortney Hughes Rinker (2014) argues, that neoliberal traits may interconnect with or draw power from particular (local) beliefs, practices, and institutions—elements that do not appear to have anything to do with neoliberal practice at first sight (see also Atia 2013; Debruyne and Parker 2015).

Neoliberalism seen as projects is not an attempt to redefine the local and its relationship vis-à-vis the global but rather an attempt to localize a phenomenon we usually ascribe to the global. By identifying projects, we can *situate* global capitalism. Identifying projects not only means that we make the connections between places around the world visible, but it also helps us to understand how all these connections produce the global situation form within different places or localities. The concept of projects makes globalization concrete, tangible, and thus also contestable. If globalization remains this abstraction, always something out there, always somewhere else, somewhere global, and thus in a way unlocated and untouchable, it becomes in the end apolitical, with the properties of a force of nature, as it were.

Different projects take place in different places, in different cities; for example, in the form of a megaproject or a slum upgrading project. But besides these two examples, projects do not always have to be so specific. The remodeling of an entire city, a national economic strategy, a particular sector, or the state itself can also be considered as projects. Yet none of these projects are constructed in isolation. None of these projects are entirely "local."

Projects explain the paradox between what globalization promises and what it produces. They explain the connection between utopian schemes of ideology and seemingly universal worldviews and the (class) interests of those who attempt to reconstruct places accordingly. This brings us straight to the second reason why I think the concept of projects explains the political nature of neoliberalism. Projects point to agency. A project refers to the complete opposite of a force of nature. It cannot be uncoupled from politics, ideology, agency, and people.

Identifying neoliberal projects is not the same as claiming that it is all caused by neoliberalism. All too often there is a tendency to anthropomorphize neoliberalism, that is, to attribute power to an imagination that does not possess that kind of power (Mayer and Künkel 2011). This act of fetishism actually hides agency and power. In contrast, projects never take shape without real human agents, the specific practices they deploy, the ideas they adhere to, and the rationalities that give sense to their actions. The concept of project implicitly suggests a certain direction, goals, and strategies. Projects are *strategic*.

Different agents are involved in different projects, and they are not necessarily confined to geographical boundaries, nation-state borders, or any other imagined or real entity. An urban development project in a particular city can attract capital, investors, and designers from all over the world. Such a project shows the interdependence, cooperation, and often also the power struggle between various agents, both private and state-related. The coming together of these actors in such a project has a significant impact on what a city is going to look like and, most important, how it is going to affect city life. Projects are thus particular articulations of "complexes of power" that give form to our contemporary global situation.

Finally, this combination of locality and agency also makes projects messy, heterogeneous, often unstable, and certainly open ended. Sometimes they can seem contradictory as the powerful struggle between each other. Obviously, they also provoke reactions, produce resistance, and create conflicts. In other words, projects are transformative articulations of power in space and time. They are changed constantly through struggles of all kinds.

Struggle is thus crucial for our understanding. Yet by "struggle" I do not only refer to obvious expressions of discontent, social protest, and so forth. In fact, social protest will not be central in the story of this book. I see struggle in a broader context. Looking at particular projects of globalization, and explaining them as projects of *neo*liberalism, only makes sense if one takes into consideration what they reacted against, what they undermined or re-created, what kind of hegemonic social order they replaced, or better, out of what kind of social order and struggles these neoliberal projects emerged.

It is in this view that David Harvey understands neoliberal projects as the "restoration of class power" on a global scale (Harvey 2006b; see also Amin 2003). In the 1980s, neoliberal projects reshaped social and political life all over the world. "Thatcherism" and "Reaganomics" became popular synonyms for two of the best-known examples of neoliberal restructuring. In the Global South, neoliberal restructurings were pushed through mainly by the World Bank and the IMF via the infamous SAPs. Neoliberalism as a set of class projects implied an attack on "big government" in the West and pressured southern countries to open their markets for capitalist interests. Yet situating different projects within a global neoliberal process does not mean that we have to homogenize different sites, spaces, and moments in time; rather, we must recognize the *global* and *political* dimensions of diversity on the ground (Tsing 2000).

Neoliberal projects not only increased globalization but also radically altered the dynamics of the process itself. The important question here is not whether the world has become more global but rather *how* globalization is (re)produced. The increased mobility of capital has allowed it to search for the most favorable conditions everywhere in the world (with respect to such factors as labor costs, institutional environment, political stability, and tax and legal regimes). This has resulted in arrangements such as outsourcing, subcontracting, and new institutionalized practices of zoning, like special economic zones. Morocco, for example, is keen to develop offshore zones in cities such as Casablanca, Fez, Rabat, Tangier, and Marrakech to strengthen the country's position as a potential destination for foreign businesses. As such, what is important for our understanding of the political transformations under neoliberalism is not so much the degree of globalization as the *form* of globalization (Massey 2005, 85).

A New Urban Order

A new urban order has emerged out of neoliberal projects. Urban politics are at the center of neoliberal globalization. Within the continual and contingent historical process in which capitalism attempts to create the preconditions of its own perpetuation, urban projects are the cornerstones of the current spatial organization of globalization (Harvey 1989b; see also Brenner and Theodore 2002; Massey 2010).

Of course, the claim that contemporary capitalism is city centric seems to state the obvious. Capitalist expansion has always been closely interrelated with urbanization. Yet the neoliberal city differs radically from the modernist and colonial city of the nineteenth century or the Fordist and developmentalist city of the twentieth century. While urban infrastructure was crucial in supporting capitalist expansion and production during the industrial age, the role of the built environment has been expanded extensively since the 1970s. Urban spaces have become highly valued consumption products on a global scale and capitalism's creative and innovative nature has been manifested through the city's dual role: as a place of consumption and as the consumption of place—two forms of growth fueled primarily by real estate speculation and increasing levels of debt (both public and private) (Lefebvre 1996, 73; see also Harvey 1989b, 2010b).

Harvey argues that the historical relationship between capitalism and urbanization should be captured in dialectical terms. Throughout our modern history, urban processes have been shaped by the logic of capital circulation and accumulation. In turn, however, these urban processes shape the conditions of capital accumulation at later points in time and space (Harvey 1989a, 3). As such, the role of cities in the history of capitalist globalization has changed significantly over time (Harvey 1989b, 19–58). To present Harvey's argument schematically (and a bit oversimplified): the mercantile city mobilized surpluses (through violent appropriation from the colonized parts of the world), the industrial city played a key role in the production of surpluses (through the exploitation of labor), and the developmental (Keynesian) city absorbed these surpluses (through the promotion of the demand side and massive public investments). Finally, the contemporary neoliberal city has become an "entrepreneurial city" in which urban government is able to respond quickly to the shifting demands of capital within an increasingly competitive world market (Harvey 1989a).[4]

The shifting priorities within capitalist organization, for example, from industrialization to financialization and capital mobility, coincided with a reproduction of urban space to facilitate these priorities. In this regard, a lot of attention has been paid to the emergence of the "global city" as a key locale in the regulation of the global economy and as evidence for the declining significance of a "national" economy (Sassen 1991).

But the impact of neoliberal capitalism cannot be reduced to the role of global cities. It has generated far-reaching transformations that concern basically every city in the world. No Moroccan city, for example, can claim that it is able to participate in, let alone determine, the direction and management of the global economy (Catusse, Cattedra, and Janati 2007). But this does not mean that cities such as Casablanca and Rabat have not experienced similar political, economic, and social transformations.

Of course, one should always be careful with the use of denotations like "the neoliberal city." It is important to stress that this specification refers not to some kind of uniform model of urban change but to a certain period of globalization. Within a significant body of literature, the neoliberal city or "neoliberal urbanism" refers to specific social and spatial transformations in the United States and Europe, namely the transition from a Fordist to a post-Fordist city characterized by deindustrialization, inner-city revaluation, real estate speculation, gentrification, and an economic development strategy mainly based on the services sector (e.g., Hackworth 2007). Yet that particular model of the post-Fordist city is not simply generalizable to the rest of the world; the histories of cities such as London and New York do not necessarily represent logical, or even inevitable, trajectories for other globalizing cities around the world.

To indicate the diversity within urban developments around the world, one might begin by arguing that the deindustrialization of Western cities actually implied the opposite in many southern low-wage countries (Chakravorty 2000). Furthermore, cities in the Global South are characterized and structured much more than their Western counterparts by such phenomena as the informal economy, extreme poverty, the impact of remittances, (forced) migration, and slums and other forms of spontaneous sprawl. These are also phenomena that are intimately related to globalization.

Additionally, one might also argue that the distinction between northern and southern cities is far from satisfactory, as many cities around the world encompass a great diversity in development, political–economic structures, social composition, and colonial histories (Chakravorty 2000). There is of course no singular Global North, nor a singular Global South, and the geographical distinction between these two concepts is far from absolute.[5]

Finally, compared to urban entrepreneurialism in Europe or the United States, local city councils in authoritarian states such as Morocco enjoy much less autonomy. This does not mean, however, that in these countries decision-making processes and state power have not been re-institutionalized and reterritorialized in important ways to give more leverage to subnational and urban scales.

Despite these obvious nuances and differences, general political-economic tendencies can still be distinguished. Neoliberal globalization has transformed cities all around the world in fundamental ways. First, the collapse of state developmentalism in the Global South and Fordism in the Global North entailed a shift from economic competition between nation-states toward an increasing competition between urban regions. In order to fix global capital flows, local government intervention shifted from redistribution mechanisms toward more market-oriented strategies and the support of private urban enterprise and private investment in the built environment (R. Weber 2002). To the degree that cities were often considered part of the problem, especially in the Global South (in terms of demographic growth and urban poverty), they had to become part of the solution (Harvey 1989b, 44).

With the collapse of state developmentalism, urban regions had to compete for investments, employment, image, and so on, by trying to lure investments, integrate into global circuits of capital, and offer attractive packages combining favorable labor conditions, tax regimes, political stability, security, physical (e.g., offices, roads) and social infrastructure (e.g., an educated labor force), and, finally, particular cultural, environmental, and lifestyle qualities (Harvey 1989b). The (re)appropriation of urban land and city centers, in Morocco as well as in many other cities in the Global South, became central in projects that promoted tourism, real estate development, the expansion of financial and other services, beautification projects, and slum relocation.

A typical strategy for the contemporary neoliberal city is the reliance on large-scale urban development projects or "megaprojects" (Flyvbjerg 2005; Swyngedouw, Moulaert, and Rodriguez 2002). They are considered key to the commercial redevelopment of the city center and the promotion of the city's "unique selling position." Megaprojects are the iconic materializations of a capital-friendly climate. They literally catch the eye. They are the city's showcases to the outside world. The promotion of an image of global outreach as part of a city-marketing strategy has become at least as important as actually "being global"; and megaprojects are the ideal instrument to encourage this imagination (Ren and Weinstein 2013).

Megaprojects are also radically reshaping Arab cities. Today, the phrase "Arab city" may still evoke a number of stereotypes, calling up images of an archaic place full of mosques and minarets, small alleys, crowded cafés, and little shops or a city characterized by chaotic planning and informal expansion. Nevertheless, the Arab city is now also becoming a place of hypermodern skyscrapers, mega shopping malls, and unabashed consumerism (Elsheshtawy 2008b, 3; Kanna 2011, 170). These phenomena are usually associated with the Gulf region, and more specifically the city of Dubai (M. Davis 2006a). The extravagant images of real estate development projects such as The World (the group of islands in front of the seashore), the seven-star hotel Burj Al-Arab, and the Burj Khalifa (the largest tower in the world today) certainly contribute to the fantasy of this "Dubai model."

No doubt, Dubai has been one of the most spectacular and most publicized cases. Yet the Emirati city is not an isolated case in the region. Dubai's urban development model was copied in the rest of the Arab world, often under the influence of oil money coming from the Gulf. Over the last decade, megaprojects proliferated in the region with flagship projects such as Downtown Beirut (Solidere), Tunis Financial Harbour, Abdali in Amman, Dreamland in Cairo, Jeddah Tower (the next tallest building in the world), The Pearl in Doha, and of course the various new stadiums in Qatar in preparation for the World Cup in 2022 (Barthel 2010; Daher 2013; Hourani 2014; Krijnen and Fawaz 2010; Parker 2009).

After the credit crunch in 2008, it seemed for a while as if the politics of megaprojects had serious limits. The first signs of overinvestment and high-risk rent-seeking urbanization became painfully clear when several ongoing projects, in Dubai for example, were either abandoned or faced serious delay in the aftermath of the financial meltdown and the global economic crisis that followed. In Morocco this also was the case, for example, with the withdrawal of a Dubai investor (Sama Dubai) from the Bouregreg project. Today, however, it appears the politics of megaprojects took only a temporary setback; there were considerable delays but the overall commitment remains, and not even the Arab uprisings managed to turn things around (Barthel and Vignal 2014).

The politics of megaprojects represents a shift not only to urban entrepreneurialism but also to important transitions within neoliberal projects and neoliberal government. The implementation of these kinds of projects required new regulatory and institutional arrangements that were radically different from the ones of the developmentalist era. Where the neoliberal reforms of structural adjustment in the 1980s aimed foremost at eradicating the former social order, the politics of megaprojects displayed some of the building stones of a new order. Within this particular transition lies the key to understanding some of the fundamental changes in contemporary politics in Morocco.

2

AN URBAN HISTORY OF
NEOLIBERAL PROJECTS
IN MOROCCO

> Urbanism is a mask and a tool: a mask for the state and political
> action, a tool of interests that are dissimulated within a strategy
> and a socio-logic. Urbanism does not try to model space as a
> work of art. It does not even try to do so in keeping with its
> technological imperatives, as it claims. The space it creates is
> political.
>
> —Henri Lefebvre, *The Urban Revolution*

> Political scientists are rarely attuned to the ways in which a
> changing cityscape might reflect emerging configurations of
> power. Yet, if one explores the new systems of movement and
> connection being etched into cityscapes across the Middle East,
> these concrete structures tell a story of transformation that has
> been lost in transition-oriented accounts of Arab political life.
>
> —Christopher Parker, "Tunnel-Bypasses and
> Minarets of Capitalism"

THROUGH THE URBAN LENS I want to understand other kinds of problems: neoliberalism; the state; government in contemporary societies, especially in the Global South; and, finally, uneven development.

One might say, compared to other regions in the world, that dynamics of urbanization remain an overlooked topic within the broader literature on political life in the Arab region. Nevertheless, there is a growing group of scholars within a broad range of disciplines that look at different aspects of urban life in the region to understand contemporary societal changes (Barthel 2010; Boumaza 2005; Daher 2013; Elsheshtawy 2008a; Fawaz 2009; Kanai and Kutz 2011; Kanna 2011; Singerman and Amar 2006a). More specifically on Morocco, there is an important body of literature, predominantly francophone, that has studied urban transformations since the 1980s (Abouhani 1999; de Miras 2005; Kaioua 1996; Navez-Bouchanine 1997; Rachik 1995; Zaki 2011a).

The primary focus of these studies is the urban condition as such. In this book, however, the city is not so much the object of study but rather my window (or my method) to understand broader political questions. My approach is thus slightly different from the works cited above (maybe with the exception of Kanna's book and Singerman and Amar's edited volume).[1] I am aiming to bridge a gap between Middle East urban studies and the wider field of political science dealing with questions of power, government, and globalization in the region.

In this chapter, I go back to the beginning of the neoliberal turn in Morocco, situate the political changes of the last four decades within a broader history of neoliberal reform, and highlight how the city became the primary object of neoliberal projects. Moreover, I describe not only the Moroccan transition to neoliberalism but also a transition within actually existing neoliberalism. The character of neoliberal projects and modalities of government today are radically different from the interventions of the 1980s.

The 1980s represented a period of political and economic crisis, a period of creative destruction and open struggle. Structural adjustment and urban mass protests marked this turbulent and very uncertain period. It prompted the monarchy to implement serious political reforms in the 1990s in order to stabilize and pacify the kingdom. These reforms, also known as the *alternance* process, followed by the accession to the throne of Mohammed VI and a changing international context (the post–Washington Consensus) are crucial political elements that contributed to the reconfiguration of neoliberal government.

Well aware of the disruptive impact of structural adjustment, the reign of Mohammed VI was characterized by the attempt to address the social limits of austerity and economic liberalization and consolidate the further development of the new neoliberal order. His reign gave rise to a radical makeover of the city, an *urbanism of megaprojects*, new forms of statecraft, and the transfer of decision-making power to new (semi) state agencies.

Political Change and the Neoliberal Turn in Morocco

The implementation of a structural adjustment program (SAP) in Morocco in 1983 is the turning point from which the current political transformations and the Moroccan state-reformation process can be explained. Before the 1980s, the Moroccan political economy contained specific characteristics of a "state-developmental model" based on the principle that the state was the main driving force for economic growth (Catusse 2009b; Richards and Waterbury 2008).

The Third World debt crisis at the end of the 1970s marked the beginning of the end of state developmentalism and opened the door to neoliberal projects, bringing about fundamental changes in (urban) society. The reforms that followed should be seen as not only an economic and a social rupture but also a political one; it should be considered as a radical economic intervention and also as the starting point of radically different modes of government.

However, in the academic literature, the most important turning point in Morocco's political history is usually situated a decade later with the beginning of the so-called *alternance*. This was a crucial moment indeed, but one that needs to be situated within a broader history of political-economic restructuring. The *alternance* not only entailed limited political liberalization but also created the conditions for the continuation and consolidation of neoliberal reform. I start with a brief sketch of the *alternance* process in order to explain its role and place within Morocco's history of neoliberalism and the transition from "rollback" to "roll-out" neoliberalism.

The Moroccan Reform Process of the 1990s

The start of a process of political change in Morocco is usually situated in the early 1990s, when King Hassan II set Morocco on a path of political and social reform. Confronted with turbulent episodes of urban unrest and violence in the 1980s, together with the continuation of the conflict in the Western Sahara, increasing international criticism on Morocco's human rights record, and the publication of Gilles Perrault's *Notre ami le roi* (1990), which denounced Hassan II's thirty years of human rights violations and criticized France's policy of turning a blind eye to these violations, Hassan II took resolute steps in the direction of political liberalization. He wanted to ensure the monarchy's survival, the credibility of its rule, and his own succession (Sater 2010).

He gave a first important political sign by creating the Conseil Consultatif des Droits de l'Homme (CCDH, Advisory Council for Human Rights), releasing many political prisoners and closing the infamous prison of Tazmamart. Furthermore, he pushed through a constitutional reform process in 1992, followed by another one in 1996. Last but not least, the monarchy undertook several initiatives to set up talks and negotiations with the opposition, leading to the *alternance* government of 1998, which brought the historical opposition parties Istiqlal, Union Socialiste des Forces Populaires (USFP, Socialist Union of Popular Forces), and Parti du Progrès et du Socialisme (PPS, Party of Progress and Socialism) into the government (Zemni and Bogaert 2006).[2] On February 4, 1998, the leader of the USFP, Abderrahman Youssoufi, was appointed prime minister.

These events sparked the hope, among both domestic and foreign observers, that a genuine process of democratization was under way despite the fact that the *alternance* government remained a very heterogeneous coalition and that the monarchy maintained the control over the so-called sovereign ministries: Interior, Foreign Affairs, Justice, and Religious Affairs.

The enthusiasm about the political reform process grew even more after the death of Hassan II. Mohammed VI, who ascended to the throne in 1999, further expanded the political reform process. He immediately got rid of the widely despised minister of interior, Driss Basri, and acknowledged the government's responsibility during the *"années de plomb"* (years of lead) (Vermeren 2002). Mohammed VI also pushed through notable reforms such as the changes made to the *Moudawana* (family code) and several measures leading to a considerable, although still limited, improvement in human rights and freedom of the press.[3]

Together with some important electoral reforms, these measures tempted many observers to speak of a Moroccan exception to the wider trend of authoritarian durability in the region. By the end of the 1990s, Amnesty International and Human Rights Watch stated that Morocco had significantly improved its human rights record; the World Bank and other international institutions lauded Morocco as being one of the "success stories" of reform in the region (Zemni and Bogaert 2006). Within academic circles this process was viewed with more prudence and skepticism but, nevertheless, some observers saw promising change (Desrues and Moyano 2001; El Hachimi 2015; Malka and Alterman 2006; Storm 2007).

This story of a Moroccan exception took a setback when several suicide bombers struck Casablanca on May 16, 2003. The attacks caused a shockwave within Moroccan society and among the political elite and marked a return to old methods of repression and authoritarian control.

Thousands of Islamist suspects were arrested; the control over the legitimate Islamist party, the PJD, was sharpened and freedom of speech in the media was restricted again. After these violent events, security became an absolute priority again, often at the expense of earlier achievements and progress made in, for example, the domain of human rights. Despite the rising criticism of the stagnation and even reversal of the reform process, some believed that Morocco's social policies implemented after 2003—as an immediate response to the sociopolitical crisis—still indicated a real transition. Policies such as the Cities Without Slums (VSB) program and the National Initiative for Human Development (INDH) were embedded within a discourse articulating a strong commitment toward democratization, good governance, poverty alleviation, and social development at the highest levels of the state (Navez-Bouchanine 2009).

A Neoliberal Transition and a Transition within Neoliberalism

I argue that these new social policy commitments are indeed evidence of a fundamental political transformation. However, the origins of this transformation should not be situated in the 1990s, in the *alternance* process, but can be traced to the beginning of the 1980s. The political process I am trying to understand here and the place of *alternance* in this process was characterized not only by a transition toward neoliberal modes of government but also by a fundamental transition within Moroccan neoliberalism.

Moreover, the political transformations produced by the neoliberal turn cannot be grasped by looking at the domestic political scene alone. Local ruling elites, international institutions, global corporations, foreign investors, NGOs, civil society, and foreign governments were all involved in the production of expanding networks and political spaces that made (urban) government more a "global enterprise" than simply a national one (Cohen and Jaïdi 2006, 3).

For the sake of analytic generalization, this ongoing process of political change could be divided into two episodes described by Jamie Peck and Adam Tickell (2002) as phases of roll-back and roll-out neoliberalism. The period of roll-back neoliberalism in Morocco corresponds with the reforms of the 1980s and early 1990s up until the start of the *alternance* process. Ever since the introduction of an SAP, Morocco entered a phase of serious economic restructuring and retrenchment. "Rollback neoliberalism" refers to this destructive moment when state power was mobilized behind austerity, fiscal consolidation, and deregulation projects. The dismantlement of direct state control over the economic sphere implied not the rollback of the state per se but rather the rollback of particular (developmentalist) state functions.

The drastic austerity measures did not come without severe social costs. In Morocco, they provoked a decade of violent urban street protests and nationwide social disturbances. Riots broke out in cities such as Casablanca (1981), Marrakech (1984), and Fez (1990). Moreover, although Morocco and other MENA countries had been prompted to liberalize their economies since the early 1980s, foreign investments and overall economic growth remained unstable (D. K. Davis 2006; Zemni and Bogaert 2009). Under pressure of these turbulent 1980s and the obvious limits of early neoliberal reform, an important reconstitution of the neoliberal project occurred from the mid-1990s onward.

This marked the period of roll-out neoliberalism. The concept refers to a more creative phase of neoliberalism, characterized by new forms of institution building, new modes of regulation, and new configurations of spatially differentiated government that transferred the ability to govern political and economic life to new governmental arrangements. The Bouregreg project is one of those arrangements.

This period of roll-out neoliberalism should be linked to the *alternance* process. In addition to those measures that aimed to improve Morocco's human rights record, the democratic deficit, and the rights of women, the Moroccan authorities also engaged in the *political reconstruction* of its market in order to attract more foreign investments and stimulate economic growth (Zemni and Bogaert 2009). As such, the *alternance* can not only be understood as the start of a (limited) process of democratic reform but also should be seen as an important political turn in the reproduction of neoliberal modalities of government and the reconstitution of neoliberalism itself in Morocco.

In contrast to the more common idea of a "retreat of the state" (Strange 1996), neoliberalization, as a market-building project, actually involves the making of a new "destructively creative" social order with the rollback of institutions and social arrangements associated with state developmentalism, followed by the rollout of new state forms, new modalities of government, and new modes of regulation (Peck and Tickell 2007, 33).

Political Change in the Context of a Post–Washington Consensus

We can observe a transition within neoliberalism in many parts of the Global South. Throughout the 1980s, programs of structural adjustment rolled back the achievements and mechanisms of many developmental states in the Global South (import-substituting industrialization [ISI], job security in the public sector, food subsidies, health care, etc.). Fiscal discipline, market liberalization, the downsizing of the public sector, and the privatization of public assets were introduced to control state-budget deficits after the Third World debt crisis.

The crisis of the 1980s and the worldwide protests against structural adjustment policies (cf. Branch and Mampilly 2015; Walton and Seddon 1994) set into motion a new political and academic discourse of "market failure" (Roy 2010). After the so-called lost decades (Easterly 2001)—the overall stagnation of economic growth between 1980 and 1998 in the Global South—a major shift occurred in development policies. The focus shifted from structural adjustment to the promotion of "good governance" and institutional reform.

In the negative aftermath of the SAP era, it was clear that mere market deregulation and price incentives were not enough to spur economic growth; under the inspiration of then chief economist of the World Bank Joseph Stiglitz, the idea emerged that supporting a free-market economy required strong state capacities (Kapoor 2008, 29). As a result, the state, first conceived as part of the problem, became part of the solution.

This change in discourse gave rise to the "post–Washington Consensus" and the recognition of the important role of governments in regulatory economic policy (Stiglitz 2004; see also World Bank 1997, 2002). The general explanation for these "second generation" neoliberal reforms was that the failure of structural adjustment was generated by the incapacity of institutionally weak states. Even though "state-dominated development has failed," the World Bank insisted, "so will stateless development" (World Bank 1997, 25). In place of advocacy for a "minimalist state," the international institution now advocated for an important role for the state in protecting and correcting markets (Panitch 1998). In the case of the MENA region, the World Bank was convinced that weak governance had contributed to weak growth because poor governance had "shackled the business environment" (World Bank 2003, 10).

The fundamentals of the Washington Consensus were not undermined. According to the World Bank and the IMF, the particular causes for the failure of SAPs had little to do with the neoliberal dogmas per se. With its new discourse on good governance, the World Bank now seemed to suggest that it was not so much the neoliberal strategies themselves that were the root of the problem (i.e., the Washington Consensus) but the domestic governance frameworks of the recipient countries (Jenkins 2002). The responsibility for "failure" was thus passed on to the "developing" countries.

The increased attention given to the state did not signify that neoliberals now accepted the definite comeback of state intervention as such. Instead, it meant that neoliberal projects would seriously influence *how* state intervention was to be deployed. Past ideas on state intervention (developmentalism, protectionism, import substitution, etc.) were replaced by more market-oriented perspectives on public policy (new public management, workfare, good governance, etc.). "Government" now had to incorporate and adjust to the principles and values of economic enterprise, including cost efficiency, technocratic management, and competition. Moroccan policymakers also adhered to these new principles. The new policy values were brought in by the appointment of highly skilled young technocrats within public institutions—often trained in the United States and France. As the former wali (governor) of Greater Casablanca, Driss Benhima, stated in weekly magazine *Maroc Hebdo* in 2001:

> In the current world, the enterprise is the framework of defining policy. In fact, it has imposed this framework upon several non-economic organizations, and several administrations are currently governed according to the running principles of enterprise. (quoted in Catusse 2008, 195)[4]

This paradigm shift within international donor institutions implied something else as well, revealing the political nature behind the technocratic language of good governance. Roll-out neoliberalism or "deep neoliberalism," as Paul Cammack called it, and the emphasis put on institutional reform by people like Stiglitz should be understood as the attempt to make the impact of neoliberal projects in the Global South more profound and sustainable in the long term from a capitalist point of view.

The key to Stiglitz's approach is the commitment to competition, between producers and between workers. Overhasty moves to liberalise and privatise prior to the introduction of regulatory regimes that will ensure competition are condemned as "shallow" and reversible, more likely to produce anti-competitive rent-seeking and monopoly than the social and institutional pressure to "compete" upon which capitalism depends. (Cammack 2004, 197)

It is for that reason that the post–Washington Consensus and people like Stiglitz advocated a more fundamental kind of "interventionism" compared to early reforms of structural adjustment. Neoliberal projects—Cammack referred to the Wolfensohn-Stiglitz project with regard to the World Bank—were supposed to aim *"at the fundamental transformation of society and institutions"* (2004, 194, emphasis added). After a destructive phase of structural adjustment, we are witnessing such kinds of fundamental transformations in Morocco, especially since the first decade of the twenty-first century, anchoring neoliberal projects in much "deeper" and profound ways in order to secure and expand opportunities for capital accumulation.

But before we continue to look at some concrete cases of this interventionism, let us look at the two periods of roll-back and roll-out neoliberalism in Morocco from a more general point of view. It will be the historical background on which the arguments of the second and third parts of the book are built.

The Urban Condition under Roll-Back Neoliberalism: Urban Unrest and the Undermining of State Developmentalism

The 1960s and the early 1970s can best be described as an era of *étatisme* and bureaucratic expansion in the MENA region (Ayubi 1997). Strong bureaucratic control over the national economy and ISI policies formed the basis for the developmental state in the region. "Arab socialism" was the dominant equivalent of Third World developmentalism. It constituted the ideological basis for popular political forces such as Nasserism in Egypt and the Ba'ath parties in Syria and Iraq. This era came to an end rather abruptly in the early 1980s when the Arab world was dragged into a severe debt crisis, together with the rest of the Third World (see Corbridge 2002; Easterly 2001; Richards and Waterbury

2008; Schatan 1987). Those countries with a lack of oil resources (e.g., Jordan, Morocco, Tunisia, Egypt) were especially hard hit.

Structural adjustment hooked even the poorest countries into the system of capital circulation (Harvey 2003). Capitalists, Harvey argues, will always try to reduce the frictions of distance and the barriers for the movement of capital. This is exactly what happened during the debt crisis. After the oil shock of 1973, great amounts of surplus capital were piling up in the Gulf States. At the same time, Organisation for Economic Co-operation and Development (OECD) investment banks saw their chance to recycle these surpluses by lending it to Third World countries that were looking to finance their expansive economic policies. When those countries eventually came into trouble, external debt rescheduling became a mechanism by which private investors, banks, and governments in advanced industrial countries continued to extract wealth from peripheral countries (Harvey 2010b; Ruccio 2011; Schatan 1987).

SAPs were introduced, for instance, in Morocco (1983), Tunisia (1986), Jordan (1989), and Egypt (1991). In the process, the implementation of those neoliberal projects implied the effective dismantling of state developmentalism. Before the era of structural adjustment, the MENA region had relatively reasonable income levels and redistribution mechanisms compared to other Third World regions. Yet structural adjustment caused an increase in the cost of living, especially in the urban areas, and the layoff of redundant labor in the public sector. Ray Bush (2004) notes that while some economic performances improved due to macroeconomic restructuring, real purchasing power parity of the average citizen fell, uneven development increased, and income inequality grew exponentially beginning in the 1980s. In other words, the neoliberal projects of structural adjustment had a profound impact on the urban condition in countries such as Morocco. Not surprisingly, they coincided very often with urban mass protests and violent disturbances, as for instance in Egypt (1977), Morocco (1981, 1984), Tunisia (1984), and Jordan (1989).

Urban Neglect in the Early Postcolonial Period

Before the neoliberal turn, Morocco's political economy could be linked to the dominant trend of "developmentalism" in the region. However, unlike other Arab countries, for example Egypt, where the influence of Arab socialism had a significant impact, Morocco never completely embraced a developmentalist model and a state-dominated economic sector (Catusse 2008; Leveau 1997; Najem 2001; Sater 2010). In contrast to most other Arab countries that opted for a planned economy, Hassan II had always opted for a controlled liberal economic system.[5] Moreover, the domestic economy continued to be dominated by foreign, mostly French, capital (Jaidi 1992). The French Banque de Paris et de Pays Bas, for example, controlled no fewer than fifty companies through its participation in the kingdom's largest holding, Omnium Nord African (ONA) (Sater 2010, 95).

Also, while important regional countries such as Egypt, Syria, Algeria, Libya, and Iraq turned to the Soviet Union for support, Morocco turned to the West. The United States and especially France were its most important allies. No other country received more French bilateral aid than Morocco after 1975 (Pennell 2000, 342–44).[6]

This did not mean that the Moroccan economy did not contain specific characteristics of a developmental state model (Catusse 2009b; Richards and Waterbury 2008). Over the years, the involvement of the state in the economy gradually increased. However, state intervention was inspired not by socialist or populist motives but rather by economic and political necessity. During the 1950s and 1960s, intervention was dictated more by the structural weakness of the private sector and by neopatrimonial practices and state clientelism than by a coherent developmentalist strategy (Ben Ali 1997; Kaioua 1996, 113; Waterbury 1970).

Most important was the role of the state in agricultural development. While other Arab countries implemented policies to promote rapid industrialization, often at the expense of the agricultural sector, the monarchy deliberately prioritized the agricultural sector during the first decades of its independence. The palace saw a stable rural landowning class as one of the foundations of its power base and pulled wealthy landowners into its patronage networks (Pennell 2000, 306; for an extensive historical analysis, see Leveau 1985). State investments in rural development were an attempt to limit the political weight of the urban-based nationalist movement and the Istiqlal party.[7] These investments also aimed to halt the rural exodus toward the cities. Consequently, authorities largely ignored the industrialization and planning of Morocco's urban agglomerates (Naciri 1984). There was no consistent urban planning strategy as late as the 1970s, even the 1980s. Politically, rural migration and the informal expansion of the city were largely neglected.

At the end of the 1960s, however, this political support for rural landowners and agriculture reached its limits. Despite the efforts, the rural exodus continued and had a significant impact on urbanization at the time. The chaotic urban expansion and the natural and structural limits of the agricultural sector (Swearingen 1987) inevitably exposed the political need to expand and deepen state intervention in the (urban) economy. Casablanca was the most salient example: its population more than doubled between the 1950s and the 1970s, the city attracted more than 35 percent of all rural migrants (Zriouli 1998), and during this period 42 percent of all urban expansion in the country was informal (Bargach 2008).

The growth of a lower urban middle class was putting severe pressure on available public services and resources in the cities. There was a real shortage of affordable housing due to limited availability and a rise in housing prices. Only about 20,000 social houses were built in Morocco between 1956 and 1965, and virtually all of them were originally planned by the colonial administration (Johnson 1972). Although the government increased their efforts to supply social housing in the 1970s, the shortfall in housing was put at 390,000 units in 1973 and was estimated at 800,000 in 1977. In order to meet the demand, approximately 70,000 new housing units were needed each year to avoid the overcrowding of existing housing and the further deterioration of urban living conditions (World Bank 1981).

This shortage and the high demand for cheap housing gave rise to a type of informal housing whose growth would be even stronger than that of the bidonvilles in the 1970s: clandestine housing or *habitats clandestins* (HC). This was a typical lower-middle-class phenomenon of urban expansion not only in Morocco but also in other parts of the region, including Egypt (Ismail 2006), Tunisia (Navez-Bouchanine 2002b), and Lebanon (Fawaz 2009). Just like the slums, the HC were originally built without official public authorization, in violation of land use regulations, and on plots without public facilities such as electricity connections, paved roads, and sewer systems. The big difference with the slums is that the inhabitants of HC own their land (albeit not legally recognized), whereas slum dwellers occupy land illegally and at best only own their shelter. Moreover, the HC were built *"en dur,"* in brick and wood, and as such, they looked a lot like formal urban neighborhoods (Abouhani 1995b; Ameur 1995, 2000; Iraki and Rachik 2005; Lahzem 1995; Navez-Bouchanine 1995).

Lamkenssa: an informal neighborhood or *habitat clandestin* in the periphery of Casablanca. Photograph by the author, 2008.

The bidonville of Douar Skouila in Casablanca. Photograph by the author, 2008.

State Developmentalism as a Response to the Urban Crisis

In a relatively short period of time, Moroccan postcolonial society had changed fundamentally. All large cities in Morocco experienced a considerable growth of their peripheries, largely due to the increase of clandestine housing. Even though the phenomenon was relatively limited in Casablanca, it applied all the more so to cities such as Salé (due to the proximity of Rabat and the increase of the public sector) and Tétouan (due to the increase of the informal sector) (Iraki and Rachik 2005; Lahzem 1995). More than 45 percent of the population of Salé lived in HC, 35 percent in Oujda, 26 percent in Fez, and 25 percent in Tétouan (Ameur 1995, 58).[8]

Rapid urban growth was putting more and more pressure on existing relations of power and patronage. The increasing exposure of the urban peripheries to the consequences of demographic growth, housing shortages, economic involution, and increasing unemployment eventually led to growing frustrations and widespread disaffection. The urban tensions that arose from this situation started to threaten the existing political order and the stability of the monarchy.

A first wake-up call came as a result of the riots of 1965 in Casablanca in which the inhabitants of Carrière Centrales, a slum situated in the industrial neighborhood of Roches Noires in the east of Casablanca, played a leading role. The immediate provocation was a ministerial circular by the minister of education prohibiting students older than seventeen from entering the second cycle of lycée (necessary to access the university). In March 1965 rioting students were joined by the inhabitants of the bidonvilles and set Casablanca on fire (Clément 1992; Pennell 2000, 323; Waterbury 1970, 311–13). The riots were brutally suppressed by the army, and little mercy was shown to those suspected to be the instigators. Hassan II saw it necessary to take over the prime ministry and called a state of emergency. He would rule by decree until 1970.

A second wake-up call was the census of 1971. It revealed a chaotic urban situation and indicated that an urban policy based almost exclusively on authoritarian control, surveillance, and harassment was not tenable anymore. Half of the houses in the Moroccan cities were deemed inadequate; most of them were informal (Rachik 2002, 93). The riots as well as the census showed that the government of Morocco's cities had become very problematic.

A final wake-up call happened with the two coup attempts by the army (in July 1971 and August 1972). Rooted in the increasing socioeconomic cleavages in Moroccan society, they were a clear and radical sign that the monarchy had to change its political strategies and change its social base (Joffe 1988). After the coups, Hassan II attempted to reduce the influence of the military in the Ministry of Interior (the then minister of interior General Oufkir was accused as one of the instigators behind the second coup). The king also turned to the urban-based nationalist movement, including the leftist Union Nationale des Forces Populaires (UNFP, National Union of Popular Forces) (which was severely repressed during the 1960s), for negotiations.[9]

As a result of these warnings and social tensions, the monarchy's attention shifted gradually from the rural to the urban areas (Naciri 1984). Already in 1967, an urban planning and housing department was founded within the Ministry of Interior. This is significant. The Ministry of Interior was the power base of the monarchy, especially during the reign of Hassan II (Waterbury 1970, 280–87). The creation of the department thus meant that there was now a stronger political potential for effective urban policy; it showed that the monarchy was beginning to take cities seriously. Also in the same year, a research and formation center (CERF, Centre d'Etude, de Recherche et de Formation [Research, Formation and Study Center]), under the direction of the French architect Alain Masson, was established with the task to develop new knowledge and strategies related to urban planning and social housing.[10] The CERF was incorporated in the department of urban planning and housing at the Ministry of Interior.

After the census and the coups, further action was taken. In 1972 urban policy was detached from the Ministry of Interior and the Moroccan authorities created for the first time since the independence an autonomous and technocratic Ministère de l'Urbanisme, de l'Habitat, du Tourisme et de l'Environnement (MUHTE, Ministry of Urbanism, Housing, Tourism and Environment). Only a year later, seven regional agencies, Etablissements Régionaux d'Aménagement et de Construction (ERACs, Regional Offices of Planning and Construction), were created to coordinate regional housing policies together with a national fund, Fonds Nationale d'Equipements et d'Achats de Terrains (FNEAT, National Fund of Infrastructure and Land Purchases), to ensure access to property for housing projects. With regard to housing projects for the slum population, the Moroccan authorities received the support of the World Bank from the mid-1960s onward (Naciri 1987). Further-more, during the 1970s, there were several attempts to elaborate a new *schéma directeur d'aménagement urbain* (SDAU, urban master plan) for the city of Casablanca. The previous master plan was still a product of the colonial administration and dated back to the early 1950s. The new master plan would provide a general scheme for land use, zoning pro-visions, new plans to build a transportation network, and new public facilities (Johnson 1972, 86). Still, it was only after the riots in 1981 that a new master plan would be put into action (see chapter 5).

The municipal reform of 1976 (Chartre Communal) was another sign of the increasing political importance of cities. It transferred some executive power from central government representatives at the local scale (the qaids and other agents under the authority of the Ministry of Interior) to locally elected government bodies. In other words, there was a transfer from traditional elite structures to a local urban elite and land-owning class. The latter had sold parts of their agricultural land in the urban peripheries as informal building plots and then used the loyalty of their new "clients," the inhabitants of the HC, to get elected to the municipal councils. In return for these votes, elected officials lobbied for certain public investments or started the necessary administrative proce-dures to formalize "their" illegal districts. Thanks to the reform of 1976, the municipal council received more authority to do so. This decentrali-zation of political power marked an important rupture with the old rural patronage system of the monarchy and further integrated an urban elite into the realm of decision-making (Abouhani 1995c, 2006; Iraki 2006a).

Finally, and perhaps most significantly, state authorities expanded their developmentalist interventions as a response to the urban crisis. Fortunately, the oil shock of 1973, which also caused a strong rise of in-ternational export prices for phosphates, provided the government with considerable resources for public spending via the state-led Office Chéri-fien des Phosphates (OCP, Sharifian Office of Phosphates).[11] It enabled the monarchy to "buy" the loyalty of the growing urban middle class (Sater 2010, 30–52). The favorable economic rents were invested, first of all, in the expansion of the public sector. Just as in other Maghreb countries like Algeria and Tunisia, public-sector employment was one of the main government instruments to redistribute wealth in Morocco (Catusse and Destremau 2010).

State-funded higher public education ensured increasing social mobility. University graduates were practically guaranteed a job in the public sector. Between 1970 and 1977 university enrolment tripled and the number of public servants grew at an average annual rate of 5.5 percent (Cohen 2003). In addition, the government continued to subsidize essential food items, and public investments went primarily to the production of basic consumer goods such as sugar, dairy products, and oil; strategic products such as cement; and strategic sectors such as mining.

These developmentalist interventions, not only in Morocco, displayed an urban bias as the bulk of public investments went disproportionately to the big cities (El-Said and Harrigan 2014; Walton 1998). The palace used public spending as a source of authority to bind the emerging urban lower middle class and a growing group of educated youth in the cities within a new social pact.

Besides substantial public investments, the monarchy also tried to strengthen the private sector. Next to the implementation of several protectionist measures (e.g., import taxes and import licenses), the government issued the so-called Moroccanization law in March 1973 to secure at least 50 percent of Moroccan ownership in domestic firms (Catusse 2008; Cherkaoui and Ben Ali 2007). By June 1975 49 percent of the targeted Moroccan companies were Moroccanized (Rami 2007, 68). In total, the law affected 1,500 companies and 400,000 hectares of farmland, while tens of millions of dollars' worth of assets went back into Moroccan hands (Clément 1986). With the Moroccanization of the economy, the monarchy sought to deepen and strengthen its ties with the urban bourgeoisie while it encouraged the controlled emergence of a capitalist elite under the wings of the state. But it also broadened the geographic origins of the urban elites by opening the door to other segments of society (e.g., the Soussis of the Agadir region). This weakened the hegemonic position of the Fassi families (Clément 1986). After all, Hassan II was reluctant to see the emergence of a strong independent bourgeoisie that could eventually form a counterforce to his political power.[12]

As a result, private capital depended on the state to improve its economic position. Access to the state apparatus and state favors became a necessary condition for success in business (Ben Ali 1997; Cammett 2007; Oubenal and Zeroual 2017). Notwithstanding the official discourse that Moroccanization was intended to encourage middle-class ownership in the private sector, these policies allowed a small segment of elite families, closely tied to the monarchy, to enrich themselves enormously. A minority of traditional economic elites and the upper echelons of the state bureaucracy managed to enlarge their holdings in the Moroccan economy and gained control over more than 60 percent of the capital involved (Cherkaoui and Ben Ali 2007).[13]

Despite the fact that Moroccan rulers always emphasized the liberal ideology behind their economic policies, the state remained the country's most important entrepreneur, banker, and employer until the end of the 1970s. This should be understood as a particular form of "state capitalism," one that cannot be confused with the more populist ISI policies such as in Egypt under Gamal Abdel Nasser (Richards and Waterbury 2008, 206–9; Waterbury 1991). The Moroccan state mainly transferred surpluses and profits to a private sector loyal to the monarchy and absorbed most of the investment risks. Moreover, compared to other populist systems in the region, the Moroccan state showed itself particularly modest in terms of redistributing national wealth and providing social security for its citizens (Catusse 2009b, 201).

Furthermore, the absence of durable and extensive rent revenues from commodities such as oil limited the monarchy's capacities to redistribute resources and exact public loyalty on the basis of a rentier social contract (Leveau 1997). The policies of state intervention in the mid-1970s were very dependent on high rents from the exports in phosphate. After the oil boom of 1973, prices quintupled within only three years' time. But even at the height of the phosphate boom, state expansion was still partly financed by foreign borrowing (Richards and Waterbury 2008, 243).

By the end of 1975, however, the international price dropped back to the level of 1973 while government expenditure continued to expand. For example, public investment increased by 340 percent between 1974 and 1978 and more than 250 public companies were created in that same period (Sater 2010, 95). Between 1970 and 1984 current expenditures of the government rose from 14 percent to 30 percent of gross domestic product (GDP) (World Bank 1987).

Consequently, toward the end of the 1970s, Morocco's state interventionist efforts began to crumble. It became clear—after several droughts, a decline in phosphate revenues, and the growing cost of the conflict in the Western Sahara—that the Moroccan government could not sustain its public spending efforts. This led to an increase of the public deficit from 19.6 percent of GDP in 1975 to a staggering 85 percent in 1983 (Cohen and Jaïdi 2006, 37; see also World Bank 1987).

Structural Adjustment and Urban Unrest

There were some attempts at the end of the 1970s and the early 1980s to reduce the deficit, but each time the government was pressured to pull back these austerity measures. The first "IMF riots" in 1981 were of course the most striking example. The government had accepted IMF austerity measures in early 1981 as a condition for further loans. The immediate trigger for the disturbances was the decision to raise prices on staple goods: the price of milk rose by 14 percent, oil 28 percent, flower 40 percent, sugar between 40 and 50 percent, and butter 76 percent (Clément 1992, 403). These measures were quickly aborted after violent disturbances broke out in Casablanca in June that year.

On June 18, 1981, a first strike in Casablanca, called by the Union Marocaine des Travailleurs (UMT, Moroccan Workers' Union), the oldest trade union and historically linked to the nationalist movement, was largely successful and peaceful. Things got out of hand, however, two days later during a nationwide general strike organized by the Confédération Démocratique du Travaille (CDT, Democratic Workers' Confederation), the other big trade union and back then linked to the socialist USFP (Clément and Paul 1984). The CDT strike assumed a much more militant and radical character, and riots broke out in the peripheries of the city of Casablanca. These quickly expanded to the city center. The rioters were mostly young and unemployed inhabitants from the poorer neighborhoods.

On the morning of June 20, 1981, cars were set on fire in the eastern periphery of the city. At noon, some three thousand people coming from the slums and the informal neighborhoods occupied one of the main highways and raised barricades. Later, banks were also set on fire, and other public and private buildings and vehicles were damaged or destroyed. The government answered with severe repression, and police forces fired on the demonstrators. The siege lasted for several days, helicopters were deployed to survey the sites of unrest, and the army was brought into action. Thousands of rioters were arrested, party newspapers were suspended, local CDT offices were shut down, and several leaders of the opposition and the trade unions, among them CDT secretary general Moubir Amaoui, were thrown in prison. Estimates of the amount of casualties varied between sixty-six deaths (official number) and six hundred to one thousand deaths (figures from the opposition and international observers) (Clément 1992, 403–4; Lust-Okar 2005, 128–30).

The social unrest might have put a temporary halt to austerity, but the budgetary problems remained. Moreover, an agricultural crisis in the early 1980s and the oil price rise due to the war between Iraq and Iran caused the government to increase its public spending and foreign borrowing. Morocco resorted to private loans from the international financial markets to cover the deficits, averaging US$800 million per year between 1978 and 1980 (Rhazaoui 1987; Swearingen 1987). Roughly $1 billion per year was spent on oil imports alone, while the conflict in the Western Sahara cost the government another $1 billion per year between the late 1970s and the early 1980s (Glasser 1995, 56–57). By mid-1983 it became clear that Morocco could no longer service its debts. The country was near bankrupt and joined the list of the fifteen most indebted countries in the world (Catusse 2009a, 62; Sater 2010, 97). Foreign creditors refused to continue to finance Morocco's deficits, and the government was obliged to turn to the IMF and the World Bank for help.

Between 1980 and 1993 there were nine IMF interventions, six official debt rescheduling exercises, and three commercial debt rescheduling exercises. These interventions entailed the typical recipes of roll-back neoliberalism: major cuts in public expenditures, investments, and consumer subsidies, public wage restraint, the promotion of exports through the devaluation of the national currency, the reduction of import taxes and customs tariffs, fiscal discipline and reform, the liberalization of the banking system (in 1985), higher taxation, the attraction of foreign direct investment (FDI) through the planning of economic free zones, and last but not least the privatization of public assets (in the 1990s). As a result, budgetary deficits were reduced from 10 percent of GDP to 7.7 percent in 1985 and 1.4 percent in 1990 (Clément 1995).

But the macroeconomic success of debt relief came with considerable social costs. The debt crisis and measures of roll-back neoliberalism exacerbated an urban crisis and coincided with a significant decline in real and relative incomes (Cohen 2004a). In 1970 40.5 percent of the urban households lived in a two-room flat. In 1985 this number increased to 54.5 percent. In 1970 31 percent of the urban population owned a house with four or more rooms; in 1985 this number decreased to only 19 percent. At the same time, the average family size in the city rose from 4.3 in 1960 and 5.2 in 1970 to 5.4 in 1982 (Rachik 1995, 96). Illegal migration increased across the Strait of Gibraltar. Shana Cohen further illustrates this social rupture with a striking demographic example: the number of single men and women in Morocco had risen spectacularly between 1982 and 1998, from 17 to 57.8 percent for the population aged twenty-five to twenty-nine and from 6.4 to 33 percent for the population aged thirty to thirty-four (Cohen 2004b, 33).

The urban character of roll-back neoliberalism was not just a Moroccan phenomenon but was typical for the Third World more generally. Whereas the urban poor and lower middle class were hit hard by the breakdown of public services, the rural population could still rely on their access to land. Moreover, while the urban poor were fed by a moral economy of growing feelings of injustice, structural adjustment did not produce this sudden and drastic change for the rural population as they were already benefiting and expecting less from the state (Branch and Mampilly 2015, 44; see also Walton and Seddon 1994).

The social impact of structural adjustment provoked new urban riots in January 1984, this time in Marrakech following a university strike. In the days that followed, the violence spread again throughout the country, especially in the North where its scale was the most significant (Walton and Seddon 1994, 195). The disturbances of 1984 were labeled as the second IMF revolts—due to the rise in prices of consumer goods— and they comprised an accumulation of revolts in more than fifty cities. In total, more than fourteen thousand people were arrested and casualties were estimated at two hundred (Clément 1992; Seddon 1989).

Six years later, a new general strike, on December 14, 1990, set the beginning of another violent explosion. The Gulf War was one of the triggers but the root causes should be traced back to the socioeconomic crisis. This time, it originated in Fez and then spread to the cities of Tangier, Kenitra, and Meknes. Again shops, banks, and state buildings were set on fire and the Moroccan army had to intervene to restore order.

The crisis continued throughout the 1990s, even though protests decreased significantly. On the human development index of the United Nations Development Programme (UNDP), Morocco dropped from 117th place in 1995 to 129th place in 2014. Absolute poverty in Morocco (people living beneath the poverty line) rose during the 1990s from 13 percent of the population in 1991 to 19 percent in 1999, or from 3.4 million to 5.3 million people, while the category of "economically vulnerable" rose from 35 percent to 44 percent (from nine to twelve million people) (Catusse 2008, 143; Cohen 2004b; El-Said and Harrigan 2014; World Bank 2001b).

The disappointing economic growth, especially during the 1990s, and the cutbacks in public investment also correlated with high rates of unemployment, while at the same time there was a significant increase of women in the labor market (Cohen 2004b; Cohen and Jaïdi 2006). Unemployment was estimated at 30 to 40 percent and especially affected young educated Moroccans who saw their prospects of working in the public administration shattered (Brand 1998; Cohen 2004a; Cohen and Jaïdi 2006).

Privatization and Changing Modalities of State Intervention

In spite of the social costs, Morocco was pushed forward by the World Bank and the IMF in the early 1990s as a success story of macroeconomic stabilization and textbook economic reform (World Bank 1990, 2001a). In general, the mobility of capital and the means of production had improved significantly and the direct control of the state over the economy was reduced. Yet, despite these reforms, overall macroeconomic recovery was still slower than previously estimated, external debt servicing continued to take a substantial portion of state revenues, and public debt even continued to grow (Brand 1998, 33). In order to service those debts, the privatization of public assets and public companies was the logical next step in the economic restructuring of the country.

Privatization policies in Morocco were not implemented until the beginning of the 1990s. The promulgation of Law 39-89 on April 11, 1990, officially kicked off the privatization policies; in February 1993 the first public company, the Société des Dérivés du Sucre, was privatized. Law 39-89 provided for the creation of three new state organisms that had to overview the process: a new ministry, the Ministry of Privatizations; a transfer commission; and an evaluation committee (Valuation Authority).[14] The latter had to set the minimum price for a company sale and enjoyed considerable legal autonomy. The Moroccan government could not oppose the price set by the Valuation Authority, only advise the committee to revise it (Catusse 2008, 77–78). As such, Hassan II kept political control over the sales and the whole process of privatization in general.

Law 39-89 listed an initial 112 businesses (77 companies and 36 hotels) for sale. It was striking that in the beginning, most of the more strategic state-led enterprises and state monopolies were missing from the list. Public authorities wished to keep control over the distribution of, among others, water and electricity, telecommunications, public transport, mining, and the social housing sector. Mainly those companies in which the state participated indirectly—via public holdings such as Société

Nationale d'Investissement (SNI, National Investment Company), Office de Développement Industriel (ODI, Office of Industrial Development), and Caisse de Dépôt et de Gestion (CDG, Deposit and Management Fund)—were listed for privatization (El Malki and Doumou 1992; Jaidi 1992).[15] Accordingly, the initial list called into question what should have been the main goal of the process, namely the elimination of inefficient public management and the dismantling of excessive and corrupt bureaucratic control (Khosrowshahi 1997, 244). The firms on the list were not those with major budget problems. On the contrary, those sectors and companies with considerable financial problems were exactly those with significant strategic and political interests. The selling of profitable firms and the holding on to strategic ones not only brought the accusation that the state was "privatizing the winners and nationalizing the losers" but also demonstrated that the monarchy was reluctant to give up its economic control too fast (246).[16]

More important, the privatization policies of the 1990s indicated how the process of economic liberalization transformed—not just rolled back—modalities of state intervention; it indicated a transition to a form of roll-out neoliberalism. The Moroccan state now tried to control the economy more indirectly through specific forms of regulation, redistribution of resources (e.g., through privatizations), and through concessions and partnerships with the private sector (e.g., the water and electricity deals with Suez in Casablanca, and Veolia in Rabat, Tétouan, and Tangier).

Furthermore, aside from indirect control, newly established institutions with direct links to the monarchy expanded the latter's control in economic affairs. For example, a substantial part of the earnings from privatization (approximately 50 percent) went to the autonomous Hassan II Fund for Economic and Social Development. This agency gave new leverage to the monarchy to reinvent its patronage politics. The Hassan II Fund was directed by royal councilors and exempted from parliamentary and government control (Hibou and Tozy 2002a).[17] The objective of the Hassan II Fund was to sponsor projects that promoted socioeconomic development (the Bouregreg project, Tanger Med, INDH, and many other infrastructural projects). But the specific procedures and strategies followed by the Hassan II Fund are not transparent. Such agencies—which also characterized Mohammed VI's Morocco—point to a kind of "agencification" of policy (García and Collado 2015) and the dominance of "technocratic structures" loyal to the palace over elected and traditional government institutions (Hibou and Tozy 2002a, 114). This proliferation of new state or semistate agencies came to characterize Morocco's phase of roll-out neoliberalism.

The Urban Condition under Roll-Out Neoliberalism: Designing a Global City

To describe structural adjustment, privatization, and the rollback of state-funded redistributive mechanisms as the start of a neoliberal turn does not necessarily mean that these types of reforms represented the "distilled essence of the neoliberal project" (Collier 2011, 13). To the contrary, as Stephen Collier argues, these measures were the product of particular historical factors; that is, a political and economic response to the Third World debt crisis: "When it was initially proposed by pragmatists at the World Bank as a program of massive *intervention* in response to economic crisis, structural adjustment was an anathema for many self-consciously neoliberal thinkers" (13).

It is thus important to understand the neoliberal turn in Morocco not as the implementation of a set of predetermined textbook-like reforms but rather as a longer-term and contingent process of profound societal change, one that continuously transforms in response to new challenges and problems.

Despite the radical economic restructurings of the 1980s, the Moroccan economy remained fragile. This was also the case for the rest of the region. Compared to other places in the world, foreign direct investments still largely bypassed the Arab world; the region remained in a rather subordinated position in the world economy (Bush 2004; Catusse 2009a; Henry and Springborg 2001; White 2007; Zemni and Bogaert 2009).

Moreover, the structural reforms of the 1980s caused poverty and inequality to rise significantly. Cities throughout the Arab region and the rest of the Global South were confronted with some serious challenges, which only deteriorated after structural adjustment. Also in Morocco, rural migration continued unabated despite the ongoing urban crisis. Fast-growing cities such as Casablanca, Salé, Tangier, and Tetouan, demonstrated that urban growth and economic development were not necessarily related. It was poverty that drove new migrants to the cities, not necessarily the need for new labor forces (Balbo and

Navez-Bouchanine 1995). The neoliberal policies of deregulation, privatization, and fiscal discipline also negatively affected the agricultural sector and therefore accelerated the rural exodus of surplus rural labor to the urban agglomerates. This lead to the privatization and concentration of large landholdings in the hands of a few elites at the cost of the fragmented and small landholding peasant majority (D. K. Davis 2006; see also M. Davis 2006b).

In order to break this pattern and the social tensions it caused, the monarchy tried to rethink its urban economy. Since Morocco could not rely on abundant natural resources, such as its neighbor Algeria, it focused on the role of its major cities as growth engines of the national economy; this meant a shift from agriculture to industry and services, particularly tourism, as dominant strategies of development (UN-Habitat 2014, 68).

In general, we can distinguish two broad features of this new urban economy, which characterizes Morocco's more creative phase of rollout neoliberalism. One feature was the reinvention of social policy. With the undermining of already limited social welfare mechanisms, the challenge for the new king, Mohammed VI, was to redefine social policy to conform to global market requirements. This resulted, among other initiatives, in the implementation of prestigious programs such as the National Initiative for Human Development and the Cities Without Slums program (for a detailed discussion, see chapters 5 and 6). A second feature was the commitment to a politics of megaprojects, such as, for example, the Bouregreg project or Casablanca Marina. Urban megaprojects had to give a boost to the attractiveness and competitive position of Moroccan cities within a global market environment.

Considering these two general features of neoliberal reform, we have seen two forms of changes within the neoliberal project. One change is an increasing "privatization of the state" (Hibou 2004b). Public authorities are working closely with private actors and delegate certain domains of governmental intervention to these actors. The state, in other words, expanded its indirect control by setting the conditions in which other societal organizations and private companies intervene (see also chapter 5). A second change is a systematic reconfiguration of the state apparatus itself to make it more efficient and operational within a competitive global market. Over the last decade, new institutional arrangements and "new state spaces" emerged, such as the Bouregreg Agency, involving new "complexes of power" that stretch well beyond the physical barriers of the city (Brenner 2004).

Morocco's Urbanism of Projects

These changes within the neoliberal project should be situated within a double political economic context: on the one hand, an international context of increasing competition between urban regions; and on the other hand, the domestic context of *alternance*.

Substantial reforms occurred in the mid-1990s as the Moroccan monarchy faced a new economic reality and increasing internal and international pressure to initiate political reform. The *alternance* government of the social democratic prime minister Abderrahman Youssoufi that came to power in 1998 attempted to break with some of the authoritarian practices of the past and displayed a great desire to reform. Gradually, this had its impact on urban government. As Pascale Philifert states:

> Aside from any talk of the dawning of a radical "new era," the series of appointments between 1998 and 2002 would appear to indicate that progressive forces were gradually getting their hands on strategic positions within the administration, particularly at central government level, and benefiting from contacts at decentralized levels (regional inspectors, directors of urban planning agencies, etc.). The arrival of professionals, academics and reformers in the departments responsible for housing and urbanism heralded a challenge to the urban planning orthodoxies that had prevailed up to then. (2014, 75)

One of the main reforms was the creation of a separate ministry for urban policy, the Ministère de l'Aménagement du Territoire, de l'Environnement, de l'Urbanisme et de l'Habitat (MATEUH, Ministry for National Planning, Environment, Urbanism and Housing), which challenged the all-powerful Ministry of Interior on issues of urban planning and housing.

Yet the initial optimism and hope invested in progressive reform was quickly tempered. With the appointment of the nonpartisan technocrat Driss Jettou as prime minister in 2002, in succession to Youssoufi, the monarchy and the makhzan made it clear that they would control reform. The liberalization process that followed the period of *alternance*, both politically and economically, entailed not a gradual transition toward liberal democracy but rather a "pluralisation of power relations" (Philifert 2014, 73): the emergence of new complexes of power, characterized by the increasing role of private actors, foreign investors, and other urban experts; technocratic planning; and new modalities of government driven by global market integration. The growing impact of globalization in this process implied at the same time a new space to negotiate those relations of power.

Within this context, efforts were set up to rethink the city altogether. A national debate was launched in 2000 by the Department of Territorial Planning at MATEUH involving fifty local workshops, sixteen regional forums, and one national forum that eventually resulted in the adoption of a national territorial planning blueprint, the *schéma national d'aménagement du territoire* (SNAT, national land use planning scheme). As Philifert (2014, 76) argues, this national dialogue inscribed itself within the main principles of urban entrepreneurialism and intended to promote "a policy that broke with previous efforts to restore territorial balance and redistribute populations, wealth and services." The SNAT stated that the concentration of economic activities, particularly in metropolitan areas along the coast, had the potential to be a driving force for the national economy and was a prerequisite for competitiveness. Boosting the attractiveness and competitiveness of strategic areas and urban regions became the main economic strategy. Spatial imbalances and the concentration of economic wealth in particular regions were not seen as a problem but as a logical stage within a long-term "trickle-down" strategy (76).

Under the impulse of King Mohammed VI, the launch of massive urban projects and large-scale infrastructural works came to characterize this new development strategy. The role of the king in urban megaprojects should not be understated. The label of "royal project," as for example in the case of the Bouregreg project, is both politically and symbolically very important. It means that a planned project cannot fail because of the "moral guarantee" the monarch represents (Bargach 2008, 108).

This reconceptualization of urban development at the beginning of the twenty-first century gave rise to an "urbanism of projects" (Cattedra 2010) or a "new culture of projects" (Barthel and Zaki 2011, 215–19). Flagship projects such as the Bouregreg Valley, Casablanca Marina, Casablanca Finance City, Tanger Metropole, Tanger Med, and the Mohammed VI Green City in Benguérir are showcases of Morocco's "urban revolution." In every local business magazine or newspaper, comparisons are made regularly by business experts, technocrats, and government officials between the Moroccan cities and global cities such as London, Paris, Rome, and Dubai.

Compared to other countries in North Africa, Morocco is a trendsetter with regard to megaprojects (Barthel and Vignal 2014; Cattedra 2010). With its strategic geographical location, Morocco aspires to attract capital from all over the world. It wants to become a place of connection between networks of capital linking Europe with the Middle East and maybe Asia and the United States. In 2009, for example, the head of the Casablanca Stock Exchange, Karim Hajji, stressed to the international press that Morocco wants to become "a stepping stone for investors from the US, Asia, Europe and the Middle East looking for opportunities to diversify investments" (Oxford Business Group [OBG] newsletter, October 29, 2009).

The urbanism of projects marks the end of traditional urban planning executed by a centralized state administration and the transition toward a more diversified and ad hoc planning of the city characterized by the exploitation of strategic locations, the creation of landmarks, and the incorporation of new actors with particular resources (e.g., capital and know-how) into the realm of decision-making.

This kind of planning culture, which depends heavily on available financial resources, turns urban government to a great extent into a cyclical process intimately connected to fluctuations in the (global) market. Urban megaprojects are thus constantly reworked and adapted to attract available capital and capture the interest of potential investors. The business plans of these projects, closely tied to the projection of a considerable return on investment, are heavily interfering with long-term policy strategies. In that sense, trade liberalization in Morocco has accelerated the "urbanization of capital" (Harvey 1989b), while at the same time it made that process in a way much more contingent.

The true impact of this urbanism of projects on urban life and the urban economy in the long-term is still uncertain, as many of these projects are still in their planning phase, under construction, or just finished. Yet, by looking at some of the proposed designs of these urban spectacles, it becomes clear that over the next two decades or so, Morocco's infrastructural endeavors will drastically reshape the face of its cities. Furthermore, major infrastructural works—highways, new train stations, tramways (in Rabat and Casablanca), a high-speed train connection (between Casablanca and Tangier), bridges, megamalls, marinas, conference centers, museums, and so on—are put in place in order to prepare the country's cities for globalization.

Flagship Urban Megaprojects

Probably the most salient flagship project that capitalizes on the country's strategic location is the Tanger Med project. The port complex aspires to be a nodal point in the maritime global network, a major hub of containerized transport and the linchpin of the country's industrial development. It is the symbol of Morocco's commitment to the global market.

The project also symbolizes, in a way, King Mohammed VI's break from the authoritarian rule of his father, Hassan II. Historically known for its rebellious nature, the northern region and the people of the Moroccan Rif lived through a troublesome and discordant relationship with the former king. While Hassan II never even visited the Rif during his reign (his last visit was in 1959 as heir to the throne leading the army to quash a revolt), Mohammed VI immediately tried to reconcile the monarchy with the people of the north when he chose to travel to the Rif for his first official visit. Three years later, in the address from the throne of July 30, 2002, he materialized this reconciliation by announcing his intention to boost socioeconomic development in the northern region with the construction of "one of the largest ports and one of the major seaside resorts of the Mediterranean."[18]

Located approximately forty kilometers from Tangier, Tanger Med I became operational in 2007. The deepwater port serves both regional and international trade flows with a handling capacity of three million twenty-foot equivalent unit (TEU) a year spread over two terminals. Container giants such as Maersk line, CMA CGM, and Mediterranean Shipping Company operate from this strategic location on the Strait of Gibraltar where 20 percent of the world's maritime traffic passes. A second port, Tanger Med II, is planned to be fully operational in 2018 and enlarges the capacity to 8.2 million TEU.[19] This would make Tanger Med the largest port of Africa. In 2009 a new passenger terminal was launched with a capacity to transport 7 million people a year, 700,000 trucks, and 2million cars (UN-Habitat 2012, 118).

Tanger Med is more than just a port. It's a multidimensional site transforming the whole hinterland. The Moroccan state transferred more than three thousand hectares of land in a radius of eighty kilometers around the port to the Tanger Med Special Authority (TMSA), a limited company under state control created in 2002. TMSA is responsible for the planning, the management, and the future development of both the international port and the industrial hinterland. It operates within a delineated territory defined by law (Law 2-02-644 of September 10, 2002).

The whole complex features several export-oriented economic zones and logistic infrastructures: a 345-hectare Tangier Free Zone for exports (already created in 1999), a 1,000-hectare industrial free zone at Melloussa-Joamaa comprising the Tanger Automotive City and Renault Tanger Med, Tétouanshore (an offshore park in the neighborhood of the city of Tétouan), a 250-hectare logistic zone (Medhub), and other parks and zones offering attractive tax benefits and exemptions from customs duties to approximately seven hundred companies.[20]

Via its subsidiaries, TMSA exercises its corporate government over specific domains and forms partnerships with other economic actors. The Tanger Med Port Authority, for example, is a joint venture between TMSA and a branch of CDG, an institution established in 1959 to manage and reinvest the pensions of public servants and other pension funds. CDG, through its many subsidiaries, is one of the investment powerhouses in Morocco's urbanism of projects (Barthel and Zaki 2011).[21]

The Tangier Free Zone is a joint venture between TMSA and a pension fund, Caisse Interprofessionelle Marocaine de Retraites (CIMR, Interprofessional Retirement Fund of Morocco); an insurance institute, RMA Watanya; two Moroccan banks, Attijari and BMCE; and ASMA invest, a Saudi-Moroccan investment company. Each time, TMSA is the majority shareholder. As promulgated in Law 2-02-644, all revenues of TMSA acquired through activities by order of the state are exempted from any state taxes and value-added tax (VAT).[22]

In addition, logistic infrastructure was provided with a new Tangier-Casablanca highway built in 2008, followed in 2009 by a forty-five kilometer rail link to the national network (UN-Habitat 2012, 118–20). A multibillion-dollar high-speed train connection between the two main economic centers of Morocco, Casablanca and Tangier, is expected to open in the next couple of years. As such, the development of the Tanger Med complex enlarges an urban corridor along the Atlantic coast including Casablanca, Rabat, and Tangier. The project Tanger Metropole launched in 2013 and the Tanger City Center project, a new residential and business district located at the heart of the city developed by the Spanish Group Inveravante, have to complete this picture.

The same urban entrepreneurial logic applies to that other economic center in Morocco: Casablanca. Over the last decade, the launch of megaprojects such as Casablanca Marina, Anfa Place (a luxury tourism and leisure complex along the corniche), Morocco Mall (one of the largest shopping centers in Africa), Casablanca Finance City (the planned reconversion of the old airport into a new financial and business district), Wessal Casablanca Port (the planned development of the port area), and the Casanearshore Park will transform the city in funda-mental ways. The latter was the first Moroccan offshore park to be offi-cially opened (in 2007). It is one of the largest offshore zones in North Africa.

Following the example of Casanearshore, offshore parks are to be created in five other metropolitan areas: Rabat, Fez, Marrakech, Oujda, and Tangier-Tetouan. Together with the other industrial free zones spread around the country, they are like islets, or more like "globalized fragments," inscribed into the urban territory with their own specific laws and regulations (Verdeil 2006, 154). Each of these globalized spaces might be considered as a particular project by which one attempts to attract and accumulate capital from around the globe (Verdeil 2006).

Besides investments in industry and services, the most prominent strategies contributing to Morocco's urbanism of projects are in tourism and real estate. Large parts of the urban transformations are based on a rentier-based model exploiting strategically located urban land. Despite the global economic crisis, the revival of religious extremism, and the region-wide uprisings exposing the vulnerability of the tourism sector and the real estate market, plans to construct resorts, golf courses, mari-nas, and other luxury projects in Morocco's most attractive tourist des-tinations continue to mushroom.

In 2010 approximately nine million tourists traveled to Morocco. Growth in the tourism industry has averaged a 9 percent contribution to the GDP in recent years and sustained a growth of 15 percent over the last decade (OBG newsletter, October 8, 2010). Together with re-mittances from the Moroccan diaspora, tourism is the biggest source of foreign currency and vital to the balance of payments (El Yaakoubi 2014). Therefore, the government launched an ambitious tourism plan in 2010, Vision 2020, in order to boost (foreign) investments, economic growth, and employment. Vision 2020 aims to double the number of arrivals in 2020 to almost twenty million and to turn Morocco in one of the top-twenty tourist destinations in the world.

In order to achieve these goals, the Moroccan authorities created another semipublic entity with private prerogatives—in a way compa-rable to the TMSA: the Fonds Marocain de Développement Touristique (FMDT, Moroccan Fund for Tourism Development). It is a limited com-pany under state control with an initial budget of 1.5 billion dirhams, two-thirds of which is provided by the state and the rest by the Hassan II Fund. This budget will be increased to 15 billion dirhams over the next ten years (decree no. 2-11-52 of February 18, 2011).[23] The FMDT lever-ages capital to invest in different tourism projects.

Gulf Capital as Political Investors

Despite a temporary setback in megaproject investments between 2008 and 2010, especially from the Gulf, petrodollar investment seems to be back in full force, ironically maybe, since nationwide protests broke out in February 2011 (Maestri 2012). Several investors from the Gulf announced projects in Morocco. According to weekly magazine *TelQuel*, projects worth 23.5 billion dirhams of foreign direct investments were announced between 2011 and 2013, equivalent to 24 percent of total FDI in Morocco. The bulk of these investments goes to real estate (41 percent) and another 14 percent to other tourism projects. Only 2 percent goes to industry (Gharbaoui 2014).

There are political reasons for this particular growth of investments and economic cooperation between the Gulf and the Moroccan monarchies. Over the past decade, the Arab Mediterranean area, together with the rest of the Middle East, was considered to be a natural safe haven for "Khaleeji Capital," especially in the post-9/11 era (Hanieh 2011). Ever since the uprisings began, the Gulf Cooperation Council (GCC) extended their strategic relations and political alliances as the political stability of the region and the political influence of the GCC became a major concern. Morocco, for its part, was facing increasing state budget problems and a slowdown of growth. GCC investments were welcome at a time when European investment decreased after the financial crisis in 2008.

The Gulf monarchies approached Morocco and also Jordan to offer their support. In May 2011 both monarchies were officially invited to join the GCC. Although Morocco declined this offer, political, economic, and security cooperation intensified significantly. In October 2012 Mohammed VI traveled to the Gulf region to visit the separate GCC members. There he secured a US$5 billion aid package spread over the next five years from Qatar, Saudi Arabia, Kuwait, and the United Arab Emirates to help the kingdom keep the uprisings at bay (El Yaakoubi 2014). In exchange, Morocco participated in the war against Islamic State (IS) (six Moroccan F-16s operated from Emirati soil) and in the Saudi campaign against the Houthis in Yemen.

One of the results of this increasing cooperation is Wessal Capital, a megadeal between Morocco and four GCC members (Abu Dhabi, Kuwait, Qatar, and Saudi Arabia). The newly created FMDT played an important part in this operation. In November 2011 FMDT signed an agreement with the sovereign wealth funds Qatar Holding, Kuwait Investment Authority's Al Ajial Investments, and Abu Dhabi's Aabar fund to create the joint venture Wessal Capital. All partners own an equal share. The Saudi Investment Fund followed later in the deal. Wessal Capital, specifically created to boost the Moroccan tourism economy, is a major private-equity–style investment fund with billions of dirhams at its disposal backed up by royal guarantee. The objective is to set up special purpose vehicles (SPV) in the form of limited liability companies for each different project in order to spread the financial risks and attract additional capital.[24] Little more than a year after its creation, Wessal Capital swung into action, announcing three megaprojects in Casablanca, Rabat, and Tangier.

Wessal Casablanca Port, a subsidiary of Wessal Capital, plans to complete the reconversion of the Casablanca port area. It pledged an investment of 6 billion dirhams to construct a real estate and marina complex around the port of Casablanca, right next to that other megaproject, Casablanca Marina. Interestingly, this luxury project, which also foresees the rehabilitation of the ancient medina located right next to Casa-Port, is supported by international institutions such as the European Bank for Reconstruction and Development, the European Investment Bank, and the World Bank.

A second subsidiary, Wessal Bouregreg, is set up to invest 9 billion dirhams in the second phase of the Bouregreg project located at the Bouregreg river banks between Rabat and Salé. Yet another marina is planned (adding to the ones that were built or planned in the first phase of the project), together with business centers, recreational areas, and retail space. The crowning touch will be the construction of the Grand Theater, offering space to 1,900 people and designed by the late "starchitect" Zaha Hadid.

Finally, a third subsidiary, Wessal Tanger Marina, will invest in a yachting marina that will replace Tangier's general shipping port. A fourth entity, Wessal Capital Asset Management, will administer all projects. In October 2014 World Finance awarded Wessal Capital with the "Sovereign Wealth Fund Deal of the Year," while their future project in Casablanca (which only existed on paper at that time) was awarded the "Social Deal of the Year" (World Finance 2014).

One of the key figures behind the construction of Wessal Capital was Yassir Zenagui, a close advisor of Mohammed VI and the former minister of tourism. In an interview in 2011 with weekly magazine *Actuel*, he elaborated on the changing role of the state through institutions such as Wessal Capital.

> Within a context of resource scarcity, it's important that the role of the state does not limit itself to a subsidizing role but that it also adopts the role of an investor looking for profitability. Along these lines, the sovereign fund [Wessal Capital] will be a vehicle to valorize public resources which can result from revenues of privatization for example. The idea is to reinvest these revenues in sectorial sovereign funds to create more wealth.

On the role of Gulf capital, he added the following:

> The engagement of Sovereign Wealth Funds . . . is not only an economic engagement but also a *political act* which confirms the confidence in the stability of our country, in the political economy and the reforms we have taken. (Kably 2011, emphasis added)

Toward a Contemporary Maroc Utile and Maroc Inutile?

All the examples described above illustrate some of the more manifest cases that characterize Morocco's urban revolution of the last decade and a half. With regard to the spatial implications, let me make some general observations. The focus on urban entrepreneurialism has brought the city to the forefront of the Moroccan economy. The urban economy has become by far the most significant producer of national economic growth. Three-quarters of the national GDP is generated within the urban economy (MHUAE 2009, 30).[25]

But this shift did not include all cities on an equal basis. Within the Moroccan urban entrepreneurial model, the coastal cities are absolutely dominant. Casablanca, Rabat-Salé, and Tangier account for 80 percent of the economic activities in industry and services. This concentration generates 75 percent of urban employment. Casablanca alone concentrates 60 percent of all industrial workers and 55 percent of the country's productive units (UN-Habitat 2012; see also Kaioua 1996). Furthermore, real estate investments predominantly flow to the large coastal cities as the shoreline has become a central feature within city marketing strategies and tourism promotion.

This geography of uneven capitalist development of the last thirty years, both within large cities and between large cities and peripheral

towns and areas, resonates in a way with the urban policies of the protectorate. A contemporary neoliberal version, or better, a continuation,
is revealed in a division between a *Maroc utile* (useful Morocco) and a
Maroc inutile (useless Morocco), a figurative image called into existence
by the first resident-general of the French protectorate, Hubert Lyautey.
In its early stages, French colonialism in Morocco required massive
investments in urban development, and Lyautey embarked on an ambitious and experimental urban project to provide the country with the
necessary infrastructure for its integration in the economic realm of the
colonial system (Abu-Lughod 1980; Rabinow 1995; Rachik 1995).

In order to extract the wealth of Morocco, mainly minerals such as
phosphate and agricultural products, colonial planning required the
creation of an entirely new urban infrastructure *(villes nouvelles)* and the
installment of industrial complexes (e.g., the port of Casablanca). In addition, the French developed road and railroad networks to improve the
transportation of goods and created an "Atlantic axis" between Kénitra
and Safi with Casablanca as its economic center (Boujrouf 1996, 39).
This part of Morocco is what Lyautey called *"le Maroc utile,"* which connected the newly developed coastal cities and the surrounding fertile
Atlantic plains that extended into the country along the riverbeds with
the colonial mother country (Abu-Lughod 1980, 202). *"Maroc inutile"*
represented the peripheral regions and remote mountain areas that were
not economically interesting and actually resisted French colonialism
until the "pacification" ended in the 1930s.

The development of colonial urban centers such as Rabat and Casablanca irreversibly changed the urban hierarchy from traditional cities
such as Fez and Marrakech and ancient trade routes toward Mali and
Mauritania to the coastal cities and their maritime trade connections.
The contemporary neoliberal projects reconfirm this hierarchy.

A lot of attention goes to the impact of neoliberal projects on inequality within cities. In Morocco, for example, both the World Bank
and UN-Habitat stated that urban inequality, especially in Casablanca,
remains exceptionally high compared to the rest of the North African
region (UN-Habitat 2012, 96; World Bank 2014). Yet one must not for-
get the impact of neoliberal development strategies on the increasing disparity between town and country, between coastal cities and inland cities,
and between different regions in Morocco. Just as in the era of the protectorate, the discrimination and deprivation of rural areas, mountain
areas, and smaller towns and villages continues (Boujrouf 1996; Naciri

1999). Today, Morocco's main highways and railroad network still bypass large, mainly rural and inland parts of Morocco. The multibillion euro project of the high-speed train connection between Morocco's two economic poles, Casablanca and Tangier, is one of the most recent examples and fits perfectly within this logic.

Consequently, Mohamed Naciri (1999, 34) notes that the distinction between a "useful Morocco" (the urban centers of the coastal areas, the touristic attractions, and large-scale industrial agriculture) and a deprived or "useless Morocco" (the urban peripheries and slums, the rural poor, and small-scale farming) still applies. This distinction will threaten Morocco's national cohesion if nothing radically changes within the next ten years, he added almost prophetically in 1999 (see also Bogaert 2015c).

Rethinking the Moroccan State

The multibillion-dollar urban makeover entails much more than just the selling or commercialization of particular strategically located metropolitan areas. The noncommittal discourses on economic growth and global competitiveness and the promises for greener, healthier, and more sustainable urban societies that accompany neoliberal projects mask strategies of political control and profit maximization. All these changes at the urban scale require us to rethink politics critically with regard to the changing relations of power that are articulated through the city.

Urban entrepreneurialism emphasizes the role of individual cities and city regions in the extraction and creation of surplus value within an ever increasing competitive global market environment. Yet the city is not an actor in itself. As Parker (2009, 113) notes: "While pavement, steel and concrete can be rolled out to enable and direct the flow [of capital], they do not set it in motion."

Thus, *who* plans the transformation of the city and *where* are those decisions made? The state plays a crucial role in the implementation of neoliberal urban projects. But the latter also entailed changing modalities of state intervention. In other words, what do we mean by the state in this new context? The cover of the 2008 special summer issue of *TelQuel*, picturing King Mohammed VI in a stylish business suit, reflects a common understanding of state power in Morocco. Underneath we can read the telling title *"L'Etat c'est lui,"* followed by a question: Does the economic boom justify absolute power? This particular image tells a great deal about the crucial role of the state and the monarch in the economic development of the country. But it also tells us something about

Cover of 2008 special summer issue of *TelQuel*. Courtesy of *TelQuel* magazine.

the specific imagination of the state: as an actor personified through the monarch himself. He has absolute power. He makes all important decisions. In other words, he *is* the Moroccan state.

Yet if we want to understand the relationship between state power and the reproduction of urban space, the state itself cannot simply be reduced to a coherent entity or single actor. Through its involvement in different neoliberal projects, the state—like neoliberalism—manifests itself differently across space. If we consider space as dynamic, open, and relational, then understanding *state spatiality* obliges us to see the formation of the state as an ongoing, relational, and dynamic—if not often discordant—process (Massey 2005; see also chapter 1). By studying the relation between state power and neoliberal projects, *the* state itself turns out to be a complex of various institutional and governmental arrangements at different scales, linking different spaces and actors.

Moreover, within our contemporary context of globalization and the increasing involvement of global capital in the reproduction of urban space, state spatiality itself obtains a more global character. This means that both foreign and domestic political forces come together through the specific ways in which state power has been spatialized (e.g., in an offshore zone or a megaproject). Just like neoliberal projects, the state itself has become a global enterprise.

One of the effects of neoliberal globalization is precisely the discrepancy between actual state spatiality and the dominant state image, or better, the mutual existence of the state as a spatially dispersed material force and as an ideologically constructed illusion of coherency and unity (Mitchell 2006; see also Bogaert and Emperador 2011; Ferguson and Gupta 2002; Hansen and Stepputat 2001). The spectacular changes within cities like Casablanca, Rabat, and Tangier coincided with important transfers of power from traditional state institutions to other kinds of governmental arrangements, semipublic entities, and autonomous state agencies. Public–private partnerships, the creation of state-controlled limited companies, the founding of new holdings and funds, and, finally, the setting up of particular ad hoc structures to manage individual projects make contemporary state spatiality in Morocco a much more complex phenomenon than roughly two or three decades ago.

Two important observations should be made here. First, important decision-making processes were moved from traditional government institutions to new—supposedly politically neutral—technocratic entities. I already mentioned vehicles like TMSA and Wessal Capital that allow the state to take on a more entrepreneurial role, as Yassir Zenagui put it. Other examples are the Bouregreg project, which is coordinated by an autonomous state agency, the Bouregreg Agency (see chapter 4), and the Hassan II Fund. The latter was created to reinvest a large part of Morocco's revenues from privatizations. Managed by royal advisors, the Hassan II Fund has been instrumental in the initial setup of mega-projects such as Tanger Med and Bouregreg. It was also involved in the creation of FMDT and Wessal Capital.

It is not a coincidence that these examples of neoliberal statecraft coincided with increasing domestic and international pressure to democratize the political system. In these times of increasing pressure to democratize, the agencies mentioned above are illustrative of the ways in which the monarchy rolled out new institutional arrangements that take authority over a significant amount of public resources and domains out of the hands of the formal—officially elected—government institutions.

Second, this urbanism of projects opened up the decision-making process to new actors. Although the process itself is still tightly controlled by the monarchy, neoliberal state spatiality in Morocco turned decision-making processes into more globally connected and more privatized endeavors. New state agencies such as TMSA or the Bouregreg Agency function as strategic–relational junctions of global connection within a geography of uneven development, spatial competition, and rule by exception. Gulf capital plays an increasingly important role, but also European capital and diplomacy, especially from France. With regard to the latter, close diplomatic and political relations between French and Moroccan state elites explain, for example, the privileged position of French multinationals such as Alstom, Bouygues, Renault, Veolia, and Suez in the Moroccan domestic market (Graciet and Laurent 2012; Tuquoi 2006; Vermeren 2009).

Against the backdrop of Morocco's urbanism of projects and the changing state spatiality, we need to rethink politics and the nature of the modern state. Or better, we need to recognize the explicitly political dimension behind those sociospatial transformations, global connections, and new practices of government that are often hidden behind abstract technocratic discourses and mainstream liberal claims about globalization. Morocco's urbanism of projects reflected not just an economic strategy but also political practices of domination, accumulation, and dispossession characterized by the privatization, fragmentation, and financialization of decision-making processes, the marketization and mobilization of public resources and land, and, finally, the transfer of state power to ad hoc arrangements and exceptional institutions.

Neoliberal projects symbolize a fundamental shift in Moroccan authoritarianism. Whereas Hassan II ruled with an iron hand during the years of lead, Mohammed VI rules via holdings, funds, and specialized state agencies. This does not necessarily mean that he is less authoritarian than his father, only different. The urbanism of projects demonstrates not only the durability of authoritarian government but also its transformation from neopatrimonial, clientelistic, and kinship-based forms of political practices toward a more globalized modality of authoritarian government. With this shift, I do not want to argue necessarily that neoliberal modalities replaced older modalities of authoritarian government; rather, already existing forms of authoritarian government converged with neoliberal ones.[26]

PART II

(STATE-)CRAFTING GLOBALIZATION

3

NEOLIBERALISM AS
CLASS PROJECTS

It has often been maintained that the classic sociological class
analysis—an analysis that draws essentially upon the insights of
Karl Marx and Max Weber—is inapplicable to Arab societies, or
that in Arab societies there are no such things as "classes." This is
a generalization apart from the evidence, at least as far as post-
World War I Arab societies are concerned. . . . To reject class
analysis out of hand, merely on account of contingent ideological
associations, is, from a scholarly point of view, inadmissible.
        —Hanna Batatu, *The Old Social Classes and the
        Revolutionary Movements of Iraq*

To prevent possible misunderstandings, let me say this. I do not
by any means depict the capitalist and the landowner in rosy
colors. But individuals are dealt with here only insofar as they are
the personifications of economic categories, the bearers *[Träger]*
of particular class-relations and interests.
        —Karl Marx, *Capital*, volume 1

NEOLIBERAL URBAN PROJECTS are class projects that (re)produce uneven
development and transform authoritarianism and state power in Morocco.
Most visibly, neoliberal projects play a central role in the production
of a wider geography of inequality and difference between a contemporary *Maroc utile* (mainly the large coastal cities) and a *Maroc inutile* (the
rural hinterland and the smaller villages and towns). But also within
large coastal cities, these projects reproduce and exacerbate social and
geographical inequality.

Politically, places like the city, and institutions like the Moroccan
state for that matter, should be understood, above all, in terms of the
social relations and practices of power articulated through these entities.
Neoliberal projects offer an entry point to explore the coproduction of

space and class and the actual relations between the making of urban places and global circuits of capital accumulation. These projects represent the coming together of particular relations and practices involved in the capitalist reproduction, exploitation, and dispossession of urban space. Class as a concept makes those relations and practices legible and also explicitly political.

In this chapter, I try to understand the social forces that reshape the Moroccan city as class forces to explain the *nature* of the agency behind neoliberal projects. The explanation for the omnipresence of neoliberal projects, not only in Morocco but on a worldwide scale, should be sought not in abstract economic theories or in the intellectual accomplishments of brilliant (Western) minds such as Friedrich Hayek or Milton Friedman but rather in the practices and interests of powerful men and women and their involvement in the undermining of existing social orders and the construction of new ones. In other words, I want to put the question of class, and not so much ideology or economic theory, at the center of our political stories on neoliberal projects.

To do so, I apply a specific reading of class. I use this concept not to describe particular groups or particular inequalities between different groups (e.g., in terms of political power, property, or income). Instead, I consider class a powerful concept to describe the specific practices and relations that are involved in the appropriation of surplus value; hence, to characterize the *production* of inequality and difference (Ruccio, Resnick, and Wolff 1990). Class, in other words, typifies not a category of people but a relation or a practice.

The Ruling Elite in Morocco:
Concepts, Specifications, and Its Changing Constitution

When it comes to the analysis of politics in the Arab world, class is rarely a prominent explanatory concept in the academic literature. In the beginning of the 1970s, James Bill (1972, 418) stressed that the "Middle East has often been represented as an area in the world where one cannot speak about classes and where class analysis is least relevant." Not much has changed since then. As mentioned earlier, contemporary politics in the region are predominantly understood as *regime* politics, characterized by family ties, patrimonial systems of rule, and resilient authoritarianism.

In the 1970s, when the developmental state model was still dominant, the postcolonial populist regimes presented themselves as "classless" in the way they claimed to represent all classes in society (Ehteshami and Murphy 1996). In reality, these political systems were characterized by the transformation of nationalist movements into a bureaucratic or state bourgeoisie that dominated the political and economic sphere, not only in the Arab world but in the whole Third World. A lively academic debate asked whether developmental state politics and the dominance of the state bourgeoisie at the time could be understood as a form of class rule (Forrest 1987; Sklar 1979).

With regard to the Arab world, critics argued that the class content of developmental state capitalism was difficult to assess using a classic sociological analysis because "in these patrimonial regimes private property was not secure from the whims of arbitrary rulers" (Henry and Springborg 2001, 11). In other words, an independent business elite did not exist: they were politically and economically tied to the ruling clique. In addition, the state bourgeoisie itself could not be considered as a "ruling class" since it did not own the means of production and failed to act as an autonomous and independent class (Waterbury 1991).

Despite the fact that *capitalist* expansion since the 1980s seriously challenged the position of the state bourgeoisie, it has not caused a significant shift to class analysis among Middle East scholars. The focus remains on regime politics and the ruling clique, largely fed by a strong reaction against those who claim that economic liberalization and structural adjustment lead to political liberalization. Many argue that the end of the developmental state did not necessarily weaken the ruling political constellation. Rather, it transformed the populist state into an overtly authoritarian state and proved the Arab regime's resilience against any pressure to democratize (Ehteshami and Murphy 1996; see also Haddad 2012; Kienle 2001; Waterbury 1991). Forms of patronage combined with heavy police control kept society in check. Moreover, contentious politics in the region are predominantly interpreted along sectarian or religious lines, not so much in terms of class struggle despite the new context of neoliberal globalization.

There are important exceptions, of course. Since the late 1970s, a growing body of literature has tried to understand the region's capitalist integration from a class perspective. People like Hanna Batatu (1978) strongly advocate a class analysis to understand Iraq's gradual transformation into an adjunct of the capitalist world system. Others, such as Ervand Abrahamian (1982), Joel Beinin (2001), and Zachary Lockman (1994), to name just a few, focus more particularly on subaltern classes and their role in the social history of the region. More recently, Adam Hanieh (2011) contends that one cannot understand the fundamental transformations in the political economy of a region like the Gulf without taking capitalist class formation seriously.

Additionally, the Arab uprisings of 2011 caused some conceptual and methodological shifts. It would be interesting to see, for example, whether class analysis becomes more prominent. In recent years, several scholars explicitly frame these uprisings within a wider neoliberal capitalist context and emphasize the class dimension of the popular uprisings (Achcar 2013; Allinson 2015; Hanieh 2013; Kandil 2012; Smet 2016; Veltmeyer 2011; Zemni 2013). They examine the events in terms of the conflicting balance of class forces in Arab societies and the role played by different social classes in the social protests (the middle class, the working class, the peasants). In this chapter, I contribute to this discussion, clarify some of the confusions about class in the literature, and explore how this concept might be useful to understand (urban) politics in Morocco.

In doing so, I use a particular notion of class. And here I differ from the more sociological approach of most scholars mentioned above. I use class not to delineate an often predefined group of actors with a set of specific characteristics (e.g., the ownership over the means of production) but rather to characterize particular practices and relations of capital accumulation and surplus-value appropriation (Resnick and Wolff 1987; Ruccio 2011; for a similar approach on the Gulf region, see Hanieh 2011). The crucial question therefore is not whether those who remodel the Moroccan city can be described as a class but whether their practices and strategies can be understood as *class practices* or *class strategies*. In other words, I use "class" as an adjective. It is analytically more productive to clarify the nature of certain relations, processes, projects, and forms of agency than to use class as a social category by which one can "classify" different groups in society and their mutual relationship (Resnick and Wolff 1987; E. O. Wright 2005).

Moreover, the concept of class is particularly helpful to understand the political context of neoliberal projects in the sense that it is not associatively linked to nation-state boundaries. Class, in contrast to the territorialized imagination of the regime or the state, has the ability to raise a different kind of geographical or spatial imagination, one that considers urban politics and the reproduction of urban space as a product not only of internal political interactions but also of relations with elsewhere, without placing these relations in an insider–outsider or global–local dichotomy (here I draw on Massey 2010, 20). Class is a concept that unifies these relations. A class project is an endeavor that brings together different forces from around the globe, as a system of relations within a particular place contributing to the making of what we call globalization. This approach to class is not to disregard the insightful and complex sociological analyses of scholars such as Batatu, Abrahamian, or Beinin but to reject the rudimental sociological critique by which other Middle East scholars reject class altogether as an explanatory concept. My approach can actually bridge the gap between regime-centered and class-centered analyses of authoritarian politics. It explains how traditional practices of patrimonial rule were complemented with and transformed into class practices of government during the neoliberal era.

But before I continue my discussion on class, let me elaborate first on how important transformations within the Moroccan elite since structural adjustment are generally analyzed and represented. Over the years, scholars such as Ali Benhaddou, Myriam Catusse, John Waterbury, Driss Ben Ali, and many others have made valuable contributions on elite formation and power during the period of economic liberalization. Their arguments are important to understand some of the fundamental societal changes in Morocco since the 1980s. However, these authors also argued explicitly or implicitly against class as an explanatory notion despite the increasing capitalist expansion of the last forty years. In my view, they are missing out on important connections and insights. Let me go along with their analyses in the first part of this chapter, only to argue in the second part that they reject class for the wrong reasons. The concept of class opens up new and important ways to grasp the spatial and social nature of the agency involved in the capitalist restructuring of Moroccan urban society.

The Kingdom's Elites and the State Bourgeoisie

Although the political and economic dominance of the Moroccan monarchy is undeniable, we cannot reduce political authority to one man or one family. Is it possible, therefore, to use class as a concept to understand the politics of the ruling elite in Morocco? In the literature on Moroccan politics, and Arab politics more generally, there has always been a strong focus on economic elites or on the role of ruling elites in controlling the national economy. Especially after the 1980s, research on the region has worked toward a more articulated understanding of state–business relations, practices of economic liberalization, and the changing role and position of economic elites (Guazzone and Pioppi 2009a; Handoussa 1997; Heydemann 2004b; Richards and Waterbury 2008). Yet the concept of class rarely featured as an explanatory concept of political change in these accounts. What's more, class analysis was often explicitly rejected on the basis of a sociological analysis of the power relations in Arab societies.

A quite common perspective on the composition of the elite in Morocco can be found in the study of sociologist Ali Benhaddou (2009). He argues that not much has changed since the beginning of the 1980s. In fact, he states, not much has changed even since the nineteenth century, since the expansion of trade relations with the Europeans. Almost the same small group of powerful merchant families continues to dominate the political economy of Morocco. Heredity prevails and family relations determine access to powerful positions within the state apparatus. Through marriages and personal ties, the Moroccan elite has managed to protect their fortunes and kept their privileged position in the political and economic order.

Benhaddou considers the Moroccan economy to be in the hands of a few powerful families with feudal features. They are more a kind of aristocracy, not an independent bourgeoisie that could eventually play a role similar to the European bourgeoisie in the eighteenth century. The Moroccan elites are intimately tied to the absolute monarchy and completely dependent on that institution for their power and wealth in society. Therefore, he argues, we cannot speak of a ruling "class." Instead, we should refer to the monopolization of power by ruling "families." Class in the eyes of Benhaddou is a more objective position of power that someone can obtain through meritocratic virtues (professionally, politically, etc.), while family rule is determined by subjective qualities like birth and kinship (2009, 61–62, 197–98).

Despite Benhaddou's insightful views on the leading political and economic elite in Morocco, the explanatory value of his study is undermined by his uncritical stance toward global capitalism. In his view, explanations for social degradation and authoritarianism in Morocco should not be sought in the abstract specters of neocolonialism, imperialism, bureaucratism, or contemporary globalization but in the sociology of the local ruling elite itself (Benhaddou 2009, 12). They are the ones who block the democratic transition toward a competitive and modern free-market society. Global capitalism remains outside the realm of Moroccan politics.

This image, of course, is problematic. It erects a static and ideal type of "democratic capitalism"—as he calls it—and completely ignores important shifts in the global situation.[1] Neither state developmentalism nor neoliberalism seem to have a significant impact on the composition of the ruling elite and their relation with the rest of society.

Few analysts would go as far as Benhaddou to deny the interrelation with the global situation. Many argue that important structural changes in the political economy of Morocco have a significant impact on the constitution of the ruling elite. Both the Moroccanization law and the record revenues from phosphate in the mid-1970s provided the monarchy with greater patronage and the means to expand its urban elite base by incorporating them in important positions in the ministries and the public sector (Henry and Springborg 2001, 172). These urban elites became dependent on the Moroccan state as their fate was conditioned by state intervention and state support, by the expansion of important state monopolies (e.g., phosphates), and by investment decisions taken elsewhere—that is, by foreign capital (mostly French-based).[2]

The considerable expansion of state interference in the economic field, especially since the 1970s, allocated substantial power and influence to state technocrats. They were incorporated in the monarchy's divide and rule strategy. In the Moroccan context, the technocratic elites were typically nonpartisan elites occupying important positions within the state apparatus and the Moroccan government. They were recruited among the powerful families (very often of Fassi descent) and directly appointed by *dahir* (royal decree). These elites occupied leading positions in state companies, state agencies, and the public administration. But they were also appointed as ministers in technocratic departments (agriculture, finance, trade, and industry) and appointed in strategically important departments (interior, foreign affairs). As such, they formed a useful counterweight to other social groups in society such as the trade unions and the working class, the rural landowning class, and an emerging private business elite.

This group of loyal technocrats is what John Waterbury and others have termed the "state bourgeoisie." According to Waterbury, the state bourgeoisie was the driving force behind state capitalism in the decades preceding structural adjustment and neoliberal reform in the Arab region. They consisted of "those top-level managers and technocrats who are in direct control of the assets owned fully or partially by the state" (Waterbury 1991, 2). They had access to the highest echelons and power centers of the regime (Haddad 2012, 232–33). Also in Morocco, especially during the Moroccanization process in the 1970s, the process of state capitalism transformed the state's high-positioned administrative bureaucracy into a state bourgeoisie that dominated the economic activities in the country (Ben Ali 1997).

As a consequence, the position of the state bourgeoisie was in many ways quite vulnerable: they owed their positions to their loyalty to the ruling regime. Precisely for this reason, Waterbury claimed, the state bourgeoisie cannot be considered as a dominant "class," because they do not own the means of state production and they cannot really secure their own incumbency or their reproduction as a state class. From a classical Marxist perspective, according to Richards and Waterbury (2008, 208), a dominant capitalist class will always try to maintain its control of the means of production and pass that control on to its offspring through the legal institution of private property. Yet members of the state bourgeoisie have no legal claim over their offices and the assets they control. They remain dependent on the state and the inner circles around the president or monarch for their power and position in society. As Ben Ali argues in the case of Morocco:

> Even though they had a clear idea of their professional interests and clung fiercely to the privileges that they enjoyed at the helm of the public sector, Moroccan technocrats did not attain the degree of homogeneity necessary to forge a social group able to break free from the Makhzen. Since managers were directly nominated and relieved by their posts by *dahir*, their dependency on the state was complete. Besides, their nomination was not only a function of their competence, but also—indeed, fundamentally—a product of their allegiance; for their tenure at the head of public enterprises was contingent upon support accorded to them by the ruling circle. In sum, being the creation of the state, these technocrats were totally dependent on it. Their existence as an autonomous group is not conceivable at the present time. By allowing them to establish rent-seeking positions as well as benefit from corruption and other gains and facilities, the Makhzen has ensured control over Morocco's technocrats. (1997, 204–5)

As such, the monarchy and the makhzan managed the economy through a neopatrimonial logic: its goal was not only to generate growth and accumulate capital through state capitalism but also to tie an important segment of Moroccan society (the urban bourgeoisie) into a network of clients by distributing positions, privileges, and rent-seeking opportunities within the state apparatus. These neopatrimonial politics eventually contributed largely to the economic distortions and state budgetary problems at the end of the 1970s.

The Impact of Privatization and Accumulation by Dispossession

Given the role of the state bourgeoisie in the expansion of state developmentalism, one might ask whether the concept of state bourgeoisie lost its relevance during the neoliberal phase of capitalist expansion. Structural adjustment and other reforms of economic liberalization radically changed the balances of power and the political practices that underpinned them. New social groups and actors emerged on the political scene, while old practices of power (state clientelism, neopatrimonialism) proved inadequate to maintain the political status quo of the pre-neoliberal era (Ben Ali 2005).

Economic liberalization and privatization were the dominant "development strategies" in the Global South to redeem state deficits after the debt crisis of the early 1980s. Within neoclassical and neoliberal discourses, these strategies were presented as necessary to roll back highly inefficient public enterprise. In addition, liberalization and privatization were also presented as antidotes against authoritarianism, corruption, and existing clientelist networks as the personal "cash cows" of a rent-seeking state bourgeoisie would be dismantled (Heydemann 2004a; Walton and Seddon 1994, 334–36). The political legitimation of structural adjustment and the rollback of developmentalist patronage and state control rested on a promise of democratization (i.e., the democracy of the market). Economic liberalization would empower an independent business elite and install a free labor market.

However, two important factors undermine this neoliberal myth. First, privatization policies, especially in the MENA region, were dictated more by the severe decline of public revenues than by the so-called inefficiency of public enterprises (Ayubi 1997). In fact, the first companies that were privatized in Morocco were some of the jewels of the public sector and had little or no efficiency or budget problems whatsoever (Catusse 2008, 2009b; Khosrowshahi 1997).

Second, although the debt crisis definitely challenged political allegiances and the networks of patronage of authoritarian regimes in the region, the political "solutions" that followed did not really undermine, in the end, the dominant position of the ruling elites. Structural adjustment and privatization policies were after all state led; those who controlled the state also controlled the process of economic liberalization (Ayubi 1997; Owen 2012). As a result, privatization also served another end besides filling up the state coffers: it became a new source of patronage.

In the wider literature on capitalist transformation, this new source of patronage is often described more generally as a process of "accumulation by dispossession," a concept linked to the work of David Harvey. By this he means "the continuation and proliferation of accumulation practices that Marx has treated as 'primitive' or 'original' during the rise of capitalism" (Harvey 2006b, 43). Harvey directs our attention to particular practices, other than the usual focus on production and innovation, through which capitalism reproduces and reinvents itself. As he recalls, "The rise of the capitalist class did not depend initially upon its capacity to generate surpluses. It rested, rather, upon its ability to appropriate them, treat them as their own private property and launch them into circulation in search for further surpluses" (90).

With regard to neoliberal reform, state-administrated austerity programs and privatization policies can also be regarded as practices of accumulation by dispossession. To the extent that state property could still be considered to belong to all citizens of that state—even though state wealth was very unevenly redistributed and controlled by a neopatrimonial state bourgeoisie—the privatization of important public assets entailed a dispossession of those public belongings. This is especially relevant when one considers the transfer of publicly owned primary goods and services such as water, electricity, public transport, and health care to profit-hungry enterprise. While imperial capitalists and states accumulated wealth through the appropriation of colonies in the nineteenth and early twentieth centuries, neoliberal capitalists use strategies such as privatization, devaluation, land-grabbing, WTO-TRIPS (World Trade Organization Agreement on Trade-Related Aspects of Intellectual Property Rights), and the commodification of culture to dispossess local communities, ethnic groups, and gender (Chatterjee 2009).

Structural adjustment, according to Harvey, was about using the power of the state and international financial institutions to orchestrate devaluations of (public) assets to permit accumulation by dispossession (2003, 151; see also Schatan 1987). In the case of Morocco, French historian Pierre Vermeren (2009, 278) has called the process of privatization an example of "true economic pillage." Many companies were sold at dumping prices. Moreover, as mentioned in chapter 2, the revenues of a large part of the privatization policies were transferred to the

Hassan II Fund and, as such, controlled directly by the monarchy and its entourage (and not by publicly accountable state institutions).

The ruling elites in Morocco and elsewhere in the region not only adapted to a new reality; they actively participated in the construction of that new reality. As the Moroccan state sold off its economic assets at bargain prices and adopted neoliberal policies, the future of the Moroccan bourgeoisie was well assured (Clément 1986; see also Catusse 2009b; Najem 2001). Most of Morocco's millionaires previously occupied privileged positions in the state administration or public sector before they turned to the private sector (Berrada and Saïd Saadi 1992). In fact, neoliberal reform further encouraged the concentration of economic wealth in the hands of a few powerful families: Benjelloun, Kettani, Lamrani, Berrada, Akhennouch, and last but not least the royal family itself.

In the process, neoliberal reform created or extended the conditions for new capitalist class practices and relations *alongside* older neopatrimonial and clientelistic practices and relations of power. These new capitalist practices and relations come together in what I call neoliberal projects. Consequently, the conceptualization of neoliberalism as "projects" does not necessarily contradict the dominant perspectives on Arab political life; rather, it emphasizes how contemporary practices of political domination are at the same time involved and entangled in the production of contemporary globalization.

Despite the fact that the ruling elite preserved its privileged position, the neoliberal transition entailed some important shifts in Morocco. First, it changed the behavior of the monarchy itself. In 1982 King Hassan II took over the consortium Omnium Nord Africain (ONA), the largest private conglomerate of the country, from its French owners. Through the king's own private holding Siger (anagram for Regis), the royal family became the majority shareholder of ONA. The king became not only the country's political leader and largest landowner but also its primary investor (Clément 1986; Leveau 1985, 257). The gross revenues of the conglomerate accounted for over 5 percent of Morocco's GDP. Moreover, ONA acquired major stakes in the country's leading commercial banks, which enabled the monarchy to control the domestic economy behind the scenes (Henry and Springborg 2001, 172).

In 2010 ONA merged with the public holding Société Nationale d'Investissement (SNI), to become even bigger, more dominant, and less transparent (both the SNI and ONA security were delisted from the Casablanca Stock Exchange in August 2010). The new conglomerate took over the name of SNI. This "royal big bang," as it was referred to by weekly magazine *TelQuel*, cost an estimated 24 billion dirhams and further consolidated the king's economic power (Iraqi and Michbal 2010). As a result, Mohammed VI became an even bigger player on the domestic market. And besides the king's own economic empire, the monarchy's control over the economy extended even further due to the increasing intervention of (semipublic) state agencies in large-scale neoliberal urban development projects (e.g., the Bouregreg project) that operate under the control of a modern state bourgeoisie.

The king's role as both the head of state and the main private investor is an ambiguous position and regularly creates conflicts of interest—from state subsidies on products manufactured and traded by ONA subsidiaries to the deregulation of the insurance or the banking sector (Sater 2010, 103; see also Graciet and Laurent 2012). Back in the heyday of the first wave of privatization, ONA was one of the principal beneficiaries of the privatization policies. Through its different subsidiaries and minority participations, ONA (and SNI today) became a major player in the retail market, banking sector, mining, tourism, real estate, automobiles, textile industry, and high technology. Since 2008, the holding also tried to break the duopoly of Méditel and Maroc Telecom in the telecommunications sector via its subsidiary Wana. It was the state regulator, the Agence Nationale de Réglementation des Télécommunications (ANRT, National Agency for the Regulation of Telecommunications), that authorized Wana (owned by ONA) to compete with the other two operators (OBG Newsletter, March 17, 2009). ANRT was another example of how the privatization of the telecom business was put in the hands of an "autonomous" state agency that operated largely outside parliamentary and government control (Hibou and Tozy 2002a).

The increasing dominance of the royal family and the makhzan in the Moroccan domestic market allowed them to regain "in the private sector the influence that policies of economic liberalization were progressively eroding in government and the public sector" (Henry and Springborg 2001, 173). The Moroccan commercial banking system was one of the most important instruments for these new practices of control. Through ONA's dominant stake in the national banking system, it monopolized the allocation of credit to the private sector (173). Consequently, elite families were less inclined to rebel against one of their most important business partners and their main political guarantor (Clément 1986). What's more, many of the leading families actually participate in the same holdings as the royal family and are bound together in an increasing corporate network of "interlocking directorates" (Oubenal and Zeroual 2017).

The Return of Global Capital and the Emergence of the Moroccan Entrepreneurs

Structural adjustment and economic liberalization not only changed the practices of the existing elite; it also introduced new actors on the scene. To begin with, the privatization policies, together with other free-market policies, entailed a de facto *de-Moroccanization* of the economy and brought international capital back into the front seat. Forty-five percent of all privatizations in Morocco realized between 1993 and 2002 were allocated to foreign investors, predominantly French investors (Hibou and Tozy 2002a). Morocco's state monopoly in telecommunications, Maroc Telecom, was sold to the French multinational Vivendi before it was later sold again to an Emirati investor. Other French companies such as Société Générale and BNP Paribas (banking sector), Axa (assurances), Accor and Club Med (tourism), Suez and Veolia (water and electricity), Alstom (transport), and Bouygues (construction) have now firmly established themselves in the Moroccan domestic market.

French companies are very active in major urban infrastructural projects. Bouygues was contracted in the construction of the industrial port Tanger Med in Tangier. Alstom, another world leader in transport and energy infrastructure, gained a contract for the construction of the tramways in Rabat and Casablanca and for the delivery of fourteen Euroduplex trains for the high-speed line between Casablanca and Tangier. Both companies have a long history in Morocco.

The excellent relations between the French political elite and the monarchy played a major role in the dominant share of French capital and French multinationals in the Moroccan economy. The relationship between King Hassan II and French president Jacques Chirac was very productive for French private interests on the one hand, and French political and diplomatic support for Morocco on the other hand (Tuquoi 2006). According to a former journalist of *TelQuel* and the economic magazine *Economie Entreprises*, Alstom, for example, owes its dominant presence in the Moroccan market due to the diplomatic efforts of former French president Michel Sarkozy (interview, Casablanca, June 5, 2010).

At the beginning of the twenty-first century, 80 percent of foreign direct investment (FDI) came from French (66 percent) and Spanish (14 percent) investors. Recently things are changing with the entry of investors from the Gulf in cities such as Casablanca, Rabat, and Marrakech. Since 2007, investments from the Gulf increased significantly. They are now the second most important source of FDI in Morocco. Between 2010 and 2014 19 percent of investments came from the Gulf (5 percent from Saudi Arabia and 14 percent from the Emirates). Spanish investments declined substantially in the same period—to only 4 percent—because of the economic crisis in Spain. French capital remains the leading investor with a cumulative share of 43 percent between 2004 and 2014 (AMDI 2015, 4).

Besides the increasing implication of foreign capital, things were also changing on the domestic scene due to economic liberalization. Melani Claire Cammett (2007) and Myriam Catusse (2008) describe how a growing group of "entrepreneurs" gained political influence within the new economic order in Morocco. Neoliberal reform opened up new opportunities for a group of export-oriented manufacturers, a relatively new component of the private sector, that sought its fortunes on global markets, largely through subcontracting relationships (Cammett 2007, 99). Cammett argues that this new group of exporters, especially in the textile industry, managed to delink itself from domestic markets and looked almost exclusively toward the global market.

The rise of this new social group of entrepreneurs did not supplant the position of the old economic elites, nor did they necessarily alter the rules of the game—personal networks were still of crucial importance for doing business in Morocco; the traditional elite families continued to dominate the capitalist economy. Yet these new entrepreneurial actors still had an impact on political decision-making: they changed the relations between the Moroccan private sector and the state as well as the interactions between private businessmen and state officials.

The new entrepreneurs often lacked high-level access to the palace and the upper echelons of the state bureaucracy. In order to establish these necessary connections, they transformed important employers' associations into powerful lobby groups. Both Catusse and Cammett demonstrate how the increasing importance of business associations in the 1990s marked these changing state–business relations. These lobby groups interacted with the state on behalf of different economic sectors and their particular interests, introducing new styles of placing demands on the state. By organizing themselves in professional associations and by redefining their modes of political action, they created a critical mass of private businessmen able to pressure the state administration (Cammett

2007, 179–81). Precisely because of their lack of access to the makhzan and the state technocrats, these associations also tried to lobby elected government officials.

Cammett argues that this did not lead to political liberalization. The new entrepreneurs did not seek to alter the political system. Instead, like most businessmen in the world, they tried to find alternative ways and strategies to pursue their private interests. The press, Cammett adds, was an instrumental channel: during the 1990s prominent entrepreneurs relied on press releases, interviews, and television appearances to express their demands and grievances.

The transformation of the Confédération Générale des Entreprises du Maroc (CGEM, General Confederation of Moroccan Enterprises) is a salient example. It evolved from a *"club de patrons"* closely tied to the makhzan into a broad interest group, a *"syndicat patronal,"* that claimed to defend the interests of the employers and private business in general (Catusse 2008, 199–244).[3] Until the beginning of the 1990s, its leaders were members of the traditional Fassi bourgeoisie who strongly relied on the state and the monarchy to protect their business interests (Benhaddou 2009). But since the mid-1990s, the CGEM expanded from four membership federations to more than twenty and integrated all kinds of new business elites.

The transformation of the CGEM characterized the increasing prominence of "atypical" business elites. A turning point was the election of Abderrahman Lahjouji as head of the CGEM in 1994 (Catusse 2008, 214–21; Sater 2002). He represented a new type of business elite that differed in outlook from the old urban bourgeoisie and the rural landowners. He was not educated in one of the Moroccan elite schools, nor was he an ex-minister, nor did he previously occupy any other high position within the state bourgeoisie. His election symbolized the rise and growing influence of this new interest group of entrepreneurs; many of the new members of the CGEM also came from more modest origins. These so-called self-made men now opposed the traditional "fat cats" (to use Cammett's denotation). They contended that they earned their living through honest and hard work rather than through the support of the state and the reliance on a privileged family background.[4]

A Shifting Balance of Power

Another turning point in the relation between the private sector and the state was the infamous "purification campaign" *(campagne d'assainissement)* or anticorruption campaign started by the government in December 1995 to fight drug trafficking and tax evasion. The campaign was launched officially by the Minister of Interior to improve Morocco's business image in the light of the recently signed free-trade agreement with Europe. The country's reputation was severely affected by rampant corruption, the informalization of the economy, and illegal economic activities like smuggling and drug trafficking.

Yet the anticorruption campaign cannot be understood only within the framework of the state's efforts to fight corruption and fraud: it must also, and maybe more important, be understood within a context of a changing balance of power between the makhzan and the growing Moroccan private sector (Cammett 2007; Catusse 2008; Hibou and Tozy 2002b; Sater 2002). The purification campaign was a powerful display of "arbitrary rule" by which the makhzan targeted specific businessmen, tried to contain the influence of the newly reformed CGEM, and attempted to strengthen its grip on new economic actors who were considered at that moment to be potential dissidents (Hibou 2004a).

The eventual signing of a "gentlemen's agreement" in June 1996 between the Ministry of Interior and the CGEM drew the boundaries of a new balance of power and further institutionalized the contacts between the professional associations and the makhzan. It is remarkable and revealing, according to Hibou and Tozy (2002b), that the elected government and the political parties were kept out of the negotiations that took place between the Ministry of Interior (the makhzan's center of power) and the CGEM.

Within this context, the gentlemen's agreement recognized, on the one hand, the political inclusion of the entrepreneurs in the realm of power (Catusse 2008, 241–42; Hibou and Tozy 2002b). On the other hand, the agreement must also be seen as the reaffirmation of the primacy of the monarchy's power (Hibou 2004a). The successors of Lahjouji as president of the CGEM were all more closely connected to the palace. Lahjouji, who was a manager of a family business in Meknes, was succeeded by Hassan Chami, who came from a respectable Fassi family and occupied important government positions before he became president of the CGEM. After Chami, Moulay Hafid Elalamy took over the leadership of the CGEM. He was the CEO of an important insurance company and had previously worked for ONA (Catusse 2008, 220). On May 23, 2009, he was succeeded by Mohamed Horani, who enjoyed the support of ONA. The two actual favorites to win that election, Mohamed

Chaïbi and Youssef Alaoui, withdrew their candidacy when Horani presented himself, leaving him as the only candidate. Horani made place in 2012 for Miriem Bensalah Chaqroun, the first female president in the history of the CGEM. She also comes from a powerful family close to the palace (Le Bec 2014).

Overall, the changes within the CGEM and the purification campaign should be situated within the broader context of economic liberalization and "the pluralization of power relations" since the *alternance* (see chapter 2). While the CGEM was practically nonexistent in the 1980s, it grew to be an influential pressure group and an important political adversary in the 1990s. Yet, in the end, the Moroccan entrepreneurs did not succeed in undermining the established political powers. To be sure, they managed to express their demands and caught the attention of the makhzan, but their autonomy from the latter was still limited. More accurately, the political struggle between the CGEM and the makhzan revealed that while the first had managed to gain political influence, the latter was still successful in co-opting potential adversaries. In fact, the main objective of the purification campaign was "to send a powerful message to the business community: the neo-liberal restructuring of Morocco's economy does not mean that entrepreneurs will be allowed to escape the grip of the Makhzan" (Denoeux 1998, 112; see also Oubenal and Zeroual 2017; Sater 2002).

More recently, a new powerful federation of entrepreneurs has entered the scene: the Fédération Nationale des Promoteurs Immobiliers (FNPI, National Federation of Real Estate Developers), the main interest group of influential companies such as Addoha and Alliances. It is now one of the most powerful pressure groups within the CGEM (Zaki 2011b); in a relatively short period of time, the private real estate sector has managed to gain considerable political leverage and influence on legislation. According to Lamia Zaki, the study of the FNPI and their complex relation with different state administrations further demonstrates that a monolithic view of the state and authoritarian power is inadequate. Of course, the monarchy remains the dominant political and economic force in the country, but the new millionaire and billionaire business elite is far from powerless (of the six richest Moroccans, three are real estate developers: Miloud Chaabi [Ynna Holding], Anas Sefroui [Addoha], and Alami Lazraq [Alliances]). They maintain an ambiguous relationship with the public authorities and the inner circle of the monarchy: while they succeed in pressing for their own interests, they still depend very much on state support and protection to maintain their oligarchic positions (Zaki 2011b).

Finally, on the other side of the political spectrum, neoliberal reform also produced important losers. The influence of other social actors, especially organized labor and the political left, diminished significantly with the introduction of structural adjustment. The balance of power built around the military, the state bourgeoisie, and organized labor that was typical for state developmentalism came under severe pressure due to the policies of structural adjustment (Ayubi 1997, 159–61). More specifically in Morocco, some social institutions, such as the press, the opposition parties (e.g., USFP and Istiqlal), and, above all, the labor unions, enjoyed relative autonomy from the state apparatus and often strongly opposed—to a certain extent, of course—the repressive politics of King Hassan II (Clément and Paul 1984). The Moroccan unions, for example, proved to be a fierce opponent during the crisis of the late 1970s and early 1980s (Cherkaoui and Ben Ali 2007, 752). They successfully pressured the government on several occasions and obliged the authorities to withdraw some economic austerity measures.

The early years of neoliberal restructuring coincided with fierce strikes and riots. The Casablanca riots in 1981 expressed increasing social discontent among the urban poor but also indicated the influence and mobilization capacities of the labor unions, in particular CDT. Some observers at the time thought the unions even had the potential to inflict a full-scale insurrection. In the period that followed, however, the monarchy managed not only to repress the unions but also to incorporate some of its leadership and that of the allied opposition parties into a general politics of consensus. By November 1983, both USFP leader Abderrahim Bouabid and Istiqlal leader M'hamed Boucetta joined the government. Subsequently, both the historical opposition parties and the major unions agreed to the new round of austerity measures imposed by the IMF (Clément and Paul 1984).[5]

As a result of the repression against the unions and the co-optation of the political opposition, the role of these actors in the subsequent riots in 1984 was marginal at the least (Clément and Paul 1984; Seddon 1989). Also in the early 1990s, neither the unions nor the emerging Islamists played a crucial role in the violent uprisings around such cities as Fez, Tangier, and Meknes. These events revealed a more general and spontaneous dissatisfaction that went well beyond the influence and scope of the unions (Brand 1998; Madani 1995).

Throughout the 1990s, as Catusse argues, the apparent class struggle of the early 1980s was further neutralized when both the unions and the CGEM were brought together as economic "partners" in an institutionalized social dialogue. On August 1, 1996, leading representatives of CDT; the Union Générale des Travailleurs du Maroc (UGTM, General Union of Moroccan Workers), which was linked to Istiqlal; CGEM; and the Minister of Interior signed a joint declaration in Rabat to install a social dialogue in order to find a common ground between their different interests. By bringing the social partners together, central power reduced its own role in the arbitration of class conflicts. They were now able to redistribute responsibilities, regulate the social risks, and supervise the process of "class collaboration" they had installed.

This new mechanism *(dispositif)* contributed to the depoliticization of socioeconomic problems in Morocco. In the name of economic growth, securitization, and social peace, the left–right divide was now put aside in favor of the consensus model (Catusse 2008, 247). The former balance of power embedded within the developmental state model was fundamentally altered. The unions and organized labor in general were among the main victims of these shifting balances of power, while the private sector, foreign capital, and a group of emerging entrepreneurs gained considerable influence. This trend was of course not limited to the Moroccan or Arab context. The diminishing power of the organized labor movements manifested itself as a global trend in relation to neoliberal projects (Harvey 2006b, 2010b; Thomas 2014).

The Nature of Politics and the Question of Class in Morocco

All these evolutions, the rise of the entrepreneurs, the decline of organized labor, the increasing influence of foreign capital—in other words, the replacement of the populist coalitions of the developmental state with new balances of power driven by increasing globalization—have made the picture of Arab politics and political agency much more complex. What conceptual tools do we have to understand the current "complexes of power"? How do we translate the structural changes of the last three decades in terms of political agency? More concrete, how do we conceptualize the agency behind the reproduction, exploitation, and dispossession of urban space?

In chapter 1, I discussed how regime-centered approaches (and the concept of the "Arab regime") underestimated the contemporary global situation and proved inadequate to unravel the diffuse, open, relational, and often global connections that constitute the outcomes of political transformation. Ironically, it was the recent *reactions against* decades of neoliberal political transformation—in the form of the Arab uprisings—that caused Middle East scholars to start questioning the dominant paradigm of authoritarian regime persistence.

Hence, can we conceptualize political agency in the Arab world differently in this era of neoliberal globalization? And how can a Marxist approach to class contribute to this tension between regime-centered approaches and the global situation?

Neoliberal Reform Leading to Capitalist Class Formation?

I am interested in the concept of class insofar as it can enable us to understand the relations of power articulated through neoliberal projects. Here we should distinguish between a stratification approach to class, which is widely accepted, and the more political approaches to class (e.g., a Weberian or a Marxist approach) that use the concept of class to explain relations of power; that is, those relations that produce conditions of inclusion and exclusion and mechanisms of exploitation and domination (E. O. Wright 2009).[6] While few people will deny the capitalist nature of some of the most significant transformations in the Arab world since the 1980s, a Marxist class analysis of these changes is much less widely accepted. References to class (working class, middle class, business class, ruling class, etc.) are abundant in many studies but rarely as explanations of the *nature* of political domination and exploitation.

In their edited volume *The Arab State and Neo-Liberal Globalization*, Laura Guazzone and Daniela Pioppi (2009a) argue that neoliberal reform has resulted in the emergence and consolidation of a new model of authoritarian regime characterized by new forms of patronage, neo-patrimonialism, and corruption and enhanced by the co-optation of an emerging business elite in the context of economic liberalization. Yet, according to the authors of the concluding chapter, this rising group of entrepreneurs under neoliberal reform, both in Morocco as elsewhere in the region, was "by no means a class in itself."

> On the contrary, it is more like the compradora bourgeoisie of old colonial times. Together with the new *infitah* elites, "old" post-independence elites still hold the reins of power. The "state bourgeoisie" or upper echelons of the public administration and security sector elites (army, security forces) are still very important in the power

structure, as are old community leaders . . . and local notables. Consequently, the increased elite variety and complexity seem to be mainly the result of a more complex society, rather than the product of new, independent, emerging classes. (Aggestam et al. 2009, 328–29)

If we follow this line of reasoning, class seems irrelevant indeed in the context of Morocco. The Moroccan economy remains largely a monarchical affair with traditional families tied directly to the monarchy and the makhzan. The most important economic decisions are always subject to the will of the king. In the beginning of the 1980s, for example, the decision to implement a structural adjustment program was made by King Hassan II personally and was perceived as a sovereign decision (Ben Ali 2005, 5). Today, most analysts agree that private actors have very little room for maneuver without the consent of Mohammed VI and his entourage: he is the one who launches "royal projects" such as the Bouregreg project, Tanger Med, and Casablanca Marina.

Moreover, the dominant influence of the contemporary Moroccan state bourgeoisie or "royal managers," as Pierre Vermeren (2009) calls them, is undeniable—they continue to dominate the (urban) development strategies of the country. The directors of important state agencies such as the Bouregreg Agency, TMSA, and CDG are some of today's most prominent economic actors in Morocco.

These royal managers do not own the means of production; they are appointed by the king and depend on his goodwill for their personal fortunes. When Mohammed VI acceded to the throne, he replaced some of the country's leading technocrats under Hassan II with his own entourage and former classmates. Over the past decade, we have witnessed the rising influence of a young group of assertive and dynamic managers with close ties to Mohammed VI. They now occupy leading positions in the state apparatus and the semipublic entities, as well as in the private sector, but can be easily replaced and displaced if it suits the political interests of the makhzan (Denoeux 2007; Tozy 2008).

In 2009, for example, just after the municipal elections, Mustapha Bakkoury was replaced by Anass Alami as director of the powerful CDG. Rumor had it that the king appointed Alami because he was a close ally of Mohamed Mounir El Majidi, the CEO of Siger and manager of the royal fortune. Yet Bakkoury, on the other hand, was an ally of Fouad Ali El Himma, also a close friend of the king, member of the royal cabinet, and one of the most influential figures in the Moroccan political landscape. Nevertheless, despite this close relationship between El Himma and Mohammed VI, the king perhaps sought to avoid too much economic and political influence in the hands of the El Himma clan (Boussaid 2009; see also Zeroual 2014).[7] Bakkoury did not disappear from the scene, however. He was later appointed chief executive of the Moroccan Agency of Solar Energy (MASEN). This example shows—whatever the reason for the reshuffle—how easily influential state technocrats can be replaced and how dependent they are on the monarchy.

The state bourgeoisie did not so much lose its influence due to the economic liberalization but changed its practices of accumulation and redefined its relations with the private sector. In the process, it attempted to control and at times hijack the projects of economic liberalization (Haddad 2012). Therefore, Bassam Haddad concludes, Waterbury's analysis of the state bourgeoisie has not been credibly challenged since it was first published "and for good reason" (2012, 234).

Still, many have tried to explain how economic reform was shaped in the region and, in return, how that reform reconfigured relations and practices of political and economic power. An interesting approach is *Networks of Privilege in the Middle East*, a volume edited by Steven Heydemann (2004b). This volume seeks to understand how economic liberalization reorganized opportunities for rent seeking and altered the ways of capturing the benefits of economic reform. Heydemann uses the concept of "networks of privilege" to tell a more complex story about the politics of economic reform and move *relationships*, rather than categories of people or social groups, to the foreground "as units of agency" (2004a, 24). One of the reasons, he states, is because the boundaries between workers, capitalists, and state technocrats as explanatory categories of politics are porous, flexible, and often ambiguous (12).

I am sympathetic to the analysis of Heydemann and others in the way they take into account the *relational* complexities of power. However, two critical comments on their conceptualization of networks of privilege should be added. First, their approach is still grounded within the boundaries of a *national* political space. Networks of privilege are perceived as "national networks" of power. There is little or no political connection to the "outside world." Second, the particular way in which networks of privilege are related to rent seeking and internal corruption creates the space for a misleading conceptual distinction between "crony capitalism," on the one hand, and a more abstract, "place-less," and ideal type kind of capitalism, on the other hand.

The concept of class, by contrast, maintains an associative link with global capitalism. I make an argument for the use of class as an explanatory concept and propose a fundamentally different reading of class than the one made by Waterbury and others. My analysis takes not only the relational but also the *spatial* complexities of power into account within the context of neoliberal projects. This reading links political change in the region, and Morocco more specifically, to globalization and situates both the politics of economic reform and a phenomenon such as "the regime" within global class relations.

Rejecting Class Analysis for the Wrong Reasons

There are three main problems with the basis on which a Marxist class analysis is rejected or ignored. First, people like Waterbury, Haddad, Benhaddou, Guazzone, and Pioppi are looking at class for the wrong reasons. In the MENA region, as their critique goes, neither the rising private entrepreneurs nor the state bourgeoisie can be considered as independent agents of political and economic change or as autonomous self-conscious classes (see also Bellin 2000; Henry and Springborg 2001, 21; Wurzel 2009). Independent agents of change, in their view, are considered those actors that can undermine and eventually eradicate the authoritarian politics of the region's regimes.

As such, this perspective remains somehow informed by questions of democracy and democratization that are implicit in the authoritarian persistence paradigm (see chapter 1). The "new models of authoritarianism" that emerged out of neoliberal reform are still regarded as residual categories of a failed transition to liberal democracy and a free market. The new groups or actors in Arab society are accounted for insofar as they can or cannot provoke democratic transition. Their failure to do so is then coupled to their failure to form an autonomous class. Benhaddou, for example, regrets that the Moroccan elite is not capable of taking on the same democratic role as the Western bourgeoisie in the late eighteenth century when they abolished the ancien régime (Benhaddou 2009, 197). Or as Guazzone and Pioppi remark from a less romanticized viewpoint: the "privatization policies in Morocco, Egypt and Jordan—to name just a few—have resulted in a shift in patronage networks and the formation of new crony capitalists, *rather than in the creation of competitive markets*" (2009b, 11–12, emphasis added). Yet class should be determined by what people actually do within the context of neoliberal projects and not by what they are "supposed" to do.

Second, it is not necessarily wrong to situate political power in the hands of a regime or a ruling elite centered around a monarch or president for life. Nevertheless, it underestimates the wider spatial dimension of the new complexes of power articulated through neoliberal projects. Most accounts of Arab political life that take into account the impact of neoliberalism consider the implementation of neoliberal reform to be a response of the regime to economic pressure coming from the outside. In other words, neoliberalism itself remains within the sphere of (global) economics or at best an economic policy, while political agency and responsibility are placed almost exclusively into the hands of a domestic regime or a state bourgeoisie.

Third, authors such as Waterbury view class too much as a rigid sociological category, giving us the illusion that one can judge the validity of the concept based on its usefulness in an empirical method of categorization (who belongs to what class and who does not). Yet using class as a static analytical category makes it not only aspatial but also anachronistic. Assessing the class content or class position of the emerging entrepreneurs or the state bourgeoisie on the basis of a set of predetermined properties (i.e., ownership over the means of production and the ability to secure their own reproduction as a class) derives from a rather simplistic reading of Marx's own class analysis in which the political cleavage between two opposing classes (workers and capitalists) is understood as an ideal type theoretical abstraction of social groups independent of historical context and not, as Marx intended it, as the characterization or "personification" of particular kinds of struggles and social relations at a particular time.[8]

Today, the specific feature of ownership of the means of production does not bring much clarity. Let me give a few straightforward examples. Even in the heartland of neoliberal hegemony, the United States, it is difficult to base a class analysis on whether one owns the means of production. CEOs and managers of multinational corporations do not own the means of production that they control (or not all of them). Moreover, they never control these means alone but are accountable to others: for example, stockholders and boards of directors. Additionally, in the contemporary phase of finance capitalism, production has become subordinated to financialization and practices of speculation. This brings to the fore all kinds of new actors (stockbrokers, day traders, hedge funds, etc.) whose class position is not necessarily only determined by the mere ownership of the means of production.

Furthermore, and more closely related to the question of the state bourgeoisie, the institutions of the European Union have proved on many occasions that they are involved in various projects to neoliberalize European political and economic life (Bogaert 2015a; Hermann 2007; K. Mitchell 2006; A. Smith 2002). Are the politics of European commissioners and Eurocrats—this rather specific kind of state bourgeoisie—then not a form of class politics? The critical question, therefore, is not so much whether neoliberal reform in the Arab region has given rise to new (independent) classes, or whether we can define certain fixed sociological categories by which we can determine the apparent class or non-class nature of certain dominant groups. Instead, the crucial issue is to understand how old and new elites transformed their traditional practices of power into class practices within a context of neoliberal reform.

Class as a Sociospatial Concept Explaining the Nature of Practices and Relations

Class is not an empirical tool but an analytical one. Class as an analytical concept explains the specific (and ever changing) nature of interests, practices, and conflicts behind labor exploitation, the appropriation of surpluses, and capital circulation. Throughout *Capital*, David Harvey notes, Marx himself was above all concerned with the *role* certain people played within the process of capitalist accumulation rather than with the actual individuals or social groups themselves who played these roles. Marx recognized therefore that one particular individual can occupy different roles, even deeply contradictory ones (Harvey 2010a, 48).

Moreover, when Marx writes about class, he does not refer to the ownership of the means of production of specific individuals but to practices of "extracting," "appropriating," and "pumping out" surplus value from those who actually produce the wealth (Resnick and Wolff 1987, 115; see, e.g., Marx 1992, 304, 411, 423, 426, 713). Class is thus not something static but *relational*. It refers to specific relations of power, domination, and exploitation. Capitalist class practices are articulated through the relations between appropriators and the dispossessed.[9]

Insofar as Marx talked about individual capitalists or particular dominating social groups in *Capital*, they were "merely personifications of economic relations" (1992, 179; see also 92, 254, 265, 342, 423, 424, 739). According to Marxist scholars such as Harvey, Resnick, and Wolff, this is absolutely crucial to understand Marx's different use of the concept of class. The more flexible use of different class categories (capitalist class, petty bourgeoisie, working class, lumpenproletariat) were used for political ends or to describe historical events (Harvey 2006a, 26; Resnick and Wolff 1987, 161–62), while Marx's understanding of class as a theoretical and analytical concept refers to the nature of particular practices and social relations between different people.[10]

Here we can make a link with Foucault. In the same way Foucault looked at power not as something that can be possessed but as something that structures relationships in space and time (see chapter 1), we can understand class as a particular form of power embedded within the relations of capitalist expansion and the restructuring of economic and political life. Not surprisingly, Foucault criticized those with Marxist tendencies who were more preoccupied with the definition of class and its delineations rather than with the understanding of the nature of the struggle itself (Marsden 1999, 24).

Class analysis is therefore not "a matter of identifying a fixed set of categories which are supposed to apply for all times and places" (Harvey 1989b, 111). To the contrary, class configurations are always contextual and embedded within the constitutive relations and transformations of actually existing capitalism. Class does not exist prior to but arises out of specific capitalist practices and relations. It characterizes social relations that are "continually in the process of coming-into-being" within the context of projects of capital accumulation and surplus-value appropriation (Hanieh 2011, 12).[11] Put differently, when we use the concept of class, we should primarily be concerned to find out *what kinds of politics and relations* we are talking about, instead of being preoccupied with the question of who fits into what category of class.

Within the context of contemporary global capitalism and neoliberal globalization, a context in which capital is hypermobile, the concept of class points to far-reaching *relational* and *spatial* consequences that stretch beyond the boundaries of the nation-state in ways much more fundamental than in the earlier period of developmentalism. Class—in contrast to concepts such as clientelism, patronage, cronyism, or networks of privilege that seem rather exotic in their use and only applicable to non-Western contexts—can point to the political and economic convergence between local economy and global capitalism or between what popular opinion often all too easily distinguishes as "us" and "them" within our contemporary global situation. Moreover, class does not really make a distinction between local and global. Class in our contemporary global situation is always articulated and produced in particular locales, while *simultaneously*, it is part of a global process (Das 2012, 27). It situates local agency not necessarily only at the receiver's end of global processes but as an active contributor to these processes.

In the case of neoliberal urban projects in Morocco, class relations arise out of the political struggles over urban space, and out of the political practices of the reproduction, exploitation, and dispossession of urban space. In the relational and spatial understanding of neoliberal globalization I am trying to advance here, placemaking ventures like the Bouregreg project, Tanger Med, and Casablanca Marina are "crisscrossings" and "collections" of "wider power-geometries that constitute both themselves and 'the global'" (Massey 2005, 101, 130). You cannot think about the changes within these particular places without the implication of capital from the Gulf, investors from Europe, foreign consultants, state support, the privileged relations between the Moroccan monarchy and emirs from the Gulf, and so on. The spatial character of neoliberal projects presents us with a multiplicity and heterogeneity of political practices and relations implicated in the production of globalization *in place* (Massey 2005). Class as a concept *unifies* these "crisscrossings" in place within a structured political analysis and links them to particular strategies of surplus-value appropriation.

In Morocco and elsewhere, neoliberal projects create opportunities to appropriate surplus value through privileged relations within the political system. But it is important to understand that these privileged relations (e.g., close ties with the regime) have their limits within certain neoliberal projects or, at the very least, cannot be reduced to mere "national" relations. An interesting example in this regard is the fact that even ONA had to reconcile with the entrance of new powerful foreign capitalist actors in the domestic market as it could not match the offer of French and Spanish multinationals in the Moroccan telecom deals at the beginning of the twenty-first century (Sater 2010, 104). This again shows the spatial complexities of power created within the context of neoliberal globalization. Class power stretches beyond the power of the regime, while in the case of Morocco, it has *at the same time* become more and more a monarchical affair connecting the regime with other class actors, for example from the Gulf (Errazzouki 2012).

All this has its consequences for "class struggle" in Morocco and the Global South more generally. As David Harvey argues, if workers would succeed to win significant concessions on wages through labor struggles—and with the increase of labor protests over the last decade in countries such as Egypt, Tunisia, and Morocco, this might seem very plausible (Ayeb 2011; Beinin 2009; El-Mahdi 2011; Zemni, De Smet, and Bogaert 2013)—these gains can be easily taken back from them by landlords, bankers, and merchants in the urban space. Through its flexibility, capital can overcome losses in the production space, among others by recovering these losses in the urban living space; for example, through rising rents of all kinds, the privatization of public services (education, health care, public transport, water, and electricity), and the benefits of taxes (the imbalance between corporate and individual taxes) (Harvey 2014, 67–68, 84).

In order to understand the urban politics in Morocco since the 1980s, I use class as an analytical tool to explore the changing nature of practices and relations of power within the context of neoliberal globalization. I do not use class as a sociological concept defined by a set of predetermined features in order to distinguish different classes in society. To the contrary, class tells us something about the particular agency, the practices, and the strategies involved precisely in the *creation* of a stratified society. The critical question is not so much whether those who remodel the Moroccan city can be described as a class but rather whether their practices and strategies can be understood as *class practices* or *class strategies*. A regime, a ruling family, the state bourgeoisie, a foreign investor—all can all engage in different class practices and strategies within the context of particular neoliberal projects.

Of course, class strategies are not necessarily concerted actions, planned to obtain one single aim (Lefebvre 1996, 77). Nor are these strategies always rational. Nevertheless, the theoretical and empirical difficulty, if not the impossibility, to *fix* class in Morocco and elsewhere does not make the *nature* of political struggle less real. The concept of class is therefore important in the way it explicitly relates political relations and practices in particular places to global capitalism. Let us look now at two specific neoliberal class projects that involve different kinds of class relations: the Bouregreg project and the national slum upgrading project.

4

IMAGINEERING A
NEW BOUREGREG VALLEY

[The city is] man's most consistent and on the whole, his most
successful attempt to remake the world he lives in more after his
heart's desire. But, if the city is the world which man created, it is
the world in which he is henceforth condemned to live. Thus,
indirectly, and without any clear sense of the nature of his task, in
making the city man has remade himself.

> —Robert Park, quoted in David Harvey, *Spaces of
> Global Capitalism*

We have, however, largely surrendered our own individual right
to make the city after our heart's desire to the rights of property
owners, landlords, developers, finance capitalists and the state.
These are the primary agents that shape our cities for us and
thereby shape us. We have abrogated our right to make ourselves
to the rights of capital to make us through the passive acceptance
or mindless embrace of the restructuring of daily life by the
projects of capitalist class interests.

> —David Harvey, *Spaces of Global Capitalism*

AT THE HEART OF TWO CITIES, the capital Rabat and its neighbor
Salé, the valley of the Bouregreg River is the place for the largest urban
renewal project in the history of Morocco. A historic natural barrier
between the imperial city of Rabat and the notorious pirates of Salé,
the river valley now portends the eventual reconciliation of two rival
cities, a historic rivalry that shapes the identity of both the Rbatis and
the Slaouis to this very day. While Rabat is the seat of government and
central power, Salé, although larger in population, is a dormitory city in
the shadow of the capital.

The Bouregreg Valley has to become a place of connection, not only
a connection between Rabat and Salé but one with the outside world as

well. The Bouregreg project is one of the icons of the country's "urbanism of projects" and claims to incorporate the rich cultural past in a harmonious way. According to the Bouregreg Agency, the site "is surrounded by panoramic views from the Hassan Tower to the Kasbah of the Oudayas, through the alleys of the souk and the medina, along the ramparts of the Chellah; it's an entire heritage that awaits you."[1]

The urban megaproject draws on historical myths to present an image of the future. Over the past few years, investments in culture and heritage have become one of the priorities of Rabat's urban development strategy. The construction of an arts district *(cité des arts)* and the Grand Theatre designed by the late "starchitect" Zaha Hadid in respectively the first and the second phase of the Bouregreg project can be placed alongside other initiatives such as the National Library and the Mohammed VI Modern and Contemporary Art Museum, which aim to turn the once dull administrative capital of Morocco into a vibrant cultural destination.

Yet this makeover of Rabat and the promotion of a new lifestyle not only makes an appeal to the past or to culture; it also draws on the myths of the present. Abstract universals such as "sustainability," "environmental protection," and "citizenship" are presented as the inspiration for the new urban lifeline that stretches fifteen kilometers into the river valley until the barrage Sidi Mohamed Ben Abdellah. These modern claims contribute to a sense of urgency, a moral obligation to prevent the further deterioration of this historical site. After all, the last decades were marked by either neglect or abuse, which threatened to turn the once luxurious valley and its diverse wildlife into a degraded, sordid, and polluted area.

The valley had become a dumping ground and a place where spontaneous and clandestine housing could thrive. "Does the agglomeration of the capital of the kingdom deserve such a future?" asked the royal commission that was charged in 2001 to come up with a new Parti d'Aménagement Global (PAG, Global Development Plan). "Do we not have the right to expect a better destination for this exceptional place?" (Royal Commission 2003, 7).[2] In the commission's perception, the valley became an impediment to future progress, one that had to be remedied and reimagined. The Bouregreg project, launched a few years later, offered a clean slate to start anew, to rethink not only the destination for the place but also urban life as such. The redevelopment of the valley promises a new way of urban life—sells it actually—to conform to the

The Kasbah of the Oudayas. Photograph by Soumia El Majdoub, 2015.

image of a moderate, open, and liberal Morocco that invites people to come and live, that invites (global) consumers and investors with a vision.

But behind the projected uniqueness and authenticity hides the structuring dynamic of an upcoming global model, a traveling political project that borrows its inspiration from the apparently limitless and futuristic optimism of global cities such as Dubai, Beijing, and Mumbai. The opening scenery of the promotional video of the Bouregreg project—the sunrise, the small fishing boats leaving the valley on their way to the open sea early in the morning, and the aerial view over the historical heritage of the city, all this accompanied by the soft tone of oriental music—is very recognizable by anyone familiar with the spectacles promoted in Dubai and elsewhere in the Gulf region.

Despite references to particularity, culture, and history, the Bouregreg project displays a well-recognized vocabulary shared by planners, architects, consultants, local administrators, politicians, and investors all over the urban world. It is based on assumptions of a universal knowledge and technical know-how, a knowledge that claims to be timeless and apolitical. Yet urban projects such as the Bouregreg project are, of course, strongly situated in an ideological and political–economic context. Behind the visible aesthetics of urban regeneration lies a whole new pattern of power. The ideas of urban entrepreneurialism invested in these designs are about the manipulation of landscapes and cultural resources for capital accumulation, consumption, and dispossession (Broudehoux 2007; Kanna 2012).

As Tarik Senhaji, CEO of the Moroccan Fund for Tourism Development (FMDT), argued in an interview for *Jeune Afrique:*

> Culture is a very important means for the valorization of Morocco as a [tourist] destination. According to several studies, 39 percent of the tourists who come to Morocco are attracted by the culture of the country. Developing these kinds of projects also allows an incredible valorization of [available] assets. Take the example of Bilbao. Fifteen years ago, the city wasn't visible on the world map of tourism. After the construction of the Guggenheim, . . . the price of real estate augmented with 500 percent in a period of 5 years, and the number of tourists in the city multiplied by six. (Michbal 2014)[3]

I am interested, primarily, in the Bouregreg project as an example of innovative neoliberal statecraft, as a project in which class relations from all over the world can come together and design the city of their interests. I focus more particularly on the new role of the state and the formation of "new state spaces" as a new model for capitalist development. The Bouregreg project is a particular case of a more globalized form of authoritarian government. In the second part of this chapter, I elaborate on this changing character of urban government and its dependence on the caprioles of global capital. This has a significant impact on long-term policy and turns urban planning more and more into an ad hoc "business." Finally, although it might be still too early to assess the social impact of the project, I conclude with some preliminary observations and hypotheses.

The Whereabouts of (State) Power and the Creation of a Global Place

The planning of a new and idyllic Bouregreg Valley not only tells us something about the aesthetic transformation of the Moroccan city; it also provides us with a view on the dynamics of globalization *in place* and its impact on mechanisms of decision-making and state power. The Bouregreg project is emblematic of the more creative phase of government and institution building that followed the destructive phase of structural adjustment and austerity.

The philosophy of contemporary neoliberal policy and urban entre-preneurialism encourages each strategic place or city to be exploited according to its place-specific assets and competitive advantages. Tanger Med aspires to be a vital logistic hub in global commodity chains and international transport, while Casablanca wants to compete with finan-cial centers such as Johannesburg to become the leading business and financial gateway to the African market. Rabat wants to be the cultural, educational, and residential showcase of a modern and global Morocco.

Institutional innovation is required to accomplish these "locational policies" (Brenner 2004, 202–3): hence, the crucial role of the state. By drawing on the case of the Bouregreg Valley, this chapter investigates the dynamics of agency formation implicated in the creation of a *new state space* and considers what it reveals about changing forms of state spatiality and the rise of new governmental arrangements outside the scope of conventional state institutions.

Mapping the New State Space of the Bouregreg Valley

For a long time, urban planning in coastal cities such as Rabat and Casa-blanca turned its back on the coast (Mouloudi 2015b, 62–67). Water-front development was not a priority. This would radically change with the accession to the throne of Mohammed VI: the urban seashores be-came strategic locations and an important asset. Moreover, Mohammed VI wanted to change the image of Rabat from being a rather boring, mainly administrative center to a dynamic and vibrant destination that meets the global city standards of consumption and investment (Bargach 2008). The redevelopment of the Bouregreg Valley is one of the models of Morocco's commitment to waterfront development and "showcase urbanism" *(urbanisme de vitrine)* (Barthel and Mouloudi 2009, 56).

On January 7, 2006, Mohammed VI officially launched the Boure-greg project. The Agency for the Development of the Bouregreg Valley (AAVB) was established two months earlier and has to coordinate this megaproject. This state agency is responsible for the development of a territory of approximately six thousand hectares alongside the Bouregreg riverbanks. Seventy percent of the delineated area is located on the ter-ritory of Salé. The project will be implemented in six phases. The pre-liminary plans foresaw the construction of, for instance, several marinas, luxury hotels, apartments, villas, commercial centers, a conference cen-ter, a museum, a theater, offices, an amusement park, a technopolis, a golf course, and ecotourism facilities. The first phase, "Bab Al Bahr" (gateway to the sea), and the second phase, "Al Saha Al Kabira" (the large square), are currently under construction.

The First Phase: Bab Al Bahr or La Marina Morocco

Bab Al Bahr is designed to be a new downtown at the heart of the two cities. It is located at the estuary of the Bouregreg River, between the two ancient medinas of Rabat and Salé and the historical Kasbah of the Oudayas, which is located in front of the medina of Rabat at the sea front and dates back to the twelfth century. This first phase of the project covers a surface of 70 hectares and comprises a real estate program of 540,000 square meters, including 1,700 residential units, two marinas, hotels, and various commercial, tourist, and cultural facilities. According to the retail brochure of the project, the site will become an attraction pole with more than 60,000 square meters of retail space complemented with underground and surface car parks to accommodate around 2,500 visitors a day.[4]

The construction began on May 12, 2009, and was initially scheduled to be finished by 2013. Due to the global financial crisis and the slowdown of the high-end market in real estate, the first phase will probably not be finished before 2020. The Bab Al Bahr real estate project, recently renamed La Marina Morocco because of the involvement of a new investor, comprises three main districts that will be finished in the near future: the Marina Front, the River Front, and the Arts and Crafts District. The latter will become a kind of gated community. Additionally, a Fairmont luxury hotel including branded residences is scheduled to open in 2019. The ocean side of the first phase will be developed later. The whole area will become home to nearly ten thousand residents.[5]

The architectural plan of the site was designed by the world-famous UK-based firm Foster & Partners together with two Moroccan firms (Confluences and Créachi). According to the developer, it represents a synergy between modern-style living and traditional Arab-Andalusian styles inspired by the narrow streets and alleys of the ancient medinas of Rabat and Salé.

Since the beginning of 2010, sales are open. After an initial phase of success, the pace of purchases slowed down significantly, with a negative effect on the advancement of the project. In the business model of Bab Al Bahr, the financing of the later stages in the project depends on the valorization of already finished districts (Bouchaf 2013).

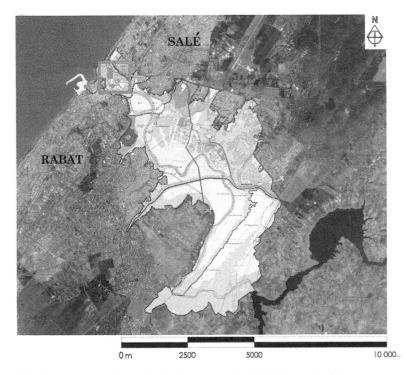

The Bouregreg project, with the first phase, Bab Al Bahr, marked by a rectangle. Copyright Béatrice Platet.

Together with the real estate project, the first phase also included a new bridge (Moulay Hassan), two tramlines, and a tunnel underneath the historic kasbah to improve the mobility between Rabat and Salé. These infrastructural works were finished in 2011. The public authorities invested approximately 3.75 billion dirhams (1.5 billion from the state budget, 1.0 billion from the Hassan II Fund, and 1.25 billion from the general direction of the local communities).[6] The improvement of mobility between the two cities formed an important part of the marketing and the promotion of the project. Every day, approximately 700,000 people cross the Bouregreg River for work or other purposes. Many residents, especially from Salé, consider this part of the project an important step forward. In the long term, an extension of the tramlines is planned to connect the two cities with the subsequent stages of the project.

New apartments at the River Front. Photograph by the author, 2013.

The Second Phase: Al Saha Al Kabira

The second phase, Al Saha Al Kabira, is located right behind the new Moulay Hassan bridge. The excavation works had already started in 2006. However, due to the global financial crisis, the then main investor, Sama Dubai, a subsidiary of sovereign wealth fund Dubai Holding, was liquidated. The Dubai investors had originally planned a luxurious residential islet that was baptized Amwaj (the waves), subdivided—Venetian style—in smaller waterways. The residents would be able to reach their villas by boat. The total cost of Amwaj was estimated at US$2.5 billion.

This real estate fantasy has now been completely abandoned and replaced by a new one. New plans have been drawn with the majestic Grand Theatre, designed by Zaha Hadid Architects, as the centerpiece. The fluid sculpture form inspired by the Bouregreg River will serve as a new landmark for the city. Besides the Grand Theatre, public funds will also be invested in the building of a Museum of Archaeology and Science. The necessary funds for the theater will be provided by the Ministry of Interior (550 million dirhams), the general state budget (400 million dirhams), and the Hassan II Fund (400 million dirhams). The museum will be financed by the Hassan II Fund, the *wilaya* (governate), and the Bouregreg Agency, each for 70 million dirhams, and the general state budget for 90 million dirhams (Decree 2-15-245). Bouregreg Cultures, a subsidiary of the Bouregreg State Agency created in April 2015, will be coordinating the construction of both landmarks.

Besides the new theater and museum, the second phase will also contain new residences, a business center, a new shopping mall, urban parks, and a new marina. In 2013 Wessal Capital announced plans to invest 9 billion dirhams in the second phase of the Bouregerg project, following the creation of its subsidiary Wessal Bouregreg. The four other phases of the project are still in their study phase.

A State within a State

The Bouregreg project was not the first attempt to work out a comprehensive development plan for the valley. The current project builds on a history of thinking about the valley's role. Between 1954 and 1998, six urban development initiatives were presented. The last two plans (1994 and 1998) took into consideration for the first time the planning of the whole river valley between the estuary and the barrage (Royal Commission 2003, 24). The 1998 plan was based on a study done by the Institut d'aménagement et d'urbanisme de la région d'Île-de France (IAURIF, Institute for Urban Planning and Development of the Île-de-France Region). It resonates the most with the project developed by the royal commission in 2003.

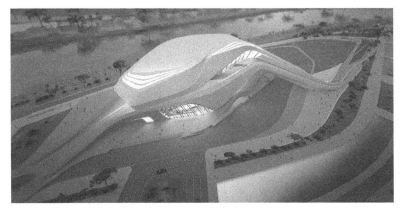

Design of the Grand Theatre in phase two of the Bouregreg project. Courtesy of Zaha Hadid Architects.

However, none of these earlier initiatives went beyond a preliminary planning phase. Natural constraints such as the danger of flooding, the poor natural drainage of the wetlands, the instability of some of the slopes on the river banks, and a high level of salinity of the river water complicated the eventual development of these plans. Yet the main obstructions were financial, political, and institutional (Mouloudi 2015b, 72–75). The institutional complexity and the rivalry between local elected bodies (city councils) and parallel structures controlled by the Ministry of Interior (the prefectures of Rabat and Salé) were perceived as the main obstacles for success. In the eyes of the makhzan, the local elected representatives were perceived incompetent to deal with the size and complexity of such a project.[7]

At the beginning of the twenty-first century, the Bouregreg Valley became a royal priority. On the initiative of the late Abdelaziz Meziane Belfkih, one of the most influential royal advisors, and under the direction of Lemghari Essakl, the Société d'Aménagement de la Vallée du Bouregreg (SABR, Company for the Planning of the Bouregreg Valley) was established in 2001 with the specific assignment to finance the elaboration of a master plan for the future of the valley. SABR was a branch of the state-owned investment vehicle CDG.

This master plan would be the work of a royal commission established under the leadership of Belfkih. It assembled a very broad range of actors, among others the wali (governor) of Rabat-Salé, the director of CDG, the director of SABR, local officials, and both domestic and foreign experts, architects, and consultants (from France, the United States, Jordan, and Spain). One of the most important recommendations of the royal commission was the creation of a single agency *(opérateur unique)* that would lead the coordination and commercialization of the project. Given the great diversity of governmental aspects that come into play with a project of such magnitude (e.g., the reallocation of land, the realization of public infrastructure and public space, the sale of building lots, and the cooperation with private developers), the project could not be left in the hands of "a multiplicity of state entities" *(une multiplicité d'organismes étatiques)* with potentially different visions, interests, and backgrounds (Royal Commission 2003, 151). Or as the Head of Project Finance and Partnerships of the Bouregreg Agency explained it:

> The problem in Morocco is that a public debate is nearly impossible. What do we have to do? Talk to the municipal representatives? They only think in their own interest. We have to force things, force

everybody. We don't have another choice. We are not ready yet for local democracy. We need a structure such as the agency. (interview, Rabat, September 23, 2013)

On November 23, 2005, the AAVB was established as a financially autonomous state agency by Law 16-04 and promulgated by *dahir* (royal decree). The director of SABR, Lemghari Essakl, was appointed by the king as director of the AAVB.[8] Article 26 of Law 16-04 dictates that the AAVB "takes all necessary measures for the realization and the honoring of the development plan."[9] Basically, Law 16-04 prescribes that the agency has exclusive authority over the project within its legally determined territorial boundaries (i.e., the six thousand hectares). Moreover, all state-owned land—Habous land or land owned by the state or the municipalities—was transferred to the Bouregreg Agency free of charge (article 46).[10] The rest, 52 percent of the designated territory, was privately owned (Royal Commission 2003, 1).

But more important, all responsibilities of the local municipalities, the prefectures, and the Urban Planning Agency of Rabat-Salé were transferred to the new state agency. The AAVB is authorized to elaborate a zoning plan, organize the public inquiry, provide public infrastructure, allocate the land for construction, deliver construction permits, regulate all deeds of sale, and expropriate private land within its territory necessary for the development of the project. "We are the state in this site," as the then director of Bouregreg Marina, a subsidiary of the AAVB, made it clear to me (interview, Rabat, May 20, 2010).

The case of the Bouregreg Valley argues for a more complex understanding of the nature of the Moroccan state. It directs our attention to the ways in which state power is geographically dispersed and deployed differentially. The evidence presented here encourages us to understand political agency in relation to the continuous transformative dynamics of state spatiality and the particular ways in which state power entangles with other—seemingly outside—networks and relations of power.

A Qualitative Transformation of Moroccan State Power

State developmentalism in Morocco and elsewhere took the national economy and the national territory as the target of comprehensive state action and state regulation, while neoliberal state strategies do not necessarily treat the national territory as a uniform political space (Brenner 2004; Ong 2006). Consequently, at the level of the city, the transition toward "urban entrepreneurialism" turned particular strategic localities into self-promoting islands of entrepreneurship, while others were left aside. In this process, the state, as the primary institutional mediator of this geography of uneven development, has been rolled out into new institutional arrangements in order to act more quickly and efficiently.

Institutionally, this new geography of power has manifested itself through what Neil Brenner calls "new state spaces" (2004) or what Aihwa Ong has conceptualized as "graduated sovereignty" (2000, 2006). It is the result generated by neoliberal state reformation, flexible decision-making, and the reorganization of political authority in relation to the interests and dynamics of global capital, global production processes, and global financial circuits. Exemplary forms of new state spaces or graduated sovereignty are state-produced exceptional zones of government to the benefit of private (multinational) capital that exist inside or alongside spaces of conventional government (e.g., the national territory, a region, a city). Special economic zones, qualified industrial zones, free trade zones, offshore zones, and urban development zones are some of the characteristic territorial products that emerged in the Arab region over the last two decades and resulted in particular regimes of graduated sovereignty in which populations and labor are often subjected to diverse modes of government (Daher 2013; M. Davis 2006a; Kanna 2011; Parker 2009; Sidaway 2007).[11]

The Bouregreg Valley is such an exceptional zone of government. To fulfil its tasks, the AAVB enjoys exceptional prerogatives. One of the first tasks of the AAVB was the elaboration of the Plan d'Aménagement Spécial (PAS, Special Development Plan). This is a complete zoning plan for the whole six thousand hectares that determines the location and planning of the buildable areas, the maximum height of the residential and urban areas, the zoning of public spaces and public infrastructure, the agricultural zones, the greenbelts, and so on. Between the promulgation of Law 16-04 in 2005 and the publication of the PAS in the Moroccan bulletin of acts in 2009, all private transactions within the designated zone were suspended with the exception of those done by the AAVB itself (articles 4–8 of Law 16-04). The AAVB had already started the preparation of the terrain of the first two phases and the expropriation of private property.

According to normal legal procedures, the publication of the PAS had to be preceded by a public inquiry. The local municipalities were invited to give their advice on the zoning plan within one month of the announcement of the PAS in October 2008. Yet they were stripped of any powers by Law 16-04 to co-determine the zoning plan (as regulated in Law 12-90) and their involvement was reduced to an advisory role. Law 16-04 overwrites normal legislation and gives the AAVB the exclusive authority to take any recommendations of the public inquiry into consideration (article 19). The agency was judge in its own cause (Mouloudi 2015a).

Nevertheless, the PAS provoked a lot of debate among locally elected officials, especially those of Salé, as the project mostly affected their territory. However, according to Hicham Mouloudi, who describes in detail how these debates in Salé evolved, they were nothing more than a theatrical performance. On the one hand, the oppositional stance of the representatives of Salé in October 2008 gave them some credibility and an opportunity to prove themselves a few months before the local elections of 2009. On the other hand, it gave the AAVB necessary political legitimacy and provided a semblance of democratic participation. In the end, however, the eventual modifications to the PAS in response to the debates were minimal and merely a façade (Mouloudi 2015b, 403–72).[12]

In addition to this, Law 16-04 grants the AAVB other exceptional prerogatives, such as the possibility to participate in private enterprises via subsidiaries within its designated area (article 50). In 2007, for example, the agency created a subsidiary to exploit the marina and in 2009 it created the Société du Tramway de Rabat-Salé (STRS, Rabat-Salé Tramway Company) to coordinate and commercialize the tramway project. The STRS was responsible for the design, the financing, and the realization of the construction works as well as the management of the tramway together with its French partner Transdev.[13] Besides private investors, the tramway project also attracted international donors such as the European Investment Bank, the EU, and the Agence Française de Développement (AFD, French Development Agency). The Bouregreg Agency is thus at the same time urban planner, developer, and private investor. "It is the flexibility of the private sector conjoined with public prerogatives," as I was told by the director of the Bouregreg Marina (interview, Rabat, May 20, 2010).[14]

The powers of the AAVB also exceed those of traditional state institutions that are subjected to public law in another aspect of urban planning. Law 16-04 adopted a special expropriation procedure. First, Morocco's compulsory purchase act states that expropriation can only occur when its purpose is declared as a public interest (d'utilité publique). In accordance with this act, Law 16-04 (article 34) and Decree 2-05-1514 (article 10) make it possible for the AAVB to declare all territories that are integrated in the PAS as a public interest. Yet while regular law states that the declaration of "public interest" is allowed only with regard to the realization of roads, green zones, public infrastructure (e.g., schools and hospitals), and zones that need to be restructured or renovated, the declaration of "public interest" in Law 16-04 comprises *all* operations necessary for the development of the zone, more specifically with regard to its urbanization (article 24; see also Mouloudi 2015b, 128).

Second, the special expropriation procedure allows the AAVB to expropriate land at a fixed price determined by the market value at the time of the publication of Law 16-04 (November 2005). As such, future expropriations are not affected by the rise of land prices due to the advancement of the project. Third, the AAVB is not obliged by Law 16-04 to compensate tenants, something that is foreseen in regular law (although the agency did it in some cases). Finally, the period of time that prohibits the construction of new buildings or the renovation of existing buildings on land that is declared public interest without the permission of the agency was extended to ten years (the normal procedure is two years) (Mouloudi 2015b, 120–31). The only limitation to its power is that the AAVB does not collect land taxes; these are still to be paid to the proper municipality.

According to a former high-ranking official of the Ministry of Housing, the creation of the AAVB had the explicit intention of excluding the locally elected municipal councils and centralizing the political decision-making process (interview, Rabat, May 7, 2009). Despite the fact that the agency is supervised by an administrative council presided over by the prime minister, this council, according to a French consultant and former member of the royal commission, should be seen as "divided between those members directly appointed by the king who make the important decisions and those who are there just to nod their heads and approve the decisions made" (interview, Rabat, May 12, 2010; this is also confirmed by Mouloudi 2015a).[15]

Reassembling State Power through the Bouregreg Agency

A common explanation for these kinds of reforms is that Morocco must compete with other countries in the region to attract foreign investments and adapt to a global competitive climate. Morocco cannot afford to stand still and has to assure a continuous flow of capital toward its cities. A megaproject such as the Bouregreg project has to accelerate the rhythm of investments.

One increasingly important target is investments from the Gulf. After 9/11, American and to a lesser extent European suspicions vis-à-vis oil-rich countries and investors from the Gulf have compelled these wealthy and powerful actors to look for new investment outlets (Baabood 2009). Morocco has willingly presented itself to these investors as a reliable alternative and stimulated foreign direct investments with numerous fiscal benefits. Before the global financial crisis of 2008, Morocco managed to attract 80 percent of all Middle Eastern investments in the Maghreb region (Vermeren 2009, 262–64).

Although the crisis slowed down the pace of investments, it did not halt the process altogether. More recently, since the Arab uprisings, Gulf investments in Morocco are on the rise again, partly because of the monarchy's ability to control discontent and partly because of the Gulf monarchies' own interests in a politically and economically stable Morocco. The announcement of new investments in the Bouregreg project from Wessal Capital and Abu Dhabi fund Eagle Hills seems to confirm this.

In order to secure this capital flow, the AAVB is a structure that—to quote a Moroccan geographer—"concentrates only on the attraction of capital . . . : central power is adapting itself to the economic context" (interview, Rabat, October 19, 2009). Speed, efficiency, economic necessity, and the incompetence of locally elected governments were the explicit rationales for bypassing more democratic procedures and reforms. As an official of the AAVB argued: "The people that govern [the project zone] are not elected and that is why we can work in the long run without indulgences to any political color" (interview, Rabat, May 18, 2010). Even the former mayor of Rabat, Omar El Bahraoui, emphasized this necessity and defended the establishment of the AAVB in 2006 in a documentary on the Bouregreg project in the program *éclairages* on the Moroccan television channel 2M.

> We consider that it is the only way to proceed more quickly, to proceed very fast, and to transcend all the difficulties and the administrative procedures that are very slow. . . . We have seen several projects that are completed, whether in Paris, London, Rome, Dubai. Well, they all have created an institution that enables the concentration of all competences in order to be able to authorize very quickly.[16]

When asked about the implication of this reorganization of state power, the general director of the Bouregreg Agency, Essakl, answered as follows, in an interview on the same program:

> We have to remember one important thing. We are in a very sensitive location. We are in a very complex administrative arrangement: three urban districts on the right bank, three urban districts on the left bank. To give investors the opportunity tomorrow to have only one party to negotiate with, we had to create a unique structure, one single operator. This is the agency [AAVB]. . . . It is going to be the main partner for the investors and it is going to be the facilitator of all the development operations.[17]

During that interview, the journalist asked Essakl how the two mayors of Rabat and Salé responded to the decision of being deprived of their prerogatives. Wasn't the AAVB infringing on their powers? she asked.

> We do not infringe upon their prerogatives. We are going to help the municipalities to do development. Today, we have a particularly good relationship with the mayor of Rabat, the mayor of Salé. In reality, we recuperate *some* prerogatives. The fiscal receipts, for example, that return to the urban districts on the right bank and the left bank will continue to go to these urban districts. We are not going to take possession of the whole territory of Rabat or the whole territory of Salé. We intervene specifically in a site well delimited.[18]

Such a reorganization and rescaling of state power as in the Bouregreg project is very rarely explained as a political maneuver by those in charge but more commonly as a technocratic intervention to do what is necessary and even inevitable, given the contemporary global situation. As the director himself stated, the AAVB only helps "to do development." Of course, this is far from being a purely technocratic or politically neutral matter. The project entails the formation of a new political space where authority is not only exercised by the newly created state agency but also shared and negotiated with private investors.

We should not fall into the trap of reifying these new state spaces and new exceptional zones of political authority in the same way that the nation-state has been reified so often. In that case a rescaling or reinstitutionalization of political sovereignty would present a picture of state power that has just been replaced more or less intact between different scales, territories, or zones, allowing little scope for questions of agency, strategy, and (global) connection (Allen 2004).

The creation of a new state space such as the Bouregreg Valley is more than just a top-down transmission of state power to lower or higher echelons or scales. In contrast to a scaled understanding of state power, John Allen advocates for what he calls a "topological view" on state spatiality, one that understands state power and state space in terms of reach, not height. The powers of reach are not a metrical property of space but relational.

> Power relationships, in topological terms, are not so much located in space or extended across it, as *compose* the spaces of which they are a part. . . . On this account, spatiality itself is imbued with power; proximity, distance and reach are inseparable from the practices of power which define them. Topology has little interest in the measurable spans of the globe or the metrics which give physical shape to our environment; rather it is concerned with how the global is folded into the local, how power and authority register their presence through a variety of spatial twists and turns. (Allen 2009, 206)

The Bouregreg project, a place with clear delineated boundaries, does not enclose all the relations of power that produce it. The power relations invested in the creation of the new place are not necessarily all located *in* that place but rather are those that are inseparable from the composition of that place (Allen 2011b; see also Allen and Cochrane 2010). In other words, the gap between "here" and "there" or the "local" and the "global" is something that can be measured not by miles and kilometers but rather by the character of the social relationships, exchanges, and interactions involved (Allen 2011a, 2011b).

In order to understand all these relations, exchanges, and interactions in placemaking projects as a whole, one should see them as an "assemblage." An assemblage of power does not refer to a coherent entity or formation but grasps how a complex and heterogeneous arrangement of social relations and connections "can hold together *without* actually forming a coherent whole" (Allen 2011a, 154). The formation of such an assemblage where both different private and public actors come together, "where elements of the central and local state are 'lodged' within the region" or within a new state space, is a very open ended, often ad hoc, therefore unstable political formation (Allen and Cochrane 2010, 1078).

Different actors with different backgrounds, interests, and objectives participate, sometimes in a discordant way, in the creation of a global place. The increasing globalization of capital and its volatile nature is one of the driving forces behind this unstable and open interplay.

Authority, such as in the Bouregreg Valley, is thus a particular relational effect of interaction between local, regional, national, and international actors rather than the sovereign exercise of an "Arab regime" as the sole locus of power (Allen 2011a).

What John Allen and Allan Cochrane describe as new assemblages of state power resonates with Christopher Parker's conception of "complexes of power" (see chapter 1). Both analyses consider these new assemblages or complexes of power as somehow decentered, but at the same time not disconnected, from the regulatory scope of national state institutions and the institutional hierarchy within the general state apparatus (Allen and Cochrane 2010, 1075; Parker 2004, 35). In other words, the specific assemblage of power within a new state space will not necessarily be disconnected from national decision-making processes but is relatively autonomous.[19]

Such a view of state power in Morocco does not necessarily suggest that power and authority are slipping away from traditional power centers. To the contrary, central state power has not been undermined, only reconfigured and reassembled. It does not discard the centrality of the Moroccan monarchy or the authority of the makhzan, only explains how its power is entangled, negotiated, and shared with other forces such as Gulf capital, French diplomacy, the European Union, multinational corporations, international donors, and so forth. The increasing implication of Gulf capital, for example, has not undermined the role of the Moroccan state nor weakened the position of the monarchy. In contrast, it aims to strengthen both of them. And in the process of doing so, it contributes to the reconfiguration of state power.

In the case of the Bouregreg project, the AAVB originally set up a joint venture in the first phase, Bab Al Bahr, with the Abu Dhabi–based property development company Al Maabar. Both partners owned an equal share in the Bab Al Bahr Development Company charged with the realization of the real estate project.[20] One of the reasons why the Bouregreg Agency gave away so much control, according to the Head of Project Finance and Partnerships, was because they were not dealing here with an ordinary private investor but with a "brother country" (*pays frère*) (interview, Rabat, September 23, 2013). In the summer of 2015, the AAVB sold another 41 percent of the Bab Al Bahr project, now renamed Marina Morocco, to the investment Fund Eagle Hills after the latter took over Al Maabar in 2014.

The Amwaj company in the second phase used to be, before the Gulf investor withdrew, a joint venture between Sama Dubai (50 percent), CDG (20 percent), the Moroccan public pension fund (10 percent), and the AAVB (20 percent). When Wessal Capital arrived in 2013, it set up a private company, Wessal Bouregreg, to develop a new real estate and tourist project for the second phase. In early 2015, Wessal Bouregreg signed an agreement with the Moroccan Groupe Aksal to set up a joint venture for the realization of a new shopping mall in the project. Aksal Group is directed by Salwa Akhennouch, wife of the Moroccan minister of agriculture Aziz Akhennouch. The Akhennouch family is one of the richest Moroccan business families and they are loyal figures within the makhzan. Aksal Group also built the futuristic Morocco Mall in Casablanca together with Saudi-based Al Jedaie Group.

Global Agents of Political Change

Government in these urban spaces becomes accountable to investors over and above the citizens whose lives are influenced by their operations. This is a salient feature of the neoliberal urban logic. The urban space is reshaped more by the logic of the market than by the needs of its residents (Bayat and Biekart 2009, 817). Ironically, as Asef Bayat and Kees Biekart point out, "many of the agents of change (such as global capital) are not even residents of these cities" (818). Al Maabar (now Eagle Hills), for example, has extensive "powers of reach" within the particular institutional configuration of Bab Al Bahr (now Marina Morocco). It enables them to be present and influential regardless of their actual physical location or geographical distance from Morocco and the Bouregreg Valley (Allen 2011b).

These private investors are not mere economic actors. As the AAVB's own press release on Bab Al Bahr makes clear:

Al Maabar is considered as one of the most innovating real estate development companies in the region. Through big-size projects under construction in Morocco, Libya and Jordan, Al Maabar has already gained a reputation of an important economic and *political* actor. Honoring the patrimony, the culture as well as the values of Abu Dhabi, the "Business Model" of the company targets attractive and sustainable economic opportunities and offers in this way a strong potential for growth for all its partners and shareholders. (Bab Al Bahr Development Company 2011, 11, emphasis added)[21]

The increasing privatization of public space involves, not only in Morocco but throughout the contemporary urban world, the growing control over urban space by "non-democratically-elected owners" (Massey 2005, 152). Subsequently, given the urban designs themselves, it may also result in the exclusion of certain social groups whom we might have expected to be allowed there if these spaces were publicly owned and democratically controlled. As a result, the Bouregreg Valley may be a globalized space, in the sense that it connects different actors from other parts of the world, but this does not mean it is an open space, a space that will be easily accessible, let alone affordable by those people who lived in its immediate surroundings before the project was launched (190).

For Massey, the real sociopolitical question "concerns less, perhaps, the *degree* of openness/closure (and the consequent question of how on earth one might even begin to measure it), than the *terms* on which that openness/closure is established" (2005, 197). What comes to the fore in the Bouregreg project is less the transmission of state power in a downward movement, from one scale to another, but rather the complex interplay, the coming together of agents of the state and their non-state partners lodged within a territory of six thousand hectares. The processes of decision-making and placemaking result in a specific configuration of sovereignty, a particular assemblage of distributed authority, which has been continuously negotiated and renegotiated (Allen and Cochrane 2010)—the struggles between AAVB and Sama Dubai over the expropriation and withdrawal of the Dubai investor being a telling example (Belghazi 2010).

While these politics and struggles may take place at the local level, they are not mere local politics but the localization of regional, national, or global actors who are coming together in a neoliberal project. The powers that the ordinary citizens of Rabat and Salé are subject to, and the pressures of uneven development produced by the Bouregreg project, are not simply emanating from a seemingly coherent institutional entity such as the "Arab regime" but are shaped and designed by a whole range of particular interest groups, private actors, and class forces.

Ad Hoc Urbanism and the Production of Uneven Development

By taking into consideration the more complex and relational production of (urban) spaces, the interaction of different actors (both public and private) that are drawn within reach through a new state space like

Bouregreg, we are confronted with a more complex and variegated politics. Moreover, we are confronted with a form of political agency that has little to do with the commitment of "a modern Morocco that fights against poverty"—as explained by the director of the Bouregreg Marina (interview, Rabat, May 20, 2010)—but with a totally different kind of political choice.

Urban aesthetics and the creation of landmarks play an important role in strategies of commodification, privatization, and even dispossession. The city has become "an object of cultural consumption for tourists, for a estheticism, avid for spectacles and the picturesque," as Henri Lefebvre (1996, 148) remarked long ago. In contrast, those people who are dependent on the city for their daily lives are disregarded by those who redesign the contemporary Moroccan cities. The city has become prone to the fluctuations in the global market. Long-term policy agendas and concerns make place for the immediate satisfaction of potential investors.

Four Guiding Principles for Political Intervention

Officially, four central components or guiding principles determine the overall model of government applied by the AAVB: environment, citizenship, history *(mémoire de lieu)*, and transport. These four components are integrated in the logo of the agency.

The first one refers to the mission of the Bouregreg Agency to preserve the environment of the valley. More specifically, it means protecting the valley from "human encroachment" *(agression humaine)* (interview with the director, Rabat, September 16, 2013). The valley had been neglected for decades and, as a result, gradually turned into a clandestine garbage dump. Furthermore, parts of the valley were occupied by slums and other forms of informal housing, the river was severely polluted due to all kinds of human activity, and stone pits were exploited without authorization. "We have to stop them," the director told me, referring to the people using and abusing the valley. "Our first and most important mission is the ecological question *(la question écologique),*" he added. The goal is to transform the valley into a green lung for both Rabat and Salé.

In second place came citizenship. As stated on their website, this means that the agency "takes into consideration the demographic, social and economic characteristics of the population concerned in order to assure an equal balance between supply and needs."[22] Part of this commitment actually entailed the replacement of some of the mostly informal daily users of the valley. The rehabilitation of the ancient medina of Rabat—or at least the area in front of the project—resulted in the resettlement of 152 families, 55 individuals, and 52 small businesses. Furthermore, the families of Douar Jdid, an informal housing settlement, had to be resettled and indemnified to make place for a maintenance center for the tramway. For the fishermen, the agency built a new small fishing port at the edge of the project in front of the medina of Salé. Before, they were selling their fish in the estuary between the quay of Rabat and one of the shores where now the Marina Morocco (formerly Bab Al Bahr) real estate project is situated. Finally, the ferrymen were forced to stop their activities for two years because of the start of the construction works in Bab Al Bahr. They were also indemnified and would eventually be reintegrated into the project as a tourist attraction. After all, they were part of the "charm of the site."[23]

The third component, history, refers to the harmonious coexistence between the project and the historical sites and monuments (the kasbah, the Hassan Tower, the mausoleum of Mohammed V, the Chellah, and of course the two medinas). Several initiatives were taken to renovate these sites, such as the reconstruction of the Bab Lamrissa square in front of the medina in Salé. In front of the Kasbah of the Oudayas, the agency planned to create a pedestrian zone and divert most traffic via the tunnel underneath it. Additionally, the Bouregreg Agency claims to take into account the cultural heritage of the place when it comes to the architecture of the real estate projects. The architectural designs of Marina Morocco strive for a harmonious synergy between Morocco's rich cultural past and its modernizing aspirations.

Fourth, the component of transport symbolically refers to the reconciliation of the capital Rabat with its dormitory neighbor Salé through the construction of the bridge, the tunnel, and the tramway. These new public works have to facilitate the mobility between the two cities and its populations. In the second phase, the infrastructural upgrading of the site will be pursued through the extension of the tramlines and the construction of a new connecting road between the city center of Rabat and the airport of Salé.

The "Business Model" of the Bouregreg Agency

There is a fifth guiding principle, however, which integrates the four official components. It is put much less in the spotlight, yet it is definitely the primary driving force behind the project. A class project of surplus-value appropriation actually determines how the environment becomes an entry point to appropriate a mass of strategically located land, how citizenship becomes a pretext to replace informal inhabitants and daily users by wealthy consumers, how memory of place and heritage become mere assets to make those places more attractive and marketable, and, finally, how transport and public services become an added value to the anticipated accumulation strategies of urban redevelopment. Massive public funds are mobilized for infrastructural improvement and the creation of landmarks (e.g., the Grand Theatre and the museum) to the benefit of land and real estate speculation.

This class project required a particular governmental approach, one where—typical for *neo*liberalism—the boundaries between public and private were blurred and bended in such a way it would serve the class interests behind it. In the beginning, the AAVB was largely funded by public money, but now it operates as a financially autonomous entity. "Today we don't want the help of the state anymore; we are now following a purely commercial logic," says the director of an agency that has the power to declare all its activities an *"utilité publique"* (public interest) (interview, Rabat, September 16, 2013).

Rabat is a city with less competitive and commercial advantages than Casablanca or Marrakech. It does not attract a lot of businesses or tourists. But there is a massive amount of unused and undervalued landed property. It was the task of the Bouregreg Agency to "produce and reproduce wealth" and create "a surplus value on the land" *(plus-value du foncier)* (interview with the director, Rabat, September 16, 2013). With this objective in mind, the AAVB prepares the land (excavations, soil remediation, removal of garbage dumps, allocation) to make sure it becomes attractive to private investors.

The surplus value created on public land or expropriated land generates an income for the AAVB and provides the necessary funds to continue the rest of the project. "This created surplus value belongs to the agency," the director told me. "That is why we declared the whole zone as a public interest." After all, the logic goes, the Bouregreg Agency does all the work. "Why would we let others benefit for something they cannot take credit for?" he added, referring to the private landowners who were expropriated (interview with the director, Rabat, September 16, 2013). This also explains why Law 16-04 allows the agency to expropriate land at the market price of 2005 and why all private land transactions were suspended until the publication of the PAS.

The logic of the state as a public institution is put upside down here. As a state agency, the AAVB is considered to act in the public interest. In this case, however, state power is used to dispossess both public and private land in order to bring the valley into the global circulation of capital in a way a private investor could never do. In other words, the task of the Bouregreg Agency is "to liberate the land" and bring it into the global real estate market (interview with the Head of Project Finance and Partnerships, Rabat, September 23, 2013). The imagined end result has little to do with the public interest.

For example, the first phase of the project (Marina Morocco) is targeting exclusively upper-middle-class consumers. According to the director and one of his staff members, there was definitely not enough purchasing power in Rabat alone. The project also depended on the foreign market. "We cannot focus exclusively on the domestic market," the director explained. That's why the project has been held up. "The European crisis, for example in Portugal, Spain, etcetera, has caused a delay in the project" (interview, Rabat, September 23, 2013). In times of crisis, the market in luxury real estate *(haut standing)* is the first segment to suffer (interview with the Head of Project Finance and Partnerships, Rabat, September 23, 2013).

This business model has put the Bouregreg Agency in an awkward situation. "We are rich," the Head of Project Finance and Partnerships explained, referring to the land the agency now controls. "The only problem is that we don't have liquid assets." A slowdown of the sales slows down the entire project. "Our income hasn't been what we expected." As a result, he added, "we have two options at the moment. We could either sell our land at a loss or wait. We choose to wait" (interview, Rabat, September 23, 2013). This was before both Wessal Capital and Eagle Hills announced new investments in the project.

How does this focus on wealthy consumers, high-end residential units, and international real estate markets correspond with the citizenship component of the project? How does it relate to the mission statement on the AAVB's website claiming that the agency would take the demographic, social, and economic characteristics of the local population into consideration and assure an equal balance between supply and needs? To the Head of Project Finance and Partnerships, it was clear: "Creating wealth is also a public interest," he told me (interview, Rabat, May 20, 2010). The question is of course for whom?

Ad Hoc Urbanism in an Economy of Appearances

Usually, megaprojects such as in the Bouregreg Valley start off with an ambitious concept plan (the PAG), very often quite detailed, reflecting the great ideas and dreams of planners and policymakers. But this is before the necessary investors are attracted—it is part of the game. Megaprojects always start by selling an idea and a prospect (for profit). In the end, however, the final result often turns out to be less ambitious or focused on different priorities. The promised urban utopias then often make way for a more realistic "cost-benefit" and "market-conform" design.

Megaprojects like the Bouregreg project are part of what Anna Tsing calls an economy of appearances. It drives on performance, materialized for example in fancy brochures, flashy billboards, and cinematic promo videos presenting picturesque landscapes and state-of-the-art infrastructure. The whole idea, according to Tsing, is to self-consciously imagine a spectacle and dramatize the potential of a place as an investment opportunity in order to attract the necessary capital: "In speculative enterprises, profit must be imagined before it can be extracted; the possibility of economic performance must be conjured like a spirit to draw an audience of potential investors" (Tsing 2005, 57).

"Starchitecture" plays an important role in this spectacle. What might seem—at first sight—as a radical and progressive experimentation with urban aesthetics actually functions as an instrument within the marketing agendas of contemporary urban entrepreneurialism. In fact, architecture itself is used "as a marketable commodity (something with which, to be sure, individual architects are complicit)" (Kanna 2011, 101). The publicly funded Grand Theatre, designed by Zaha Hadid, is an exponent of this trend. Before the Grand Theatre was presented as central and crucial in the reimagination of Rabat as a cultural world-class destination, the site was being prepared to become an exclusive archipelago-like residential domain centered on waterways and yachting (such as the Amwaj project of Sama Dubai).[24] Apparently, cultural performance was then much less of a priority.

With regard to the first phase of the project, we see a similar development. The royal commission gathering politicians, state managers, planners, architects, urbanists, consultants, and royal advisors worked out an ambitious plan for the Bouregreg Valley and drafted a 165-page document that can still be consulted on the website of the AAVB (the PAG). The first phase, Bab Al Bahr, was already worked out in detail and the commission anticipated the construction of a central public space just in front of the medina of Salé along the shore of the river. It had to be a green esplanade where palm trees would provide shade, designed for the local population to use and suitable for activities such as picnicking, games, and strolling. It had to be a place where people came together and where the overall objective of enhancing the solidarity between the two river banks was physically and socially materialized (Royal Commission 2003, 33). It was important, the commission stated, that the new public place would be "planned with less density than the shore of Rabat to allow a larger variety of uses by the population of the city" (40).[25]

Yet, in the end, the future city will not so much be decided by planners, urbanists, politicians, or even taxpayer's money but by private investors looking for a high rate of return. In the case of Bab Al Bahr, the Head of Project Finance and Partnerships of the AAVB admitted that this phase had to be revised, that the building site had to be densified in order to increase profitability (interview, Rabat, September 23, 2013). Today, nothing is left of the original green esplanade and the open public space envisioned by the royal commission.

Consequently, the end result very seldom appears to be what was actually promised. This kind of urban planning culture, which depends heavily on its ability to attract the necessary investments, turns urban government to a great extent into a cyclical and ad hoc process sensitive to market trends and fluctuations. Urban megaprojects are thus constantly reworked, readjusted, and adapted to (new) investors' desires. In other words, the future of this sort of urban government is thus rather contingent because some investors may withdraw or fail to live up to the expectations, conflicts can arise between investors and their state partners, and new investors can arrive with a completely different view.

A Flexible Political Economy of Urban Spectacles

An urbanism of projects determines urban government more and more, not only in Rabat but all over the country. And new state spaces are created to bring this into practice. Another example is the Tanger Med Special Authority (TMSA) established in 2002 to develop the international port of Tangier and its industrial hinterland. To a similar degree, TMSA is responsible for the planning, development, and management of a territory of 550 square kilometers. TMSA also takes over the competences of local municipal authorities and has the right to expropriate people on its territory (Planel 2011).

TMSA, however, does not have the unique status of AAVB. TMSA is indirectly state owned via the participation of the CDG and the Hassan II Fund. The most important difference between AAVB and TMSA is that the latter is a public limited company controlled by the state and endowed with public authority prerogatives while the first is a fully fledged state agency that replaces all other governmental institutions. Yet both agencies represent new political spaces where particular (global) relations of power come together and where opportunities are created for privileged (corporate) interest groups, outside the jurisdiction of traditional government bodies.

The specific institutional and practical difference behind these two governmental arrangements constitutes the reality of government in this era of neoliberal projects. TMSA and AAVB are what Aihwa Ong calls zoning technologies of neoliberal government: ad hoc structures established to think about and act on specific challenges and problems in a particular locale and to open possibilities for a greater flexibility in rule. Graduated sovereignty is precisely the effect of the contingent outcomes of different neoliberal projects (Ong 2006, 97–118).

The particular government model of the AAVB (or the TMSA) is still not widely applied in Morocco. Other prestigious projects such as Casablanca Marina or Casablanca Finance City are also coordinated and managed by some form of case-specific authority. However, neither of these arrangements has the same extensive powers of the AAVB. Nevertheless, the model of the Bouregreg Agency may become the rule rather than the exception in future development schemes. As I was told by the Head of Project Finance and Partnerships, this model is a test case, "a laboratory to test certain issues which fail based on private initiative alone" (interview, Rabat, May 20, 2010).

In July 2009 King Mohammed VI launched the Marchica Med project. Similar to the Bouregreg project, the lagoon of Marchica will be developed in seven phases and the delineated area of two thousand hectares will be administrated by the Agency for the Development of the Lagoon of Marchica. Law 25-10, creating the Marchica agency, is practically a replica of Law 16-04. It also contains a special expropriation procedure and transfers all competences of the municipality and the Urban Agency of Nador to the Marchica agency.

Hence, despite its still unique configuration, the AAVB gives an indication of how state power in Morocco is being reshaped and respatialized at the local scale and how real decision-making power is being shifted from more conventional state institutions—which are under pressure for democratic reform—to new state spaces that are not at all subject to popular control. This increasing agencification and flexibility of rule in Morocco is of course not unique in the region. Examples such as the Aqaba Special Economic Zone in Jordan (Debruyne 2013), Solidere in Beirut (Krijnen and Fawaz 2010; Makdisi 1997), and the parastatals in Dubai (Kanna 2011) are but a few of the zoning technologies applied in the rest of the Arab world.

Bouregreg as Statement

If we are to believe the urban developers themselves, these zoning technologies are subordinated to the concern for the environment in the first place and the citizen in second place. "We are not a private company," I was told by the Head of Project Finance and Partnerships. "We are trying to keep the middle ground here. We invest, for example, in the tunnel, the bridge, etcetera. That is money we lost. If we only followed a commercial logic, then we would only think about profits. Investing in real estate is of course much more lucrative than planning [aménagement]" (interview, Rabat, September 23, 2013).

He is right, of course. The Bouregreg Agency has to valorize not only the valley as such but the city as a whole. In this way, the Bouregreg project contributes to the creation of a particular image of the Moroccan capital. The project offers us a window through which dominant discourses, ideologies, and social power relations become legible. As Darel Paul observed, such projects "narrate and advance a particular definition and interpretation of the city." The Bouregreg project imposes a vision of "cosmopolitanism, global connectivity and wealth embodied in transnational capital" and tries to cultivate it in the minds and actions of its urban residents (Paul 2004, 575).

The role of "starchitecture" is important to understand here. It does not so much set the standards of a new urban era; it represents (a new) power. Starchitecture is far from apolitical or even progressive, let alone revolutionary (as it is sometimes presented). As Lefebvre observed, the architect does not define "a new approach to life"; rather, it is the other way around: new (neoliberal) approaches to urban life determine the work of the architect. The latter often functions as a social accelerator of hegemonic ideologies and the interests of the powerful (Lefebvre 2003, 99–100). Starchitecture thus mostly reflects, reproduces, and legitimates in very aesthetic ways existing power hierarchies. Starchitecture is the ultimate aesthetic materialization of how capital is taking over the city. As such, the planned built environment in the Bouregreg Valley with its specific architecture is not only an appearance but also a "statement" (Hirst 2005, 156–58). Buildings like the Grand Theatre and the specific forms, styles, and spatial orders designed in the built environment of the valley are like political statements that strengthen power's claim over the urban space, while at the same time that space becomes a resource of power (Kanna 2011, 103).

This is not something new, of course. Throughout history, cities and their built environment were always intended to reflect hegemonic power. This was the case for the ancient empires and the medieval church, as well as for capitalist urbanization more recently. The capitalist city both integrated the mechanisms for the reproduction of capital and reflected the value systems that legitimated the social conditions of that reproduction. Just as the movement of metropolitanism in the nineteenth century redeveloped urban space to increase its exchangeability and reflect colonial bourgeois values (Rotenberg 2001), the current aspirations to create global urban spaces reflect the values and interests of a transnational capitalist class.

The rebuilding of the metropole of the colonial motherland had to propagate the power, success, and desires of the emerging bourgeoisie vis-à-vis the aristocracy on the one hand and the growing labor force on the other, while the rebuilding of the contemporary city in the Global South reflects the ambitions of the ruling elite in the South to breach into the worldwide urban hierarchy and position themselves vis-à-vis a transnational (or Western) capitalist class and the global flows of capital. Obviously, Rabat does not aspire to become London, New York, or Dubai. Nevertheless, the Bouregreg project aims to reposition the city among the great cities of the Mediterranean basin (Royal Commission 2003, 25).

A New Narrative for/on the City

A megaproject like the Bouregreg project does not only look to the outside world. It also attempts to impose a new lifestyle on the city itself and its everyday life. Human degradation, spontaneous urbanization, and informal encroachment had to make place for a "modern" way of life (in their perception).

The contemporary urban transformations we observe in the Middle East and North Africa, and the Bouregreg project in particular, can be read as part of a new hegemonic discourse, a neoliberal one, for imagining city life. The rising towers and the mushrooming of urban megaprojects in the region radically rewrite orientalist narratives and perceptions of the Arab city. The promoted "Dubai model" impacts our urban knowledge. Does it matter, Ahmed Kanna asks when he writes about Dubai, that a region long stereotyped as "archaic" or "Bedouin" is suddenly one of the references for the "skyscraper silhouette," the "hyperurban or supermodern" city (Kanna 2014, 170)? "Such representational devices do not simply reflect the realities to which they refer, but rather help to constitute the object we call, and act upon, as 'the city'" (170).

Kanna attributes an ethico-moral aspect to the Dubai model of urban development, one that constantly interpellates individuals as subjects of the country and its ruling power. Drawing on Louis Althusser, who argued that ruling class ideologies were translated and passed on via "state ideological apparatuses" (the educational system, law enforcement, etc.), Kanna argues that people are subjectified not only through ideology or coercion but also through space (2011, 18).[26] The Dubai urban model interpellates a refined, cultivated subject who "properly negotiates the complexity of Arab identity . . . , discarding those aspects incapable of resolution with the neoliberal universal" (Kanna 2009, 215). In the same way, the Bouregreg project interpellates a Moroccan identity true to its culture and traditions but at the same time compatible with the consumerist lifestyle of contemporary capitalist society.

As such, neoliberal narratives do not necessarily replace the older narratives of the Arab city but integrate and alter them through their interaction with new narratives of entrepreneurship and neoliberal modernization. The rich architectural and cultural past of many Arab cities is turned into important assets to promote the unique selling position of these cities as places where tradition and modernity coincide and combine the best of both worlds. In the process of doing so, however, a very real history (as human struggle) and a very real culture (as everyday practice) is ignored (Kanna 2012).

Urban life in the Bouregreg Valley has to obey new rules and regulations imagined from the drawing tables of the project itself and dictated by the profit motive. The fish market has been removed and replaced by quays and marinas with fancy cafés, the fishermen are resituated in a

Billboard of the Amwaj project of Sama Dubai picturing Western styles of consumerism. Photograph by the author, 2008.

Billboard of La Marina Morocco picturing a Moroccan upper-middle-class family living in the new project. Photograph by the author, 2016.

new site at the edge of the project in order not to intersect with the waterways of the marina, while the traditional ferrymen who took people from one medina to the other for just one dirham are now supposed to be integrated in the project as a tourist attraction. They even got new boats and suitable ("traditional") costumes.

In this regard, the old slogan "redefining skylines, redesigning life-styles" of Sama Dubai, the ex-partner in the Amwaj project (second phase), should be taken almost literally (Bogaert 2012). The valley was to represent a "new style of living."[27] Localized versions of neoliberalism are often being aligned with local structures of meaning and become part of a self-cultivating and entrepreneurial version of Morocco's so-called modern identity (Kanna 2009).

The specific architecture of the project tries to make a link with (or reinvents) local or Mediterranean styles of living. The Bouregreg project is about reinvigorating Morocco's cultural heritages and cultural authenticity. What's more, the objective is to bring "authenticity" and "culture" into a new destination, as Tarik Senhaji, CEO of the FMDT and board member of Wessal Capital, put it in an interview for Bloomberg.[28] Yet this reinvigoration and "bringing in" of authenticity has to be compatible with the market demands of the modern and global present as the billboards surrounding the project highlight so clearly. They picture Western styles of living, featuring foreigners or upper-middle-class consumers.

Statements such as the Bouregreg project also address the outside world. The unique selling position of the city depends heavily on an attractive urban imaginary. It was striking that in several interviews with AAVB officials, the project was presented as a counterbalance to the image of a "Maroc Islamiste" (interview with the director of Bouregreg Marina, Rabat, May 20, 2010).[29] And this was done not only as a rejection of Islamist viewpoints but also in terms of a recognition of the social causes of religious extremism and jihadism. In the same way that the director of the Bouregreg Marina claimed that the Bouregreg project is much more than just a construction project—it is also a fight against poverty—an official of the Bab Al Bahr Development Company tried to legitimize the project by referring to its wider social, economic, and even cultural implications for the cities of Rabat and Salé (interview, Rabat, May 28, 2010). Investing in the Bouregreg project meant more prosperity for everyone. This was a kind of argument that I heard many times during my interviews with officials of the AAVB. As another official told me:

The project is a fight against poverty, informal housing *[habitats clan-destins]*, . . . and for the development of the country. We give Salé a new face. In the past, Salé was only known for its prison, its hospital, the bidonvilles, and the *habitats clandestins*. Even the airport of Salé is systematically referred to as the airport of Rabat. . . . The Bouregreg [project] thus actually serves a noble purpose. [The area] used to be a floodplain which was enormously polluted. . . . It was an agricultural area which wasn't used to its full capacity just because of the pollution. A lot of the housing in the area was also responsible for this pollution. There were no sanitary fittings and people dumped their waste in the river. (interview with the Head of Project Finance and Partnerships, Rabat, May 20, 2010)

It should be clear that in many cases the socioeconomic objectives in these discourses are not just part of an empty discursive picture trying to cover up other interests but form part of a deeply entrenched govern-mentality. Many officials of the AAVB sincerely believe that they are doing something good for the city, the country, and the economy. More-over, they are using their powers and influence, their class status, to de-fend and materialize those beliefs. As such, the very "imagineering" of the Bouregreg project cannot be separated from the power behind it.[30] Imagineering refers to the combination of imagination and engineering and is, at its core, a political act (Paul 2004, 574). The imagineering of the valley makes an appeal to the global, the universal, and the local through its reference to the four central guiding principles. The lan-guage and images that are reproduced by these four core values of the project (environment, citizenship, history, and transport) are presented in such an apolitical way that no one can really object.

Underneath this universalist discourse, a hegemonic project aspires to align the valley with the virtues of consumerist cosmopolitanism. And these dreams have a very real material effect. The vast infrastructural patterns laid out by the Bouregreg project will restructure urban life and determine the mobility and movement of people, goods, and capital for the coming decades. It creates real physical and spatial boundaries between those with the capability to consume and those who can merely desire. Once finished, a new user of the city will replace the old one.

The Social Impact of the Bouregreg Project

When I left the AAVB director's office after our interview in 2013, he gave me an example of how the project created new opportunities to bring people in the city together in a harmonious way. Recently, the director told me, he ran into a minister who had a small yacht in the Bouregreg Marina. The minister told the director that the man who now maintains his boat was actually someone with whom he studied in elementary school. Normally, they would probably never have had the chance to see each other again as they both lived in a different neighborhood, but thanks to the project, they were now brought together again.

This is a discourse you often hear among the advocates of the project. The Bouregreg project creates opportunities, especially for the people of Salé who can now go and work as waiters and cooks in the restaurants and bars of Marina Morocco. The critical question is: what kind of harmony are they actually envisioning? And what are the contradictions between the place itself and this imaginary?

It is still too early to draw final conclusions about the Bouregreg project and its overall social impact. Nevertheless, there is an extensive body of literature that is highly skeptical about the outcome of these kinds of megaprojects (Flyvbjerg 2005; Ren and Weinstein 2013; Swyngedouw, Moulaert, and Rodriguez 2002). In the case of the Bouregreg project, the association Sala Al Mustaqbal (Arabic for the future of Salé), tried to encourage critical debate on the project. Sala Al Mustaqbal brings together professionals, experts, and members of political parties from Salé. In 2006 the association organized a roundtable on the Bouregreg project in order to express some major concerns.

With regard to the spatial concept of the first phase and its implementation, Sala Al Mustaqbal argued, in contrast to what the AAVB asserts, that the project actually turns its back on the historical medina of Salé and creates a barrier between the city center and the riverside. Marina Morocco is built right next to the ancient medina of Salé. But the height of the planned buildings actually hides the medina from the view of people looking from the quays of Rabat. The construction is three stories high, while the urban area just behind it is on average only two stories high. As a result, the buildings of Marina Morocco form a huge physical wall that separates the medina of Salé from the sight of the quays of Rabat and the Oudayas. This goes against the recommendations of the royal commission, which sought to restore the view on the medina of Salé from the shore of Rabat by redeveloping the site less densely (Royal Commission 2003, 40).

Another concern is that the medina of Salé is an impoverished area. When one walks through this medina, one quickly notices the difference

Marina Morocco seen from the quays of Rabat. Photograph by Soumia El Majdoub, 2015.

from the medina of Rabat and the well-known medina of Marrakech with their specialized shops in Moroccan arts and artisanal products. It is a beautiful medina, yet people are poor and very few tourists are around.[31] Moreover, the whole population of Salé is generally much poorer than the population of Rabat. Salé is primarily known for its bidonvilles, informal neighborhoods, and low-cost housing. As such, the social composition of the urban area immediately surrounding the Bouregreg project will contrast strongly with the lifestyle and prestige promoted by the developers. The popular medina of Salé will be enclosed by luxury and its corridors, with Marina Morocco on one side and the bridge and the tramway on the other.

Just as the French had built their new modern cities around the Arab medina during the protectorate, imposing a design of spatial and social segregation (Abu-Lughod 1980; G. Wright 1991), the current project imposes a similar segregation. As a result, the project "turns its back on the historic patrimony of Salé" and will most likely turn out to be the creation of "heaven next to hell," as I was told by a Moroccan architect and one of the initiators of Sala Al Mustaqbal (interview, Rabat, April 27, 2009).

In addition, there are serious questions about the so-called social and public dimension of the project. The expropriation of land for private purposes (the construction of hotels, marinas, and apartments) has little to do with the public interest. This particular form of accumulation by dispossession can also be seen as a way to socialize the risks related to the development of the Bouregreg Valley and privatize the benefits. It is thanks to public funding that the former marshland area of the first phase was made suitable for building; it was also provided with all the necessary physical infrastructure (e.g., quays, tunnel, bridge) in order to make it a profitable site for investment.

Public power and money were also involved in the relocation and resettlement of some of the original users of the valley. The fishermen, for example, were relocated to a new small fishing port. Yet, according to the fishermen, the AAVB never consulted them about their new location and the facilities they needed. They complained about the inadequate construction of the cove and the landing place, the fact that they were now hidden behind the new bay, and that they often damaged their engines due to the shallow water and the rocks in the cove (Mouloudi 2015b; Vanderelst 2010).

Furthermore, the Bouregreg Agency expropriated the people and businesses of the quarter of Kardona just in front of Bab Lamrissa, one of the ancient gates of the medina of Salé, to make way for the new bridge Moulay Hassan and new apartments (Juiad 2010). Some informal housing was also relocated. Among the resettlements, 137 families were moved to make place for the maintenance center of the tram, while 259 households and small businesses in the ancient medina of Rabat were relocated or compensated for their expropriation. According to AAVB officials, this was done, each time, with the full participation of the occupants.

The resettlement of poorer citizens and the attraction of a more affluent resident might have a wider gentrifying impact on the neighborhood. Gentrification is not only a central and worldwide feature of contemporary urban entrepreneurialism and urban megaprojects (N. Smith 2002); it is often also a state-promoted process in order to attract a wealthier consuming and tax-paying class to the city center (Hackworth and Smith 2001; Krijnen and De Beukelaer 2015). The Bouregreg Agency seems to play a similar role. The Head of Project Finance and Partnerships, for example, explained to me that the construction of the Moulay Hassan bridge and the Grand Theatre could revalue the urban land in the surrounding neighborhood and as such generate more profit for the Bouregreg Agency and its private partners. He also compared the potential of the Grand Theatre with the impact of the Guggenheim in Bilbao (interview, Rabat, September 23, 2013).

Gentrification has already accelerated in the medina of Rabat and the Kasbah of the Oudayas, mostly due to the influx of foreigners.[32] As a result, prices rose almost tenfold over the last ten years in the case of some historical houses (McGuinness 2013). Other indicators also point in the direction of gentrification. Alongside the trajectory of the tramway, new apartments are being built and new shops and restaurants emerge that are clearly targeting a more affluent consumer.[33]

Finally, the new quays in Rabat that provide a view over Marina Morocco are often presented as a place where the inhabitants of Rabat and Salé can meet each other, stroll, and have a coffee together in one of the cafés. However, a quick look at the prices makes clear that these new spaces of consumption are not meant for ordinary citizens. A regular coffee easily costs two to three times more than in a regular bar in the medina. The pricing mechanism in those restaurants and bars introduces a certain social selectivity and attracts a type of consumer who would normally not frequent those kinds of public spaces before the Bouregreg project (M'Hammedi and Karibi 2012). A waiter who works in one of the bars expressed it as follows:

> There used to be restaurants along the river. Now, people don't really eat here anymore. They stroll along the quay and drink one coffee. I used to be a kitchen help. Now I am a waiter. My wage dropped from 2,000 to 1,600 dirhams. My salary thus declined. . . . Shopping center or theater . . . what's the difference? . . . I cannot afford it with my wage. I have to pay for a house and maintain a family. Sometimes, I can consume something here [talking about one of the new bars along the quay] because I work here and I get a free coffee. All these changes, . . . they are not for us. These are all luxury things. They are meant for people with money, not for the average citizen. (interview, March 12, 2016, quoted in Amara Hammou 2016)

Taking all these elements into account, the Bouregreg project will set out and defend the demarcations between those who can afford to invest, live, and consume in these newly created urban spaces and those who fall by the wayside (see Bargach 2008, 114). The result—and this is becoming clearly visible today—will most likely be a spatial segregation between an enclave that is tailored to the benefit of international investors and rich tourists, and the average Moroccan citizen who will be largely absent from this area or, at best, be rather inconspicuous in the role of one of the serving jobs such as waiters, receptionists, and cleaners. Urban development strategies such as the Bouregreg project lead to the juxtaposition of privileged zones of inclusion where capital can design luxury and grandeur into its space, and the outside spaces where urban poverty and exclusion constitute the flipside of this spatial division of consumption.[34]

Many ordinary citizens know this very well. In her research, Kenza Amara Hammou argues that many residents of the medinas of Rabat and Salé consider the Bouregreg project as "another world," a place not for them (2016, 49). I once asked a car-park attendant on the construction site of Bab Al Bahr (now Marina Morocco) what the advantage of the project was for the people of Salé. "We don't earn money with the bourgeois," he said. "They want to stay in their hotels with hotelkeepers with diplomas. But we don't have diplomas. They are not going to come to our hotels" (interview, Salé, October 25, 2009). A young man who used to live in the Oudayas looking over the valley told me that Bouregreg was "a project of false promises. . . . It's a project merely for the rich while the ordinary Moroccan will be victim of this project" (interview, Rabat, June 23, 2008).

The Bouregreg project affects our notion of distance. In a topological world, Allen (2011b, 285) argues, distance is not always a good indicator of either separation or proximity. The global space created at the valley of the Bouregreg might be very close (distance wise) to the pockets of poverty in the medina of Salé and the clandestine housing in the proximity of the riverbanks, but the lived world that is going to be created is situated miles away (figuratively speaking) from the lived world in most of the neighborhoods of the rest of the city. The latter are excluded by design but also by the black iron fences that surround the Bouregreg Marina and by the security guards who control its entrance. At the same time, a space like Marina Morocco might be familiar, connected, and much more accessible to other parties and consumers coming from outside the city, from far away.

The promised ideal of borderlessness in many neoliberal discourses is a fetish that obscures the actual creation of new borders, this time determined not so much by geographical distance but rather by social access and political power. The Bouregreg Valley will be in all probability a globalized space but not an open space.

The Bouregreg project is a salient example of a neoliberal class project. Such placemaking projects are products of the ideas and practices of an elitist collaboration between planners, urbanists, local rulers, (foreign) capital, and wealthy consumers, of global connections that come together and materialize in a particular place. The language of environmental protection and inclusive citizenship masks the ways in which class power redesigns not only an underdeveloped and "quasi-empty" piece of land between two cities but the social and political relations within those cities as a whole.

Capturing the constitutive dynamics of such global urban spaces requires attention to both the particularities of place and people as well as a careful analysis of the broader structures and dynamics that connect these places to other places and actors around the world. It requires us to think of politics and placemaking as being both local and global at the same time and what this means with regard to the ability of people to decide over their own urban futures.

PART III

TRANSFORMING URBAN LIFE

5

CHANGING METHODS OF AUTHORITARIAN POWER

[The development of capitalism] would not have been possible without the controlled insertion of bodies into the machinery of production and the adjustment of the phenomena of population to economic processes. But this was not all it required; it also needed the growth of both these factors, their reinforcement as well as their availability and docility; it had to have methods of power capable of optimizing forces, aptitudes, and life in general without at the same time making them more difficult to govern.

—Michel Foucault, *The History of Sexuality*

For the city's planners the poor were a public danger, their potentially riotous concentrations to be broken up by avenues and boulevards which would drive the inhabitants of the crowded popular quarters they replaced into some unspecified, but presumably more sanitary and certainly less perilous locations. . . . For building entrepreneurs and property developers the poor were an unprofitable market, compared to the rich pickings from the new specialised business and shopping districts and the solid houses and apartments for the middle class, or the developing suburbs.

—Eric Hobsbawm, *The Age of Capital*

IN CHAPTER 2 I describe a transition from a phase of roll-back neoliberalism (with projects aiming to dismantle developmentalism) to a phase of roll-out neoliberalism (with projects involved in the creation of a new order). The latter was characterized not only by a transformation of state institutional power (e.g., the Bouregreg arrangement) but also by the aim to transform urban life itself. This entailed a fundamental shift in methods of power and techniques of government. While the reign of Hassan II and the policies of structural adjustment were predominantly underpinned by repressive methods, the *alternance* and the urbanism of projects under Mohammed VI marked the introduction of new methods of intervention, control, and economic expansion.

This paradigm shift manifested itself especially in the field of social policy. The beginning of Mohammed VI's reign was characterized by important social reforms and the launch of ambitious projects such as the National Initiative for Human Development (INDH) and the Cities Without Slums (VSB) program. The objective was to replace the old social contract of the developmental state, in which citizens had certain social privileges and rights in exchange for their loyalty (e.g., public employment), with a new contract between state and citizens in which people were "responsibilized" and encouraged to seize the opportunities of the (free) market. State power had to be redeployed and reorganized, not only to exploit strategic locations and redesign urban skylines but also to create neoliberal citizens (self-reliant, entrepreneurial, individualized) and facilitate their integration into the formal market ("inclusive growth").

The "reinvention of social policy" under Mohammed VI contributed to the contrasting image between the new "modern" monarch and his authoritarian father. Hassan II pushed through structural adjustment and did not hesitate to use excessive force to smother any form of resistance against his sovereign decisions. Order and stability had to be secured by overt repression and the display of sovereign power. In contrast, his successor's rule was characterized by the attempt to replace the destructive policies of the father with more reconciliatory policies and new forms of state intervention in order to make the neoliberal order more stable. As a result, neoliberal reform in Morocco, especially since the reign of Mohammed VI, was not necessarily antisocial but fundamentally reconfigured the social question and the question of urban government.

Taking into account this political context of neoliberal reform, it is important to emphasize that the new methods of (urban) government developed during the neoliberal era were generated not only by the economic pressures of the 1980s and the changes within international finance but also by security concerns, the will to control, and more specifically by the problem of slums. In the modern history of Morocco, the slum population and the urban poor more generally were consistently involved in outbreaks of social protest and urban violence (Belarbi 2015; Clément 1992; Madani 1995). They were perceived (or stigmatized) as the dangerous classes (Bayat and Denis 2000).

Two watershed moments of urban unrest and violence accelerated the elaboration of new governmental practices: the bread riots of 1981 and the suicide bombings of 2003, both involving slum dwellers, and both occurring in Casablanca. Consequently, the increasing urbanization of capital entailed a double shift: it reflected not only capital's preference to guarantee its smooth circulation but also the concern to protect the established political order (and by extension capital's interests) from possible threats. The political interventions under both Hassan II and Mohammed VI have to be understood as different ways to "pacify" the riotous city of the 1980s and neutralize the jihadist threat of the early twenty-first century.

In this chapter, I turn the chronological order around. I start in the 1990s with the reinvention of social policy at the beginning of Mohammed VI's reign. Projects such as INDH and VSB enable us to understand the particular convergence between an authoritarian and a neoliberal governmentality under pressure of enduring social crisis and continuous political instability. In the second part of the chapter, I focus more particularly on urban government and go back to Casablanca of the 1980s, a city confronted with the social consequences of structural adjustment and mass revolt. The ways in which the city was "securitized" help us understand the "biopolitical vacuum" that coincided with structural adjustment and the dismantling of developmentalism. This vacuum provided the backdrop for the rollout of new methods of government and social control dealing with the problems of urban poverty, informal housing, and urban violence.

Neoliberal Practices, Authoritarianism, and the Problems of Modern Government

Many observers saw in the renewed attention to poverty alleviation under Mohammed VI and the launch of large-scale social projects such as INDH and VSB not only a break with the harsh reforms of structural adjustment but also evidence of a promising political transition (Martín 2006; Navez-Bouchanine 2009). On a broader level, Florian Kohstall, for example, saw in Morocco's new social policies a pluralization of power relations that played an important role in the country's ability to "reform more efficiently" and adapt to what he called "an international normative order" (i.e., Western policy models). Although he considered these social reforms not necessarily as a form of democratization, they were at least inherently contradictory to authoritarian rule (Kohstall 2010, 197).

The social policies of the last decade did feed the image of Moroccan exceptionalism. The general idea was that the political system showed a double face, as it were: on the one hand, a system with characteristics of an authoritarian regime still in place, and on the other hand, liberal and social reforms that could form the basis of a genuine democratic transition (Alicino 2015; see also Charai 2011; El Hachimi 2015).

I fundamentally disagree with this point of view. It is without a doubt that over the last decade we witnessed a growing attention to social policies and poverty reduction in Morocco. Yet I argue that these efforts should not be considered as a form of political liberalization but rather as a particular field through which we can understand the qualitative transformation of authoritarian government.

Moreover, despite the fact that these new social policy interventions were deliberately addressing the limits of structural adjustment, it is important to understand them not as some kind of paradoxical conjunction with neoliberal reform, or as a compensation for that matter, but rather as an attempt to *consolidate* the neoliberal order in the long term and even expand its scope. While structural adjustment in the 1980s dismantled the old social order, causing massive uprisings and rising poverty, the reinvention of social policy in Morocco during the first decade of the twenty-first century formulated an answer to these "limits" of market liberalization. It was part of a larger political process attempting to deepen neoliberal projects, to embed them by creating the necessary institutional infrastructure and by making society more receptive, more stable, and more integrated.

The convergence of an authoritarian and a neoliberal governmentality will be the focus of the next two chapters. Neoliberal rationalities and authoritarian measures are not inherently contradictory. Rather than viewing neoliberalism as a normative political philosophy, committed to the idea of individual freedom, limited government, and market liberalization, I examine neoliberal governmentality as a practice or a way of doing things that has the "free market" (i.e., capitalist globalization) as an organizing principle for authoritarian intervention (Dean 2007, 110–12; Foucault 2008, 116–21).[1]

The Reinvention of Social Policy

The reinvention of social policy in Morocco should be situated within a changing national and international context. At the national level, a socialist prime minister from the historical opposition took office in the *alternance* government of 1998, while Mohammed VI, who acceded to the throne in 1999, immediately made it clear he wanted to break with his father's authoritarian image by implementing wide-scale reform. Both events installed hope and optimism with regard to the aspirations of a democratic process. Furthermore, they created the political space to rethink Morocco's policy approaches toward the (urban) poor.

At the international level, an important discursive shift occurred during the 1990s with the promotion of good governance by institutions like the World Bank. The harsh rhetoric of the Washington Consensus on austerity and privatization was discredited, even by the World Bank itself, and new ideas were pushed to the forefront that recycled the political ideas of an earlier era: self-help housing, microenterprises, and community building (Roy 2005, 150).[2]

The euphoria concerning the so-called end of history and the infallibility of free-market capitalism made space for a new engagement to "end poverty" (Roy 2010). The World Bank president at the time, James Wolfensohn, expressed, in a key speech in 1998 titled "The Other Crisis," his concerns about a looming crisis that the world had failed to notice: the crisis of poverty. He called for a worldwide prioritization of poverty alleviation (Roy 2010, 16, 74–83). At the subsequent Millennium Summit in 2000, all 192 member states of the United Nations agreed on eight Millennium Development Goals to halve poverty in the world by 2015.

This broader context, together with the memory of the social tensions of the 1980s, created the political space for a reflection on the social dimension of economic reform; it set the stage for important political transformations within Moroccan neoliberalism. The late 1990s and early twenty-first century were characterized to a great extent by an increased political attention to the "social question" (Catusse 2005, 2009a, 2011; de Miras 2007; Hibou and Tozy 2015; Navez-Bouchanine 2002a). More government attention was given to the negative social impact of market-oriented reform, while new modes of public intervention were rolled out to address the limits of structural adjustment. Since the public sector had clearly lost its leverage as a provider and redistributor of accumulated wealth, the challenge for the new king and his entourage was to reform and redefine policies of social development to conform to the norms of "the market."

According to Myriam Catusse, new social policy initiatives were taken in two domains: in the improvement of social legislation and in poverty alleviation. In the first domain, there were some improvements in labor conditions with an increase in the minimum wage, the adoption of a new labor code in 2003, and initiatives to improve health insurance—only 25 percent of the qualified population had the right to a pension and approximately 85 percent did not have access to healthcare (Catusse 2005, 2008, 2009a). However, the results were rather limited and confined to the wage-earning population.[3] Therefore, the state-led initiatives taken in the domain of the fight against poverty were probably more significant. INDH and the VSB program were two of the most important initiatives within this second domain.

In his royal discourse of May 18, 2005, Mohammed VI announced the launch of a National Initiative for Human Development, calling poverty alleviation one of the most important challenges for the future. He also made explicit reference to "extremist tendencies" *(velléités extremistes)* that found fertile ground in social misery and economic marginalization, thereby linking the political targets and priorities of INDH directly to the Casablanca suicide attacks of 2003. The political implications of INDH are significant as the king defined the program as a *chantier de règne* (a reign-long policy area), linking this initiative with the entire duration of his rule and giving it royal prestige (Bono 2010b; World Bank 2012).

INDH specifically aims to tackle pressing social problems such as unemployment, poverty, illiteracy, and social exclusion. To do so, the initiative includes international partners, local elected authorities, and grassroots organizations in the elaboration and funding of microprojects all over the country. The second phase of the project was launched in June 2011. An overall budget of 17.1 billion dirhams was allocated to finance this phase, a considerable increase compared to 10 billion dirhams allocated to the first phase (2006–10).[4] Fifty-five percent of the second phase is financed by the central government, 33 percent by local governments, 6 percent by other public agencies, and another 6 percent by external grants (from the World Bank and others).[5]

INDH consists of five subprograms: a rural subprogram targeting rural poverty and attempting to improve the living conditions in 702 rural communities; an urban subprogram fighting social exclusion in 532 urban neighborhoods *(quartiers)* around the country; a cross-cutting subprogram "promoting the social and economic inclusion of poor and vulnerable persons in poor areas not targeted under other subprograms"; a vulnerability *(précarité)* subprogram "to improve the quality of life of vulnerable persons in [specifically] targeted categories (widows, disabled

persons, orphans, street children, drug users, and HIV affected people)";
and finally a territorial upgrading subprogram "to improve the living
conditions of populations in mountainous and isolated areas through
investments in basic infrastructure in 503 isolated rural communes"
(World Bank 2012, 9–10).

There is a lot of skepticism toward INDH and the amount of resources made available. Some observers consider it too little to solve the
pressing socioeconomic problems of the country (Martín 2006). A prominent Moroccan economist called INDH "just a drop in the ocean" (interview, Rabat, October 26, 2009, conducted with Egon Gussé). Finally,
James Sater argues that, with regard to the first phase, no extra state
funds were allocated to INDH. Instead, the initiative was financed solely
from existing resources that were diverted from other ministries. Furthermore, the estimated cumulative loss of state revenues and social costs
due to the signing of free trade agreements with the EU and the United
States are actually a multiple of the value and the impact of the entire
2006–10 INDH program (Sater 2010, 108–11).

Rethinking Politics and Government through INDH

A critical analysis of the INDH initiative, however, should go beyond
the mere question of numbers. What is more important is to understand
the ways in which such schemes alter state–society relations, practices
of urban government, and social subjectivities. Neoliberal projects such
as INDH should be considered as a contemporary framework through
which urban life is raised as a problem of (authoritarian) government
(cf. Collier 2011, 125).

A social program like INDH, just like the VSB program for that
matter, has two interrelated objectives.[6] First, it enhances control over
a population that is perceived as a threat to political stability. Second,
it attempts to create a more self-reliant and entrepreneurial citizen.
Instead of giving the urban poor the tools to claim collective rights and
focus on issues of class struggle, any form of social activism should be
ideally reduced to an individual responsibility. New forms of state intervention and new governmental practices have to facilitate citizens to
take matters into their own hands. Three points further illustrate the
importance of these issues.

First, increased state intervention within the framework of the
INDH program did not compensate or undermine the fundamentals of
neoliberal projects in Morocco. To the contrary, King Mohammed VI

explicitly stressed in his address to the nation of May 18, 2005, that the increased efforts in social development do not imply a break with the overall macroeconomic direction of the country, which is based on economic growth, free-market reform, and trade liberalization.

> If the level of economic growth is insufficient and inequitable in the sense that not all people and regions of our country benefit from its dividends, all the more because some continue to suffer from marginalization and social degradation, it is important to note, at the same time, that the desired level of inclusion should not be considered, according to a simplistic and narrow vision, as a weight that burdens [economic] growth, but rather as its condition and catalyst.[7]

Two years later, in his address from the throne on June 30, 2007, the king called "economic liberalism" one of the fundamental pillars of the Moroccan *"état de droit"* (constitutional state) and part of the Moroccan "national consensus" (Vermeren 2009, 57–58). For the monarchy, the economic direction the country had taken since the 1980s was not negatively linked to conditions of poverty and marginalization. What's more, the logic behind a program such as INDH made it clear that *more* market integration was required to fight the country's social problems.

Second, INDH contributes to the depoliticization of the economic vision that underpins it. Not only is it inconceivable that a royal project be questioned by other political actors in the country—Mohammed VI sees INDH as part of the "national consensus" (Bono 2010b)—but this kind of development scheme also passes on the final responsibility from the public authorities to other actors (the private sector and the beneficiaries). In his speech of May 18, 2005, the king framed this within the broader concept of good governance.

> We also call on them [the government] to adopt an action plan [INDH] based on the principles of good governance, namely responsibility and transparency, the rules of professionalism, the broad participation of the population, integration and the rationalization of the interventions of public institutions and organizations, as well as the permanent followup and evaluation of the realizations.[8]

The principles of good governance were presented as an alternative to the bureaucratic, corrupt and clientelist central government of the past, turning public action and state-funded programs into a collaborative endeavor at the local level (Bergh 2012, 411). A social development scheme such as INDH relies strongly on cooperation between the state, civil society, and the private sector in order to create alleged win-win situations for both beneficiaries and private investors. Lydec in Casablanca, a subsidiary of the French multinational Suez, is integrated, for example, in the INDH program to provide informal housing with basic services such as water and electricity. What's more, Lydec actually needs state partners and neighborhood organizations to facilitate its access to this side of the market.

This shift in responsibility is further illustrated by the encouragement of a "marketization" of development, based on stimulating competition between beneficiaries to obtain funding, performance-based contracting and management, as well as demanding co-financing from the private sector and civil society (Bergh 2012, 411).

Two key words are central in a program such as INDH (and also VSB): *responsibilization* and *participation*. Schemes such as INDH, according to Claude de Miras (2007, 18), turn the fight against poverty into a "fight of the poor against their own poverty," a fight that does not concern or relate to the condition of other social classes anymore and, as such, disconnects the question of social development from broader political and structural questions.

Here, we see a definite break with the social policies and objectives of the developmentalist era, and a clear link with the post–Washington Consensus. The goals of full employment and social welfare set forth by the developmental state based on principles such as social rights, collective solidarity, and a class compromise—in theory at least—are replaced by corporate social responsibility, public management, and the economically liberated individual (Catusse 2011, 69).

Third, a program such as INDH precisely reconfigures and enhances political control through the promotion of "participation." It is true that social development schemes such as INDH brought forth new social actors in the field and opened up new spaces for political and social action. However, these new spaces were also immediately constrained by new boundaries and limits.

Yasmine Berriane demonstrates that through INDH "new actors who were not part of the traditional local notability have been able not only to climb the social ladder but also become part of the local decision making apparatus as political actors" (2010, 98). This seems to confirm a general trend in Morocco of a kind of political transformation "from below."

Since the end of the 1970s, we have seen a substantial growth of associational life in Morocco and an increase in new neighborhood associations and other civil society organizations, especially in cities. Several reasons can be given: the increasing rural exodus toward the cities, the emergence of a new urban middle class, important urban reforms that gave more authority to local elected governments (e.g., the new Communal Charter of 1976), the *alternance* process of the 1990s, and finally the gradual rollback of the developmentalist welfare functions of the state, which obliged citizens to explore alternatives and take matters into their own hands to improve their neighborhoods and livelihoods (Abouhani 2006; Ameur 2000; Iraki 2006a, 2006b; Navez-Bouchanine 1995). Initiatives such as INDH, which distributes its funds via local associations and nongovernmental organizations (NGOs), further stimulated this growth of neighborhood associations (Bergh 2012; Berriane 2010; Bono 2010a).

However, this does not mean that we are witnessing some kind of burgeoning democratization. Despite the widespread rhetoric of participation, good governance, and transparency, the actual control over and the distribution of INDH resources take place via the Ministry of Interior (the historical powerbase of the monarchy) and its representatives at the regional, prefectural, and provincial level. The coordination of INDH depends on a pyramid structure that includes all levels of decision-making but is ultimately controlled in a centralized matter by the Ministry of Interior. Even though this state program encourages participation and the creation of new associations, these new actors are still politically controlled and have to conform to the predefined rules. As Berriane remarks:

> At the very top of the ladder, the Ministry of Interior oversees NGO activity while at the bottom it is the mqaddem[9] who keeps a close eye on an NGO's daily activities, taking part for example in general assemblies, conferences and festivities that are organized by associations. Furthermore, a central database designed to contain all the information about each association was launched a few years ago. From this point of view, we could argue that *the growing number of NGOs signifies a greater control over society by the state.* (2010, 100, emphasis added)

Sylvia Bergh (2012, 412) seconds this argument. INDH has strengthened the position of the Ministry of Interior at the expense of locally elected officials and served to co-opt a large part of civil society and the local elites. The program exemplifies the reorganization and redefinition of public action and fundamentally restructures power relations between people, between those who govern and the governed (see also Hibou and Tozy 2015).

Moreover, by targeting and defining the "poor" as a primary category of intervention or primary "population" to be governed, and by promoting an entrepreneurial logic and corporate management, INDH is not contradicting or compensating neoliberal reform in Morocco but rather extending it to other areas of society (Bono 2010a).

This political dimension of INDH is enhanced through other aspects. Through different mechanisms, such as the delivery of licenses and authorizations, the allocation of resources, and so on, the Ministry of Interior intervenes in associational life and potentially filters out those actors and organizations it considers not politically suitable or desirable. In reality this means that those associations with a clear political agenda or a certain political affiliation are excluded from the distribution of resources (Berriane 2010).

The program was also used as a counterweight against the growing influence of the Islamists and Islamic charity by increasing the visibility of the state in poor neighborhoods through local partners and NGOs of their own choosing (Iraki 2013; see also Hibou and Tozy 2015). Furthermore, a program such as INDH deprives the Ministry of Social Affairs, run by an elected representative, of an important part of its core business as some redistribution policies were recentralized within the sovereign Ministry of Interior.

Finally, this program also allows international aid from, for example, the EU or the World Bank, to be redistributed via a central power apparatus. As such, international donor funds do not really affect central power's control over the space of social intervention (Bono 2007).

Within the context of these kinds of transformations, access to state power still plays a crucial role but not in the same way as in the developmentalist era. The INDH program is a salient example of what Béatrice Hibou (2004b) has called the "privatisation of the state" in which certain domains of public action are entrusted to private agents while the state opts for an indirect form of control.[10]

Privatization should thus be understood as a new form of state intervention and not so much as a phenomenon that indicates a retreat of the state. The growing involvement of (foreign) private actors, in the form of NGOs, grassroots organizations, or private businesses, entailed not a loss of state autonomy but a transformation of state modes of intervention. In other words, what we observe in Morocco through social programs such as the INDH and the like is a change in techniques of government and the appearance of new actors on the scene of "government (Hibou 2004b; Lemke 2002, 58).

As a result, the privatization of the state entailed a renegotiation of power relations and an increasing entanglement of different kinds of political actors (both public and private) within the domain of urban government. The coalescence between these different actors within different projects of neoliberalism makes clear conceptual distinctions between public and private, market and state, and finally between the economic and the political much more difficult. Writers such as Tsing (2000) and Massey (2005) would add that it also confuses the conceptual distinction between local and global.

The privatization of the state and the reinvention of social policy in Morocco led to the creation of new types of institutions by which those in power actually bypass traditional state institutions and formal democratic control. I mentioned the Hassan II Fund earlier. The establishment of the Mohammed V Foundation for Solidarity is another example. Both agencies were created at the end of the 1990s and invest in the INDH program.[11] Officially, such organizations are created in the name of national solidarity and intend to confront the pressing socioeconomic problems. In reality, these kinds of agencies not only bypass standard budgetary procedures and controls but also establish important connections between state elites and private interests groups and alter the mechanisms for patronage and economic intervention as they are placed under the direct authority of the monarchy and its entourage (Hibou and Tozy 2002a, 2015; see also Catusse 2011).[12]

New Forms of Power:
The Role of Biopower in Capitalist Expansion

Neoliberal projects involve attempts to make the state more entrepreneurial and to privatize government. At the same time, they also attempt to make citizens more reliable, to turn them into productive economic subjects and into consumers of and in urban space. The political analysis of Morocco's urbanism of projects cannot thus be reduced to an analysis of state spatiality alone. Neoliberal projects like INDH imply not only a reengineering of the state but also the reengineering—if you like—of the urban citizen. The second issue is intimately related to a security dimension and perceived potential threats to the neoliberal order.

Throughout Morocco's modern history, the urban peripheries of major cities, the poor working-class neighborhoods, and the slum areas represented spaces of "high risk" (Rachik 1995). The urban mass riots of the 1980s obviously fed this perception. The bombings in Casablanca allegedly demonstrated this once again and very forcefully. These moments of urban violence may not directly target the newly planned urban megaprojects and economic growth strategies for the city, but we cannot consider them entirely separate phenomena. This would deny the urban complexity of contemporary capitalist society.

The first political question that informs neoliberal urban projects (how can we maximize the process of capital accumulation in the city?) is complemented with an equally important political question: how do we deal with the existing urban population in order to stabilize the class project of capital accumulation? The city is thus not only a vehicle to generate growth but also an instrument of political control. This double shift produced new methods of power that coincided with the broader transition within Moroccan neoliberalism itself.

Linking these issues of capital accumulation and political control together requires a methodological expansion introducing a focus on the "art of government" (Foucault 2007). For Foucault, the concept of "government" referred not to the state as such, nor its institutions, but rather to particular techniques of management and security that take the population as their object. In other words, government in the Foucauldian sense refers to power in terms of its specific methods rather than its institutional forms (T. Mitchell 2006, 179). The concept of government thus incorporates all kinds of techniques, ranging from practices of "governing the self" to "governing others" (Lemke 2007, 45).[13]

Power is central to an analytics of government. Yet Foucault wanted to avoid a sort of schematism that sought to locate power (in a state apparatus) or assume that power is possessed by some center (the regime). Instead, he preferred to explore the "micro-physics of power": the anonymous strategies, the specific form of its exercise, and the very sites where power is exercised over individuals (Jessop 2008; Lemke 2002). The study of these micro-physics, as Foucault argued in *Discipline and Punish*, presupposes that "power is exercised rather than possessed." Moreover, the power exercised on a body (e.g., in the case of prison space) or on a population (e.g., through particular modalities of urban government) was not so much a property but a *strategy* (Foucault 1979, 26–27).

In other words, Foucault did not necessarily want to give a face to power (e.g., *the* state or *the* capitalist class); he only wanted to explain *how* it works. Power has a productive effect. From a Foucauldian perspective, control and domination have to do not only with repression or the use of force but also with the very mechanisms through which power penetrates the bodies of subjects, the ways technologies of power determine the government of their lives, and the effectiveness with which subjects internalize the "truth" of the arrangements in which they find themselves (Agamben 2009, 12; Allen 2004, 23).[14]

As such, Foucault's concept of governmentality—that is, the inseparable interrelation between technologies of power and the different modes of thought or political rationalities that underpin them (Lemke 2001, 191)—illustrates how neoliberalism is much more than just an ideology generated by the state or a dominant class. A neoliberal order materializes through forms of power that reach into our daily lives and can be retraced in the quotidian experiences of capitalist society. The purposes of those technologies of power is to create a new subjectivity that allows a neoliberal rationality to extend across other social spaces (beyond the realm of the market) to become an image of society (Read 2009).[15]

The theoretical strength of the concept of governmentality lies in its ability to understand neoliberalism "as a political project that endeavors to create a social reality that it suggests already exists" (Lemke 2002, 60). *Neoliberal* governmentality is then a new form of governmentality, a new way in which people are subjectified: the homo-economicus—the man of exchange—is turned into an *entrepreneur*, an entrepreneur of himself in which he is his own "capital," his own producer, and lives his life responsibly according to his own capabilities (Read 2009; see also Foucault 2008, 226).[16] In other words, "neoliberal citizens" are created through techniques of self-government and the promotion of autonomous behavior within a market society (Hughes Rinker 2014). At least, this is the rationale integrated in projects such as INDH and VSB (see also chapter 6).

Historically, the development of new technologies of subjectification can be situated within a fundamental shift from a political focus on territory (which was the subject of sovereign power and sovereign politics) toward a focus on population as the defining object of government. Foucault observed in the genealogy of modern politics a gradual shift from the preoccupation of the sovereign "prince" to establish control over his territory (epitomized by Machiavelli's masterpiece) to a new art of government in which the control over human life itself became the main concern. While the relation between the prince and his territory used to be central in pre- and early capitalist society, with the population that inhabited the territory in a secondary role, modern governmentality dealt with the population and life itself as political problems (Elden 2007a; Rose-Redwood 2006). This shift entailed what Foucault understood as the emergence of "biopower" or "biopolitics."

Biopower, and government as a form of biopower more specifically, gradually became dominant over the use of sovereign power. Consequently, "power would no longer be dealing simply with legal subjects over whom the ultimate dominion was death, but with living beings" (Foucault 1990, 143). In contrast to sovereign power, which has the capacity to decide over life and death, biopower had a productive impact on life. It is "the power to make life" (Foucault 2003, 247).

Foucault described the methods and technologies of modern government as "apparatuses of security." Security, in this sense, refers to "the future-oriented management of risks" (Valverde 2007, 172). Foucault himself gave several examples of security apparatuses such as town planning and the specific strategies to cope with food shortages and epidemics (e.g., through market regulation and vaccination campaigns). The safety (*sûreté*) of the prince and his territory made place for the security (*sécurité*) of the population (Foucault 2007, 65).

To Foucault, this security or well-being of the population was intimately related to the governmental problem of popular discontent, sedition, and riot. The discontent of the people was one of the main problems of modern government: "And one aspect of government will precisely be taking responsibility for this possibility of riot and sedition" (Foucault 2007, 271).

It would be wrong to see these different forms of power, that is, sovereign power and biopower, as mutually exclusive. Sovereignty as a form of power, especially in authoritarian political systems, did not simply disappear with the emergence of "life-administering power" (Agamben 1998; Mbembe 2003). Yet "government" eventually became dominant over all other types of power, even in authoritarian systems, because biopower was without a doubt indispensable for the further development and expansion of capitalism. The development of capitalism, as

Foucault stated in the epigraph of this chapter, "would not have been possible without the controlled insertion of bodies into the machinery of production and the adjustment of the phenomena of population to economic processes" (Foucault 1990, 141).

The intimate relation between the rise of capitalism and the rise of the modern nation-state can thus also be situated within these processes of gradual governmentalization: "It is as though power, which used to have sovereignty as its modality or organizing schema, found itself unable to govern the economic and political body of society that was undergoing both a demographic explosion and industrialization" (Foucault 2003, 249). Consequently, Foucault's analysis can also be read "as continuations of rather than departures from Marx's arguments concerning the rise of a disciplinary [and administering] capitalism in which workers have to be socialized and disciplined to accept the spatiotemporal logic of the capitalist labor process" (Harvey 2010a, 149).

By making this particular claim about the importance of biopolitics for the expansion and development of capitalism, Foucault goes into dialogue with Marx and Marxism. Instead of rejecting Marx, he actually gives an additional insight on the particularity of their different, or rather complementary, visions on the rise of the modern state and modern political society. While Marxist accounts tend to focus more on the institutions of power, he wants to point our attention to some of the methods or techniques of power that coincided with those institutions and were equally important for the expansion of capitalist relations.

> If the development of the great instruments of the state, as *institutions* of power, ensured the maintenance of production relations, the rudiments of [disciplinary power] and bio-politics, created in the eighteenth century as *techniques* of power present at every level of the social body and utilized by very diverse institutions (the family and the army, schools and the police, individual medicine and the administration of collective bodies), operated in the sphere of economic processes, their development, and the forces working to sustain them. They also acted as factors of segregation and social hierarchization, exerting their influence on the respective forces of both these movements, guaranteeing relations of domination and effects of hegemony. The adjustment of the accumulation of men to that of capital, the joining of the growth of human groups to the expansion of productive forces and the differential allocation of profit, were made possible in part by the exercise of bio-power in its many forms and modes of application. (Foucault 1990, 141)

With regard to neoliberal techniques of government, one has to understand it in terms of a continuation and consolidation of capitalist expansion and transformation—only this time not so much in a geographical sense, like under colonialism, or in the disciplinary sense, like under early industrialization, but rather in the sense that neoliberal techniques integrate more and more (public) domains into the market economy (through structural adjustment, public–private partnerships, etc.), promote competition in all spheres of society (through the privatization of the state, new public management, etc.), and create new subjectivities that guarantee new effects of hegemony (from homo-economicus to a self-governing entrepreneur).

Neoliberal Governmentality in Authoritarian Rule

A neoliberal governmentality might be perfectly compatible with authoritarian political systems because it promotes a very narrow conception of freedom. Within neoliberal rationality, the freedom of the individual was no longer a necessary precondition for rational government, as argued by the liberal thinkers of the eighteenth and nineteenth century, but rather a condition that could be created artificially *through* government, that is, by promoting entrepreneurial and competitive behavior between economically rational individuals (Foucault 2008; Lemke 2001, 200).[17] Freedom, in other words, was reduced to a freedom of entrepreneurship within a market society. The techniques of government that ensure and consolidate competition and market expansion are not necessarily the same ones that promote individual and political freedom.

Within the context of neoliberal globalization and increasing global market integration, authoritarian political systems have to take the "government" of their populations seriously. Modern politics in a well-functioning state, whether it is a form of liberal democracy or a more authoritarian system of rule, can simply not escape the fact that they have to deal in some way or another with the biological and social processes of their populations. Like (neo)liberalism, Mitchell Dean argues, "authoritarian governmentality" is a particular articulation of sovereign power and biopower (1999, 131).

In contrast to more liberal forms of rule, nonliberal and authoritarian forms of rule seek to operate through obedient rather than free subjects by giving more weight to particular methods of sovereignty, domination, and repression (Dean 1999, 131). However, the notion of authoritarian governmentality still points to the preeminence of techniques of "government" over those of mere subjugation, repression, and violence. The techniques embedded within programs such as INDH and VSB specifically target particular populations and have a neoliberal political economy as its major form of knowledge (cf. Foucault 2007, 108–9). With regard to Morocco, a country that is increasingly integrated into the global capitalist system and pretends to draw on a "liberal" regime of government, a governmentality approach provides us with a conceptualization of the relation and shifts between sovereign power and biopower within the neoliberal era. King Mohammed VI's speech from the throne on July 30, 2007, is insightful in this regard and provides us with a view on the ruling power's vision on the transformation of Moroccan society. The king emphasizes that the political order in Morocco is founded on a "national consensus." Yet his conceptualization of this national consensus clearly demonstrates how elements of sovereign politics and biopolitics articulate. Mohammed VI defined this national consensus as follows:

> It concerns, particularly, the Constitutional State and its institutions, a citizenship based on a respect for human rights and the duties of men, an economic liberalism, and the liberty of entrepreneurship. This besides solidarity, social justice and an openness to the rest of the world. It is up to Us [the monarchy] to watch over the permanency of these values, whatever the consequences and its fluctuations may be. This is . . . our conception of *la Monarchie citoyenne*.[18]

He then concludes at the end of his speech:

> I will remain, dear people, just like you have always known Me, the Citizen-King, leading the militants who are working on the field, in all regions of the country, just like abroad. Likewise, I commit Myself to consolidate the pillars of unity and democracy, to strengthen the dynamics of development, progress and solidarity, and to reaffirm the capacity of Morocco to act in synergy with the outside world and the changes that occur, without ever abandoning the authentic Moroccan identity.[19]

Here we clearly see how the king, as the symbol of absolute power in Morocco, refers to modern technologies of government that he personally promises to preserve or implement. Sovereign power, in other words, is promised to be used to assure the continuation of government (biopower). Sovereign power "protects" the national consensus. These royal words give an indication of how nondemocratic political systems constitute their own mixture of sovereign and biopolitical technologies of power to rule their territory and their population within the context of capitalist globalization.

A political analysis of the convergence of neoliberal and authoritarian governmentalities in Morocco helps us understand the differences in the ways of rule between Mohammed VI and his father, Hassan II. The latter supported more overt methods of sovereign power to control the political domain, while the former has increasingly shifted his technologies of control from the formal political domain into the economic domain. A focus on techniques of neoliberal government explains *how* this was done in particular domains and within particular projects, such as Cities Without Slums (see chapter 6).

Power, Territory, and Control at the Urban Scale

The differentiation between different forms of power and methods of government becomes especially useful when one studies the political changes in an urban setting. Foucault taught us a great deal about the organization and politics of space (Elden 2007b). He attributed a central role to the city, or rather the town, as a key problem for government and security. Growing problems like epidemics, food scarcity, rural migration, and so on turned public health, urban planning ("town planning"), and the mobility of goods and people in a market system into central mechanisms of security (Foucault 2007, 55–86).

What's more, the conceptual distinction between sovereign power and biopower is particularly helpful in understanding a particular moment of radical political transformation and creative destruction in Moroccan history, namely the transition from a developmentalist to a neoliberal social order. The dismantling of the developmentalist order through structural adjustment required an increasing reliance on methods of sovereign power in order to maintain control over the urban space and compensate for the rollback of particular apparatuses of security associated with the developmental state (public services, public employment policies, and all kinds of mechanisms of wealth redistribution; for example, food subsidies). In other words, the breaking up of the biopolitical techniques of the developmentalist era required a strong involvement of sovereign power in order to impose and protect the project of rollback neoliberalism. This period of destruction was eventually followed by a constructive phase rolling out new political arrangements, among others INDH, VSB, and the Bouregreg project, implementing new technologies of biopower.

As I already mentioned, two moments of disruption and violence, the bread riots of 1981 and the suicide bombings of 2003, are the starting points for understanding significant differences in the way the Moroccan city was controlled and stabilized. While the methods of control taken after the riots of 1981 were more focused on the physical environment through which people move, that is, the urban territory, those implemented after the bombings of 2003 targeted the slum population itself as a calculable subject for a general strategy of control, trying to turn the slum dweller into a self-reliant and entrepreneurial citizen.

These different methods of power targeting the slums between the early 1980s and the early twenty-first century can be best explained with Mariana Valverde's distinction between what she calls *"sovereign city planning"* and *"cities of security."* Drawing on the Foucauldian notions of sovereignty and security, she argues that sovereign city planning relies predominantly on techniques that capitalize a territory and emphasize monumental state architecture in order to incite submission to the sovereign. In contrast, cities of security involve planning that assembles techniques that are more concerned with the biopolitical management of the urban population and the future risks related to that population (Valverde 2007, 168). In short, whereas sovereign city planning in the 1980s dealt with individuals as a set of legal subjects within a designated *territory*, technologies of security deployed in the first decade of the twenty-first century will precisely constitute and target a specific *population*, in this case, the slum population.

Casablanca is the most obvious case study. First, the white city has been the main stage in numerous eruptions of social unrest that then spread throughout the country. Second, Casablanca was and is exemplary for large-scale urbanization in the Global South: rapid urban demographic growth without a proportional redistribution of economic growth. The coastal city expanded rapidly during the twentieth century to become Morocco's biggest urban environment. Until 2003, Casablanca was not only the economic center of the country; at the same time it also accommodated more than 30 percent of Morocco's slum dwellers.

Because of this specific social situation and because of Casablanca's dominant position in the national economy, the city has always been a *"ville laboratoire,"* a test case and model for other Moroccan cities (Catusse, Cattedra, and Janati 2005). Over the course of the past thirty years, new strategies of social and spatial organization "tested" in Casablanca were adopted afterward in other major Moroccan cities.

Toward an Urbanism of Control:
Sovereign City Planning in the 1980s

A radical turn in urban politics began in 1981. During the 1970s the Moroccan authorities gradually paid more attention to its urban regions. Yet most observers agreed that there was still no overall and coherent urban vision at the national political level (Abouhani 1995a; Kaioua 1996; Naciri 1987; Rachik 2002). Urban informality and informal expansion were still largely tolerated. Due to a lack of housing on the formal market and a nontransparent and slow bureaucracy, spontaneous and informal urbanization became the real motor behind urban expansion in Morocco and the Arab region more generally. There was a real divergence between "planned" urbanization and "actual" urbanization (Navez-Bouchanine 2005a).

However, urban informality was not only a result of a lack of resources and public services. Toleration was also a strategy to maintain social peace and political stability. It was a form of "management by absence," as Lamia Zaki calls it: "By maintaining the inhabitants on the legal margin, the state creates a latent insecurity which sustains the shantytown dwellers' fragility and limits the assertion of collective demands" (2008, 118).

Repression was the only other means to keep the city under control. Until the late 1970s, government "solutions" were predominantly based on the premise that a good repression meant ten years of social peace (Clément 1992, 402). As a result, Moroccan urban policy insufficiently dealt with the complexity of increasing urbanization. It failed to provide sustainable solutions for a growing lower middle class looking for affordable housing outside the expensive *ville nouvelle* (the colonial city).

The structural conditions and the crisis at the beginning of the 1980s marked an end to the benign neglect of the urban periphery, its slums, and spontaneous urbanization in general. The riots of 1981 were the starting point for a radical governmental shift, leading to a tighter control over urban territory. The informal urban areas became the primary focus of a general political urban restructuring strategy that symbolized the transition from an "urbanism of tolerance" toward an "urbanism of control" (Abouhani 1995a) or an "urbanism of urgency" (Rachik 2002; see also Naciri 1987).

Of course, this did not mean that spontaneous urbanization was halted completely. I want to emphasize above all a change in governmental attitude and strategy, a change that was provoked by a moment of severe political crisis. The general strike and the social disturbances that followed violently exposed the convergence of the tensions that were emerging within the city and the growing cleavage between an emerging urban entrepreneurial elite with considerable political influence, benefiting from economic liberalization, and the rest of the urban population bearing the costs of neoliberal reform and the rollback of welfare policies.

As in 1965, the riots that followed the strike of 1981 were severely repressed by police and army forces. But in contrast to 1965, the use of repression and physical violence was not the only answer the government had in store. After 1981, the marginalized peripheral urban areas—the slums, the informal housing quarters, and the working-class areas—became a primary focus within a general master plan for the restructuring of Casablanca.

Sovereign city planning is exercised through grand principles that break open the riotous city. Moreover, sovereign interventions attempt to emphasize and glorify the sovereigns' power, among others through monumental state architecture such as the magnificent Mosque Hassan II in Casablanca (discussed later in this chapter). These kinds of strategies tried to compensate for the loss of "security." The primary objective was not so much to control the conduct of a specific population—that potential had been reduced temporarily by rolling back welfare policies—but to subjugate dissent, clear the streets, and supervise the city as a whole through the implementation of a new sovereign master plan.

There were three core components of sovereign planning in Morocco during the 1980s: a thorough administrative redivision of the city, the setting up of new institutions of control, and the improvement of urban circulation and the construction of state architecture.

The Deconcentration of State Power at the Urban Scale

Within months after the riots, the urban territory of Casablanca was divided into smaller administrative units (prefectures) in order to increase administrative control and state presence in the urban peripheries and informal areas. The riots had demonstrated the political urgency of bringing the "administration closer to those administered" (Ministry of Planning, quoted in Claisse 1987, 40). The eastern periphery of Casablanca, where a large number of shantytowns and clandestine housing was concentrated, became a central focus of attention.[20]

The direct reorganization of state power at the urban scale involved the division of Casablanca into five administrative prefectures (until then Casablanca counted only one prefecture and five urban municipalities).[21] Furthermore, the new prefectures were integrated shortly thereafter in a newly established administrative superstructure: the *wilaya* (governate) of Greater Casablanca. The *wilaya* became the highest authority at the subnational level in Morocco. At that moment, there were only two *wilayas*, one in Casablanca and one in Rabat-Salé, which was created at the same time.

This intervention aimed to achieve two things. First, further administrative division had to extend the official city borders. Due to the informal urban sprawl of the preceding decades, the administrative borders of Casablanca did not reflect the actual urban footprint anymore. Many shantytowns and informal areas had expanded beyond official city borders and physically connected Casablanca with its rural hinterland.

Second, the aim was to recentralize and strengthen the state's presence at the urban level to increase the control and supervision over those political forces that defied the monarchy's power (e.g., the trade unions, the opposition parties, local civil society organizations, the Islamists, and the slum population). By bringing the "administration closer to those administered," the *wilaya* became the watchdog of the Ministry of Interior at the urban scale (Naciri 1989; Rachik 1995, 2002; Zriouli 1998).

This expansion of control can be seen in the light of a longer historical process of administrative politics that characterized the transformation of the Moroccan state and its power structures since the independence. After colonialism, one of the main challenges for the monarchy was to reconstruct the Moroccan state and establish the structural and institutional foundations of its rule. The building of a new machinery of state power was characterized by a double process: a *decentralization* of state power and a *deconcentration* of state power (Catusse, Cattedra, and Janati 2007; see also Findlay and Paddison 1986; Planel 2009). Understanding the difference between those two processes of state reformation is crucial to understanding the administrative element of sovereign city planning after the 1981 riots.

Decentralization refers to a process that transfers public competences and resources from the central government to elected authorities at a subnational level. In theory, decentralization is thus based on the democratic principle of subsidiarity. It suggests a reduction of administrative supervision by a central state authority and a genuine transfer of power to a separate and relatively autonomous government entity on a lower scale.

The creation of *communes* (municipalities), *prefectures* (urban), and *provinces* (rural) at the end of the 1950s and the beginning of 1960s entailed that some political leverage was given to an elite loyal to the monarchy, and it replaced the more traditional sociological power structures of Moroccan society (the tribal structures) as the foundation of the Moroccan state apparatus (Rousset 1992; see also Naciri 1987). These two levels of territorial authority received legal recognition with the Constitution of 1962.

In 1971 the Moroccan authorities created a third territorial entity: the region. The growing demands for development and economic growth and the multiplication of prefectures and provinces required a higher subdivision. In the same way as the other decentralized entities, the region was politically efficient to control peripheral dynamics in the country through the renewal of elite networks (García and Collado 2015).[22]

Since the municipal reform of 2002 (Chartre Communal de 2002), there are basically three "Moroccan-style" decentralized levels. First is the city council, which is headed by a president (mayor). In cities with more than 500,000 inhabitants, the urban territory is further divided in different *arrondissements* with limited jurisdiction. The establishment of one city council in every city meant a significant break with the administrative fragmentation of Moroccan cities before 2002 and also drastically reduced the number of local elected officials. While Casablanca still counted twenty-nine urban municipalities and six rural communities with a total of 1,147 elected officials in 1997, the city counted only 131 elected city councilors after the local elections of 2003 (Catusse, Cattedra, and Janati 2007).[23]

The second decentralized level is the prefectural or provincial assembly. This assembly has limited competences and is composed of indirectly elected city councilors and representatives of the professional chambers (Catusse, Cattedra, and Janati 2007). The third decentralized level is the regional council. This council is also indirectly elected, although this changed with the project of "advanced regionalization" announced by the king in 2010 and implemented in 2015 (García and Collado 2015).

Overall, the decentralized authorities have little power. The regions, for example, exist to collect data and develop economic plans that require approval from central government. Basically, they function as large chambers of commerce (McMurray 2014). The space of maneuver for the decentralized authorities is very limited. Only a fraction of total public expenses (11 percent in 2007) was spent by the decentralized authorities (Iraki 2010, 82).

Deconcentration, on the other hand, refers to a rescaling (and thus not a transfer) of competences, resources, and executive power from the national scale to subnational scales *within* the central state administration, more specifically the Ministry of Interior. The main principle is not that of democratic subsidiarity but rather the expansion or reorganization of central state power at the local or urban level. In short, deconcentration thus involves a sort of rationalization of state power at different scales.

It is thus crucial not to confuse decentralization with deconcentration. Governmental power at the local urban level is predominantly situated within the deconcentrated institutions. Various police forces operate under its control and officials are usually appointed by the Ministry of Interior. This kind of reform was in a way a logical consequence of increasing decentralization within a context of authoritarian government.

The decentralized entities were always subordinated to the deconcentrated authorities. The governor is the highest representative of central power at the local level. He has the executive authority within the region, province, or prefecture. The decentralized assemblies and elected organs are placed under his tutelage but he himself is not elected. A governor is directly appointed by *dahir* and, as the "representative of His Majesty," he or she becomes automatically the most powerful authority within the decentralized government body.

At the lower levels, the Ministry of Interior and the governor control a top-down system of appointments and patronage relations going from qaids, sheikhs, and eventually *mqaddems* at the street level. The latter is supposed to know every household in his jurisdiction (McMurray 2014). These local state agents perform functions that are not always stated in the law but exist in practice, for example the function of a mediator.

With the municipal reforms of 1976 and 2002, these local state agents lost some of their prerogatives (e.g., the qaid's authority to deliver construction permits). Yet the paradox of decentralization in Morocco is

DECENTRALIZED AUTHORITIES	DECONCENTRATED AUTHORITIES
City Council In cities with more than 500,000 inhabitants, the territory is subdivided into *arrondissement* councils.	*Qaids and Pashas* Urban district level. At the street level, they are represented by *mqaddems*.
Prefectural and Provincial Assemblies Indirectly elected.	*Prefecture and Province* Headed by a governor. He has direct authority over the local *agents d'autorités*, i.e., the qaids and pashas.
Regional Council Indirectly elected at first. Directly elected under the new project of advanced regionalization.	*Wilaya* Headed by a wali. The wali is also governor of the main prefecture. His authority is largely based on his status as direct representative of the king. The wali also directs the regional assembly.

The decentralized and deconcentrated authorities in Morocco.

that modest transfers of power to locally elected officials (e.g., the municipal reform of 1976) can easily be reversed through new rounds of deconcentration. And this is exactly what happened after the events of 1981.

The creation of the *wilaya* of Casablanca is a salient example. The wali (governor) heads the *wilaya*. He is at the same time governor of the main prefecture of the city. The *wilaya* does not have the same legal status as the prefecture or the province. It is not a separate local government body, only an interprefectural and provincial framework for the coordination of urban policies. Officially, the wali coordinates the increasing administrative deconcentration of the urban agglomerate and ensures the collaboration between the different governors of the prefectures and the provinces. That is why, legally, he has the same administrative rank as the other prefectural and provincial governors. Symbolically, however, the wali enjoys far more authority than the other governors. He is the main representative of the king at the urban level and he has much closer ties with the Ministry of Interior compared to his colleagues.

Today, the wali has three main tasks. First, he has to coordinate the policies of the prefectures and provinces in his jurisdiction, and he supervises the locally elected municipal governments. With regard to the latter, the wali directly carries out the supervisory function of the Ministry of Interior. The local city councils are dependent on the Ministry of Interior for the redistribution of resources, and their budgetary, technical, and juridical affairs are supervised by the Direction Générale des Communautés Locales (DGCL, General Direction of the Local Communities) (Catusse, Cattedra, and Janati 2007).[24]

Second, in 2002 the tasks of the wali were extended with the promotion of economic development and industrialization. The king ordered the creation of Centres Régional d'Investissement (CRI, Regional Investment Centres), one-stop contact points for Moroccan and foreign economic investors, under the supervision of the *wilayas*. As a result, the technocratic and economic ministries were dispossessed of some of their prerogatives, which were transferred to the *wilaya*. This resulted in the appointment of several "techno-walis" or "super-walis" who were supposed to bring a new technocratic and management culture to the job (Catusse 2008, 130; 2009b, 197–98).

Finally, the wali is responsible for the preservation of security and public order on his territory. He directs and controls the deconcentrated network of the *"agents d'autorités"* (qaids, pashas, *mqaddems*, etc.) and the various police forces. After 1981 the wali became the most important political actor within the city. As a deconcentrated authority and representative of the state, he not only overrules the local elected government but also replaces some of the national ministries in many policy domains of urban planning and urban government.

Casablanca expanded to six prefectures in 1985, seven in 1990 (after the riots in Fez), and nine in 1997. Today, Greater Casablanca is divided into twelve prefectures.[25] During that same period, the central authorities also effectively decentralized the urban scale of Casablanca and multiplied the amount of municipalities. In 1976 Casablanca was divided into five municipalities. In 1985 there were twenty-three urban and rural municipalities, while in 1997, as I mentioned earlier, there were thirty-five, effectively breaking up potential political alliances and weakening the territorial strength of locally elected councils.

This double process of deconcentration (the reinforcement of central state power at the urban scale through the *wilaya*) and decentralization (the crumbling of the municipal constituencies in Casablanca) had a perverse effect on the power balances in the city. It reversed the municipal reform of 1976, which had sought to integrate the emerging urban middle class into the realm of decision-making (Cattedra 2001; Kaioua 1996; Naciri 1987). The immediate goal of the monarchy and the makhzan was to weaken the alliance between the historical opposition parties, especially the socialist USFP and the nationalist Istiqlal, and the trade unions that had demonstrated their strength during the turbulent years of the 1980s. With the municipal reform of 2002, this divide and rule strategy was partly reversed. But the political damage was already done.

Following the perceived effectiveness of the reforms in Casablanca, this administrative model was applied to other cities during the 1990s. After the violent riots of December 1990, in which the inhabitants of the bidonvilles in Fez played an important role, three new *wilayas* were established in the cities of Fez, Marrakech, and Meknes. In January 1994 another four *wilayas* were created (Oujda, Agadir, Tétouan, and Lâayoune). This time, however, there was no direct provocation. It was more a preemptive measure anticipating the creation of regional governments in 1996 (Zriouli 1998).

The New Master Plan and Its Executive Agencies

The second important element of sovereign city planning in the 1980s involved the creation of several governmental agencies and new urban planning instruments to enhance urban control and supervision. Within a month after the riots, King Hassan II entrusted the French urbanist Michel Pinseau with the elaboration of a new *schéma directeur d'aménagement urbain* (SDAU), a new general master plan, to map out Casablanca's future for the next two decades. This was the first fully elaborated SDAU since Morocco's independence.

The SDAU had three objectives: a solution for the housing problem and the problem of spontaneous informal urban expansion, the improvement of the quality of public spaces and buildings, and the improvement of mobility within the city. The planning of a metro line was one of the most remarkable parts of the master plan.[26] With this master plan, Pinseau's team received the explicit mission to "securitize the city" (Cattedra 2001, 130–31; Philifert 2016).

The intention was obvious. Issues of urban planning and urban reorganization had become a top priority and the central administration needed specific instruments that concentrated the resources, the expertise, and the political power to govern the urban terrain from a more technical perspective. Following the elaboration of the SDAU, two important agencies were created in 1984 to implement the new urban strategies. The first, the Agence Nationale pour l'Habitat Insalubr (ANHI, National Agency for Degraded Housing), was charged with the eradication and reintegration of the slums and the informal neighborhoods. It was placed under the control of the Ministry of Interior but operated as a financially autonomous public institution. The requirements of structural adjustment implied, after all, a radical decrease of state subsidies for social housing programs. This meant a clear break with some of the state-led housing policies before the implementation of the SAP in 1983.

In the following years, the real estate market and the construction sector were largely privatized; the Moroccan state disengaged more and more from direct financial intervention (Philifert and Jolé 2005). With the liberalization of the housing market, ANHI would work closely with the emerging private sector in order to provide social and low-cost housing.

Additionally, the establishment of the ANHI implied a return to programs of slum resettlement that had been popular during the final years of the protectorate (Navez-Bouchanine 2002c). This meant a break with the strategies applied during the 1970s when preference was usually given to a restructuring in situ, a policy strongly promoted by the World Bank at the time, also in Morocco (Naciri 1987). Due to the new economic climate of the 1980s and the rapid expansion of Casablanca—which caused the absorption of many bidonvilles into the urban fabric—some of the leading architects and urban planners at the time considered that the restructuration of shantytowns in situ would imply the permanent *"bidonvillisation"* of the city center and, as a result, this would negatively impact the future economic development of Casablanca, that is, within a neoliberal spatial logic (Navez-Bouchanine and Berry-Chikhaoui 2005, 66). Ben M'sik, a large "restructured" slum in the eastern part of the city, was one of the epicenters of the 1981 disturbances and this probably contributed to the shift in focus from restructuration to relocation (Naciri 1987).

A second agency that was created following the elaboration of the new master plan, the Agence Urbaine de Casablanca (AUC, Urban Agency of Casablanca), was of even greater significance. The AUC was Morocco's first technocratic urban planning agency. Its main task was the implementation and elaboration of the recommendations prescribed by the new master plan. The Moroccan authorities needed an agency with the capacity to map the urban territory as well as its demography to increase visibility. One of the tasks of the AUC was to gather all the economic, social, demographic, and financial statistics about the city of Casablanca (Cattedra 2001, 140).

Politically, the creation of the AUC should not be misunderstood. It was granted extensive powers in urban planning and policy at the cost of the decentralized government bodies (Philifert 2016). The director of the AUC has the status of a governor. He is nominated by the king and directly accountable to the Ministry of Interior. Next to the wali of Casablanca, the governor of the AUC is the most powerful person in the city. As such, the AUC was another example of how the Ministry of Interior established its domination over the urban territory of Casablanca at the expense of all other local actors. The AUC disposes of considerable public powers: it has the right to expropriate, the right of preemption, and also the autonomy to expand its own property reserves. The AUC could also intervene in the market and influence land prices by selling or buying land on its own account (Moujid 1989).

The AUC model was subsequently adopted in other Moroccan cities. Following the *dahir* of September 10, 1993, all major cities in Morocco established their own urban agency in the following years. The policies and interventions issued by the urban agencies and the powers they exercise are often a source of conflict between them and the locally elected representatives who consider the urban agencies as local agents of central power. The agencies, for their part, claim to be an alternative to the clientelist practices of local politicians and their lack of an overall and integrated urban policy (Philifert 2011).

In comparison to the other urban agencies, the AUC remains unique. While the other urban agencies are placed under the authority of the Ministry of Housing, the AUC still remains, to the present day, a deconcentrated department of the Ministry of Interior. And unlike the AUC governor, none of the directors of the other urban agencies have the status of governor. The AUC thus remains the privileged instrument of the Ministry of Interior to control the increasing complexity of Casablanca's urbanization.

This role of the Ministry of Interior cannot be understated. It acts as the sovereign power on Casablanca. In April 1985 this was demonstrated again when the government transferred the ministerial authority over urban planning from the then Ministry of Urbanism, Housing, Tourism and Environment back to the Ministry of Interior. The former was reduced to a Ministry of Housing.[27] Moreover, it was no coincidence that the master plan, published in April 1984, was only ratified in May 1985, one month after the transfer of power from the Ministry of Urbanism to the Ministry of Interior (Cattedra 2001, 141).

After the administrative division of the city and the establishment of the *wilaya*, the AUC, and the ANHI, central power managed to get a firm grip on the urban planning of Casablanca. It ensured spatial visibility and, consequently, political stability.[28] To quote Raffaele Cattedra, the ministry effectively succeeded after 1981 in "territorializing its own power" (2001, 141–42). And until the end of the 1990s, sovereign city planning was the dominant mode of operation.

A first sign toward a paradigm shift was the creation of a new and stronger Ministry for National Planning, Environment, Urbanism and Housing under the *alternance* government of 1998 (see chapter 2). The new government transferred the powers over urban planning from the Ministry of Interior back to a technocratic ministry under control of the elected national government. However, this form of democratization should not be overestimated, according to a Moroccan urbanist: "It is [still] the Ministry of Interior who really governs the cities. . . . The ministry of urbanism has the possibility to define the norms, but nothing really more than that" (interview, Rabat, April 21, 2009, conducted with Sami Zemni).

Urban Restructuring and State Architecture in Casablanca

Sovereign city planning in Morocco had significant spatial implications. Administrative division and the agencification of urban authority would only make sense if the territorialization of power would also be visible. In spite of the then economic crisis, public authorities invested heavily in the spatial reorganization of Casablanca (Kaioua 1996; Moujid 1989; Naciri 1987, 1989; Rachik 1995, 2002). The restraints of the public deficit and the pressures of the IMF to cut back public spending did not constrain Moroccan authorities from intervening in the restructuring of the city. For the first time, the authorities planned the integration of *all* bidonvilles—at least they talked about it—and they planned the elaboration of a whole new road network for the city.

In the following years, new social housing projects, new roads, the installation of police stations in the urban peripheries, and above all the construction of the majestic prefectural headquarters gave a face to the state in those neighborhoods where it was previously absent (Naciri 1989). Urban redevelopment and renovation—especially the renovation of the Mohammed V and the United Nations squares—were meant to give testimony to the greatness and prosperity of Casablanca (Rachik 1995, 71–72).

Two additional objectives were delineated in the SDAU: the renovation of the city center and the construction of new prefectural buildings. These buildings, their decoration, their grandeur, and the open space that surrounds them stand out in stark contrast to the impoverished and monotonous apartment buildings in the immediate surroundings.

According to Mohamed Naciri, these buildings represented not only the preoccupation of central power with the control of the peripheries of the country's most important city but also the desire to implant new beacons of modernity in the midst of degraded urban areas, often stereotyped as the antithesis of modernity. The new majestic prefectural edifices demonstrated the state's clear intention to be overtly and physically present in peripheral districts such as Ain Sebaa, Ben M'sik, and Aïn Chock (Naciri 1987). Moreover, these prefectural palaces were considered the first step in the creation of additional urban centers within the territory of Greater Casablanca and eventually attractions for private investment.

At the same time, these spatial interventions turned the urban territory into a more calculable and governable space. The urban restructurings sought to improve the control over urban residents and their movements. For example, in an attempt "to curb the habits of [the] unruly inhabitants," some specific urban interventions disentangled the densely populated peripheries by opening up Casablanca's impoverished peripheries, making them more accessible and improving the connection between different nodes of capitalist production and exchange throughout the city (Ossman 1994, 30).

This not only opened up urban space but also drew new boundaries in the process. For example, a new highway between Rabat and Casablanca finished in the mid-1980s, connecting the capital with the airport of Casablanca, literally splitting the city in two, and forming a physical barrier between the predominantly working-class periphery and the city center (Cattedra 2001, 143; Ossman 1994, 30–31).

Today, the urban space of Casablanca is split up by large boulevards. This not only improved the mobility of capital and labor but also increased the speed of urban life in general—with the boulevard as its symbolic pinnacle—leading to the constant circulation of goods, capital, and people. Yet, on the other hand, it has reduced people's capacity to stand still, wonder, think, and—if necessary—mobilize.[29] The enlargement and renovation of the road network in Casablanca in the 1980s specifically aimed to make urban circulation more fluid, ensure spatial visibility, and improve the physical integration of (and consequently the control over) the urban periphery (Rachik 1995, 80–82).

Additionally, monumental state architecture aimed to incite loyalty to the Moroccan sovereign. Two megaprojects in particular symbolized this rationality of sovereign city planning in the 1980s: the Mosque Hassan II and the project of the Royal Avenue. These two large-scale "neo-Haussmanian" projects had to represent the power of the sovereign at the urban scale (Catusse, Cattedra, and Janati 2005).

The Mosque Hassan II

The first project, the impressive Mosque Hassan II, was a royal project imposed on the city by a sovereign decision of the king himself. Not even the master plan elaborated by Michel Pinseau mentioned any plans to build the mosque.

The Mosque Hassan II is located at the shoreline right in front of the old medina and is constructed partially on the water. Today, it is the second largest mosque in the world and it has the largest minaret (two hundred meters). It took six years (1987–93) and fifty million man-hours to build the mosque. Designed by Pinseau, the impressive mosque can accommodate up to twenty-five thousand people, while another eighty thousand can be received on the extensive esplanade (Roberson 2014, 75). In order to finance the project, King Hassan II launched the idea of a national subscription, a "voluntary contribution" by every Moroccan citizen. Those who contributed were awarded a special certificate.[30] After forty days, officials claimed they had raised approximately 3 billion dirhams, or two-thirds of the then estimated total budget of the project (Cattedra 2001, 177).

Raffaele Cattedra shows how the Mosque Hassan II played an important symbolic role in what he calls the "reconfessionalization" of the city. It was the showpiece by which the city was reclaimed ideologically. The appeal of the radical left and secular politics among a large part of the emerging middle class and trade union militants, on the one hand, and the proliferation of new mosques and the emergence of Islamist movements

Mosque Hassan II in Casablanca. Photograph by the author, 2009.

in the urban peripheries, on the other hand, were considered important political threats to the stability of the monarchy. Moreover, events on the international scene, more specifically the Iranian revolution, had demonstrated the real danger of political Islam (Roberson 2014).[31]

The signature mosque was supposed to give back the city of Casablanca—a city that had been turned into a financial and economic center since the protectorate without much consideration for local tradition and culture—its image of a Muslim city. During the protectorate, the French never provided the space in the *ville nouvelle* for the building of religious monuments. Consequently, the city lacked the necessary infrastructural symbols to be perceived as a Muslim city in the collective imagination (Cattedra 2001). Now dominating the skyline of Casablanca, the Mosque Hassan II became a new focal point that was clearly Muslim and reminded all those who approached the city, by land or by sea, that they had arrived in an Islamic country (Roberson 2014, 74–75).

At the same time, the mosque had to reestablish the religious authority of the king as the "Commander of the Faithful." The mosque's architectural grandeur was in itself a reflection of the monarchy's power and a material reference to its religious ideology as one of its main pillars of legitimation: "Given the turbulence of the 1970s and 1980s, it is not surprising that Hassan II sought new ways to visually cement his position and distract from dissent" (Roberson 2014, 73). It lent, Jennifer Roberson argues, "a sense of permanence and legitimacy to the king, who was both a political and spiritual leader and a descendant of the Prophet Mohamed's family" (60).

Finally, the mosque was not only instrumental in the creation of a national identity loyal to the monarch. The project also fit perfectly in a new neoliberal development strategy for the city as it sought to draw tourists to Morocco and bolster the local economy. It was one of the first projects in Morocco that exemplified a new vision: waterfront development. Today, the mosque is a tourist landmark and the only mosque in Morocco open to non-Muslims (Roberson 2014, 80).

The Royal Avenue

The second project, the Royal Avenue, also characterized the new neoliberal spatial logic for the city of Casablanca. Again, it entailed a rather sudden sovereign decision by Hassan II, as this project was not mentioned in Pinseau's master plan either. The project itself, however, never materialized. Nevertheless, it already reflected the new project-based approach to urban planning that would become paradigmatic under Mohammed VI's reign.

This urban renewal project involved the creation of a completely redesigned axis, 1.5 kilometers long and 60 meters wide, connecting the shoreline in front of the medina and the Mosque Hassan II with the inner city center and the United Nations square. The Royal Avenue was to be situated alongside the historic medina and entailed the redevelopment of Casablanca's center in order to meet the desires of tourists, investors, and the city's upper-class residents.

Besides the image of an Islamic city, this project had to present another image to the outside world: an image of a vibrant and dynamic city, not that of a violent and riotous city. The project included among other things the construction of high-end and middle-class apartments, a new commercial center, a conference center, and a theater. The realization of all these plans would require the relocation of more than twelve thousand families (sixty thousand people) out of the historical city center. Faced with the complexity and magnitude of the project, the public authorities entrusted the Société nationale d'aménagement communal (SONADAC, National Company for Municipal Planning)—a semipublic agency created in 1991 and placed under the supervision of the Ministry of Interior—with the coordination of the project (Berry-Chikhaoui 2010, 219).

A first resettlement program was launched in 1995. The urban residential estate of Attacharouk became home to 530 resettled families. Since 1997, the plan was to relocate the remaining people to the new site of Nassim, almost ten kilometers from the city center (Berry-Chikhaoui 2010; Navez-Bouchanine and Berry-Chikhaoui 2005). Between 1998 and 2002 about two thousand households were relocated. Since then, however, the project has slowed down considerably due to operational and financial problems and increasing resistance from the inhabitants. By 2009, no more than three thousand households were relocated out of the total twelve thousand planned in the beginning (Berry-Chikhaoui 2010).

Françoise Navez-Bouchanine and Isabelle Berry-Chikhaoui (2005) detail the authoritarian and sovereign character of this kind of development strategy. Preference was clearly given to the market value of the urban site, while the original inhabitants of the site did not take part whatsoever in the decision-making process. They were informed neither before nor during the course of the project.

The inhabitants themselves resisted the project and the conditions of their relocation. The site of Nassim was much less interesting than their current living place because it was located at the periphery of the city; relocation would disrupt the social and economic links that were established with neighboring central districts, and in particular with the souks of the old medina (Berry-Chikhaoui 2010, 224). Local residents used a wide variety of tactics to delay the advancement of the project (see Navez-Bouchanine and Berry-Chikhaoui 2005, 53–57). In the end, the project failed. Today, the only remnants of the project are a big empty space and some worn-out billboards. As such, the failure of the Royal Avenue illustrated why entities such as AAVB in the Bouregreg project are deemed necessary.

To summarize, the urban renovations of the 1980s with flagship projects such as the Mosque Hassan II and the Royal Avenue—but also the construction of the prefectural headquarters, the renovations of major squares, and the expansion of the road network—materialized sovereign city planning in the 1980s. Together with the administrative division of the city and the creation of new state agencies, these interventions

The remains of the billboard announcing the project of the Royal Avenue. Photograph by the author, 2009.

The Royal Avenue. Photograph by the author, 2009.

symbolized the territorialization of power with an authoritarian vision of urban renovation. The mosque and the Royal Avenue were royal projects subject to the decision of the Moroccan sovereign and constructed to glorify the monarchy.

The use of sovereign power during the era of structural adjustment in the 1980s was an attempt to stabilize the temporarily unstable and disturbing period between the dismantlement of the old social order of developmentalism and the creation and consolidation of a new one based on a neoliberal governmentality. It did so by monopolizing urban territory and installing a new central command apparatus with the *wilaya* and agencies such as AUC and ANHI. At the same time, sovereign city planning ensured the interests of capital by guaranteeing better circulation and repressing dissent. The securitization of urban space should thus be considered as an integral part of early neoliberal reform and structural adjustment in Morocco.

In the end, however, the territorial focus of the reforms of the 1980s caused other key political and social questions to remain unaddressed. The disturbances that caused the authorities to engage in sovereign city planning were never really solved in a sustainable way. The new master plan of 1984 and the specific objectives of newly created institutions like the *wilaya*, ANHI, or AUC made clear that the Moroccan authorities would repress or deal with increased social tensions in a technocratic and sovereign way rather than in a comprehensive social and political way. As such, the era of sovereign city planning failed to take into account the social complexity of the city as a whole and avoided pressing political questions about the future of its urban population. Despite the massive reorganization of urban space in Morocco, little attention was paid to root causes like increasing social inequality, which were, after all, the basis for the riots in the first place.

6

POWER AND CONTROL
THROUGH TECHNIQUES
OF SECURITY

The bourgeoisie is not interested in the mad, but it is interested in power over the mad; the bourgeoisie is not interested in the sexuality of children, but it is interested in the system of power that controls the sexuality of children. The bourgeoisie does not give a damn about delinquents, or about how they are punished or rehabilitated, as that is of no great economic interest. On the other hand, the set of mechanisms whereby delinquents are controlled, kept track of, punished, and reformed does generate a bourgeois interest that functions within the economico-political system as a whole.
—Michel Foucault, *Society Must Be Defended*

Urban segregation is not a frozen status quo, but rather a ceaseless social war in which the state intervenes regularly in the name of "progress," "beautification," and even "social justice for the poor" to redraw spatial boundaries to the advantage of landowners, foreign investors, elite homeowners, and middle-class commuters. As in 1860s Paris under the financial reign of Baron Haussmann, urban redevelopment still strives to simultaneously maximize private profit and social control.
—Mike Davis, *Planet of Slums*

A KEY ARGUMENT IN THIS BOOK is that we can distinguish a governmental shift in the ways the city, and slums particularly, are governed over the last three decades and that this shift illustrates broader shifts within neoliberalism itself.[1] More specifically, this governmental shift illustrates the transition from a phase of roll-back neoliberalism in which the governmental apparatuses and mechanisms of state developmentalism were dismantled to a phase of roll-out neoliberalism characterized by the creation of new "apparatuses of security" aiming to consolidate neoliberal government in Morocco.[2]

The Cities Without Slums (VSB) program generally failed to fulfill its promises. Instead of reducing urban poverty it only—or even intentionally—succeeded in displacing that poverty. Moreover, in many cases it exacerbated urban poverty and underdevelopment: many resettlement projects had a negative impact on the education of youth, on the participation and integration of women in new neighborhoods, on solidarity networks between residents, on consumption patterns, on social mobility, and so forth (Bartoli 2011; Mansion and Rachmuhl 2012; Toutain and Rachmuhl 2014; World Bank 2006a). These results are not exceptional; they are comparable to the impact of slum upgrading in other parts of the Global South (Huchzermeyer 2008; Milbert 2006; Roy 2005).

However, my goal is not so much to assess the social impact or technical efficiency of slum upgrading in Morocco, its successes and failures, but to understand the political rationale behind a program such as VSB. While the social impact of VSB is of course crucial, I argue that the political significance of this program lies elsewhere. VSB symbolizes a changing relationship between those who govern and the governed, and among the governed themselves. As such, I try to understand neoliberalism here not so much as a doctrine or an ideology but as a biopolitical *practice*—as a technology of power or a political project shaped by biopower—aiming to establish both security and economic "freedom" (Wallenstein 2010, 189, 201; see also chapter 5).

I focus thus on the apparatuses or techniques of security introduced by the VSB program that were designed to govern the slum population, or at least make them more governable. These techniques mark a break with the dominant practices of the 1980s. The dismantling of the developmentalist order, through interventions of structural adjustment and privatization, heavily relied on sovereign power to impose and protect it. In contrast, the beginning of the twenty-first century was characterized by attempts to build and consolidate a new social order in which biopower replaced sovereign power again as the dominant force shaping authoritarian rule.

During the period of roll-back neoliberalism, the safety of the monarch was the main concern. This can be interpreted in two ways: symbolically, he represented the state power that pushed through radical economic reforms; literally, Hassan II himself had been the target of two coups in the early 1970s and the monarchy as an institution was profoundly shaken by the riots of the early 1980s. Yet sovereign repression and violence eventually gave way to a fundamentally different kind of exertion of power oriented toward the management of future risks, especially with regard to the slum population and the issues of radicalism and terrorism.[3]

Techniques of security "work on details" (Valverde 2007, 170). Rather than imposing a grand scheme to improve urban territorial control, they facilitate the detailed regulation of specific groups of people (e.g., the slum population). These new technologies require mechanisms of urban planning, or rather regulation, in which life is administered, regulated, and policed, almost at an individual level.

The shift I am pointing to can be situated both in a changing national and international context responding to the challenges and failures of the 1980s (see chapter 5) as well as in a new outbreak of urban violence: the suicide bombings of 2003. This time, however, the Casablanca attacks exposed a danger or threat that was not challenging the political order directly. Its motivations were much less clear compared to a general strike led by unions or a food riot. A new, more incalculable, threat was exposed, much more obscure and unexpected, a threat from within the slums and the slum population itself that seemed to aim for the destabilization of Moroccan society as a whole.

From Repression to Integration: Techniques of Security in the Twenty-First Century

The expansion of urban territorial control in the 1980s did not, in the end, bring forth a sustainable solution. The resettlement operations of ANHI were quite effective in smaller cities but less successful in bigger cities due to land scarcity, speculation, the reluctance of people to move from their original living place, and the inability of slum dwellers to finance the resettlement (Lahzem 1995; Navez-Bouchanine 2002c). Many operations in bigger cities were either postponed or delayed.

One of the reasons for the failure of slum resettlement in the 1980s can be found in the contradictions of roll-back neoliberalism itself. Despite obvious efforts to reorganize the urban space after 1981, the coinciding structural adjustment policies deprived the state of the necessary financial means to plan and fund heavily subsidized public housing programs. As such, a kind of paradox arose. On the one hand, the state strengthened its control over the urban territory (with the *wilaya*, AUC, ANHI, etc.) and, consequently, it became increasingly difficult to expand the city informally. On the other hand, this increasing territorial control coincided with the financial disengagement of the state in the provision of low-cost housing (Lahzem 1995; Nachoui 1998).

Structural adjustment led to the liberalization of the housing market and the emergence of a strong private real estate sector that gained an increasing share of the market in the beginning of the 1990s. For example, in 1994 King Hassan II launched the ambitious "200,000 houses" plan (of which 70,000 were to be built in Casablanca alone). Seventy-eight percent of this plan was realized by the private sector, while previously the public sector usually financed two-thirds of the housing projects (Zaki 2011b).

The strong growth of the private sector in the housing market undermined the affordability of real estate. Especially in cities like Casablanca, prices skyrocketed due to increasing speculation. The urban poor, for whom the housing schemes were intended, found themselves unable to afford them; their places were often taken by a better-off middle class. This was typical also in other countries where state control was replaced by market-price mechanisms (Huchzermeyer 2008; Milbert 2006). Consequently, the already significant overpopulation in existing informal settlements increased (Lahzem 1995).

It was not until the suicide bombings in 2003 that the Moroccan government seriously renewed its efforts to eradicate all slums in the country. Two important differences with the policies of the 1980s are evident. First, the state would now play a more prominent role in supporting the private sector in slum resettlement operations. In the big cities, the resettlement operations encountered serious speculative, financial, and social obstacles and required more engaged state intervention (Navez-Bouchanine and Berry-Chikhaoui 2005, 67). New state arrangements were created to manage the operations on the ground and coordinate the public–private partnerships.

Second, there was a different approach toward the slum population itself. In the past, ANHI cared little about the participation of the slum residents themselves and pushed through many operations in a very top-down and repressive manner (Philifert and Jolé 2005, 393). After the crisis of 2003, *participation* and *consent* became key concepts within the new methodology of slum upgrading.

The new methods of security not only encouraged the participation of the slum population; they also entailed an increasing administration of life in the slums itself. The main concern was how the slum population could be rendered more visible, calculable, and eventually more productive. New biopolitical techniques focused not only on territorial control but on the transformation of urban life itself.

Toward an Active Management of the Slum Population

In 2002 the then Ministry of Housing, Urbanism and Spatial Planning (MHUAE) defined the bidonville as "an anarchic ensemble of houses, built with anomalistic materials, deprived of hygiene and collective services and populated by indigent people or people badly integrated in the urban fabric" (Zaki 2005, 53).[4] This definition neglects the more structural causes for the existence of slums and places the responsibility for the lack of integration on the inhabitants themselves (Zaki 2005, 53). It is also silent about probably the most economically important characteristic of the bidonville, namely the illegal occupancy of land, and permits the official discourse to obfuscate one of the basic dynamics behind their "management by absence": toleration as a form of control (see chapter 5). This management by absence had become untenable: the crisis of 2003 had turned the *active management* of the slum space into a perceived urgency.

This active management was based on a particular "politics of truth" within neoliberal governmentality that represented the slums as not really belonging to the city (Lemke 2002). Physically, the slum space had its characteristic features (small and shabby, usually ground floor, shelters with corrugated tin roofs) that made it seem very different and separated from the formal bricked city. In the eyes of both the slum dwellers and all other urban residents, the "real city" was constructed *"en dur,"* in brick, despite the fact that slums were often located right within the city center (Zaki 2005, 52).

Moreover, this perceived exclusion of the slum dweller was not only limited to physical aspects. It was often believed that the expansion of slums (mostly due to a rural exodus) and their integration in the urban space had not led to a modern urban lifestyle (Ibrahim 1975). Slums, in other words, were stigmatized as the emblem of a creeping "ruralization" of the city: their inhabitants maintained a so-called rural mentality and were not yet adapted to modern city life (Zaki 2005, 67–69; see also Bayat and Denis 2000).

The "formal" represented the ordered city—both in terms of its urban and architectural shape as in terms of the cultural, economic, political, and social organization of space—while the "informal" represented the opposite: shapeless urban areas where economic and sociopolitical structures are unstable and where culture is characterized as more "traditional" (Hernández and Kellett 2010, 1).

This particular social and spatial imagination of the formal and the informal not only essentialized the slum as a homogenous unity threatening the city and its public life; it also presented the slum as a space to be governed separate from the spatial problematic of the city as a whole. It neglects the many ways in which both parts of the city are intimately connected socially, culturally, politically, and economically.

The new techniques of active management and slum upgrading, backed by the Millennium Development Goals (MDGs), prioritized "integration" and "participation." Not only in Morocco, but internationally, there was a shift from repressive approaches aiming to eradicate slums to one seeking to assimilate the slum population (Bolay 2006).[5] UN-Habitat (2003, 71–72), for example, advocated for a more participatory approach to development policies, "incorporating the poor within the design and implementation of development projects" as a necessary precondition to tackle urban poverty. "Participatory development," "community empowerment," and "bottom-up" became the buzzwords of development's new orthodoxy (Kapoor 2008, 60; see also Parker and Debruyne 2012).

According to Mark Duffield, this reinvention of social policy entailed a "radicalization of development" as policies and interventions not simply aimed to alleviate poverty but were directly concerned with "attempting to transform societies as a whole, reconstructing social relationships anew and, especially, changing behaviour and attitudes" (2002, 1066–67). Instead of simply trying to improve the physical conditions in which slum dwellers live, the idea was to change their mentality, their way of life. All this was driven by the concern that underdevelopment, and more precisely absolute poverty, had become a threat to modern society and its status quo (Duffield 2002, 1066).

This became painfully clear on May 16, 2003, when suicide bombings caused a shockwave within Moroccan society and among the ruling elite. Five simultaneous attacks in the center of Casablanca killed more than forty people. Eleven of the fourteen perpetrators came from Douar Thomas, one of the larger shantytowns in the district of Sidi

Moumen in the eastern periphery of the city. The events strengthened the perception of the slums as a breeding ground for radical Islamism and terrorism.

The Moroccan authorities took immediate action by arresting thousands of Islamists and pushing through a new antiterrorism law within two weeks after the bombings (Zemni and Bogaert 2006). Perhaps more important, the authorities launched, within months after the attacks and instructed by the king himself, the national Cities Without Slums program. The INDH program would quickly follow in its footsteps.

Although VSB itself was clearly a response to the events of 2003, the particular content of the program reflected an ongoing transformation. The rationality behind VSB was a product of a new development paradigm promoted by international organizations such as the World Bank and UN-Habitat. At the same time, it also reflected an ongoing policy evolution within the country itself. Between 1999 and 2001, more than sixty workshops and forums on the local, regional, and national level were organized and directed by the Ministry of Housing.[6] The aim was to develop a critical and interdisciplinary approach to public urban intervention and discuss the social impact of all dimensions of slum clearance and resettlement (Navez-Bouchanine 2002a, 2004, 2009; see also Philifert 2014; Zaki 2005). The new political space created by the *alternance* government of 1998 and the willingness to break with the "years of lead" of the Hassan II era had initiated a thorough reflection on urban planning, sustainable development, and more concretely on the social dimension of slum clearance. These debates within the Ministry of Housing resulted in the elaboration of a new concept, *"maîtrise d'ouvrage social"* (MOS, social management), which eventually constituted a policy guideline for the massive slum interventions within the framework of VSB.

MOS conceptualized an integrated approach in which both the technical and the social dimensions of slum resettlement projects are *equally* valued. Furthermore, it promoted a contextualized approach to public intervention, in contrast to centralized and standardized planning, and emphasized the participation of the local population as a key for success (Berra and Kourar 2004; Debbi and Toutain 2002; Navez-Bouchanine 2002a, 2004). The Agence de Développement Social (ADS, Social Development Agency), created in 1999, played an important role in developing a modus operandi for MOS (Bogaert 2013a).

Last but not least, this paradigm shift in social development also created the space for the cooperation with other actors on the ground such as NGOs, local associations, foreign development agencies (e.g., USAID or the French Development Agency [AFD]), international donors, and private companies (both foreign and domestic); that is, it created the space for an increasing privatization of the state (see chapter 5).

A National "Cities Without Slums" Program

The Cities Without Slums (VSB) program was launched in 2004 following an address from the throne in July 2003 emphasizing the pressing challenges and threats of urban marginalization and calling for immediate action. VSB explicitly commits itself to the MDGs (Al Omrane 2010). The program targeted 362,000 households (approximately 1.8 million inhabitants) spread over a thousand bidonvilles in eighty-five Moroccan cities and towns. The overall cost was estimated to be 25 billion dirhams, of which 10 billion dirhams is funded by the state via the Fonds Solidarité de l'Habitat (FSH, Solidarity Fund for Housing). The resources of the FSH are generated by a tax per kilo of cement sold in Morocco.[7]

Additionally, the state supports the program by making public land available for resettlement operations. As such, more than 3,500 hectares of land were integrated in the VSB program (Effina 2011, 48), to be sold at one-fifth of the market price to the eventual beneficiaries (Toutain 2014). Furthermore, VSB is supported financially (through gifts or loans) by various international agencies and donors such as the European Investment Bank, the AFD, and the World Bank. Agencies such as USAID provided VSB with foreign expertise and assistance to local governments via the nonprofit institute RTI International (Arandel and Wetterberg 2013; USAID 2007).

The deadline for the finalization of the VSB program was initially 2010 but was then quickly extended to 2012 and later 2015. Today, there does not really seem to be a deadline anymore. Nevertheless, VSB has achieved considerable results, according to its officials. In July 2016 Minister of Housing Nabil Benabdallah declared fifty-six cities slum free and claimed that more than 248,659 families saw their living conditions improved.[8] Since the launch of the program, the total slum population decreased from 8.2 percent in 2004 to 3.9 percent in 2010, according to official numbers (Toutain and Rachmuhl 2013, 2014). As a result, Morocco received the UN-Habitat Scroll of Honour Award in 2010 for delivering, according to UN-Habitat, "one of the world's most successful and comprehensive slum reduction and improvement programmes."[9]

Overall, when we look at the history of slum upgrading and slum clearance in Morocco, three particular strategies to reintegrate slums were used. First was restructuration, which means that the slum space is reorganized and improved on the spot (by improving access to services like water and electricity, paving roads, fortifying houses, etc.). But the restructuration of slums in Morocco (slum upgrading) was abandoned after the Casablanca riots in 1981 in favor of a second strategy: resettlement *(recasement)*. This implies the allocation of serviced plots to households that they have to develop themselves via assisted self-build housing schemes (very often in co-ownership). The third strategy was rehousing *(relogement)*. In these kinds of operations, the slum dwellers are transferred to new apartments in multidwelling units built for them by a public or private developer.

The resettlement, for example, of approximately 8,400 households from Casablanca's two most infamous bidonvilles, Douar Skouila (6,000 households) and Douar Thomas (2,400 households), notorious for their link with the bombings of 2003, combined the resettling of some families on the spot while moving others to Essalam, a seventy-one hectare site about seven kilometers from Douar Thomas but closer to Douar Skouila, at the outskirts of the city (Mansion and Rachmuhl 2012; Toutain and Rachmuhl 2014).

VSB prioritizes the resettlement of inhabitants (Le Tellier 2009b)—80 percent of the operations involve resettlement. Preference is given to this strategy for obvious reasons. First, there are security reasons: the slum areas were inaccessible places and the state authorities had little hold on those who lived within these densely populated spaces. The relocation of the population to new estates (less dense, with wider roads, better planned, etc.) obviously made these places and their population more visible and governable.

Second, resettlement is also the cheapest and easiest solution because public authorities only have to make sure that land is available and eventually bear the costs of public services (roads, transport, electricity, water). The beneficiaries finance the construction of their new house and sometimes part of the land price as well.

Finally, other economic interests explain the preference given to resettlement. In the past, resettlement operations turned out to be motivated more by the desire to recover valuable land occupied by slum dwellers than by a genuine concern for the social needs and problems of the urban poor. Moreover, having slums in the urban center could have a negative impact on the city's image and its "unique selling position" (Le Tellier 2009a; Navez-Bouchanine 2002c; Navez-Bouchanine and Berry-Chikhaoui 2005). Consequently, many resettlement operations were located at the outskirts of the city or even further away.

A New Coordinating State Agency: Holding Al Omrane

In the past resettlement projects coped with difficulties such as affordability, real estate speculation, the lack of public services, and the resistance of beneficiaries to move for a variety of reasons (distance, money, work-related issues) (Le Tellier and Guérin 2009; Navez-Bouchanine 2002c). Within the framework of the VSB program, a whole new series of methods, instruments, and governmental arrangements were put in place to make future operations more effective and transparent.

A first set of measures tightened administrative supervision and tried to keep the costs for slum dwellers under control. Land acquisitions were subsidized, social housing prices fixed, and private developers supported by means of financial and fiscal incentives. Additionally, slum dwellers were now required to destroy their former shelters before being allowed to move to their new place and build a new house. This implied an increase of administrative procedures and control (architectural plans, authorizations, tax registrations, etc.).

The increasing complexity of the operations on the ground required more central coordination. ANHI merged with other local public housing agencies to form Holding Al Omrane. This new state agency was placed under the authority of the Ministry of Housing but has to operate as a financially autonomous limited company (société anonyme). The agency, as an Al Omrane official explained, is "the armed force of the Ministry [of Housing]" (interview, Rabat, June 4, 2010). Al Omrane is responsible for more than 80 percent of the projects within the framework of VSB. Besides resettlement operations, the holding also invests in other real estate projects such as the creation of new towns or satellite towns (e.g., Tamesna near Rabat) and more high-end and tourist projects.

In fact, Al Omrane is one of the biggest real estate investors in Morocco. As a result, the agency often causes resentment from the private sector, which accuses Al Omrane of unfair competition because of their access to public land (Zaki 2011b). Nevertheless, Al Omrane works closely with the private sector, and VSB relies strongly on public–private partnerships (PPPs). Al Omrane usually puts state land at the disposal of the private sector, and in return, the latter commits to building a certain amount of social housing (depending on the land surface). Not only Moroccan companies profit: more than thirty-five international developers (62 percent of foreign capital in the Moroccan real estate sector) have benefited from a collaboration with Al Omrane (Effina 2011, 321).

Since the 1990s, public authorities have tried to actively involve the private sector through tax exemptions and financial incentives specifically designed to encourage private investment. Yet the VSB program intensified the participation of private capital at a scale never done before. As noted by Olivier Toutain, a French architect who worked as a consultant for the VSB program: "The partnerships set up under these programmes undoubtedly helped to re-energise the production of social housing, structure the private sector and facilitate the emergence of large Moroccan real estate groups: Addoha, Chaabi and Alliance" (2014, 25; see also Zaki 2011b).[10]

New Governance Frameworks and the Exceptional Case of Casablanca

A second set of measures within the VSB framework seeks to increase the transparency of the resettlement projects in order to break with some of the clientelist practices and corruption of the past. To give a very concrete example, one of the new measures to assure more transparency on the ground within the individual projects was the allocation of plots and apartments by public drawing lots (Le Tellier and Guérin 2009, 671).

At a more institutional level, new mechanisms were developed to deal with the multiplicity of actors on the ground. The major partners of the VSB program were, on the one hand, public actors such as the Ministries of Interior, Finance and Housing, the deconcentrated authorities (the *wilaya*), the decentralized authorities (municipalities), and the technical operators (urban agencies, regional inspections of urban planning, Al Omrane). But the VSB framework also integrated private actors such as NGOs and civil society organizations, consultants, international cooperation representatives, the private (real estate) sector, and of course the slum dwellers themselves.

To coordinate all this, a new "governance framework" was set up at different scales: a national follow-up committee presided over by the prime minister and directed by the Ministry of Housing, a regional coordination committee headed by the wali, and a provincial or prefectural committee of identification and implementation headed by the local governor (MHU 2012, 20–21). Within this new governance framework, the regional authorities (the wali and the governors) take the lead. The contribution of local elected officials is minimal and often contradictory because they fear losing part of their electorate once a slum population is relocated (Le Tellier 2009b; Mansion and Rachmuhl 2012; Toutain 2008; Zaki 2005).

A complementary initiative and so-called example of "good governance" is the "city contract," a contractual mechanism to assure the implementation of VSB objectives at the local level and to commit all partners on the ground to these specific objectives. Every contract stipulates the areas of intervention, the nature of the operations to be realized, the financial contributions of each partner, and the social assistance measures to be taken (Al Omrane 2010). In total, sixty-four city contracts were closed in the framework of the VSB program.

Interestingly, however, there is no such city contract in Casablanca. Again, the white city remains an exceptional case, which demonstrates its political importance. Despite the fact that Al Omrane is supervising large resettlement operations in the district of Sidi Moumen (e.g., Douar Skouila and Douar Thomas), the city has not signed a city contract because this would have entailed a decrease of the influence of the Ministry of Interior. Moreover, the latter reasserted its grip on the city by taking away operations from Al Omrane in the rest of Casablanca. Most of the operations in the city—concerning approximately 34,500 households—were supervised by another public agency: Idmaj Sakan. This state agency was created in 2005 and is supervised by the wali of Casablanca.

It is illustrative that the 2006 action plan of Idmaj Sakan situated its objectives explicitly within the framework of the INDH, a program coordinated by the Ministry of Interior, and not within the VSB program, which is coordinated by the Ministry of Housing (Idmaj Sakan 2006). Despite the similar social objectives between VSB and INDH, the programs reveal an interinstitutional rivalry between the Ministry of Housing and the Ministry of Interior (Toutain 2011). With regard to slum operations in Casablanca, the decision-making process was recentralized into the hands of the Ministry of Interior.

In a few other cases, slum resettlement operations are carried out by a third semipublic agency: Dyar Al Mansour, a subsidiary of CDG. Douar Al Kora, a major slum at the coastline in Rabat (in the direction of Temara and Casablanca), was one of the projects taken over by Dyar Al Mansour.[11] This project was originally supervised by ANHI, but the king ordered the CDG to take over in 2002 due to delays and conflicts between ANHI and the inhabitants. Douar Al Kora is also an example of a rehousing program. The resistance of the local population caused the authorities to abandon the resettlement plan and rehouse the slum dwellers on site (Essahel 2015).[12] According to Toutain, although Al Omrane may be responsible for the bulk of the slum projects, "the hot potatoes were always taken out of their hands" by operators with much closer ties to the monarchy and central power (interview, Rabat, September 10, 2013). When I asked the technical director of Dyar Al Mansour, he told me: "We intervene there where the state has difficulties to advance" (interview, Rabat, July 1, 2010).

Administering Slum Life through Innovative Social Engineering

A third set of measures dealt directly with the slum population itself and involved techniques to "administer" them, regulate them, and anticipate potential future risks from that population. Or to put it in the governance jargon of the program itself: new techniques *(dispositions)* of local management *(gestion des affaires locales)* that contribute to the optimization of financial means and the rationalization of human resources (MHU 2012, 14).

New mechanisms of "social engineering" replaced the old methods of force and repression. Due to the often fragile and mistrustful relationship between the inhabitants and public authorities, the new governmental methods had to intervene more at the level of the individual to facilitate cooperation, to ensure the slum dweller's acceptance of the project, to help them with their move, and even to reeducate them (Le Tellier 2009a, 2009b; cf. Le Tellier and Guérin 2009; Toutain 2009a).

First, one of the most important innovations was the methodology of *accompagnement social* (AS, social accompaniment). It emerged from the debates on the social impact of slum clearance in the early twenty-first century and the subsequent conceptualization of MOS. AS seeks to enhance the "active participation" of the inhabitants and facilitate the more technical aspects of resettlement. It involves a set of methodological guidelines to accompany—literally—the slum dweller through the whole process of moving to a new place. It aims to improve the different aspects of public intervention in the slums (identification of the beneficiaries, definition of the criteria and modalities of allocation, promotion of the technical operation) and to establish better contact and relations of trust with the inhabitants (MHU 2004).

AS is carried out by *cellules d'accompagnement sociale* (CAS, social accompaniment teams) of three to five persons set up in the shantytown.[13] They guarantee the "proximity" of public authorities and mediate between the population and a public agency such as Al Omrane (Toutain 2008). This establishment of a permanent local presence is new compared to past policies. Their job includes, among other duties, organizing workshops and information sessions with local authorities, beneficiaries, and neighborhood associations; and administrative assistance, social intermediation, and assistance with financial issues (i.e., facilitating inhabitants' access to credit and credit institutions) (Le Tellier 2009a; Toutain 2011).

A second important aspect of resettlement operations, besides the methodology of AS, was the development of new mechanisms to improve the slum dwellers' access to credit in order to purchase a new home. Ownership is central in the VSB program. Assuring home ownership and individual property rights, according to Al Omrane (2010, 5), "allows a sustained socio-economic development of beneficiary households: better access to credit, business opportunities, etcetera." The problem, however, is that the beneficiaries start off with very few means or financial capacities. Moreover, for obvious reasons, there is little trust and familiarity between the urban poor and commercial credit providers. On top of that, the interest rates that commercial banks usually charge to cover the risks are unaffordable for low-income households.

To solve this "finance gap"—a problem not unique to Morocco but applicable to many slum upgrading projects in the Global South—new arrangements were created in the wake of VSB to "bring finance to the slums" (Jones 2012). One of those was the FOGARIM convention, a guarantee fund for housing mortgages for people with low or irregular income.[14] This guarantee fund, established in 2004, allows slum dwellers to obtain a bank loan with a government guarantee up to a maximum amount of 250,000 dirhams and with an interest rate of around 6 percent. It spreads the risk between the commercial credit institutions and the state in order to facilitate access to credit for slum dwellers. FOGARIM guarantees banks a recovery of 80 percent of commercially invested capital (70 percent for non-VSB beneficiaries).

In August 2014 a total of 111,183 loans had been granted since the creation of FOGARIM, worth approximately 17 billion dirhams (MEF 2014). A large number of these loans, approximately 40 percent, went to households living in Casablanca. Yet it is important to note that FOGARIM is not limited to the VSB program alone. The number of bidonville households that used FOGARIM remains relatively limited (10 percent) compared to other populations with limited revenues, but the objective is to increase the number of slum dwellers benefiting from FOGARIM (Toutain 2009b).[15]

According to Olivier Toutain (2009b), FOGARIM is a very innovative instrument in public housing policies: there is no equivalent in the wider MENA region, albeit there are some initiatives in Tunisia and Jordan that resemble it. Morocco is one of the few countries in the world—if not the only one—where you can obtain such a loan without any proof of a stable income or guarantee of solvency. In fact, the borrower only has to deliver a declaration with his word of honor confirming the average income and the nature of his economic activities (Toutain 2009b).[16] One of the problems, however, is that instruments like FOGARIM are still little known among the poorest populations. In this regard, AS is one of the ways in which slum dwellers are informed and guided toward FOGARIM.

Besides FOGARIM, the Moroccan legislation allowed Moroccan microfinance institutions in 2004 to finance households in resettlement and restructuring operations (Le Tellier 2009a). Since the 1990s, microfinance is a booming business in Morocco, but it was only with the launch of VSB that these financial products could also be used for housing loans—although they are still a minority within the portfolio of the Moroccan microfinance institutions (MFIs). The inhabitants of the bidonvilles are a potentially valuable population for the MFIs because only 25 percent of them has access to regular banks (Le Tellier 2009a).

Compared to FOGARIM, however, there are obvious limits to microcredits. First, microcredit loans are limited to a maximum amount of 50,000 dirhams as prescribed by Moroccan law. This amount of money is never enough to finance a new apartment or a plot (with the subsequent construction), as the price of a state-subsidized housing unit varies between 140,000 dirhams and 250,000 dirhams. A state-subsidized plot still costs around 20,000 dirhams, and the construction of a unit costs at least 40,000 dirhams (i.e., the absolute basic construction) (Le Tellier 2009a). As a consequence, the majority of microcredits are used for renovations, not purchases.

Second, the interest rate is much higher (around 12 percent) than other loans such as FOGARIM. As a result, only those people with creditworthiness qualify for microfinance. This is usually also the case for FOGARIM, where only the most solvent of the urban poor have access to these kinds of loans. As a result, the success of these financial mechanisms is still limited and often too expensive for the poorest among the beneficiaries (Le Tellier 2009b, 206–10).

A final innovative mechanism was the "third-party partner" *(tiers associé)*, developed in Casablanca, more specifically in the projects of Essalam and Medinat Errahma (Toutain 2014). The principle is simple. In Casablanca, due to land scarcity and the large number of slums, two slum households (instead of one, as in most other resettlement operations) are allocated one plot. With the third-party arrangement, the two families can share their plot with a contractual partner who is ineligible for the VSB program (e.g., a small-scale developer or a real estate investor). Within the contract, the third party agrees to build a four-story housing unit for the beneficiaries, covering both their costs for the construction as well as their cost for the land. In return, the third party receives two stories (usually the ground floor and the first floor), while the two families receive one story each.

This allows poor families to obtain an apartment free of charge, while the investor benefits from the heavily subsidized land price. The third party can inhabit the other two floors, rent them, or sell them (the ground floor is often planned as a commercial space). In the context of a high-demand housing market, this arrangement potentially offers a high rate of return. The third-party partner must complete the construction within a maximum period of six months and in accordance with legal norms and requirements. In case of a delay, he or she has to cover the temporary rental costs of the beneficiaries.

Olivier Toutain (2014) argues this mechanism has been a clear success: over two-thirds of the households in the two VSB projects in Casablanca entered into a contract with a third-party partner. Moreover, the resale rate among beneficiaries *(glissements)* is significantly lower than the averages observed in other resettlement projects. Finally, although most of the third-party partners are individuals, the attractiveness of this system could well encourage more professional real estate investors and property developers to participate (Toutain 2014). With Virginie Rachmuhl, however, Toutain sketches a more nuanced image and stresses that this particular arrangement has generated a lot of disputes between the two families and the third party (Toutain and Rachmuhl 2014).

It Is All about the Numbers: The Difference between AS and MOS

It is important not to confuse the method of social accompaniment (AS) with the concept of social management (MOS) despite the fact that AS also emerged from the national debates at the beginning of the twenty-first century. MOS is an integral conceptualization of the social dimension of resettlement operations. It takes into account the social, economic, urban, fiscal, and juridical aspects of the technical operation itself, the precarious living conditions of the slum population, and the new living space to which they will be moved.

But despite the conceptualization of MOS and its extensive documentation, it has never been implemented on the ground. MOS was very ambitious and it reflected the democratic and social hopes of a new political era under the *alternance*. But just as the *alternance* government itself, the principles of MOS quickly became smothered by a neoliberal and technocratic rationale that converged with the changing political strategies of the monarchy and its new authoritarian governmentality. AS was an exponent of this evolution.

AS is far less ambitious. According to the methodological guide published by the Ministry of Housing in 2004, AS refers to a social action that is "subordinated" to the technical aspect of the resettlement operation (MHU 2004, 5). The actual transfer of the slum population to their new residence is the absolute priority. In this context, the method of AS, as I was told by the Al Omrane director in charge of quality (*directeur chargé de la qualité*), "is meant to accelerate the rhythm of social housing . . . , to put in place a measure to proceed more rapidly . . . , to put in place an arrangement to facilitate people to move." As a result, he continued, "we are now moving forty thousand households per year instead of five thousand in the past" (interview, Rabat, June 8, 2010).

In reality, it comes down to the fact that the social intermediator, for example ADS, within the AS program has to "persuade" each individual slum household to move and make him or her subscribe to the program (Mansion and Rachmuhl 2012; Navez-Bouchanine 2005b). This contrasts with the objectives of MOS, which aims at an *equal valuation* of both social and technical aspects of slum clearance. As Julien Le Tellier states:

> In reality, on the ground, it mostly comes down to making the slum
> dwellers accept the fact that they have to leave their bidonville and

that they have to destroy their shelter, but also that they have to participate in the financing of the transfer and of their new home. *In the
end*, cooperation in the projects of resettlement and rehousing materializes above all through the *financial participation* of the beneficiaries
in the costs of the operation. (2009a, 57, emphasis added)[17]

Three sorts of social intermediators were involved in AS projects: the
public Social Development Agency (ADS), NGOs, and private consultants. While ADS tried to set the standards for a comprehensive AS
methodology, Al Omrane quickly made an appeal to private consultants
by putting out public contracts based on quantifiable targets. This not
only encouraged new private consultancies to compete for these contracts but also brought about the "commercialization" of the AS procedure itself. Under these conditions, it is not surprising that, depending
on the type of social intermediator, the interpretation of the objective
of AS—a concept that has been defined rather vaguely from the beginning (Toutain 2011, 175)—and the specific approaches on the ground
differed.

In other words, there is no consensus on what AS really means.
Different actors within VSB can have different perspectives. For example, the vision of *participation* of the private consultants and public agencies like Al Omrane is limited to a passive conception of the word. Slum
dwellers are reduced to a simple audience or, at best, "clients." Moreover, for agencies like Al Omrane or Dyar Al Mansour, the whole problem of the existence of the slums in Morocco remains a technical rather
than a political or a social issue. Resettlement is the obvious solution.
On top of that, it can be measured. As Olivier Toutain stressed: "They
[Al Omrane] need to make numbers" (interview, Rabat, April 15, 2009).
Success or failure is measured that way. Consequently, Al Omrane tends
to favor contracts with private consultants in AS programs, because they
do it "faster and cheaper" and they can be held responsible for results
(Le Tellier 2009b, 205; see also Barthel and Zaki 2011).

An example of this perspective is the comparison made by a staff
member of Team Maroc (one of the private consultants involved) between his role and that of the public intermediator ADS.

> We are a private operator, we answer to calls for public contracts *[appels
> d'offres]*. We have to keep ourselves to the operational plan *[cahier de
> charge*. . . . We don't do MOS. . . . And actually we don't do AS either.
> Instead, we do administrative guidance. . . . I talk in terms of results.
> We realize a number of three hundred destroyed shelters per month,

while public actors such as ADS realize an average of ten shelters per month. We achieve five times the number of ADS. In four years' time we have eradicated more than four thousand shelters, while ADS only realized roughly a thousand over the same period. . . . We are happy with Al Omrane and Al Omrane is happy with us. . . . We are bound to an operational plan. We are obliged to deliver results. (interview, Rabat, July 2, 2010)

He continued arguing that the public intermediators, in contrast, are not bound to results, that they received assignments without any require- ment to account for any specific results, and that this was actually a form of discrimination vis-à-vis the private sector. "According to me," he stated, "that is money thrown out the window." When I asked him whether the private sector actually had a role to play in social develop- ment, he answered: "That's the market, it is a question of supply and demand; if there is a demand we try to fulfill it." One of his colleagues, working as a CAS member for Team Maroc in Casablanca, was a bit more cynical: "What other role do we have than to steer people towards credit institutions?" (interview, Casablanca, July 7, 2010).

In contrast, the approach and vision of social intermediators such as ADS and NGOs like Enda Maghreb resonate more with the objectives of MOS. This is also visible in their budgets as they spend much more money on AS than the private consultants in proportion to the house- holds they work with (Le Tellier 2009b). Nevertheless, one of the cru- cial differences between the conception of MOS and their operations within the framework of AS, according to these actors, is that MOS has to start *prior* to a resettlement operation, while they are contracted *during* the operations.

Several staff members of ADS and Enda Maghreb were critical of the way things were evolving. Yet their space of maneuver is constrained by their contract with agencies such as Al Omrane. They can never question the technical operation itself as mentioned (and even explic- itly underlined) in the methodological guidelines of AS published by the Ministry of Housing (MHU 2004, 11). One staff member of Enda Maghreb explained this as follows:

We care about the people. Al Omrane only cares about the adminis- trative support [we deliver]. That is why they work more with the private sector now. Enda pays attention to women's rights. We work to find sustainable solutions. We respect the human rights and also help people in generating new revenues, etcetera. . . . The private sector only does what Al Omrane asks from them. . . . They have only a role as service provider *[un rôle uniquement de prestataire de service]*. They carry out their research, they make an inventory *[recensement]*, they send in their polltakers *[enquêteurs]* and focus primarily on quantitative data. . . . When they finish their job, they are gone. (interview, Rabat, July 2, 2010)

The more political questions related to issues of social welfare and human development are generally pushed to the background, while the objectives of VSB are reduced to a mere housing question for which technical solutions are supposed to suffice (Barthel and Zaki 2011). At the Ministry of Housing, they are quite open about this. A staff member of the cabinet argued that the Ministry of Housing "is a technical ministry, we deliver houses. . . . All other social aspects should be provided by other ministries. We don't do education, health care, etcetera. . . . We just do housing" (interview, June 9, 2010). Ironically, this negates the whole philosophy behind the national debates on the social dimension of slum resettlement set up by the Ministry of Housing itself during the *alternance* period.

As a consequence of this failure or reluctance to implement the principles of MOS, ADS decided to end its cooperation with Al Omrane. NGOs such as Enda Maghreb quickly followed in their footsteps, resulting in a decline in AS operations on the ground (Toutain 2011, 177). Today, the actual implementation and results of VSB seem miles away from the original objectives of social and urban integration that were pushed forward so promisingly with the conceptualization of MOS at the beginning of the century.

Mixed Results: The Impact of Ten Years of Cities without Slums

The new practices of urban government and innovative techniques of social engineering did not really achieve what was anticipated at the start of the VSB program. The results of VSB are rather ambiguous. Official accounts, and especially the Ministry of Housing, emphasize the (mainly quantitative) achievements (e.g., fifty-six cities declared a city without slums, more than 70 percent of the program realized, a reduction of slum households from 8.2 percent to 3.4 percent, an increased average demolition rhythm from five thousand to twenty-five thousand shelters a year) (MHU 2012).

One cannot deny that the physical living conditions of most people who were resettled have improved significantly. Aesthetically, the new social housing projects are undoubtedly an improvement for the city's image compared to the chaotic and miserable image of bidonvilles. Regular access to water and electricity and the construction of sewage systems has obviously improved the conditions of hygiene and security (Toutain and Rachmuhl 2014).[18]

Yet the positive picture of the social impact of VSB, as often presented by state officials and international institutions such as UN-Habitat, should be nuanced. According to Toutain and Rachmuhl, these quantitative results say nothing about the qualitative changes in people's living conditions. First, almost all the residents of the nine projects they evaluated experienced a deterioration of their living conditions due to the absence of collective services such as schools, health centers, ovens, and bathhouses (hammams). These conditions are exacerbated by the fact that most new relocation sites are often situated at the outskirts of the city and are poorly connected to the city center. Many households were dependent on their original living place or the presence of a souk (traditional market) in the city center for petty trade activities or worked in the informal sector. As such, a resettlement often contributes to feelings of isolation and marginalization (Toutain and Rachmuhl 2014, 8).

Second, moving means new costs, which put pressure on already modest family budgets. People have to pay new taxes, and fees for water, electricity, and public transport (if available). As such, the transfer often means a decline in incomes and an increase in expenses. Toutain and Rachmuhl determined that approximately 30 percent of the households experience more difficulties in meeting daily expenses and risk being even more impoverished (see also Bartoli 2011). Additionally, projects experience a considerable number of "absentees" as the poorest among the slum population opt out or are not reached (between 10 and 20 percent). These people return to the bidonville or end up in other forms of informal housing (Toutain and Rachmuhl 2014, 21).

Among those who do move eventually, a considerable number of households were compelled to cut expenses on primary consumption goods and services such as education (for the children) and healthcare. In some projects, there was a decline in families connected to electricity networks due to rising bills (Toutain and Rachmuhl 2014, 32, 40). Moreover, many beneficiaries in resettlement operations have to find temporary accommodation to bridge the time between the obligatory destruction of their shelter and the construction of their new homes. This brings extra costs that are often difficult to bear as the average time is ten to fifteen months (Le Tellier 2009b; Mansion and Rachmuhl 2012, 87; Toutain and Rachmuhl 2014, 69). As a result, only 50 percent of the resettlement projects evaluated by Toutain and Rachmuhl were occupied by VSB beneficiaries at the time of their research; the rest of the houses and plots were either vacant or already occupied by other families (Toutain and Rachmuhl 2014, 28).[19]

Third, the transfer often means the breaking up of solidarity networks and social relations that existed in the shantytowns before resettlement (Iraki 2006b). This element has a gender component. In the new sites, women have more difficulty integrating and end up staying at home more often (Toutain and Rachmuhl 2014, 34–35). One can ask whether rehousing really improved the situation at all. In the words of an ADS official:

> They always talk about a war against degraded housing [guerre contre l'insalubrité]. But the state is losing this war. . . . In the new sites, there we can really talk about real poverty. There we can really talk about social exclusion. In a bidonville there is less exclusion because the inhabitants live close to a market, there is economic activity, a health center, etcetera. But the new sites [often] don't have public services and there are no transport possibilities. In those sites, there is not even the bare minimum. (interview, Rabat, September 12, 2013)

Fourth, financial instruments such as FOGARIM still fail to reach and integrate the majority of the urban poor. Many of them still prefer to borrow money from relatives and finance the construction with their own savings (Bartoli 2011). Only 20 percent of the households in the evaluation of Toutain and Rachmuhl applied to FOGARIM. The more than 110,000 loans granted under the FOGARIM program so far is nowhere near the anticipated 50,000 loans per year as announced in 2006 by the then minister of housing Ahmed Taoufik Hejira (Karim Douichi 2006). Additionally, the number of defaulters is on the rise, creating some anxiety among several banks (Harmak 2013; Toutain and Rachmuhl 2014).

Finally, despite the claim that the integrated urban vision of VSB is a crucial and innovative element that distinguishes this program from all previous ones, a critical observation is necessary. In the end, many observers agree that the main goal is simply to eradicate the slums and relocate the slum population. Al Omrane is judged primarily on the number of shelters it demolishes. The new housing blocks are carefully parceled to fit as many households as possible, which makes the actual apartments or plots too small for the larger families (Toutain and Rachmuhl 2014, 26).

"Everything has been built over with apartments," a journalist and former bidonville inhabitant told me once when we were driving through the district of Sidi Moumen in Casablanca. "There is no space provided for green spaces, parks, trees, for playgrounds, youth centers and other places where people can meet each other" (interview, Casablanca, May 16, 2008). Many of these new social housing projects and resettling operations transform the urban periphery in a monotonous mass of low-cost apartments. According to a prominent Moroccan economist, "[Morocco is] making the same mistakes as the French. We are creating *banlieues*" (interview, Rabat, September 26, 2009; see also Laval et al. 2010).

Neoliberal Practices of Maximizing Profit and Social Control

Despite the poor results of VSB, it is clear that other interests, motives, and calculations are at play. To parallel the opening epigraph of this chapter: the ruling class is not interested in the slum population but is interested in power over that population. They are above all interested in the system of power, the biopolitical techniques of control embedded within development policies and poverty alleviation strategies. From this perspective, the reinvention of social policy, with programs such as VSB (and also INDH), is not paradoxical or contradictory to neoliberal reform but characterizes the transformative reality of the neoliberal project itself. These contemporary social development programs display the technical practices and knowledges that try to guarantee relations of domination and effects of hegemony (Foucault 1990, 141).

Characteristic of biopolitical technologies of power is that they do not have absolute control or domination as their raison d'être. It is rather about governing uncertainties, possibilities, and future risks. With regard to his case studies in Istanbul, Ozan Karaman (2013) argues that there is a disciplinary element in the way slum dwellers are targeted and governed. Through resettlement programs, slum dwellers are not only reintegrated into the formal housing market; these programs also seek to regulate and discipline the conduct of beneficiaries to conform to the norms of formal market behavior (see also H. Weber 2002).

Yet disciplinary techniques, in the way Foucault understood them, are always limited beyond the enclosuring capacities of total institutions (e.g., the panoptic prison). Discipline, or the disciplinary problem of how deviant behavior can be corrected, becomes more problematic in open space (e.g., the city). Consequently, the main objective in modern government will be not the repression or disciplining of conduct but rather its *control* (Deleuze 1992). Within neoliberal government, the attempt to control conduct, or possible future conduct, is then administered, calculated, and regulated through the market economy, through the expansion of market relations, through the circulation of capital, or, more concretely, through the expansion of the housing market and the integration of the informal into the formal city.

Exhaustive control and mere repression are no longer desirable. Neither is it legitimate within the context of new global discourses on democratization, good governance, and poverty alleviation. Yet threats remain and the question is then—a question that has been dealt with throughout this book—how does the ruling order deal with a crisis situation in an innovative and creative way? And in the process of doing so, how does it build a new order, a more sustainable one? Or from the perspective of the problem of slums, how does it deal with the perceived terrorist threat coming from within the bidonvilles?

The VSB program was one of those creative answers. And it had to take into account two aspects or problems: serving the vested interests embedded within the new neoliberal order, that is, exploiting new markets and new frontiers of capital accumulation; and consolidating those interests not only by making the surveillance of threats more effective but also by focusing on normalization and integration. The best way to protect a new hegemonic order is by making everyone part of it. Mere repression and the use of sovereign power cannot do this. Neither can it be done by simply "buying" social peace. Something else is needed, something more fundamental.

It is in this sense that Karaman (2013) stresses that the urban development strategies behind slum clearance are not just about dispossession and displacement—even though it often ends up doing so—but also about the integration of slum dwellers into the formal market and about the marketization of their conduct. Social intervention and social policy within neoliberal projects entail a sort of "inverted social contract" (Foucault 2008, 202). The goal is not to redistribute accumulated wealth in order to counterbalance market distortions or simply to support those who are excluded from the market; the goal is to *impose* the rules of the game—the competitive market society—on every citizen and prevent them from dropping out again. As such, we are dealing here with a different kind of power compared to sovereign city planning of the 1980s. The new modalities of urban government are not so much driven by "the power to take life" (i.e., sovereign power, the power to oppress indiscriminately) but rather by "the power to make life" (i.e., the entrepreneurial version) (Foucault 2003, 247).

Poverty Capital: Social Development as an Economic Opportunity

In a project such as VSB, market-based housing solutions and the participation of private capital are presented as the way forward to address the shortfall in the low-income market and avoid the failures of public housing programs in the past. However, the private sector usually shows little inclination to invest in this segment of the market. The problem is not so much the lack of economic potential. According to McKinsey & Company (2012), affordable housing is a global economic opportunity worth hundreds of billions of dollars. The problem is not so much the demand either. To the contrary, as Simon Walley, senior housing finance specialist at the World Bank, argues: "Demand is almost limitless—those without housing need shelter and those with it want more room or improved conditions" (2014, 3). In Morocco, the shortfall in social housing was estimated to be between 800,000 and 1 million units (Philifert 2014; Toutain 2014).

The real challenge, however, is "turning this need or desire into effective demand" (Walley 2014, 3). In other words, the private sector is deterred by issues such as legal uncertainties, slow bureaucratic procedures, limited access to affordable land, and a group of "clients" that has very little means and difficult access to credit. Creative innovation is needed, proponents advocate, to find new development models, technologies, and services that deliver profits, provide easy credit, and are supported by effective public policies and stable regulatory frameworks creating an environment that is favorable to private investment (Bigourdan and Paulais 2014; Sarda 2014). What's more, the role of the state is absolutely key here. The establishment of new public–private partnerships has the capacity to unlock "dead capital" both in the form of public property as well as in the form of informal capital (De Soto 2001).

With regard to Morocco, the innovative combination of methods such as AS and financial mechanisms such as FOGARIM and microcredits for housing are crucial elements in what Ananya Roy calls the alliance that lies at the very heart of "poverty capital." This alliance brings together those who "control access to the poorest" (e.g., the CAS teams, microfinance providers, Al Omrane, and the local authorities) and those who "control access to capital" (e.g., the commercial banks) (Roy 2010, 31). In other words, the form of participation promoted by AS is in reality above all a matter of improving the relationship between supply (social housing) and demand (the slum dwellers' diverse social situations and expectations) (Mansion and Rachmuhl 2012, 77). The alliance behind poverty capital has to explore and exploit a "new frontier of capital accumulation," that is, the inclusion of the urban poor in the urban economy: those people who had not been served by financial systems and markets before (Roy 2010, 53; see also Elyachar 2002).

The complex but crucial question at hand, according to Roy, is whether poverty capital will ensure the financial inclusion of the poor on fair and just terms, or whether these financial innovations are just new ways to exploit them. Is VSB a scheme to grant even the poorest among the urban residents access to property, or rather a pretext to break open a new market? More generally, is the support of the state in VSB—via subsidies, tax cuts, and financial guarantees—a way to give the urban poor a new hope for the future, or is state support a (class) instrument to privatize benefits and socialize risks and losses? There is probably no black-and-white answer. Nevertheless, the critical task is to look beyond the promises of the VSB project relative to its impact and pay attention to the underlying restructuration of relations of capital and relations of government.

The exploitation of poverty capital becomes a more viable option for market growth in this context of global financial crisis. After an apparent boom in the first decade of the twenty-first century, Morocco's construction and real estate sector experienced a slowdown in more recent years, especially in the sector of high-end urban development and urban megaprojects. As a result, the Oxford Business Group (OBG), a global publishing and consultancy company focusing on emerging markets in the Arab region and Asia, indicated that both state officials and private developers were looking to offset the drop in demand for high-end development projects by stepping up their support for social housing projects (OBG newsletter, August 25, 2009).

The constant high demand for affordable housing offered a reliable alternative to the business in tourist and luxury residential projects, which had suffered under the global financial and economic crisis. To address the demand, the Moroccan government strengthened its commitment to provide low-cost housing and increased the construction of social housing to an average rate of more than 100,000 units a year (UN-Habitat 2013). In February 2009 the government signed two new agreements, allocating a total of 52 billion dirhams for social housing projects and liberating 3,853 hectares of public land for the building of 200,000 units in thirty-two different cities across the country (OBG newsletter, August 25, 2009). In January 2011 the king himself urged increasing efforts and set the target for 300,000 units a year between 2011 and 2015 as it became clear that the original targets of VSB were not going to be reached (Chaoui 2011).

According to OBG, finance programs such as FOGARIM and other initiatives are essential to enable Moroccans to purchase homes and to "take advantage of the potential in the lower end of the market" (OBG newsletter, August 25, 2009). In this same newsletter, OBG also emphasized that some officials have argued that even more should be done to encourage private investors:

> Deputy and parliamentary committee finance member Abdelhamid Mernissi told local media that the state should reduce land prices and increase bonuses from 30,000 [dirhams] (€2,665) to 40,000 [dirhams] (€3,553) for those who target social housing. Others have called on the government to ease its quantitative measurements for affordable units. Currently, it is defined as properties of 100 sq metres at a price of 200,000 [dirhams] (€18,000), while low total property value housing has a price of under 140,000 [dirhams] (€12,600) and an area of less than 60 sq metres. With space scarce in major cities, the area could be reduced to 40 sq metres, while the price could be raised to 300,000 [dirhams] (€27,000) to increase developers' profits.

From this statement, it is clear that the needs and desires of the slum population are not driving a program such as VSB as much as market opportunities. OBG continues:

> Still, even without these added incentives, investing in the affordable segment seems like a solid option, despite lacking the same potential for high returns as more lucrative, high-end projects. *Until the economy improves,* and big risks once again offer the prospect of great rewards, *social housing, and Morocco's underprivileged citizens, stand to benefit.* (emphasis added)

In 2008 some important tax exemptions supporting the sector were revoked (Zaki 2011b), followed by a significant drop in constructions and new projects (Benmehdi 2010). Between 2008 and 2009 the construction of social housing plunged from 129,000 to 35,000 units. The 2010 Finance Act and the subsequent Act of 2011 aimed to resurrect the sector of social housing with new tax exemptions.

Also, the new maximum price for a social apartment was raised to 250,000 dirhams (Toutain 2014) rather than the former 200,000 dirhams benchmark dating from 1995. According to observers, this price raise was justified because the price of land had increased by 50 to 100 percent over the last fifteen years (Benmehdi 2011). What these new government decisions showed, however, was that poverty capital depended heavily on state support stimulating both the demand side (through FOGARIM, microcredit, etc.) and the supply side (through tax benefits, price regulation, etc.).

Development schemes such as VSB, and the technologies of government they produce, facilitate the merger of development capital and financial capital. They mark out and open up new spaces of investment in order to solve current or future "capital surplus absorption problems" (Harvey 2010b; see also Roy 2010). The needs and desires of the beneficiaries, the social dimension, in other words, represent merely the instrument or entry point through which new market opportunities are to be exploited.

A staff member of Al Omrane in Rabat explained that the semipublic company wanted to enter the stock market (which still has not happened). When asked whether this would jeopardize the social dimension of their work—after all, the stock market is driven exclusively by the profit motive—he answered, a bit excitedly: "No, on the contrary . . . this social dimension is our competitive advantage. . . . The social dimension *[le social]* is very profitable" (interview, Rabat, August 27, 2007, conducted with Sami Zemni).

During another interview, an employee of the private company Lydec, a subsidiary of SUEZ in Casablanca delivering water and electricity to shantytowns and informal neighborhoods in the framework of INDH, explained that it was her task to make sure that these people were turned into customers. The social dimension of it all, she argued, was that Lydec, at the moment, did not make any profit. Their products were delivered under the market price. Instead, Lydec adopted a long-term vision, expecting these people to become valuable costumers in the long run (interview, Casablanca, May 13, 2008).

Unlocking Dead Capital:
The Making of New Relations of Power

Poverty capital is embedded within the wider practices and methods of neoliberal government that aim to bring all human action into the sphere of the market. According to influential thinkers such as Hernan De Soto or C. K. Prahalad, the poor dispose of an enormous amount of "dead capital" (De Soto 2001) and there is a "fortune [to be made] at the bottom of the pyramid" (Prahalad 2005). These thinkers give you a privileged gaze into the creative neoliberal mindset: in these two perspectives, "the poor *have* assets" and they "*are* assets" (Roy 2010, 64).

To Prahalad, the poor are a "latent market," an emerging consumer base that is both underserved and large. By the mere "virtue of their numbers, the poor represent a significant latent purchasing power that must be unlocked" (Prahalad 2005, 11). The problem is that these markets have remained invisible for so long and that the private sector basically lacked the knowledge and the technologies to see the poor as an opportunity, as a commercially viable operation. The solution, for Prahalad, lies not only in creating new services and products but also in an innovative collaboration between the private sector and both civil society organizations and local governments. The latter two then operate as intermediaries between private enterprise and the poor.

Local and national governments "have to create the enabling conditions for active private-sector involvement in creating this [bottom of the pyramid] market opportunity" (Prahalad 2005, 99–100). Social development schemes such as VSB cannot be understood only as initiatives (successful or not) to improve poor people's lives; they are also political instruments to integrate that very attempt into a neoliberal project. This is the very logic or ideology behind poverty capital.

More concretely with regard to the housing sector, De Soto argues that the poor are unable to access their wealth (what they own informally) because they do not possess formal property titles. Their capital is dead capital because "it exists in a universe where there is too much room for misunderstanding, confusion, reversal of agreements, and faulty recollection" (De Soto 2001, 14). This capital is useless according to De Soto because it cannot be employed as collateral to secure a bank loan, nor guarantee the payment of water, electricity, or any other infrastructural service. Therefore, he pleads to give the poor legal land titles and property rights so they can put their assets to work in the formal capital market.

De Soto's idea of land titling resonates with the objective of VSB to turn slum dwellers into legal homeowners (Al Omrane 2010). At first glance, De Soto's plea for formalization seems to be a laudable call for property rights. Yet, as Ananya Roy has pointed out, in reality it "is not so much about property rights as it is about the right to participate in property markets" (2005, 152). There is a crucial difference and it is related to power.

If we follow Marx's definition of capital (in this case property), then we should understand it not as a thing but as a social relation. A piece of land or a house only becomes "capital" when it is put into circulation and integrated in a process of production and exchange in order to accumulate more capital. Hence, a piece of land or a house only becomes capital when it mediates social relations between people. And this is exactly what De Soto has in mind. Inevitably, power comes into play: "Between equal rights, force decides" (Marx 1992, 344).

Low-income populations are particularly vulnerable or powerless in processes of capitalist urbanization, urban development, and property exchange. Both in the Global North as in the Global South, critical scholars have argued that once the urban poor are turned into legal homeowners and supposedly gain control over a valuable asset, speculation takes over; gentrification, for example, transforms the neighborhood and forces out low-income populations (Harvey 2003, 158; see also Fawaz 2013).

De Soto's scheme can thus easily be transformed into a machine of dispossession, transferring assets from the poor to the wealthy (T. Mitchell 2004). Especially in the case of financially vulnerable households, property titles could be a legal basis for creditors to seize the assets of those unable to keep up debt payments. Legal property rights thus not only increase the access and possibilities of the poor vis-à-vis their own assets; it also makes these assets *visible* and accessible to more powerful players in the market such as property and real estate developers, or simply the urban middle class.[20] The assets of the poor are not a source of wealth creation, as suggested by De Soto, but the *means* through which the reorganization and accumulation of wealth is carried out (T. Mitchell 2004).

For years, even decades, many slum dwellers in Morocco have lived outside the formal market economy. Many of them have no property rights, no regular job, no legal water connection, and so on. But if the poor are not finding their way to the formal market, the new methods of social engineering are now helping to bring the market to the poor. And, if necessary, the market products will be adapted to the capacities of the poor (and not necessarily their needs).

The creation of an additional housing program in 2008, setting the price of apartments at 140,000 dirhams, was an attempt to serve even the lowest-income groups within the VSB program (Toutain 2014). In a country where the majority of the poor population still does not have a bank account, concepts like debt and credit are introduced among the lowest-income classes with instruments such as FOGARIM and micro-credits for housing. Insofar as the bidonville is seen to represent the "ruralization" of the city, the solution is presented as one of shepherding its inhabitants toward market integration.

This kind of approach creates new forms of exclusion, as Lamia Zaki argues: "It [transforms the slum dwellers] from citizens to consumers by replacing the notion of absolute (human) rights with that of a right to services." Consequently, this development philosophy tends to atomize the notion of right by creating conflicting interests between those who are able to afford market inclusion and those who are simply too poor and thus remain excluded (Zaki 2008, 134).

Finally, what will happen when beneficiaries are no longer able to pay their loans? A new apartment implies a lot of extra costs; for example, registration fees, property taxes, a legal connection to the electricity and water distribution networks, and public transport. While it is not dramatic yet, the number of defaulters is on the rise (Harmak 2013; Thiam and Faquihi 2013; Toutain and Rachmuhl 2014). Additionally, on a more general level, *TelQuel* published official estimates in 2015 that predicted that more than 85 percent of Moroccan households will have difficulty saving in 2016.[21]

The Depoliticization of "Development" and the Expansion of State Bureaucratic Control

Besides money power, there is another kind of power the ruling class is interested in. It is also acquired through the new methods and technologies of government produced by VSB. The implementation of a program like VSB is not only a way to exploit the economic opportunities of the "lower end of the market." The specific timing reveals other motives and calculations that are more related to the consolidation of the interests of money power and the concern to protect the established social order from possible threats in the future.

VSB entailed an increasing administrative control over the slum population. The new methods of social engineering facilitated the entrance of governmental agency into the slums. In the past, the bidonvilles had always been impenetrable spaces. The crisscross of shelters and very narrow aisles, often unpaved, make the shantytowns inaccessible to fire engines, police cars, ambulances, or army vehicles. "The bidonville is an uncontrollable site," argued a Dyar Al Mansour official. "Even the police couldn't enter there" (interview, Rabat, October 27, 2009). Promoted as a fight against poverty, VSB paved the way to stage the deconstruction of these impenetrable and ungovernable spaces.

The daily presence of the CAS teams ensures the embeddedness of governmental influence in the slums and facilitates bureaucratic administration and control. According to Toutain (2011), the immediate goal of social accompaniment for the local authorities was to neutralize mobilizations and protests against the resettlement projects (see also Essahel 2015). In some cases—for example, in the rehousing program of Ennakhil—the CAS facilitators stayed on site for two years and in the process they established personal ties with the beneficiaries and came to understand the complexity of the solidarities and conflicts between the households (Arandel and Wetterberg 2013). The CAS teams conduct surveys, make inventories of the population, and explain to people how the resettlement project will proceed. They inform them of the next steps and assist the population in all the necessary administrative procedures. In other words, the CAS teams are one of the crucial elements in the process of making the slums more transparent and increasing the knowledge about the slum population.

One of the added values of the AS approach, according to the methodological guide, is precisely the "improvement of the quality of information [on the slum dwellers] available to the decision-makers" (MHU 2004, 25). Poverty was thus not only a market opportunity, as suggested by thinkers like De Soto and Prahalad, but also an entry point for the state to expand its bureaucratic control (Ferguson 2006). Similar to Ferguson's analysis of the development apparatus in Lesotho, the VSB apparatus was not necessarily a "machine" (to use Ferguson's word) for eliminating poverty and improving the lives of slum dwellers, which incidentally

Resettled beneficiaries from Douar Skouila had to destroy their shelters before they were allowed to move. Photograph by the author, 2008.

Others were still living between the ruins. Photograph by the author, 2008.

A former owner had to make a hole in the wall to prevent somebody else from occupying his shelter; his neighbor still lived above. Photograph by the author, 2008.

coincided with more state-bureaucratic presence, but rather a machine for reinforcing and expanding bureaucratic state power, which incidentally took poverty as an entry point (Ferguson 2006, 273). The result, Ferguson argues, may be that state intervention has no real effect on poverty, at least not a sustainable effect, but that does not mean it has no other effects.

The effect is actually twofold. Besides increasing state presence, VSB and AS also reduce the issue of poverty to a purely technocratic matter, a matter of providing adequate housing. By embracing abstract principles such as good governance, transparency, and participation, the radical political nature of a development scheme such as VSB is actually obfuscated.

> By uncompromisingly reducing poverty to a technical problem, and by promising technical solutions to the sufferings of powerless and oppressed people, the hegemonic problematic of "development" is the principal means through which the question of poverty is de-politicized in the world today. At the same time, by making the intentional blueprints for "development" so highly visible, a "development" project can end up performing extremely sensitive political operations involving the entrenchment and expansion of institutional state power almost invisibly, under cover of a neutral, technical mission to which no one can object. (Ferguson 2006, 273)

Yet this does not necessarily mean that the spatial expansion of state presence through biopolitical methods of government is successful or effective, that "the state" has actually increased its power over the slum population. As Ferguson continues:

> The expansion of bureaucratic state power, then, does not necessarily mean that "the masses" can be centrally coordinated or ordered around any more efficiently; it only means that more power relations are referred through state channels—most immediately, that more people must stand in line and await rubber stamps to get what they want. What is expanded is not the magnitude of the capabilities of "the state," but the extent and reach of a particular kind of exercise of power. (282)

The Power to Make Life:
The Remodeling of the Urban Citizen

People resist resettlement all the time. They are not just passive victims but strategic and realistic urban agents who know how to mobilize both family and political networks to their own benefit (Navez-Bouchanine 2003). The ordinary still quietly encroaches on the ruling classes' project and the latter's hegemonic vision of the city (Bayat 2000; on Morocco, see Berry-Chikhaoui 2010; Essahel 2015; Navez-Bouchanine and Berry-Chikhaoui 2005; Zaki 2008). In other words, although state control may be expanded through various methods and institutions in a *quantitative* manner, this does not necessarily mean that the methods implemented under VSB automatically have a *qualitative* effect.

Yet the new biopolitical methods of VSB do actively strive for a qualitative change. It is not just about plain surveillance; it is a societal project of introducing a new way of urban life for the slum population, one that thrives in a "market-based ecosystem," as Prahalad likes to call it. The new knowledge produced on the slum population and on urban poverty becomes instrumental in the production of "the (new) truth": this knowledge became the currency of an authoritative complex of experts, governments, and international donors who produced a powerful narrative that became common sense and part of a new taken-for-granted worldview (Roy 2010, 56). They determine the "best practices," embracing so-called universal principles such as sustainable and social development, participation, good governance, and so on, while in reality they impose standardized and normative "methodological packages" that can be applied everywhere independent of the economic, political, and social needs and desires of the targeted population (Navez-Bouchanine 2007).

The neoliberal governmentality that underpinned the process of reinventing social policy in Morocco was based on two of those best-practice goals: participation and integration. These two—at first sight—progressive goals were integrated in a system of power that aims not to empower life but to make it fit the new "ecosystem." It is exactly the opposite of empowerment.

"Sustained behavioural change" is a key objective for Al Omrane. "Through the implementation of *Cities without slums*, Al Omrane enables a reinforcement of the capacities of the urban poor," the group states. "Access to ownership allows slum dwellers to improve their living conditions and induces a *new social behaviour* as well as an increased involvement in local affairs" (Al Omrane 2010, 6, emphasis added). According to Al Omrane, AS strengthens the capacities of slum dwellers and "induces positive behaviours" (5). What Al Omrane means by "positive" is not clarified in the document itself, but it is clear that it consents to the "truth" produced by institutions such as the World Bank as well as thinkers such as De Soto and Prahalad.

Access to land and assets is essential for the poor to become "active citizens, good clients and municipal taxpayers," according to George Gattoni, former director of the World Bank's Urban Poverty Thematic Group (quoted in Werlin 1999, 1531). Generally, the idea behind the conception of urban "integration," as I was told by a former official of ADS, is that once people are good consumers they will eventually become responsible citizens with a proper job and a proper lifestyle (interview, Rabat, April 16, 2009, conducted with Sami Zemni). As such, the market becomes the norm by which good citizenship is measured. It fits within the neoliberal dogma of "helping the poor help themselves" (M. Davis 2006b, 72).

Governmental practices and methods such as AS are never only about intervention. They involve both intervention *and* formation (Dikec 2007, 287). The formation of the responsible good citizen comes with the conviction that the slum dwellers need to be reeducated. In the words of the technical director of Dyar Al Mansour: "We have to teach them a new way of life, first of all by teaching them to live vertically [i.e., in apartments] instead of horizontally [i.e., in shelters occupying too much land]" (interview, Rabat, July 1, 2010).

When talking to public officials and private actors, one often gets the impression that slum dwellers are not capable of engaging in public life and that they themselves are responsible for this situation. Another official of Dyar Al Mansour told me: "We have to guide them and be with them constantly. They are like babies" (interview, Rabat, May 28, 2008). An official of Al Omrane complained to me that the inhabitants sometimes refuse to move to their new homes because living in a bidonville is "a way of life, it is a social and cultural problem. There are people who like living in the bidonvilles" (interview, Rabat, August 27, 2007, conducted with Sami Zemni). Another Al Omrane official confirmed this, stating that "the [slum] population is culturally as well as traditionally difficult" (interview, Rabat, June 30, 2008). Finally, a staff member of Lydec explained that delivering these people water and electricity also requires putting a lot of effort in education—teaching them how to use their new services and how to pay for them (interview, Casablanca, May 13, 2008). In many cases, but not all, there is a real contempt for the slum dweller among the public and the technical agencies (Navez-Bouchanine and Berry-Chikhaoui 2005).[22]

The problem here is situated within the confrontation between the urban projects envisioned and implemented by the powerful and the various ways in which the newly created spaces are eventually used, twisted, and reappropriated by all other people who live, work, and survive in the city—ways often not intended or desired by those in power. The modes and patterns of circulation and exchange that eventually give life to the mass of urban infrastructure and the built environment are not necessarily those that were anticipated by the urban design itself. It is within the most densely populated areas that these frictions reach their high point. It demonstrates the complex relationship between those who rule and the governed, a power relationship that is dictated by both fear and the drive to bend or bypass existing or enforced norms (Navez-Bouchanine 2010).

The CAS teams, for example, receive the explicit mission to pay attention to the pedagogical role of their communication with slum dwellers; that is, to pay attention to "the sensibilization and the responsibilization of the inhabitants" (USAID 2007, 87). Likewise, as stated in the methodological guidelines, AS comprises not only a financial and a logistic guidance but also a psychological guidance. After all, "a change of domicile often constitutes a psychological trauma and a loss of orientation for the people involved. This is even more true if such a change concerns the mode of living and even life itself" (MHU 2004, 14).[23] Slum dwellers are thus reeducated to comply with the norms of the new market ecosystem. The VSB program aims to include the slums in the formal urban space where the state can define, defend, and regulate the norms and boundaries for social life.

Empowerment and participation are notions that are often used to legitimate and promote a program such as VSB. Yet the slum dwellers have very little to say in the whole process of their relocation. Often, these concepts are turned into buzz words used by local governments to meet the requirements of international donors and gain access to international finance (Mansion and Rachmuhl 2012, 77). In the VSB program, participation is limited to consultation and is politically controlled (47). The crucial decisions concerning why, when, and where the "beneficiaries" are to be resettled, and who is to be included and excluded from these state-subsidized operations, are all taken without the slum dwellers' input and are usually not open for negotiation (Arandel and Wetterberg 2013, 146; see also Mansion and Rachmuhl 2012, 80).[24]

Nabil Kerdoudi of Al Omrane in Casablanca left no doubt about what he understood by citizen participation and about the specific practices of slum dwellers that resist resettlement.

> The households have retorted by allowing a densification, even inside their shelters. The parents accommodate their children, but also their spouses and their descendants. In fact, while we offer them one plot or one apartment destined for an average household, they refuse and wait for a more interesting opportunity in terms of surface. Despite the method of social accompaniment [AS] provided by the ministry [of Housing], which is meant to convince them to accept rehousing, we found ourselves obliged, recently, to turn to the judiciary for those cases where beneficiaries refuse the proposed accommodation. (Kerdoudi quoted in Blal 2010)[25]

This explanation and the other examples cited above illustrate the intrinsic authoritarian character of the contemporary government of slums, not in the classical sense of the word but in its transformation through new modalities and technologies of government. Here, I disagree with Christian Arandel and Anna Wetterberg (2013), who argue that the methods of VSB occupy a middle ground between the authoritarian methods of the past and the ideal of community empowerment. They consider VSB as a gradual and somehow linear improvement toward more democratic methods of government. In contrast to their argument, I emphasize the fundamental transformation within authoritarian modalities of government, this time dictated more by market requirements than by a concern for the safety of the sovereign.

Security and stability are still central within this authoritarian project of behavioral change and capitalist expansion. The principle that residents should "be made to pay" for their rehousing is based on the assumption that "beneficiaries will be much more mindful of how money is used if it comes from their pockets rather than public funds" (Mansion and Rachmuhl 2012, 105). Or, considered from another point of view, indebted citizens are less likely to stage a revolt (Karaman 2013).

Put in the context of the Arab uprisings of 2011, one can ask whether VSB has had an impact on the situation in Morocco. In contrast to the great revolts of 1952, 1965, 1981, and 1990, the slum dwellers were, for the first time, not really involved as a group in the mass protests of 2011. Despite the fact that slum dwellers often contest the particularities of the slum upgrading projects in which they are involved, the dominant feeling among the slum population at the moment, according to Toutain and Rachmuhl, is not one of anger or a willingness to revolt comparable to those who participated in the Arab uprisings of 2011 but one of hope that despite the many difficulties and problems on the ground, their situation will improve in the end (Toutain and Rachmuhl 2013, 104). That is maybe how we should understand VSB's intention in the first place and its actual success. Whether this apparent success will be sustainable in the long term is another question, because, from a poverty alleviation perspective, all VSB has done is to shift poverty to the outskirts of the city. Moreover, by moving the poor out of the urban center, capital could reclaim Morocco's urban centers for commercialization and megaproject development. This is a class project in which the poor have no right to placemaking.

To summarize, VSB did not solve the internal contradictions of capitalist development and expansion, but it fundamentally altered the relations between those who govern and those who are governed. Since the end of the 1990s, and definitely with the launch of the VSB program, the slum *population* rather than the urban *territory* became the politicized subject. But the claims, demands, and desires of that population are now very much depoliticized and reduced to technical questions of housing, property rights, and market integration. As such, the right to the (formal) city is an imposed right for slum dwellers in which entrepreneurship, market integration, responsibilization, and social control are considered crucial elements for success.

In the end, however, urban poverty still is a political problem intimately related to and even reproduced by contemporary hegemonic models of "development." Real problems such as a lack of quality education, healthcare, and employment are still largely ignored. In the words of an inhabitant of Douar Al Kora (Rabat):

> In a society the problems are social. In the hospital there are no doctors, no nurses, there is a lack of medicines. . . . In education the teachers receive a very low salary. . . . The classrooms are overpopulated, often fifty students. . . . [But] we don't have a choice. They decide. If they give you two rooms, you don't argue; you take it. (interview, Rabat, October 15, 2009)

A NEW GEOGRAPHY
OF POWER

> Who can ignore that the Olympians of the new bourgeois
> aristocracy no longer inhabit. They go from grand hotel to grand
> hotel, or from castle to castle, commanding a fleet or a country
> from a yacht. They are everywhere and nowhere.
>
> —Henri Lefebvre, *Writings on Cities*

THE AIM OF THIS BOOK is to understand both neoliberal globalization and the transformation of authoritarian government. Despite the fact that these two abstract phenomena inform the work of so many political scientists, geographers, anthropologists, economists, area specialists, and others, their convergence in the Arab region remains understudied and often poorly understood.

Of course, there is a strong awareness about the impact of globalization in the region, especially when it relates to geopolitics. Nevertheless, insofar as the global situation is taken into account, local economies and local political systems are usually seen as somehow subordinated to the dynamics of globalization (Hazbun 2012). The local can either resist or adapt to these dynamics; Morocco is generally considered to be among the latter.

My main concern was to tell a story not about the "impact" of globalization but about how globalization is produced *in places*—cities like Rabat and Casablanca. In other words, this book tells a story about globalization as inseparable from place itself. Neoliberalism and globalization are not supernatural forces that operate in a separate sphere far above any locality. To the contrary, these phenomena are always grounded, constituting connections between very material things (infrastructure, commodities, people) and their relation to immaterial processes (ideas, ideologies). The Bouregreg project, for example, is a political and institutional laboratory that formulates answers to the challenges of the neoliberal world and, in return, helps to shape that world.

The making of contemporary globalization is a continuation and intensification—albeit in radically new ways—of uneven capitalist development. This process of uneven development in the Arab region, or Morocco more specifically, cannot be ascribed to an incomplete, authoritarian, or a not yet fully implemented version of neoliberalism *in contrast* to some kind of ideal type or neoliberal reference model (see Dahi and Munif 2012; Dillman 2002; Schwedler 2012). This is a false point of departure. There is no distinction between local versions and a global model. The variegated outcomes of neoliberal projects on the ground are part of the very logic of global neoliberalism tout court.

I took the city as my entry point. The modern city is not just an epiphenomenon of national, regional, and/or global processes; it is one of the instruments itself, if not the most important one, behind the production of those processes. The urban space is a key arena for all kinds of struggles and its material constitution is always a reflection of contemporary as well as historical hierarchies of power.

Over the past few decades, Moroccan cities have transformed rapidly and fundamentally. Yet what matters here are not just the material changes in the urban landscape. A slum resettlement project is not just a new space of the built environment; it is not just a huge mass of concrete implanted in the urban fabric, a series of apartment buildings carefully parceled next to each other within the periphery of the city. It is much more than that. A slum resettlement project embodies an assemblage of social forces and power relations coming together in place and involved in placemaking. A social housing complex represents the materialization of relations of power between slum dwellers, government officials, economic elites, technocratic experts, civil society organizations, international donors, and others.

Similarly, the Bouregreg megaproject is not just a wasteland that was built over and turned into a modern real estate project with "authentic" Arab-Andalusian architectural accents. It represents the creation of a global space and of globalization, one that opens up and reaches out to the rest of the world, while at the same time drawing new social, economic, and spatial boundaries between the original residents on the one hand, and political elites, foreign investors, and global consumers on the other hand. Understanding the materialization of the city as a thing and a physical structure forces us to look at the spatially grounded social processes of urbanization in which a wide range of agents—both foreign and domestic, both physically present and absent—with different agendas, interests, and objectives give shape to the city, and in return, are shaped by the city as well (those who shape the urban are in the end also constrained by their own creations) (Harvey 1989a, 3).

In this relational geography, places such as Casablanca and Rabat are not starting points but nodes of connection in the global flow of ideas, methods, and struggles that make our neoliberal social order into what it is today. As the director of the Bouregreg Agency told me, the Bouregreg project was directly inspired by the Lebanese experience of Solidere in Beirut (interview, Rabat, September 16, 2013). Yet Solidere itself can be situated within a more global trend, also within Western countries, to circumvent and undermine traditional democratic channels and institutions of accountability with regard to the development of megaprojects (Ong 2006; Swyngedouw, Moulaert, and Rodriguez 2002). The Bouregreg project itself already serves as a model for other projects in Morocco, such as the Marchica Med project, and it might be used as a source of inspiration in other countries as well.

The same logic applies to the issue of slum upgrading. The VSB program won the 2010 UN-Habitat Scroll of Honour Award. UN-Habitat awarded Morocco this prize "for delivering one of the world's most successful and comprehensive slum reduction and improvement programmes. In a concept already being replicated in Egypt and Tunisia, the Moroccan programme widely considered the best of its kind in Africa, is spearheading Morocco's Cities without Slums drive."[1] UN-Habitat contributes to the promotion of the Moroccan modus operandi as a possible model for other countries dealing with similar challenges.

The nature of contemporary politics in Morocco is hidden within the relational complexes that produce urban spaces such as the Bouregreg Valley and give shape to social programs like Cities Without Slums. These urban politics characterize the transformation of authoritarianism over the last decades: from a system primarily based on the use of sovereign force (the years of lead under Hassan II) and a limited redistribution of public resources (state developmentalism) to a system based on increasing global market integration and neoliberal government (personified by Mohammed VI). Within the context of this transformation, authoritarian *government* has thus become more and more a globalized affair.

Neoliberalism as Projects

Thinking about globalization and neoliberalism as a set of "projects" offers us an interesting approach to grasp the political changes we have observed over the past three decades. Instead of relying on a predetermined definition of neoliberalism, the concept of projects allows us to focus on the actual practices, connections, and governmental technologies that constitute contemporary globalization and the making of a neoliberal order. Paying attention to different kinds of projects allows us to understand actually existing neoliberalism as something radically different from the ideal type. Hence, the concept of projects keeps us committed to understand the locality, the agency, and the contingent messiness of neoliberalism.

First, the differences between the imagination and promises of the Bouregreg project or Cities Without Slums and their actual materialization on the ground expose the contradictions of neoliberal ideal-type imaginaries, principles, and assumptions. These contradictions show us, for example, how government according to neoliberal principles of market freedom, private entrepreneurship, and individual responsibility does not necessarily imply less government, but rather a different kind of government; they show us how globalization is very much state crafted. Hence, our contemporary global situation has not necessarily produced a crisis of the state, maybe only a radical transformation of its modes of intervention. Moreover, by paying attention to the ways in which state power is *spatialized* in various ways, the state itself is exposed as this heterogeneity in space.

It is within the context of these new forms of government and state power that we have to rethink seemingly straightforward conceptual counterparts such as freedom and control, democracy and authoritarianism. The slum populations, for example, are now governed by benchmarks, targets, and new methods of "participatory development." They are managed and regulated by public–private partnerships and less by an authoritarian public administration that does not care about what these people think and do. Yet urban citizens in Morocco are not necessarily freer but rather are controlled and dominated differently. The final result is not less authoritarianism, let alone some kind of democratization, but authoritarian government with a different face.

Second, seeing neoliberalism as projects immediately evokes the association with agency and strategy. The label of "project" shatters the illusion that globalization is this kind of intangible process that acts like a force of nature. At the same time, the concept of project also transcends the tendency to anthropomorphize neoliberalism. Neoliberalism does not do things; people do: projects do not take shape without actors, the specific practices they deploy, the ideals they adhere to, and the rationalities that give sense to their actions. Neoliberalism is just a term by which we can understand some kind of coherency, convergence, and structure within diverse and in many ways contingent political histories.

Moreover, looking at particular projects of globalization, and explaining them as projects of *neo*liberalism, only makes sense if one takes into consideration the process of creative destruction. In other words, we have to take into account what these projects reacted against, what they destroyed, what kind of hegemonic social order they replaced, or better, out of what kind of social order and struggles these neoliberal projects emerged. Structural adjustment fundamentally undermined the developmentalist order and the "techniques of security" embedded within that order. Later projects, such as the Bouregreg project and VSB, tried to rebuild an alternative order and rolled out a new institutional infrastructure, one that created new balances of power and new techniques of government.

The current reshaping of Moroccan urban space and the reconfiguration of its urban economy is the result of deliberate and conscious political choices. These are not always determined beforehand or entirely autonomous from the global situation, but neither are they completely subordinated to the global logic of an alleged external force we call globalization. Hence, the conceptualization of neoliberalism as projects suggests a certain direction, goals, and strategies.

I used an additional concept to describe and understand this agency; that is, the concept of class. Neoliberal projects are class projects. As I explained in chapter 3, class here refers not to a particular sociological group that can be defined by a set of fixed characteristics (e.g., ownership over the means of production). Instead, class describes a particular political process of capital accumulation and surplus-value appropriation. Class clarifies the nature of certain relations, processes, projects, and forms of agency. The important political question therefore is not whether those who remodel the Moroccan city can be described as a class but rather whether their practices and strategies can be understood as class practices or class strategies. This does not mean of course that class agency cannot be connected to other forms of agency.

Class is thus, first and foremost, a relational concept, but one that evokes a spatial imagination that stretches well beyond the territorial boundaries of a nation-state. Class relates more directly to the political reality of contemporary global capitalism. Projects are specific sites where global class relations come together. The Bouregreg project, for example, enables us to trace the whereabouts of power without being constrained by a geographical landscape of fixed distances and boundaries. Moreover, understanding the Bouregreg project as a particular assemblage of class relations does not disregard the heterogeneous formation of different places and new state spaces. The mapping of a political assemblage where different private and public actors such as Eagle Hills, Wessal Capital, CDG, and the Bouregreg Agency come together in a new institutional state arrangement, while others such as the local municipalities and the local residents of Salé are excluded, gives us an insight into the dynamics of placemaking and statecraft in the service of the caprioles of global capital. Following the topological perspective of someone like John Allen, the power relations invested in the creation of the new Bouregreg Valley are not those who are necessarily all located *in* space but rather those who are inseparable from the composition of that space (Allen 2011b).

Political authority, such as in the Bouregreg Valley, is thus a particular relational effect of interaction between local, regional, national, and international forces, rather than the sovereign exercise of a sole entity of power (the Arab regime or the monarchy). The institutional infrastructure of the Bouregreg megaproject forms part of just one particular islet in a more scattered landscape of graduated sovereignty. State reformation and respatialization leads to the creation of all kinds of exceptional zones, governmental arrangements, forms of privatizing the state, and so on, where capitalist class forces are allowed to connect and seize the opportunities of local places in relation to the global mobility of capital.

Finally, these emphases on agency, strategy, choice, and calculation open up a perspective that depicts neoliberalism as a rather messy business, ad hoc and in many ways unstable. Situating the class projects I discussed in this book within a more global process of neoliberal globalization does not imply homogenization or generalization but rather the recognition of the *global* political dimensions of *diversity* on the ground. This is how we have to understand "neoliberalism as projects" and its intimate connection to local systems of power.

Neoliberal projects have given rise to a kind of ad hoc urbanism or "incentivized urbanism" where urban spectacles such as the Bouregreg project or market-creating schemes such as VSB have to entice (global) capital (Easterling 2014). As I elaborated in chapter 4, this kind of urbanism is based more on an economy of appearances, preimagined performances, and a drive to compete with other urban spaces than on long-term planning and vision. It makes these projects in many ways opportunistic, ad hoc, and volatile.

An economic crisis, for example, can lead to a damaging slowdown or the withdrawal of a vital partner, as we have seen in the case of Sama Dubai in the second phase of the Bouregreg project. The entrance of a new investor can completely alter the direction and urban design of a place like Marina Morocco (phase one of the Bouregreg project). Previously planned public spaces can be densified to augment profitability, or an exclusive residential islet (the Amwaj project of Sama Dubai) can be replaced by a top-notch cultural destination such as the Grand Theatre (phase two). Of course, these new directions are presented as if they were always part of the bigger picture—as if they were the result of vision, expertise, and a careful plan for the future. This is part of the whole "performance."

Because of all these different elements of neoliberal projects, I have paid explicit attention to the question of space. A critical spatial perspective looks at the relational, interruptive, and dislocating dynamics of contemporary politics. In this view, politics are not necessarily unpredictable but certainly open ended. A spatial perspective transcends the constraints of a reading of history that is framed within mere temporal sequences or sequential stages (developing/developed; authoritarian/democratic; traditional/modern) and that ignores to a large extent the contingency and coevality of political trajectories.

Neoliberalism and the Transformation of Authoritarian Government

Neoliberal projects cause reactions, conflicts, and resistance. In turn, these reactions will set in motion new kinds of projects. The project of structural adjustment provoked fierce riots and urban violence in the 1980s. Two decades later, the Casablanca suicide bombings were another violent expression of the failure to deal with the problem of slums. These events show very clearly what Foucault argued more generally; namely, that the development of a neoliberal order cannot escape the central problem of modern capitalist society: how to govern human beings? As such, neoliberal projects should also be understood within the history of biopolitics or the attempt to govern a populations' welfare and its socioeconomic function within a modern market society. Biopower, Foucault argued, was essential to the well-being and expansion of global capitalism.

Social projects such as INDH and VSB tried to fill the lacuna left by the destructive projects of the 1980s. They attempted to tackle the problem of (urban) poverty and also to transform urban life and urban society itself by elaborating new biopolitical techniques of governmental intervention. These projects illustrated important transformations within neoliberalism itself. The methods deployed in the early twenty-first century differed radically from those in the 1980s. While the latter *enforced* neoliberalism through projects of structural adjustment, the apparatuses of security embedded within VSB and INDH aimed to *stabilize* or *consolidate* the neoliberal order. The space of habitation was a key arena for the reproduction of a neoliberal and authoritarian governmentality.

Neoliberalism thrives in authoritarian contexts because it promotes a very narrow form of freedom. Yet, at the same time, neoliberal projects transform authoritarian "government" in fundamental ways. Of course, when it comes to understanding politics in Morocco, one cannot go around the monarchy as an institution and the king as the dominant political actor. Yet viewing the monarchy as the "possessor" of absolute power might actually obscure more than it illuminates. It might neglect the different ways in which this figure, and his institution, is entangled within a much broader complex of power *relations.*

This does not necessarily mean that the monarchy in Morocco has less power than in the past, only that the structures and mechanisms of domination and exploitation in which it engages changed fundamentally. Power, in both the Marxist and the Foucauldian sense, is not something that can be possessed but something that structures social relations. The monarchy or the makhzan for that matter are not thing-like entities that possess power but constellations of social relations, global connections, and struggles that imply constant change, even though this change might not always be the desired one (i.e., from a liberal democratic perspective).

The key to understanding contemporary authoritarianism in Morocco lies thus not only in the monarchy as a core institution, in its religious authority or its neopatrimonial power and its clientelistic networks; it also lies in the class projects of urban renewal, slum up-grading, poverty alleviation, gentrification, structural adjustment, market liberalization, market integration, foreign capital investment, and the creation of a good business climate. The monarchy, obviously, plays an important role in these latter projects of political change but is not a sufficient explanation.

Instead of focusing on how much power the monarchy possesses, we should try to understand how its methods and techniques of rule have changed within the context of our contemporary global situation. The creation of a "good business climate" became key for the ways in which authoritarianism in the region was transformed and the ways in which the interests of ruling domestic elites and global economic elites became increasingly intertwined.

From this perspective, the takeover of ONA by King Hassan II in the early 1980s is probably one of the most significant shifts in the exercise and practices of power of the Moroccan monarchy. It signified a shift of intervention—or at least a very important expansion of the monarchy's activities—from the conventional state-institutional realm to the private realm of business and market control. This was in fact a logical step as structural adjustment was destroying the social order of state developmentalism and the techniques of control embedded within the public sector and the state bureaucracy. Today, King Mohammed VI has become the primary capitalist of the country. He answers more to the image of an "economic predator" than to the image of an absolute sovereign who rules with an iron fist (Graciet and Laurent 2012).

Besides transforming authoritarian government, neoliberal projects are also instrumental in the construction of a new political narrative and the establishment of political legitimacy. The crisis of the 1980s, the *alternance* government, and the changed international context with the end of the Cold War not only pushed those in power to change their methods of rule but also provided them with the necessary political space and discourse to create this image of Moroccan exceptionalism. The reinvention of social policy, the adherence to the principles of the free market and good governance, and the investor-friendly politics of megaprojects served the monarchy to present itself as a model reformer, committed to market-oriented growth and serious about poverty alleviation. Moreover, by reducing the issues of economic growth and poverty to mere technical problems, those in power effectively used the technocratic language of "development" to depoliticize their strategies of capital accumulation and social control (Ferguson 2006).

Neoliberal projects are thus not just about imitating new global standards or serving the interests of the ruling elite; they are also about the appropriation of these standards for the further entrenchment of political authority and legitimacy. Both Bouregreg and VSB are "statements"—in different ways, of course—upon which a new narrative of modernity, religious moderation, cosmopolitanism, and hope for a better future is built. Both projects are showcases of a benevolent monarchy with a clear economic vision (Bouregreg) and a caring heart for the socially disadvantaged (VSB). They are showcases of a monarchy that does not rely on the army or a ruthless police force to secure its power but in fact acts as an economic powerhouse to strengthen its social, political, and cultural position (Feliu and Parejo 2013, 89). Of course, by no means should its success be taken for granted, as the Arab uprisings have shown very clearly.

Considering the Global Situation

To conclude, how can this book make a contribution to the broader field of MENA studies? I would like to end with two general observations. First, with regard to the notion of the region as a unique and separate territorial and cultural world: the understanding of politics in the Arab world still suffers from this aura of exceptionalism. To put it a bit bluntly, politics are usually reduced to some form of neopatrimonial family rule or exotic authoritarianism, epitomized by the "regime," while the political economy of the region is often all too easily put aside as "crony capitalism." Yet these kinds of narratives do not necessarily enlighten us with a deeper understanding of the complexity of the region but rather serve as a kind of mirror: "When difference is put in exceptionalist terms, in short, the referent is universalized" (Daniel Rogers, quoted in Hazbun 2012, 208). In the ways in which "the other" is often characterized as authoritarian and corrupt, the West is represented implicitly as the opposite: democratic and righteous. Western political systems are then turned into ideal types and we remain blind to our own inconsistencies, contradictions, and involvements.[2]

For example, one should pay attention to the fact that while most European leaders consider liberal democracy as the solution for the Arab region, in their own continent they are slighting the conviction that it is up to democratically elected leaders to resolve the economic crisis that started in 2008. Instead, they now look to unelected technocrats, the IMF, and the European institutions for salvation. In the case of Italy, it was stressed openly that the new cabinet of Prime Minister Mario Monti, appointed in November 2011, was made up "only of experts, no politicians" in order the assure the markets (Bogaert 2013b, 219). In Greece, even more astonishingly, it became very clear that the European political and economic project—lauded by so many prominent leaders in Europe who seize every opportunity to represent it as beneficial to all European citizens—*had* to be respected at all times, *even if* it means the destruction of a whole society, notably the Greek one. The democratically elected government was openly crushed by the "Troika" or "the institutions" (the EU, the IMF, and the European Central Bank) and the Greek financial system sabotaged when Syriza did not want to conform to the recommended reforms and austerity policies. Democracy and sovereignty were subordinated to the governing law of the memorandum. In contrast to the contemporary myth of the European Union—that is, presenting the union as a democratic transfer of authority from the national to the European scale—the European elite orchestrated a seizure of power from within the institutions, mainly in the interest of a powerful financial sector (Bogaert 2015a).

This book does not deny the authoritarian nature of Arab politics, nor the crony character of global capitalism, but points to the interrelations between "their world" and "our world" in the constitution of neoliberal projects and neoliberal globalization more generally. Neither does this book ignore or downplay the role of monarchs, "presidents for life," and their inner circles; rather, it situates them within wider and more global complexes of power. From that perspective, the political transformations explored in this book make the region, in the end, not so exceptional as it looks at first sight. The book opens up space to analyze the region, in all its diversity, in terms of dynamics found elsewhere, or better, in terms of *global* dynamics (Hazbun 2012).

Second, although I have paid little attention to the many forms of social protest the region, and Morocco more specifically, has seen over the past thirty years, the insights and arguments presented here do make a valuable contribution to a deeper understanding of some of the root causes of the Arab uprisings and, more concretely, to the history of social protest in Morocco.

The outcry for change in the region since 2011 was rooted in the political changes of the last thirty years. The uprisings were not just a revolt against authoritarian regimes but also expressions of a systemic crisis, a structural crisis of the social order of neoliberal globalization. The demands of protesters in the first weeks and months of the uprisings were formulated in clear political terms: remove the incumbent regime, install free and fair elections, end corruption, and so forth. Implicit in these demands, however, was the desire for greater social and economic justice. People were drawn to the streets by strong feelings of injustice and indignation provoked by more than thirty years of neoliberal projects depriving the urban poor, the working classes, and the middle class.

The Moroccan protests that followed those at Tahrir Square and Avenue Habib Bourguiba were not just a domino effect but should be situated and contextualized within a larger history of resistance against uneven capitalist development that can be traced back to the early 1980s. Moreover, we have seen a significant change in the geography of protests: while the disturbances of the 1980s were largely an urban phenomenon, the center of gravity shifted to smaller towns and the rural hinterland in the twenty-first century.

The reason is twofold. First, as I described in chapters 5 and 6, the marginalized urban areas—the slums, the informal neighborhoods, and the working-class areas—became the primary focus within an urbanism of control and security. Second, neoliberal urban projects in Morocco not only reshaped the city but also reproduced a historical relationship between town and country. By neglecting most of the countryside— the *Maroc inutile*—these projects shaped the structural relationship between Morocco's urban centers and the marginalized hinterlands. Neglect should be seen here as a form of action that provoked reactions. Migration was one aspect; the significant increase of socioeconomic protest in small towns was another (Bogaert 2015c).

The increasing protests in Morocco's peripheries cannot be considered separately from the neoliberal projects that produce uneven development. The social crisis in Morocco is not about socioeconomic grievances as such but about the contemporary form of globalization, the class politics, and the relations of power, exploitation, and dispossession that produce those grievances. The "revolt of small towns" in Morocco is about not only economic self-interest but also fundamental political issues related to economic marginalization, redistribution of wealth, and access to public services (Bogaert 2015c)—or in this case, about equal access to the "urban fabric" (Lefebvre 2003).

Any political and emancipatory struggle against authoritarianism cannot be separated from the underlying socioeconomic dimension, as the authoritarian shape of the Moroccan state, or any other state in the region, is instrumental in the politics of "accumulation by dispossession." The transformation of authoritarian government in Morocco is characterized not only by a lack of freedom to express your opinion, to vote, to choose your own political leaders, or to organize and mobilize politically but also by a lack of access to the city, by dispossession in urban space, and its exploitation and reproduction. An emancipatory counterproject should not only (re)claim the common liberal democratic rights but also reclaim the city as a whole and take it back out of the hands of (global) capital. The neoliberal city reflects a political project for society as a whole. As such, reclaiming *the right to the city* is not just a project to claim back the individual city but rather a revolutionary ideal to liberate society, recognizing that it has to start from within the city, targeting the new structures and systems of domination implanted by neoliberal projects and financial globalization (Lefebvre 1996, 2003; see also Bogaert 2014).

NOTES

Introduction

1. The following paragraphs draw on material published in *Jadaliyya* (Bogaert 2015b).

2. See "Casablanca Marina Project," August 5, 2009, http://www.youtube .com/watch?v=0mdHAMs3I2U.

3. It is important to emphasize that this neglect during the first decades after the independence contrasts quite strongly with colonial times. During the rule of the French, urbanization and urban planning were absolutely central. The French used their protectorate to experiment with new forms of urban planning. Moreover, French colonial urbanism gave way to a politics of design that resulted in a social and spatial segregation of the indigenous and the European populations that continues to have an impact on contemporary urbanization. The French "experimental" urban planning project actually laid the foundations for subsequent sociospatial struggles (see Abu-Lughod 1980; Rabinow 1995).

4. I refer to the Global South when I am talking about the former Third World in the contemporary post–Cold War context. I use the term "Third World" when I am referring to the postcolonial context during the Cold War or to particular concepts in the literature such as the "Third World debt crisis."

5. State developmentalism was somehow the counterpart of the welfare state in the Global North. It is a model broadly based on principles of state capitalism, import substitution, and a (limited) redistribution of wealth in the form of health care, public sector employment, and subsidized primary consumer goods.

6. This reputation as "king of the poor" has lost its currency today. It characterized, above all, his first years of rule. Today, Mohammed VI's supporters focus more on his role as national symbol and safety valve against political instability and the possible breakup of the country if the monarchy would disappear (due to issues such as the Amazigh question, the conflict in the Western Sahara, and the increasing influence of the Islamists).

7. I consider "urban politics" as it is understood by David Harvey, namely "in the broad sense of political processes at work within a fluidly defined but

nevertheless explicit space" (1989b, 127). In this view, the urban space is not exclusively defined by the urban territory and political agency is not reduced to local or national authorities.

8. I consistently use the concept of government when I refer to the practices, technologies, and methods of power that try to govern a population or a certain space such as the city. In this sense I apply a broader meaning of "government"—that is, as a general form of power—usually ascribed to the writings of Foucault (2007).

9. I want to emphasize that I use the terms "Arab society" and "Arab politics" out of convenience. I recognize that the reference "Arab" is far too limited to describe the region and somehow harms its great cultural, linguistic, and ethnic diversity.

10. I want to thank Christopher Parker for this comment.

11. Overall, I conducted over two hundred interviews. They included a wide range of actors and "experts": public officials from different state agencies, ministries, semipublic agencies, nongovernmental organization (NGO) workers and civil society activists, members of political parties and social movements, journalists, academics, members from private companies and consultants, and, finally, members from international development and donor agencies (e.g., United States Agency for International Development [USAID], French Development Agency, European Commission). Some of my respondents wished to remain anonymous. For reasons of security and integrity, I decided to quote anonymously from most of my interviews, mentioning only the function of the person I talked to. When names are mentioned, it was with the explicit consent of the interviewee or because he or she had already published or publicly expressed similar opinions and analyses.

1. Considering the Global Situation

1. Explanations ranged from an emphasis on culture and religion (Huntington 1993a; Lakoff 2004; Lewis 2001), to the nature of the economy and the dependency on rents such as oil and foreign aid (Beblawi 1990; Luciani 1990), to the involvement of foreign imperial powers (e.g., the United States) who supported authoritarian leaders to serve their interests (Quandt 2004), to the internal regime survival tactics and domestic political structures (Albrecht and Schlumberger 2004; Brownlee 2002; Brumberg 2002; Ghalioun 2004), and, finally, to the lack of a vibrant, independent, and democratic civil society (Hawthorne 2004; Kamrava and Mora 1998). Additionally, some have investigated the particular characteristics of authoritarian rule in the Arab monarchies (Anderson 2000; Herb 1999; Lucas 2004; Ottaway and Dunne 2007).

2. Or, at best, globalization is imagined as an abstract force coming from the West. As Clement Henry and Robert Springborg argue, "While [the MENA region] is closest geographically to Europe, it has adapted less successfully to globalization than regions more distant" (2001, 226).

3. This perceived disconnection between politics and economics can be related to the World Bank's Articles of Agreement, which state that "the Bank

and its officers shall not interfere in the political affairs of any member." Article IV, section 10, concludes that therefore "only economic considerations shall be relevant to [the World Bank's] decisions." International Bank for Reconstruction (IBRD), Articles of Agreement, February 16, 1989, http://siteresources.world bank.org/EXTABOUTUS/Resources/ibrd-articlesofagreement.pdf.

4. Such schematic generalizations of capitalist development divided into "historical stages" harms the truth in many aspects. Harvey, of course, recognizes that the reality is much more complicated and nuanced. "Though the emphasis may vary," he argues, "appropriation, mobilization, production and absorption are ever separate moments in an integrated process. How they hang together in space and time is what counts" (1989b, 53–54). The colonial city is obviously missing in this schema. Nevertheless, it had its own specific features and was instrumental in the extraction of surpluses from the colony, the organization of a violent regime of dispossession, and the subjugation of the colonized to colonial administration and government.

5. Based on the typical stereotypes of the southern city, one might wonder, for example, whether some cities in the south of Europe, in countries such as Greece, Spain, and Portugal, are not increasingly resembling cities in the Global South due to the impact of austerity and economic reform.

2. An Urban History of Neoliberal Projects in Morocco

1. This does not mean, of course, that the studies mentioned above do not take into account a broader political–economic context to understand the changing dynamics of urbanization from its many different angles.

2. Istiqlal ("Independence") was the oldest party in Morocco and dates back to the nationalist struggle against the French. The USFP originated indirectly out of a progressive left-wing split within the nationalist movement. The PPS was the smallest of the three opposition parties and originated out of a split within the communist movement. Since 1992 these parties were unified as opposition in the so-called Koutla al-demouqratiyya or Democratic Bloc.

3. Over the past few years, however, this extended freedom of the press has been under severe pressure again. Critical magazines and journalists have been fined or even imprisoned for showing a lack of respect for the king, the religion, or the national state boundaries (i.e., the issue of the Western Sahara). Weekly magazine *Le Journal*, for example, had to close its doors in 2010 because of fines and juridical battles. New online media such as *Lakome*, among others, also faced repression, with the arrest of their editor Ali Anouzla in September 2013. More recently, outspoken journalists such as Hicham Mansouri were imprisoned, while the well-known political analyst and human rights activist Maati Monjib went on a hunger strike to denounce the lack of political freedom.

4. "Dans le monde actuel, le cadre de définition de la gestion est celui de l'entreprise. En effet, celle-ci a imposé ce cadre à plusieurs organisations non économiques, et plusieurs administrations sont gérées actuellement selon les principes en cours dans les entreprises." All translations in the book are mine, unless noted otherwise.

5. During the first five-year plan (1960–65), import-substituting industrialization and agrarian redistribution of land were pushed forward as key strategies for economic independence. These policies were established under the socialist Ibrahim government. However, after only six months these plans were already shelved when Hassan II dissolved the government and opted for agricultural modernization in the form of irrigation (Sater 2010).

6. Despite the clear alliance with the Western bloc, C. R. Pennell notes that Hassan II did not ignore the Soviet Union and kept good relationships with the Russian leadership. In 1978 Morocco singed an important fishery deal with the Soviet Union that turned out to be one of the largest commercial deals between the Soviet Union and a developing country ever to be signed (Pennell 2000, 344).

7. Through the monarchy's support of landownership, it even managed to drive a wedge between more conservative Istiqlal members and the leftist wing around Mehdi Ben Barka. Among the former there were many landowners—such as Istiqlal's agriculture minister Omar Abdeljalil—who benefited from the state's promotion of the agricultural sector. The more leftist members of Istiqlal advocated a land reform—among them former prime minister Abdellah Ibrahim—to the benefit of the (landless) peasants. This eventually led to a split within the party and the creation of the UNFP.

8. These are numbers from the beginning of the 1980s, but it gives a good indication of the size of informal housing in Moroccan cities.

9. As a result of the search for a new political consensus between the monarchy and the nationalist movement, the UNFP broke up and one of the fractions formed the USFP. This new leftist party distanced itself from the "revolutionary option" defended ten years earlier by Mehdi Ben Barka.

10. The CERF was made up primarily of foreign (French) researchers, trained as architects and planners. Certainly in the beginning there was very little mingling with other disciplines such as sociology and economy. In general the plans of the CERF were too ambitious and took into account little of the political and economic reality of the country (Johnson 1972). According to Raffaele Cattedra (2001, 81) and Katherine Marshall (1972, 71), CERF is the abbreviation for Centre d'Experimentation, de Recherche et de Formation. However, Mohamed Naciri (1989, 239) gives CERF as the abbreviation for Centre d'Etude, de Recherche et de Formation. I use this latter form.

11. Today, the OCP remains the most important public company in the kingdom with more than twenty thousand employees. It produces 3 percent of Morocco's GDP and represents 30 percent of Moroccan exports (Catusse 2009a, 63).

12. It must be noted that the Moroccanization law did not necessarily imply a significant loss of influence of foreign capital in the Moroccan economy. Although the law encouraged Moroccans to take over foreign businesses, many of them actually established strategic partnerships with foreign capital, allowing the latter to retain and in some cases even increase its holdings in the Moroccan economy. Nevertheless, the Moroccanization did radically improve the participation of Moroccan private capital in the economic realm (Cammett 2007, 98; Clément 1986; Rami 2007).

13. The benefits of the Moroccanization policies were not exclusively monopolized by the traditional elites. The new emerging group of petty tradesmen and small businessmen from the Souss area also profited from the new economic opportunities (Sater 2010, 95).

14. Valuation Authority is the name used by Cameron Khosrowshahi (1997, 247).

15. SNI was a holding created via the Moroccanization law and is one of the dominant investors in Morocco today. In 2010 SNI merged with ONA, the business consortium controlled by the royal family.

16. Toward the end of the 1990s and during the first decade of the twenty-first century, some of these more strategic sectors would also be privatized (telecommunications) or incorporated into public–private partnerships (water and electricity).

17 In the beginning the Hassan II Fund was completely disconnected from the national state budget. As such, part of the public revenue from the privatization of the telecommunication sector was not even inscribed in the state budget. Yet this was restored quickly after the death of Hassan II following criticism from international actors such as France and the World Bank (Hibou and Tozy 2002a).

18. Mohammed VI, address from the throne, July 30, 2002, http://www .maroc.ma/fr/discours-royaux/discours-de-sm-le-roi-mohammed-vi-à-loccasion -du-troisième-anniversaire-de.

19. Heba Saleh, "Morocco's Tanger-Med Container Port Provides Bridge to Europe," *Financial Times*, March 22, 2016.

20. Saleh, "Morocco's Tanger-Med Container Port Provides Bridge to Europe."

21. Since the beginning of the twenty-first century, CDG has been involved in numerous megaprojects such as Casablanca Marina, Casanearshore, Fès Shore, Rabat Technopolis, the Zenata new town, Tanger Med, and the initial setup of the Bouregreg project. Its CEO is directly appointed by the king, and the holding operates as a financially autonomous entity.

22. Around 98 percent of Morocco's external trade takes place via ports. In the wake of the Tanger Med project, the authorities aim to create many more maritime clusters in order to boost economic growth and regional development. With the National Port Strategy 2030, launched in 2012 by the Ministère de l'Equipement et des Transports (MET, Ministry of Infrastructure and Transport), Morocco wants to (re)construct new major ports divided over six regional nuclei, and give each nucleus its own strategic objectives. With this national plan, coordinated by the National Port Agency, new major port facilities are planned in cities such as Nador, Kenitra, Safi, and Jorf Lasfar. The latter two are important logistical hubs in the export of phosphates (for a more detailed overview, see MET 2011). See also Oxford Business Group, "Morocco Advances on Regional Port Projects," October 27, 2015.

23. One U.S. dollar is equal to 9.82 Moroccan dirhams; one euro is 10.86 dirhams (exchange rate of June 28, 2016).

24. SPVs are legal constructions created by the main company to securitize investments and reduce financial risks and bankruptcy costs. By breaking up the financing of different projects, the parent company transfers assets to the SPV in order to carry out some specific purpose or activity.

25. MHUAE is the Ministère Délégué Chargé de l'Habitat, de l'Urbanisme et de l'Aménagement de l'Espace (Ministry of Housing, Urbanism and Spatial Planning), or the new MATEUH, as it were. Over the years this ministry has changed names several times, often in relation to the competences it receives from central power (e.g., Ministry of the Interior).

26. Erik Swyngedouw, Frank Moulaert, and Arantxa Rodriguez argue that new systems of urban government and ruling networks under neoliberalism in Europe also make possible more discretional forms of management—lobbies, family ties, business connections, and forms of clientelism (2002, 565). In Morocco we see a reversed evolution; that is, the transformation of already existing discretional forms of elite government into more market-oriented forms.

3. Neoliberalism as Class Projects

1. This image is also completely ahistorical. It ignores the class politics and class antagonisms at the heart of world history and the making of our global economy (see Pijl 2012; and of course Marx 1992).

2. These changes are not necessarily denied by Benhaddou, yet they did not seem to alter the very nature of family rule. The expansion of an elite base in Morocco did not affect the power of the traditional ruling families but added more elites into their circle.

3. The establishment of the CGEM dates back to 1933, during the protectorate, as the country's main private sector organization.

4. This image should be nuanced. Although many of these "self-made men" did not have connections within the upper echelons of the Moroccan political elite, they were still well connected and coming from wealthy backgrounds (Cammett 2007, 171–72).

5. The political reform process of the 1990s (the *alternance*) had a similar effect. Their definite co-optation into the realm of monarchial power caused the historical opposition parties (Istiqlal and USFP) to lose a lot of their appeal among the general public and undermined their capacity to pressure the monarchy.

6. The stratification approach pictures class principally in terms of individual attributes and living conditions, but attributes such as sex, ethnicity, education, social income, religion, and geographical location (e.g., the urban–rural divide) can also be considered factors that explain social class positions in society. Such an approach does not posit a causal relation between the social conditions of the different classes. Classes are just ranged from upper classes over middle classes to lower classes and finally the underclass (whose living conditions are not secure with respect to their most basic needs) without any further systemic link between these different social positions (E. O. Wright 2009).

7. In an interview, a close contact within the CDG confirmed for me that the allegiance of Alami to the El Majidi clan was probably one of the reasons for the dismissal of Bakkoury (interview, Rabat, May 17, 2010).

8. Likewise, how empirically sound are concepts such as the regime, the makhzan, or the state bourgeoisie? In the case of Morocco, where does the makhzan actually end and the state bourgeoisie begin?

9. In a way this is a very logical outcome of Marx's very definition of capital. Capital for Marx is not a thing (e.g., a stock of assets) but a process, a social relation. A certain thing (a resource, a house, an amount of money) only becomes capital when it is put into circulation and integrated in a process of production and exchange in order to accumulate more capital. As Marx himself stated: "Capital is not a thing, but a social relation between persons which is mediated through things" (1992, 931). Class then refers to the specific ways this accumulated capital is generated.

10. A lot of the misconceptions concerning Marx's own use of the concept of class lie in the fact that he used this concept in different ways in his own writings. One has to make a distinction between Marx's political writings (e.g., *The Communist Manifesto*), where he uses class "to refer to more or less unified groups of people in social conflict," and his more theoretical writings (e.g., *Capital*), where he articulates a concept of class that does not refer to a particularly defined group of persons but rather to particular social relations and practices of capital accumulation (Resnick and Wolff 1987, 109). The latter use of class points to the conflictual nature of capital *circulation*, to the agency behind capital's *movement* in space, and as such class cannot be something fixed itself. By contrast, in his political writings he presented political change as a necessary struggle between the working class and the capitalist class. He did so from a strategic and political viewpoint, not so much a theoretical one. In his more theoretical work, he wanted to understand the particular nature of struggle and unravel the key social relations of domination and exploitation that determined that struggle. According to Marx, capitalist production was not merely the production of commodities but, "by its very essence, the production of surplus-value" (1992, 644). Following this observation, he distinguished necessary labor (labor necessary to keep oneself alive) from surplus labor (actual unpaid work that goes into the production of surplus value). The concept of class in *Capital* refers to the very relations and practices involved in the exploitation of surplus labor and the production and appropriation of surplus value (Resnick and Wolff 1987, 110; Ruccio 2011, 223).

11. Central to Marx's analysis, Harvey argues, "is that a concept such as 'class' can take on a meaning only in relation to the historical context in which it is to be applied." In other words, class "has a contingent meaning depending upon whether we are considering feudal, capitalist, or socialist modes of production" (1989b, 111). We could argue in today's context that the meaning of class will vary whether we are considering actually existing state developmentalist or neoliberal forms of capitalist expansion (see Chatterjee 2016). In both cases, capitalist accumulation will take place differently and by different kinds of actors. Within a neoliberal project, for example the megaproject in the Bouregreg

Valley, class forces obtain a more transnational character. Under a regime of import substitution, class forces will obviously have a more national character.

4. Imagineering a New Bouregreg Valley

1. Quoted from the promotional film of the Bouregreg Marina, "Projet d'aménagement et de mise en valeur des deux rives du bouregreg," December 27, 2010, https://www.youtube.com/watch?v=K7JJI1UWHJo.

2. "L'agglomération de la capitale du Royaume est-elle digne d'un tel avenir? N'est-on pas en droit d'attendre de ce lieu exceptionnel un meilleur destin?"

3. "La culture est un moyen de valorisation très important pour la destination Maroc. Selon plusieurs études, 39% des touristes qui viennent au Maroc sont attirés par la culture du pays. Développer ce genre de projets permet aussi une incroyable valorisation des actifs. Prenez l'exemple de Bilbao qui, il y a à peine quinze ans, n'était pas visible sur la carte du tourisme mondial. Après la construction du Guggenheim, . . . , le prix du résidentiel a augmenté de 500% en l'espace de 5 ans, et les arrivées touristiques dans la ville ont été multipliées par six."

4. "Brochure Retail: Bab Al Bahr," https://www.yumpu.com/fr/document/view/16675700/brochure-retail-bab-al-bahr/5.

5. The project comprised eight districts in the beginning, but these have been regrouped into three districts and a hotel area. Since the launch of the first phase the master plan has been changed several times, as well as the main website of the project. The latest brochure of the Marina Morocco project is available at https://www.eaglehills.com/our-developments/morocco/la-marina -morocco/master-plan.

6. The total budget of 3.75 billion dirhams is approximately US$400 million.

7. The project's designated territory was part of the jurisdiction of six urban districts (three in Rabat and three in Salé) and fell under the authority of the locally elected city councils of both Rabat and Salé. Especially since the municipal reforms of 1976 and 2002, local elected bodies had received more competences to deal with issues of urban planning and development. At the same time, however, the monarchy and the Ministry of Interior kept firm control over the city councils through a parallel state–institutional network of provinces, prefectures, and *wilayas*. This will be elaborated on in chapter 5.

8. Essakl resigned from his post in March 2017 and was succeeded ad interim by Said Zarrou, who is also the director of the Marchica Med project (see below) and who used to be a former executive of ONA.

9. "L'Agence pour l'aménagement de la vallée du Bouregreg prend toutes les mesures nécessaires pour la réalisation et le respect du plan d'aménagement." Dahir 1-05-70 (November 23, 2005), article 26.

10. Habous is an Islamic legal institution of religious mortmain property. The property is administered by the Ministry of Habous.

11. Sovereignty, defined by thinkers such as Carl Schmitt (2007) and Giorgio Agamben (1998) as the ultimate power to call a state of exception to the law,

should be interpreted here in the positive or productive sense; that is, as the power to create exceptional opportunities, usually for a privileged minority, to pursue those political goals, and to enjoy those political advantages that are not valid in the rest of the national territory and that are not granted to the majority of the population (Ong 2006, 101).

12. Every two years the PAS can be revised by the Bouregreg Agency in accordance with the objectives of the project (Mouloudi 2015b, 131).

13. The AAVB owns a 99.99 percent share in STRS. The two municipalities each own one symbolic share; the Moroccan state owns two (interview with the director of STRS, Rabat, May 26, 2010).

14. In one case, the authority of the AAVB even extends beyond its legally determined jurisdiction. The STRS obtained the mandate from the two city councils to coordinate and manage the development of the tramway stretching into the territories of Rabat and Salé (interview with the director of STRS, Rabat, May 26, 2010).

15. Besides the prime minister, the council is composed of all local and national government bodies affected by the project, including the Minister of Interior, the wali of the region Rabat-Salé-Zemmour-Zaer, the governors of the prefectures of Rabat and Salé, the director of the Urban Agency, and the presidents of the locally elected city councils of Rabat and Salé.

16. "Nous estimons que c'est le seul moyen d'aller plus vite, d'aller très vite, et transcender toutes les difficultés et les procédures administratives qui sont très lentes. . . . Nous avons vu un certain nombres des projets qui sont fait, que ça soit à Paris, à Londres, à Rome, à Dubaï. Eh bien, ils ont créé une institution qui a permis donc de concentrer toutes les attributions pour pouvoir autoriser très rapidement." "Émission Éclairage," January 2006, part 1, https://www.youtube.com/watch?v=u53i6WjT7NI.

17. "Il faut rappeler une chose très important. Nous sommes dans une zone très sensibles. Nous sommes dans un découpage administrative très complexe: trois communes sur la rive droite, trois communes sur la rive gauche. Pour permettre demain à des investisseurs d'avoir un interlocuteur unique, il fallait de créer une structure unique, un seul opérateur. C'est l'agence. . . . Ça va être le principal interlocuteur des investisseurs et ça va être le facilitateur de toutes les opérations de développement." "Émission Éclairage," January 2006, part 2, https://www.youtube.com/watch?v=_9MQdBw62O4.

18. "On empiète pas sur leurs prérogatives. Nous allons aider les communes à faire de développement. Aujourd'hui, nous avons une relations particulièrement parfaite avec le maire de Rabat, le maire de Salé. En réalité nous récupérons quelques prérogatives. Les recettes, par exemple, fiscales aux communes de la rive droite et de la rive gauche continuent à aller vers ses communes. Nous allons pas prendre possession de tout le territoire de Rabat ou de tout le territoire de Salé. Nous sommes spécialement intervenant dans une zone bien délimité."

19. The way in which Allen and Cochrane refer to the "powers of reach" or the "reach of government" (Allen 2009, 198; Allen and Cochrane 2010, 107) can also be understood in another way, in terms of the ability to produce new "politics of truth" (Lemke 2002), permeate everyday life (Painter 2006), and

govern "at a distance" (Rose 1999). It is obvious that "reach" refers here to the impact of specific technologies and methods of government, and that government is understood as a form of power invested in the regulation of the population, the creation of neoliberal citizens, and the privatization of the state. These aspects of government will be elaborated in detail in chapters 5 and 6.

20. The public works (the bridge, tunnel, and tramway) were still the sole responsibility of the AAVB.

21. "Al Maabar est considérée comme une des sociétés de développement immobilier les plus innovantes de la région. A travers des projets de grande envergure en cours de réalisation au Maroc, en Libye et en Jordanie, Al Maabar gagne déjà une réputation de grand acteur économique et politique. Honorant le patrimoine, la culture ainsi que les valeurs d'Abu Dhabi, le 'Business Model' de l'entreprise s'oriente vers des opportunités attrayantes et durables sur le plan économique offrant ainsi un fort potentiel de croissance pour tous ses partenaires et actionnaires."

22. "l'Agence prend en compte les caractéristiques démographiques, sociales et économiques des populations concernées, afin d'assurer l'adéquation entre l'offre et les besoins." "Citoyenneté," AAVB, http://www.bouregreg.com/citoy ennete/.

23. See "Émission Éclairage," part 2, https://www.youtube.com/watch?v=_9MQdBw62O4.

24. For a sense of the Amwaj project, see photos available at "Amwaj Bouregreg Development–Morocco," *Premier Art*, 2009, http://lepremierart.com /amwaj-bouregreg-development/.

25. "Moins densément aménagé que la rive de Rabat pour permettre une plus grande variété d'utilisation par la population de l'agglomération."

26. The process through which individuals are transformed into subjects is called "interprellation" by Althusser. To give a simple example, interpellation can be "imagined along the lines of the most commonplace everyday police (or other) hailing: 'Hey, you there!'" By the mere act of turning around, the hailed individual becomes a subject because he recognized that the hail was addressed to him and not someone else (Althusser 2006, 105).

27. This was one of the billboard slogans promoting the Amwaj project.

28. Chancy Roy, "Wessal Capital Wants to Support Moroccan Tourism," June 28, 2015, http://www.dailymotion.com/video/x2vr09i.

29. I heard a similar message in interviews with the Head of Corporate and Finance Partnerships and the Director of Juridical Affairs (Rabat, May 20, 2010).

30. The term "imagineering" was coined by the Walt Disney Studios to combine the ways of imagination with engineering (Paul 2004, 574).

31. Many of the historical medinas in Morocco, also in Rabat and even in Marrakech, have socially degraded over the years. They have become transit zones for rural migrants and are inhabited by many poor tenants (Ameur 2000; Balbo and Navez-Bouchanine 1995).

32. At the same time, the Moroccan middle class is leaving these historical sites or is not interested in buying there. Instead, the middle class is looking for more modern housing accommodations either in the perimeter of the old

colonial city center or the middle-class neighborhood of Agdal. Consequently, social inequality in the medina of Rabat and the Kasbah is rising fast with poor tenants, on the one hand, and foreign investors looking to start romantic B&Bs, on the other hand (McGuinness 2013).

33. This is merely based on observations and pictures taken between 2007 and 2013. No detailed research has been done to confirm these observations so they have to be taken with caution. Nevertheless, some other observations seem to confirm this trend (McGuinness 2013).

34. The prices of units in the Marina Morocco project vary between 1 and 9 million dirhams (Bouchaf 2013). To compare, the cost of a social apartment varies between 140,000 and 250,000 dirhams (between US$14,784 and 26,401).

5. Changing Methods of Authoritarian Power

1. "One must govern for the market, rather than because of the market," as Foucault explained the fundamental difference between neoliberalism and classical liberalism (2008, 121).

2. In the early 1970s, the World Bank prioritized for the first time the improvement of slums in situ as an essential part of poverty alleviation strategies (M. Davis 2006b; Milbert 2006). Interestingly, the inspiration for this came from the British anarchist architect John F. C. Turner, who advocated the rollback of state intervention in public housing projects and preferred housing projects with a strong focus on participation and the autonomy of local inhabitants. The role of government had to be restricted to the facilitation of the inhabitants' access to resources (see Turner 1976). His anarchist view on self-help had turned into a new World Bank strategy to advocate a departure from heavy state-subsidized public housing projects and emphasize slum upgrading in situ to make housing more affordable (M. Davis 2006b, 72).

3. Moreover, employees in the public sector enjoyed better conditions and more social protection than those in the private sector. Yet the bulk of the Moroccan workforce is active in the private sector, excluding the informal sector, where there is no protection at all.

4. In May through December 2005, 1,104 projects were already set up with a budget of 250 million dirhams.

5. During the first phase, the national state budget was responsible for 60 percent of the resources, the local authorities 20 percent, and the other 20 percent of the budget was covered by loans and gifts from foreign donors and international organizations (the World Bank, the EU, Saudi Arabia, etc.) (World Bank 2006b).

6. In this chapter I focus mainly on the INDH program as an example. In the next chapter, the focus shifts to VSB to further elaborate on some of the points raised in chapter 5.

7. "Si le niveau de croissance économique est insuffisant et inéquitable dans la mesure où ses dividendes ne profitent pas à l'ensemble des populations et des régions du pays, d'autant que certaines continuent à pâtir de la marginalisation et de la dégradation des conditions de vie, il importe de noter, en même

temps, que l'inclusion souhaitée ne saurait être considérée, selon une vision sim-
pliste et étriquée, comme un fardeau qui pèse sur la croissance, dès lors qu'elle
en est à la fois la condition et le catalyseur." King Mohammed VI, address from
the throne, May 18, 2005, http://www.maroc.ma/fr/discours-royaux/discours-de
-sm-le-roi-mohammed-vi-à-la-nation-0.

8. "Nous l'appelons aussi à adopter un plan d'action fondé sur les principes de bonne gouvernance, à savoir la responsabilité et la transparence, les
règles de professionnalisme, la large participation des citoyens, l'intégration et
la rationalisation des interventions des établissements et organismes publics,
ainsi que le suivi et l'évaluation permanente des réalisations."

9. The *mqaddem* is a representative of the Ministry of Interior at the local
neighborhood level. He acts as the eyes and ears of the ministry.

10. Similar schemes are also to be found in the rest of the Arab region; for
example, the National Solidarity Fund (the famous 26.26 Fund) in Tunisia
(Hibou 2006) and the Social Fund for Development in Egypt (Elyachar 2002).

11. The Hassan II Fund also invests in large infrastructural projects (Tanger
Med and Bouregreg), social housing, agriculture, and cultural and sporting
events. The Mohammed V Foundation has realized projects for more than 3.3
billion dirhams and invests in social welfare domains such as sustainable development, formation, medical care, and education. These institutions are (semipublic) hybrid structures financed by exceptional resources and directed by private
entrepreneurs, close advisers of the king, and a technocratic "state nobility"
(Catusse 2009b, 206; Vermeren 2009, 90).

12. It is within this context of entanglement and hybridization that Hibou
points to the deinstitutionalization of the state (2004b, 41). However, she
sketches only part of the picture. The changing modes of state intervention
result not only in more indirect forms of government and political control, as
Hibou argues, but also in the reinstitutionalization of state power depending
often on the particular neoliberal project, as we have seen, for example, in the
case of the Bouregreg project. Different neoliberal projects require different
kinds of statecraft.

13. Foucault's approach has often been described as antistatist and post-
structuralist as he rejected any attempt to develop a general theory of the state.
Obvious tensions seem to arise when one combines his approach with neo-
Marxist approaches on state-institutional power and change. Yet this is a mis-
conception. His work on governmentality and biopolitics actually proved his
interest in changing forms of statehood and statecraft (Jessop 2007). It provides
us with many new insights on contemporary neoliberal projects. Foucault
intended to show how the modern state and the modern individual codeter-
mined each other's emergence, not by limiting the field of power relations to the
government of the state but by showing how some power relations concentrated
themselves historically in the form of the state—without ever being reducible to
it (Lemke 2002, 58). There is, however, a crucial difference between these two
approaches. While people such as Brenner, Harvey, and others stress that state
institutions are the motor behind the (re)production and regulation of capitalist
space and neoliberal globalization, a Foucauldian approach would argue that it
is not so much the state (or state institutions) that produces and monitors the

contemporary market economy, but it is market society itself, and more specifically the practices and rationalities that arise from it, that helps to constitute the contemporary state form. With regard to urban entrepreneurialism, people such as Brenner stress that new state spaces are the motor behind the production of capitalist space and neoliberal globalization (Brenner 2004). A Foucauldian approach would argue slightly differently. It would emphasize that it is neoliberal globalization itself, the practices and governmental methods that emerge from within it, that demands and generates state-institutional change within and across space.

14. John Allen clarifies this internalization of "the truth" as follows: "If people whether in hospitals or clinics, universities or prisons, or public sector housing estates for that matter, accept the 'truth' of the arrangements in which they find themselves, then those selfsame arrangements provide a guide as to what kind of behaviour is thought acceptable and what is not" (2004, 23). Power manifests itself through indirect techniques of self-regulation that prompt us to behave in certain ways, which makes it difficult to behave in any other way.

15. Cortney Hughes Rinker, for example, shows how Moroccan women reproduce and incorporate neoliberal principles of self-government and individual responsibility through reproductive practices and strategies of family planning. They do so not because they just obediently follow top-down strategies promoted by INDH but because they use their own elements of culture and identity; for example, religion. Hughes Rinker demonstrates that religion did not occupy a space outside neoliberal transformation but became a facilitator of it; a neoliberal governmentality was reproduced through Islamic understandings that women used to justify their personal decisions. Women's decisions, in other words, were made autonomously and in accordance with their religious beliefs but mirrored, at the same time, the government's neoliberal agenda for social development. In this process, women "produce new meanings of development and new notions of Islamic neoliberal citizenship" through their reproductive practices (Hughes Rinker 2014).

16. This can be related to the human or social capital theory. From a Marxist perspective, however, this concept is contradictory because an essential feature of "capital" is that one can live off its interest (capital as a property relation always has that option). There is no way of accumulating wealth and income from particular talents or competences *without* laboring for it yourself or putting someone else to work with your talents (Harvey 2014, 185–86).

17. Neoliberal governmentality differs radically from classical liberalism. Neoliberal thinkers transformed classical liberalism in a fundamental way: they decoupled the principle "laissez-faire" from the market economy in the way that their main goal was to *create*, *produce*, and *regulate* "a concrete and real space in which the formal structure of competition could function" (competition was not considered a natural state but the object of governmental intervention). According to Foucault, "Neoliberals should not therefore be identified with laissez-faire, but rather with permanent vigilance, activity, and intervention" (2008, 131–32).

18. "Il s'agit, notamment, de l'Etat de droit et des institutions, de la citoyenneté fondée sur le respect des droits et des obligations de l'Homme, du libéralisme

économique, et de la liberté d'entreprendre. Outre la solidarité, la justice sociale et l'ouverture sur le monde. C'est à Nous qu'il échoit de veiller à la pérennité de ces valeurs, quelles que soient les circonstances et leurs fluctuations. C'est cela, du reste, Notre conception de la Monarchie citoyenne." King Mohammed VI, address from the throne, July 30, 2007, http://www.maroc.ma/fr/discours-roy-aux/discours-de-sm-le-roi-mohammed-vi-à-la-nation-à-loccasion-du-ème-anniversaire-de.

19. "Je resterai, cher peuple, tel que tu M'as toujours connu, le Roi-Citoyen à l'avant-garde des militants oeuvrant sur le terrain, dans toutes les régions du pays, comme à l'extérieur. Je M'attacherai également à consolider les piliers de l'unité et de la démocratie, à conforter la dynamique de développement, de progrès et de solidarité, et à raffermir la capacité du Maroc à agir en synergie avec le monde extérieur et les mutations qui s'y opèrent, sans jamais se départir de l'identité marocaine authentique."

20. The western part of Casablanca has always been a more residential area, while industry was mainly concentrated in the east. This had its roots in the protectorate. The west was reserved for the European residents, the south was for the Moroccans, and the east and northeast were developed as industrial zones. This partition had an enduring effect on the social fabric of the city. Today, sociospatial fragmentation still reflects this historical east–west divide (Rachik 1995, 2002). In the west, you will find luxurious residential neighborhoods such as Anfa, where the upper class of Casablanca resides. They represent approximately 5 percent of the urban population. This is a more open part of the city with parks and public spaces, and many houses have huge gardens. The architecture is diverse and modern. The east, with districts such as Ben M'sik and Sidi Moumen, is characterized by bidonvilles, clandestine housing, and low-cost housing blocks. The bulk of Casablanca's poorest population (approximately 20 percent of the urban population) lives here. It is much denser. The architecture is more monotonous. Many of the numerous apartment blocks located in the east are the result of state-sponsored housing policies, and over time a lot of the public spaces were taken over by informal housing. This east–west divide is also perceptible in the names given to neighborhoods and streets. In the west you can find areas with Western names such as Californie, Bourgogne, Gauthier, and Racine. In the east, Arab names are more common; for example, Sidi Othman, Ben M'sik, Jamila, Lalla Mériam, Moulay Rachid, and Sidi Moumen. It is as if the west of Casablanca is associated with Western modernity and characterizes the city's openness toward Europe, while the east of Casablanca is associated with Moroccan tradition and its links with the rural hinterland (Nachoui 1998).

21. The five prefectures were Casa-Anfa, Ain Sebaa-Hay Mohammedia, Ben M'Sik-Sidi Othman, Aïn Chock-Hay Hassani, and Mohammadia-Zénata.

22. Yet it still lasted until the constitutional amendments of 1992 and 1996 that the regions and the regional government obtained the official status of local government (Hinti 2005, 170).

23. In large cities such as Casablanca, the presidents and the vice presidents of the urban municipalities were assembled in a supramunicipal administrative

body: the Urban Community. But this entity did not have the same prerogatives as the city council after 2002.

24. The DGCL was a department of the Ministry of Interior established by Driss Basri in 1976 in order to maintain control over the extended competences of the local municipal governments established with the municipal reform of 1976. For example, the local tax system, which dealt mainly with the granting of licenses, urban taxes, and the redistribution of VAT fees, depended on the redistribution of the resources by the Ministry of Interior. This deprived the local councils largely of any margin for autonomous decision-making (Catusse, Cattedra, and Janati 2007).

25. The *wilaya* of Greater Casablanca is subdivided into four large prefectures (Casablanca, Médiouna, Nouaceur, and Mohammédia). The prefecture of Casablanca is further subdivided into eight smaller prefectures: Hay Mohammadi-Ain Sebaa, Sidi Bernoussi, Anfa, Ain Chock, Mers Sultan, Hay Hassani, Ben M'Sik, and Moulay Rachid).

26. This metro was never realized and has been replaced by a tramway today. The first two lines were completed in December 2012.

27. The MUHTE was founded in 1972 and took over urban policy from the Ministry of Interior (see chapter 2).

28. These were some of the most obvious examples, but not the only ones. Other institutions and instruments were created during the 1980s and 1990s to increase territorial control and centralize urban planning (the regional inspections, the prefectural departments of urbanism, etc.) (see Catusse, Cattedra, and Janati 2005; Philifert and Jolé 2005; Rachik 1995, 2002; Zriouli 1998).

29. The urban space of the street is a place for communication and movement that can eventually lead to "street politics," but streets—as the French philosopher Henri Lefebvre reminded us—can also be a repressing place where cars are hunters and pedestrians become the hunted (Lefebvre 2003, 21).

30. This move quickly turned into an instrument of the makhzan to enforce an additional tax on the entire Moroccan population because not having such a certificate could become the subject of public scrutiny and suspicion (Cattedra 2001, 171–80).

31. Several studies argue that mosques played a crucial role in the emergence of bidonvilles and informal neighborhoods. The building of a mosque protected the neighborhood from being torn down and destroyed. It also provided a central meeting place from which new forms of mobilization and association could emerge (Cattedra 2001; Iraki 2006b; Naciri 1987). In twenty years (1960–80), there were more mosques built in Morocco than in the two preceding centuries. The recurrent stigmatization of the slum population—for example, as breeding places for Islamist extremists—played a crucial role in the decision to build the Mosque Hassan II (see Cattedra 2001).

6. Power and Control through Techniques of Security

1. Both this chapter and the previous one are based on a thorough revision and deepening of arguments published elsewhere (cf. Bogaert 2011, 2013a).

2. I use the concept of "security" in the Foucauldian sense, as the future-oriented management of risks (see chapter 5).

3. Again, let me stress that this distinction between sovereign planning and techniques of security is far from absolute. Both sovereign power and bio-power are always copresent in modern societies. What I emphasize is a shift in the particular type of power that becomes dominant (sovereignty in the 1980s and biopower in the early twenty-first century).

4. "Ensemble anarchique d'habitations sommaires, édifiées à l'aide de matériaux hétéroclites, privées d'hygiène et d'équipements collectifs, où vivent des populations démunies ou mal intégrées dans le tissu urbain."

5. Target eleven of the MDGs aimed "to have achieved a significant improvement in the lives of at least 100 million slum dwellers" by 2020 (UN-Habitat 2003, 7). It was based on a global initiative launched a year earlier by Cities Alliance, a global multidonor coalition of cities and their development partners promoted by the World Bank and UN-Habitat. The initiative, known as the Cities Without Slums Action Plan, was endorsed by 150 member states (Morocco was one of them).

6. The Ministry of Housing has changed names and competences many times. Therefore, I will use the term "Ministry of Housing" to refer to the contemporary ministry, unless stated otherwise in the text.

7. This tax was raised by the FSH from five to fifteen cents per kilo in 2012, collecting 1.5 billion dirhams in 2012 (Toutain and Rachmuhl 2014, 15).

8. On the number of cities, see "Nabil Benabdallah: 56 villes déclarées sans bidonvilles jusqu'à présent," July 27, 2016, http://maroc-diplomatique.net/nabil-benabdallah-56-villes-declarees-bidonvilles-jusqua-present/; on the number of households, see Wadii Charrad, "Benabdellah: '54 villes se sont débarrassés de leurs baraques,'" *TelQuel*, November 18, 2015, http://telquel.ma/2015/11/18/benabdellah-54-villes-se-debarrasses-leurs-baraques_1470828.

9. UN-Habitat, "The 2010 Scroll of Honour Award Winners," http://mirror.unhabitat.org/content.asp?typeid=19&catid=827&cid=8816. Despite these optimistic numbers, other sources in the media (e.g., *L'Économiste*) have questioned the numbers of the Moroccan authorities and argued that new bidonvilles continue to emerge in cities like Casablanca, Marrakech, and Tangier (Alami 2010). In July 2016 the Minister of Housing himself deplored the fact that 120,000 new households moved into slums since the start of VSB. See "Nabil Benabdallah: 56 villes déclarées sans bidonvilles jusqu'à présent."

10. Already in 1999 the Ministry of Housing launched a program that granted complete exemption from taxes for real estate developers who delivered units with a minimum of three rooms and a floor area of fifty to one hundred square meters at an agreed price of 250,000 dirhams or US$26,401. In 2008 this scheme was complemented with a low-cost housing program priced at 140,000 dirhams (minimum two rooms and a total floor area of fifty to sixty square meters). The real estate developers could benefit from the same tax exemptions on the condition that they build at least five hundred units (Toutain 2014). Social mixture *(péréquation)* is another strategy used in resettlement operations to diversify the population in the relocation sites and create space to finance the

projects. It enables developers to increase their profits or reduce their costs as they can sell a certain portion of the apartments (usually of a higher standard) at a market price.

11. Dyar Al Mansour was responsible for three projects during my field-work in Morocco, one in Rabat (Douar Al Kora) and two in Temara (the Annasr project and the Mers El Kheir project).

12. CDG created the Société de Développement al Kora first, which later became Dyar Al Mansour. They are more specialized in operations of rehousing *(relogement)*, while Al Omrane, as mentioned, specializes primarily in operations of resettlement *(recasement)*.

13. This method is not applied in every slum upgrading project. AS was implemented in approximately 20 percent of the resettlement operations nation-wide, but more than half of the targeted population lived in Casablanca (Toutain 2008, 27). Coordinating agencies such as Al Omrane decide where to apply the method of AS. "In some smaller operations we don't need to use social accom-paniment," I was told by the Al Omrane director in charge of quality. "There are also people who like to leave" (interview, June 8, 2010).

14. FOGARIM stands for Fonds de garantie des prêts au logement en faveur des populations á revenus modestes et/ou non réguliers (Housing loan guarantee fund for moderate or non-regular income populations).

15. The average monthly payment of a loan with a FOGARIM guarantee cannot surpass 1,750 dirhams per month for beneficiaries outside the VSB pro-gram and 1,000 dirhams per month for VSB beneficiaries. The minimum wage in Morocco is approximately 2,000 dirhams per month.

16. An official of ADS told me that this had to be signed by a representative of the state (the qaid), who often exaggerated the exact income in order to make sure the person in question got his loan (interview, Temara, May 31, 2010).

17. "En réalité, sur le terrain, il s'agit surtout de faire accepter aux bidon-villois le fait qu'ils doivent à la fois quitter le bidonville et démolir leur baraque, mais aussi participer au financement du transfert et du nouveau logement. *In fine*, l'adhésion aux projets de recasement et de relogement se matérialise avant tout par une participation financière des bénéficiaires aux coûts de l'opération."

18. Nevertheless, despite the improvement of the dwellings, the new houses are still built at an absolute minimum cost. In one of the projects I visited in May 2010, the Annasr project in Temara done by Dyar Al Mansour, some of the residents invited me into their homes to show the cracks in the walls and the humidity stains. Nearly all the apartments of the rehousing project had them, they told me, after being finished only two years. On top of that, the sewage system was leaking, which gave off a really unpleasant smell. The homeowners did the best they could to repair the damage themselves. In some apartments, I noticed holes in the walls where they had to reconfigure electricity.

19. Moreover, there is also the problem of tenants who risk being left out. Technically speaking, the owner of a shelter enters the VSB program while ten-ants, on the other hand, pay their monthly rent and eventually are threatened to end up with nothing (Mansion and Rachmuhl 2012, 6). Somewhat related to the tenant problem is the issue of speculation. Some people tend to profit from the

VSB program by investing in shelters. The allocated plots are then resold and the process starts anew (Laval et al. 2010).

20. Interestingly, the beneficiaries of VSB do not always prioritize the immediate formalization of their newly acquired properties. They put it off for all kinds of reasons, not in the least because it brings with it new taxes (property taxes) and additional registration fees (Toutain and Rachmuhl 2013, 102; 2014, 36).

21. "85.3% des ménages marocains incapables d'épargner en 2016," *TelQuel*, November 19, 2015, http://telquel.ma/2015/11/19/85-3-menages-marocains-incapable-depargner-2016_1470590.

22. To be fair, in the case of the Lydec official, I noticed no contempt for the slum dwellers at all.

23. "Un changement de domicile constitue souvent un traumatisme psychologique et une perte de repères pour les personnes concernées. Ceci est d'autant plus vrai lorsque ce changement concerne le mode même de logement, voire de vie."

24. Projects are sometimes changed when residents resist and manage to mobilize strongly enough against the public agency.

25. "Les ménages ont trouvé la parade en créant une densification à l'intérieur même des baraques. Les parents hébergent leurs enfants, mais également leurs conjoints et leurs progénitures. De fait, lorsque nous leur proposons un lot de terrain ou un appartement destiné à un ménage moyen, ils refusent et attendent une opportunité plus intéressante en termes de superficie. Malgré le travail d'accompagnement social prévu par le ministère qui a pour objectif de les convaincre d'accepter un relogement, nous nous sommes trouvés contraints, récemment, de recourir à la justice pour des cas de bénéficiaires qui refusaient l'habitation proposée."

Conclusion

1. UN-Habitat, "The 2010 Scroll of Honour Award Winners," http://mirror.unhabitat.org/content.asp?typeid=19&catid=827&cid=8816.

2. I am writing this conscious of my position as a white researcher within a field of study still dominated by Western scholarship.

BIBLIOGRAPHY

Abouhani, Abdelghani. 1995a. "Introduction: Urbanisation, habitat spontané et mouvements sociaux au Maroc." In *L'Etat et les quartiers populaires au Maroc: De la marginalisation a l'emeute; Habitat spontané et mouvements sociaux*, edited by Abdel ghani Abouhani, 5–8. Dakar: Council for the Development of Social Science Research in Africa.

———. 1995b. "Le mouvement associatif dans les quartiers populaires marocains." In *L'Etat et les quartiers populaires au Maroc: De la marginalisation a l'emeute; Habitat spontané et mouvements sociaux*, edited by Abdelghani Abouhani, 121–40. Dakar: Council for the Development of Social Science Research in Africa.

———. 1995c. "Médiation notabilaire et habitat clandestin au Maroc." In *L'Etat et les quartiers populaires au Maroc: De la marginalisation a l'emeute; Habitat spontané et mouvements sociaux*, edited by Abdelghani Abouhani, 11–27. Dakar: Council for the Development of Social Science Research in Africa.

———. 1999. *Pouvoirs, villes et notabilités locales: Quand les notables font les villes.* Rabat: Urbama.

———. 2006. "Les nouvelles élites urbaines: Le rôle des notables et des cadres associatifs dans le système politico-administratif local." In *Pouvoirs locaux et systèmes municipaux dans le monde arabe*, edited by Abdelghani Abouhani, 55–75. Rabat: Institute National d'Aménagement et d'Urbanisme (INAU); San Domenico di Fiesole: Centre Robert Schuman pour les études avancées.

Abrahamian, Ervand. 1982. *Iran between Two Revolutions.* Princeton, N.J.: Princeton University Press.

Abu-Lughod, Janet. 1980. *Rabat: Urban Apartheid in Morocco.* Princeton, N.J.: Princeton University Press.

Achcar, Gilbert. 2013. *The People Want: A Radical Exploration of the Arab Uprising.* Berkeley: University of California Press.

Agamben, Giorgio. 1998. *Homo Sacer: Sovereign Power and Bare Life.* Stanford: Stanford University Press.

———. 2009. *The Signature of All Things: On Method.* New York: Zone Books.

Agence Marocaine De Développement Des Investissements (AMDI). 2015. "Le Maroc en bref." *Guide de l'investisseur,* July 28. http://www.mre.gov.ma/ sites/default/files/Fichiers/Pages/Guide%20de%20linvestisseur.pdf.

Aggestam, Karen, Laura Guazzone, Helena Lindholm Schulz, M. Cristina Paciello, and Daniela Pioppi. 2009. "The Arab State and Neo-liberal Globalization." In *The Arab State and Neo-Liberal Globalization: The Restructuring of State Power in the Middle East,* edited by Laura Guazzone and Daniela Pioppi, 325–50. Reading: Ithaca Press.

Alami, Mailika. 2010. "Bidonvilles: Ils prolifèrent toujours et pas qu'à Casablanca!" *L'Economiste,* no. 3307 (June 28). http://www.leconomiste.com/ article/bidonvilles-ils-proliferent-toujours-et-pas-qu-casablanca.

Albrecht, H., and Oliver Schlumberger. 2004. "'Waiting for Godot': Regime Change without Democratization in the Middle East." *International Political Science Review / Revue internationale de science politique* 25, no. 4: 371–92.

Alicino, Francesco. 2015. "Morocco: An Islamic Globalizing Monarchy within the Elusive Phenomenon of Arab Spring." *Oriente Moderno* 95, nos. 1–2: 145–72.

Allen, John. 2004. "The Whereabouts of Power: Politics, Government and Space." *Geografiska Annaler, Series B: Human Geography* 86, no. 1: 19–32.

———. 2009. "Three Spaces of Power: Territory, Networks, plus a Topological Twist in the Tale of Domination and Authority." *Journal of Power* 2, no. 2: 197–212.

———. 2011a. "Powerful Assemblages?" *Area* 43, no. 2: 154–57.

———. 2011b. "Topological Twists: Power's Shifting Geographies." *Dialogues in Human Geography* 1, no. 3: 283–98.

Allen, John, and Allan Cochrane. 2010. "Assemblages of State Power: Topological Shifts in the Organization of Government and Politics." *Antipode* 42, no. 5: 1071–89.

Allinson, Jamie. 2015. "Class Forces, Transition and the Arab Uprisings: A Comparison of Tunisia, Egypt and Syria." *Democratization* 22, no. 2: 294–314.

Al Omrane. 2010. "Al Omrane: Leading Actor for Settlements Upgrading." Rabat. http://mirror.unhabitat.org/downloads/docs/11592_1_594601.pdf.

Althusser, Louis. 2006. "Ideology and Ideological State Apparatuses (Notes towards an Investigation)." In *The Anthropology of the State,* edited by Aradhna Sharma and Akhil Gupta, 86–111. Oxford: Blackwell.

Amara Hammou, Kenza. 2016. "Urbanisering in het Globale Zuiden, armoede en ontwikkeling: Case marokko." Master's thesis, Ghent University.

Amcham Morocco. 2007. "Morocco Trade and Investment Guide 2007." https: //issuu.com/amchammorocco/docs/tradeandinvestmentguide2007/4.

Ameur, Mohamed. 1995. "Habitat clandestin: Problèmes et possibilités." In *L'Etat et les quartiers populaires au Maroc: De la marginalisation a l'emeute; Habitat spontané et mouvements sociaux,* edited by Abdelghani Abouhani, 57–73. Dakar: Council for the Development of Social Science Research in Africa.

———. 2000. "Les associations de quartiers: Un nouvel acteur au milieu urbain." In *Gouvernance et sociétés civiles: Les mutations urbaines au Maghreb,* edited by Mostafa Kharoufi, 59–79. Casablanca: Afrique Orient.

Amin, Samir. 2003. *Obsolescent Capitalism*. London: Zed Books.

Anderson, Lisa. 2000. "Dynasts and Nationalists: Why Monarchies Survive." In *Middle East Monarchies: The Challenge of Modernity*, edited by Joseph Kostiner, 53–70. Boulder: Lynne Rienner.

Arandel, Christian, and Anna Wetterberg. 2013. "Between 'Authoritarian' and 'Empowered' Slum Relocation: Social Mediation in the Case of Ennakhil, Morocco." *Cities* 30 (February): 140–48.

Atia, Mona. 2013. *Building a House in Heaven: Pious Neoliberalism and Islamic Charity in Egypt*. Minneapolis: University of Minnesota Press.

Ayeb, Habib. 2011. "Social and Political Geography of the Tunisian Revolution: The Alfa Grass Revolution." *Review of African Political Economy* 38, no. 129: 467–79.

Ayubi, Nazih. 1997. "Etatisme versus Privatization: The Changing Economic Role of the State in Nine Arab Countries." In *Economic Transition in the Middle East: Global Challenges and Adjustment Strategies*, edited by Heba Handoussa, 125–66. Cairo: American University in Cairo Press.

Baabood, Abdullah. 2009. "The Growing Economic Presence of Gulf Countries in the Mediterranean Region." In *Med. 2009: Mediterranean Yearbook*, 203–9. Barcelona: Institut Europeu de la Mediterr'ania (IEMed); Fundació CIDOB (Barcelona Centre for International Affairs).

Bab Al Bahr Development Company. 2011. "Bab Al Bahr: Etat d'avancement du projet septembre 2011." Press release, September 2011.

Balbo, Marcello, and Françoise Navez-Bouchanine. 1995. "Urban Fragmentation as a Research Hypothesis: Rabat-Salé Case Study." *Habitat INTL* 19, no. 4: 571–82.

Barari, Hassan A. 2015. "The Persistence of Autocracy: Jordan, Morocco and the Gulf." *Middle East Critique* 24, no. 1: 99–111.

Bargach, Jamila. 2008. "Rabat: From Capital to Global Metropolis." In *The Evolving Arab City: Tradition, Modernity and Urban Development*, edited by Yasser Elsheshtawy, 99–117. London: Routledge.

Barthel, Pierre-Arnaud. 2010. "Arab Mega-Projects: Between the Dubai Effect, Global Crisis, Social Mobilization and a Sustainable Shift." *Built Environment* 36, no. 2: 133–45.

Barthel, Pierre-Arnaud, and Hicham Mouloudi. 2009. "Waterfronts de Casablanca et de Rabat: Un urbanisme de projet." *Urbanisme*, no. 369 (November–December): 52–56.

Barthel, Pierre-Arnaud, and Leïla Vignal. 2014. "Arab Mediterranean Mega-projects after the 'Spring': Business as Usual or a New Beginning?" *Built Environment* 40, no. 1: 52–71.

Barthel, Pierre-Arnaud, and Lamia Zaki. 2011. "Les holdings d'aménagement, nouvelles vitrines techniques de l'action urbaine au Maroc: Les cas d'Al Omrane et de la CDG Développement." In *L'action urbaine au Maghreb: Enjeux professionnels et politiques*, edited by Lamia Zaki, 205–25. Tunis: Institut de Recherche sur le Maghreb Contemporain; Paris: Karthala.

Bartoli, Sarah. 2011. "'Eliminer les bidonvilles = Éliminer la pauvreté,' Ou les charmes pervers d'une fausse évidence." *L'Économie politique* 49, no. 1: 44–60.

Batatu, Hanna. 1978. *The Old Social Classes and the Revolutionary Movements of Iraq: A Study of Iraq's Old Landed and Commercial Classes and of Its Communists, Ba'thists, and Free Officers.* Princeton, N.J.: Princeton University Press.

Bayat, Asef. 2000. "From 'Dangerous Classes' to 'Quiet Rebels': Politics of the Urban Subaltern in the Global South." *International Sociology* 15, no. 3: 533–57.

———. 2002. "Activism and Social Development in the Middle East." *International Journal of Middle East Studies* 34, no. 1: 1–28.

Bayat, Asef, and Kees Biekart. 2009. "Cities of Extremes." *Development and Change* 40, no. 5: 815–25.

Bayat, Asef, and Eric Denis. 2000. "Who Is Afraid of Ashwaiyyat? Urban Change and Politics in Egypt." *Environment and Urbanization* 12, no. 2: 185–99.

Beblawi, Hazem. 1990. "The Rentier State in the Arab World." In *The Arab State*, edited by Giacomo Luciani, 85–98. London: Routledge.

Beinin, Joel. 2001. *Workers and Peasants in the Modern Middle East.* Cambridge: Cambridge University Press.

———. 2009. "Workers' Protest in Egypt: Neo-liberalism and Class Struggle in 21st Century." *Social Movement Studies* 8, no. 4: 449–54.

Belarbi, Wafae. 2015. "Les mobilisations sociales dans les territoires périphériques de Casablanca pendant les années 1990." *L'Année du Maghreb*, no. 12: 137–53.

Belghazi, Naoufal. 2010. "Amwaj: Bye-Bye Sama Dubaï, le projet saucissonné." *La Vie éco*, June 14. http://lavieeco.com/news/economie/amwaj-bye-bye -sama-dubai-le-projet-saucissonne-16861.html.

Bellin, Eva. 2000. "Contingent Democrats: Industrialists, Labor, and Democratization in Late-Developing Countries." *World Politics* 52, no. 2: 175–205.

Ben Ali, Driss. 1997. "Economic Adjustment and Political Liberalization in Morocco." In *Economic Transition in the Middle East: Global Challenges and Adjustment Strategies*, edited by Heba Handoussa, 183–217. Cairo: American University in Cairo Press.

———. 2005. "Civil Society and Economic Reform in Morocco." Zentrum für Entwicklungsforschung, Bonn. http://www.zef.de/fileadmin/webfiles/down loads/projects/politicalreform/Civil_Society_and_Economic_Reform.pdf.

Benhaddou, Ali. 2009. *Maroc: Les élites du royaume: Enquête sur l'organisation du pouvoir au Maroc.* Paris: Riveneuve éditions.

Benmehdi, Hassan. 2010. "Parliament Considers New Funding for Moroccan Affordable Housing." *Magharebia*, January 5.

———. 2011. "Morocco Eyes Social Housing Development." *Magharebia*, January 14.

Bergh, Sylvia I. 2012. "'Inclusive' Neoliberalism, Local Governance Reforms and the Redeployment of State Power: The Case of the National Initiative for Human Development (INDH) in Morocco." *Mediterranean Politics* 17, no. 3: 410–26.

Berra, Hicham, and Saïd Kourar. 2004. *Accompagnement social des opérations de lutte contre l'habitat insalubre: Guide méthodologique.* Rabat: Ministère Délégué Chargé de l'Habitat et de l'Urbanisme (MHU).

Berrada, Abdelkader, and Mohamed Saïd Saadi. 1992. "Le grand capital privé marocain." In *Le Maroc actuel: Une modernisation au miroir de la tradition?*, edited by Jean-Claude Santucci, 325–91. Paris: Editions du Centre national de la recherche scientifique.

Berriane, Yasmine. 2010. "The Complexities of Inclusive Participatory Governance: The Case of Moroccan Associational Life in the Context of the INDH." *Journal of Economic and Social Research* 12, no. 1: 89–111.

Berry-Chikhaoui, Isabelle. 2010. "Major Urban Projects and the People Affected: The Case of Casablanca's Avenue Royale." *Built Environment* 36, no. 2: 216–29.

Bigourdan, Isadora, and Thierry Paulais. 2014. "Promoting Housing Policies Coordinated with the Private Sector." *Private Sector & Development*, no. 19 (July): 9–12.

Bill, James A. 1972. "Class Analysis and the Dialectics of Modernization in the Middle East." *International Journal of Middle East Studies* 3, no. 4: 417–34.

Blal, Myriam. 2010. "Bidonvilles: Encore 45 villes à traiter d'ici 2012." *La Vie éco*, July 12, 2010. http://lavieeco.com/news/economie/bidonvilles-encore -45-villes-a-traiter-dici-2012-17135.html.

Block, Fred. 2001. "Introduction." In *The Great Transformation: The Political and Economic Origins of Our Time*, edited by Karl Polanyi, xviii–xxxviii. Boston: Beacon.

Bogaert, Koenraad. 2011. "The Problem of Slums: Shifting Methods of Neoliberal Urban Government in Morocco." *Development and Change* 42, no. 3: 709–31.

———. 2012. "New State Space Formation in Morocco: The Example of the Bouregreg Valley." *Urban Studies* 49, no. 2: 255–70.

———. 2013a. "Cities without Slums in Morocco? New Modalities of Urban Government and the Bidonville as a Neoliberal Assemblage." In *Locating the Right to the City in the Global South*, edited by Tony Roshan Samara, Shenjing He, and Guo Chen, 41–59. New York: Routledge.

———. 2013b. "Contextualizing the Arab Revolts: The Politics behind Three Decades of Neoliberalism in the Arab World." *Middle East Critique* 22, no. 3: 213–34.

———. 2014. "From Carbon Democracy to the Right to the City: On the Struggle against Neoliberalism." *Jadaliyya*, March 14. http://www.jadaliyya .com/pages/index/16878/from-carbon-democracy-to-the-right-to-the -city_on.

———. 2015a. "Breaking the Myths of Power: The Struggles of the Haitians, Algerians, and Greeks." *Jadaliyya*, July 9. http://www.jadaliyya.com/pages/ index/22139/breaking-the-myths-of-power_the-struggles-of-the-h.

———. 2015b. "Paradigms Lost in Morocco: How Urban Mega-Projects Should Disturb Our Understanding of Arab Politics." *Jadaliyya*, June 4. http:// www.jadaliyya.com/pages/index/21784/paradigms-lost-in-morocco_how -urban-mega-projects-.

———. 2015c. "The Revolt of Small Towns: The Meaning of Morocco's History and the Geography of Social Protests." *Review of African Political Economy* 42, no. 143: 124–40.

Bogaert, Koenraad, and Montserrat Emperador. 2011. "Imagining the State through Social Protest: State Reformation and the Mobilizations of Unemployed Graduates in Morocco." *Mediterranean Politics* 16, no. 2: 241–59.

Bolay, Jean-Claude. 2006. "Slums and Urban Development: Questions on Society and Globalisation." *European Journal of Development Research* 18, no. 2: 284–98.

Bono, Irene. 2007. "The Support to NGOs in the Euro Mediterranean Partnership: Investigating Possible Scenarios of Power Redistribution and Political Stability." Paper presented at the 6th Pan-European International Relation Conference, University of Toronto, September 12–15. http://www.eisa-net.org/be-bruga/eisa/files/events/turin/bono-Bono_ecpr.pdf.

———. 2010a. "L'activisme associatif comme marché du travail: Normalisation sociale et politique par les 'Activités génératrices de revenus' à El Hajeb." *Politique africaine*, no. 120: 25–44.

———. 2010b. "Pauverté, exception, participation: Mobilisation et démobilisation 'dans le cadre de l'INDH' au Maroc." In *L'Etat face aux "débordements" du social au Maghreb: Formation, Travail et protection sociale*, edited by Myriam Catusse, Blandine Destremau, and Eric Verdier, 149–63. Paris: Karthala.

Bouchaf, Ouafae. 2013. "Mise en place d'une stratégie de communication commerciale au sein de la société 'Bab Al Bahr Development Company.'" Master's thesis, Université Mohammed V.

Boujrouf, Said. 1996. "La montagne dans la politique d'aménagement du territoire au Maroc." *Revue de Géographie Alpine* 84, no. 4: 37–50.

Boumaza, Nadir, ed. 2005. *Villes réelles, villes projetées: Villes maghrébines en fabrication*. Paris: Maisonneuve & Larose.

Boussaid, Farid. 2009. "The Rise of the PAM in Morocco: Trampling the Political Scene or Stumbling into It?" *Mediterranean Politics* 14, no. 3: 413–19.

Branch, Adam, and Zachariah Mampilly. 2015. *Africa Uprising: Popular Protest and Political Change*. London: Zed Books.

Brand, Laurie. 1998. *Women, the State, and Political Liberalization: Middle Eastern and North African Experiences*. New York: Columbia University Press.

Brenner, Neil. 2004. *New State Spaces: Urban Governance and the Rescaling of Statehood*. Oxford: Oxford University Press.

Brenner, Neil, and Nik Theodore. 2002. "Cities and the Geographies of 'Actually Existing Neoliberalism.'" *Antipode* 34, no. 3: 349–79.

Broudehoux, Anne-Marie. 2007. "Spectacular Beijing: The Conspicuous Construction of an Olympic Metropolis." *Journal of Urban Affairs* 29, no. 4: 383–99.

Brown, Nathan J. 2013. "Egypt's Failed Transition." *Journal of Democracy* 24, no. 4: 45–58.

Brownlee, Jason. 2002. ". . . And Yet They Persist: Explaining Survival and Transition in Neopatrimonial Regimes." *Studies in Comparative International Development* 37, no. 3: 35–63.

Brumberg, Daniel. 2002. "The Trap of Liberalized Autocracy." *Journal of democracy* 13, no. 4: 56–68.

Bush, Ray. 2004. "Poverty and Neo-Liberal Bias in the Middle East and North Africa." *Development and Change* 35, no. 4: 673–95.

Cammack, Paul. 2004. "What the World Bank Means by Poverty Reduction, and Why It Matters." *New Political Economy* 9, no. 2: 189–211.

Cammett, Melani Claire. 2007. *Globalization and Business Politics in Arab North Africa: A Comparative Perspective*. New York: Cambridge University Press.

Carothers, Thomas. 2002. "The End of the Transition Paradigm." *Journal of Democracy* 13, no. 1: 5–21.

Cattedra, Raffaele. 2001. "La mosquée et la cité: La reconversion symbolique du projet urbain à Casablanca." PhD diss., Université François Rabelais de Tours.

———. 2010. "Les grand projets urbains à la conquête des périphéries." *Les Cahiers d'EMAM*, no. 19: 58–72.

Catusse, Myriam. 2005. "Les réinventions du social dans le Maroc 'ajusté.'" *Revue des mondes musulmans et de la Méditerranée*, nos. 105–6: 221–46.

———. 2008. *Le temps des entrepreneurs? Politique et transformations du capitalisme au Maroc*. Paris: Maisonneuve & Larose.

———. 2009a. "Maroc: Un état social fragile dans la réforme néolibérale." *Alternatives Sud* 16, no. 2: 59–81.

———. 2009b. "Morocco's Political Economy: Ambiguous Privatization and the Emerging Social Question." In *The Arab State and Neo-Liberal Globalization: The Restructuring of State Power in the Middle East*, edited by Laura Guazzone and Daniela Pioppi, 185–216. Reading: Ithaca Press.

———. 2011. "Le 'Social': Une affaire d'état dans le Maroc de Mohammed VI." *Confluences Méditerranée* 78, no. 3: 63–76.

Catusse, Myriam, Raffaele Cattedra, and M'hammed Idrissi Janati. 2005. "Municipaliser les villes? Le gouvernement des villes marocaines à l'épreuve du politique et du territoire." In *Intégration à la ville et services urbains au Maroc*, edited by Claude de Miras, 313–61. Rabat: Institut National d'Aménagement et d'Urbanisme (INAU).

———. 2007. "Decentralisation and Its Paradoxes in Morocco." In *Cities of the South*, edited by Barbara Driesken, Franck Mermier, and Heiko Wimmen, 113–35. London: Saqi Books.

Catusse, Myriam, and Blandine Destremau. 2010. "L'état social à l'épreuve de ses trajectoires au Maghreb." In *L'état face aux débordements du social au Maghreb: Formation, travail et protection sociale*, edited by Myriam Catusse, Blandine Destremau, and Eric Verdier, 15–52. Paris: Karthala.

Cavatorta, Francesco. 2004. "Constructing an Open Model of Transition: The Case of North Africa." *Journal of North African Studies* 9, no. 3: 1–18.

———. 2005. "The International Context of Morocco's Stalled Democratization." *Democratization* 12, no. 4: 548–66.

Chakravorty, Sanjoy. 2000. "From Colonial City to Globalizing City? The Far-from-Complete Spatial Transformation of Calcutta." In *Globalizing Cities: A New Spatial Order?*, edited by Peter Marcuse and Ronald van Kempen, 56–77. London: Blackwell.

Chaoui, Mohamed. 2011. "Logement social: Le Souverain reprend le dossier en main." *L'Economiste*, no. 3456 (January 31). http://www.leconomiste.com/article/logement-socialbrle-souverain-reprend-le-dossier-en-main.

Charai, Ahmed. 2011. "The Moroccan Exception." Foreign Policy Research Institute, February 3. http://www.fpri.org/article/2011/02/the-moroccan-exception/.

Chatterjee, Ipsita. 2009. "Social Conflict and the Neoliberal City: A Case of Hindu-Muslim Violence in India." *Transactions of the Institute of British Geographers* 34, no. 2: 143–60.

———. 2014. *Displacement, Revolution, and the New Urban Condition: Theories and Case Studies.* New Delhi: SAGE.

———. 2016. "Beyond the Factory: Struggling with Class and Class Struggle in the Post-Industrial Context." *Capital & Class* 40, no. 2: 263–81.

Chekir, Hamouda, and Ishac Diwan. 2014. "Crony Capitalism in Egypt." *Journal of Globalization and Development* 5, no. 2: 177–211.

Cherkaoui, Mouna, and Driss Ben Ali. 2007. "The Political Economy of Growth in Morocco." *Quarterly Review of Economics and Finance* 46, no. 5: 741–61.

Claisse, Alain. 1987. "Makhzen Traditions and Administrative Channels." In *The Political Economy of Morocco*, edited by William I. Zartman, 34–58. New York: Praeger Publishers.

Clément, Jean-François. 1986. "Morocco's Bourgeoisie: Monarchy, State and Owning Class." *MERIP Middle East Report* 16, no. 142: 13–17.

———. 1992. "Les révoltes urbaines." In *Le Maroc actuel: Une modernisation au miroir de la tradition?*, edited by Jean-Claude Santucci, 393–406. Paris: Editions du Centre national de la recherche scientifique.

———. 1995. "Les effets sociaux du programme d'ajustement structurel marocain." *Politique étrangère* 60, no. 4: 1003–13.

Clément, Jean-François, and Jim Paul. 1984. "Trade Unions and Moroccan Politics." *Middle East Report*, no. 127 (September–October): 19–24.

Cohen, Shana. 2003. "Alienation and Globalization in Morocco: Addressing the Social and Political Impact of Market Integration." *Comparative Studies in Society and History* 45, no. 1: 168–89.

———. 2004a. "The Moroccan Subject in a Globalizing World." *Thesis Eleven* 78, no. 1: 28–45.

———. 2004b. *Searching for a Different Future: The Rise of a Global Middle Class in Morocco.* Durham, N.C.: Duke University Press.

Cohen, Shana, and Larabi Jaïdi. 2006. *Morocco: Globalization and Its Consequences.* London: Routledge.

Collier, Stephen J. 2011. *Post-Soviet Social: Neoliberalism, Social Modernity, Biopolitics.* Princeton, N.J.: Princeton University Press.

Connell, Raewyn, and Nour Dados. 2014. "Where in the World Does Neoliberalism Come From?" *Theory and Society* 43, no. 2: 117–38.

Corbridge, Stuart. 2002. "Third World Debt." In *The Companion to Development Studies*, edited by Vandana Desai and Robert B. Potter, 477–80. New York: Oxford University Press.

Daher, Rami. 2013. "Neoliberal Urban Transformations in the Arab City: Meta-Narratives, Urban Disparities and the Emergence of Consumerist Utopias and Geographies of Inequities in Amman." *Environnement urbain / Urban Environment* 7:99–115.

Dahi, Omar S., and Yasser Munif. 2012. "Revolts in Syria: Tracking the Convergence between Authoritarianism and Neoliberalism." *Journal of Asian and African Studies* 47, no. 4: 323–32.

Das, Raju J. 2012. "From Labor Geography to Class Geography: Reasserting the Marxist Theory of Class." *Human Geography* 5, no. 1: 19–35.

Davis, Diana K. 2006. "Neoliberalism, Environmentalism, and Agricultural Restructuring in Morocco." *Geographical Journal* 172, no. 2: 88–105.

Davis, Mike. 2006a. "Fear and Money in Dubai." *New Left Review*, no. 41 (September–October): 47–68.

———. 2006b. *Planet of Slums.* London: Verso.

Dean, Mitchell. 1999. *Governmentality: Power and Rule in Modern Society.* London: SAGE.

———. 2007. *Governing Societies: Political Perspectives on Domestic and International Rule.* Maidenhead: McGraw-Hill.

Debbi, Fathallah, and Olivier Toutain. 2002. *Guide méthodologique d'intervention en matière d'habitat insalubre: Etude relative á la redéfinition des méthodes d'intervention en matière de résorption de l'habitat insalubre.* Rabat: Ministère de l'Aménagement du Territoire National, de l'Urbanisme, de l'Habitat et de l'Environnement.

Debruyne, Pascal. 2013. "Spatial Rearticulations of Statehood: Jordan's Geographies of Power under Globalization." PhD diss., Ghent University.

Debruyne, Pascal, and Christopher Parker. 2015. "Reassembling the Political: Placing Contentious Politics in Jordan." In *Contentious Politics in the Middle East: Popular Resistance and Marginalized Activism beyond the Arab Uprisings,* edited by Fawaz A. Gerges, 437–67. New York: Palgrave Macmillan.

de Certeau, Michel. 1984. *The Practice of Everyday Life.* Berkeley: University of California Press.

Deleuze, Gilles. 1992. "Postscript on Societies of Control." *October* 59 (Winter): 3–7.

de Miras, Claude, ed. 2005. *Intégration à la ville et services urbains au Maroc.* Rabat: Institut National d'Aménagement et d'Urbanisme (INAU).

———. 2007. "Initiative nationale pour le développement humain et économie solidaire au Maroc." *Revue Tiers Monde* 190, no. 2: 357–77.

Denoeux, Guilain. 1998. "Understanding Morocco's 'Sanitisation Campaign' (December 1995 to May 1996)." *Journal of North African Studies* 3, no. 1: 101–31.

———. 2007. "Corruption in Morocco: Old Forces, New Dynamics and a Way Forward." *Middle East Policy* 14, no. 4: 134–51.

De Smet, Brecht. 2016. *Gramsci on Tahrir: Revolution and Counter-Revolution in Egypt.* London: Pluto Press.

De Soto, Hernando. 2001. "Dead Capital and the Poor." *SAIS Review* 21, no. 1: 13–43.

Desrues, Thierry, and Eduardo Moyano. 2001. "Social Change and Political Transition in Morocco." *Mediterranean Politics* 6, no. 1: 21–47.

Diamond, Larry. 2003. "Universal Democracy?" *Policy Review*, no. 119 (June 1): 3–25.

———. 2010. "Why Are There No Arab Democracies?" *Journal of Democracy* 21, no. 1: 93–104.

Dikec, M. 2007. "Space, Governmentality, and the Geographies of French Urban Policy." *European Urban and Regional Studies* 14, no. 4: 277–89.

Dillman, Bradford. 2002. "International Markets and Partial Economic Reforms in North Africa: What Impact on Democratization?" *Democratization* 9, no. 1: 63–86.

Doornbos, Martin. 2001. "'Good Governance': The Rise and Decline of a Policy Metaphor?" *Journal of Development Studies* 37, no. 6: 93–108.

———. 2003. "'Good Governance': The Metamorphosis of a Policy Metaphor." *Journal of International Affairs* 57, no. 1: 3–17.

Duffield, Mark. 2002. "Social Reconstruction and the Radicalization of Development: Aid as a Relation of Global Liberal Governance." *Development and Change* 33, no. 5: 1049–71.

Durac, Vincent. 2009. "Globalizing Patterns of Business, Finance and Migration in the Middle East and North Africa." *Mediterranean Politics* 14, no. 2: 255–66.

Easterling, Keller. 2014. *Extrastatecraft: The Power of Infrastructure Space*. London: Verso.

Easterly, William. 2001. "The Lost Decades : Developing Countries' Stagnation in Spite of Policy Reform 1980–1998." *Journal of Economic Growth* 6, no. 2: 135–57.

Effina, Driss. 2011. "Marché immobilier résidentiel et investissements directs étrangers: Cas du Maroc." PhD diss., Université Mohammed V.

Ehteshami, Anoushiravan, and Emma C. Murphy. 1996. "Transformation of the Corporatist State in the Middle East." *Third World Quarterly* 17, no. 4: 753–72.

El Hachimi, Mohamed. 2015. "Democratisation as a Learning Process: The Case of Morocco." *Journal of North African Studies* 20, no. 5: 754–69.

El-Mahdi, Rabab. 2011. "Labour Protests in Egypt: Causes and Meanings." *Review of African Political Economy* 38, no. 129: 387–402.

El Malki, H., and A. Doumou. 1992. "Les dilemmes de l'ajustement." In *Le Maroc actuel: Une modernisation au miroir de la tradition?*, edited by Jean-Claude Santucci, 313–23. Paris: Editions du Centre national de la recherche scientifique.

El-Said, Hamed, and Jane Harrigan. 2014. "Economic Reform, Social Welfare, and Instability: Jordan, Egypt, Morocco, and Tunisia, 1983–2004." *Middle East Journal* 68, no. 1: 99–121.

Elden, Stuart. 2007a. "Governmentality, Calculation, Territory." *Environment and Planning D: Society and Space* 25, no. 3: 562–80.

———. 2007b. "Rethinking Governmentality." *Political Geography* 26, no. 1: 29–33.

Elsheshtawy, Yasser, ed. 2008a. *The Evolving Arab City: Tradition, Modernity and Urban Development*. London: Routledge.

———. 2008b. "The Great Divide: Struggling and Emerging Cities in the Arab World." In *The Evolving Arab City: Tradition, Modernity and Urban Development*, edited by Yasser Elsheshtawy, 1–26. London: Routledge.

El Yaakoubi, Aziz. 2014. "UPDATE 1-Wessal Capital to Invest $1.10 Bln in Morocco Tourism." *Reuters*, May 12. http://in.reuters.com/article/morocco-tourism-investment-idINL6N0NY4MJ20140512.

Elyachar, Julia. 2002. "Empowerment Money: The World Bank, Non-Governmental Organizations, and the Value of Culture in Egypt." *Public Culture* 14, no. 3: 493–513.

Entelis, John P. 2007. "The Unchanging Politics of North Africa." *Middle East Policy* 14, no. 4: 23–41.

Errazzouki, Samia. 2012. "A Monarchical Affair: From Morocco to the Arabian Peninsula." *Jadaliyya*, April 10. http://www.jadaliyya.com/pages/index/4980/a-monarchical-affair_from-morocco-to-the-arabian-p.

Essahel, Habiba. 2015. "Évolution des registres de l'action, de la ruse à la mobilisation de la notion 'droit' par les habitants des bidonvilles au Maroc." *L'Année du Maghreb*, no. 12: 115–35.

Fawaz, Mona. 2009. "Neoliberal Urbanity and the Right to the City: A View from Beirut's Periphery." *Development and Change* 40, no. 5: 827–52.

———. 2013. "Towards the Right to the City in Informal Settlements." In *Locating the Right to the City in the Global South*, edited by Tony Roshan Samara, Shenjing He, and Guo Chen, 23–40. London: Routledge.

Feliu, Laura, and M. Angustias Parejo. 2013. "Morocco: The Reinvention of an Authoritarian System." In *Political Regimes in the Arab World: Society and the Exercise of Power*, edited by Ferran Izquierdo Brichs, 70–99. London: Routledge.

Ferguson, James. 2006. "The Anti-Politics Machine." In *The Anthropology of the State*, edited by Aradhana Sharma and Akhil Gupta, 270–86. Oxford: Blackwell.

Ferguson, James, and Akhil Gupta. 2002. "Spatializing States: Towards an Ethnography of Neoliberal Governmentality." *American Ethnologist* 29, no. 4: 981–1002.

Fikri, Mostapha. 2005. *La bonne gouvernance administrative au Maroc: Mission possible*. Mohammedia: Espace Art & Culture.

Findlay, Allan M., and Ronan Paddison. 1986. "Planning the Arab City: The Cases of Tunis and Rabat." *Progress in Planning* 26:1–82.

Flyvbjerg, Bent. 2005. "Machiavellian Megaprojects." *Antipode* 37, no. 1: 18–22.

Forrest, Joshua B. 1987. "The Contemporary African State: A 'Ruling Class'?" *Review of African Political Economy*, no. 38 (April): 66–71.

Foucault, Michel. 1979. *Discipline and Punish: The Birth of the Prison*. New York: Vintage Books.

———. 1990. *The History of Sexuality*. Vol. 1, *An Introduction*. New York: Vintage Books.

———. 2003. *Society Must Be Defended: Lectures at the Collège de France, 1975–76*. New York: Picador.

———. 2007. *Security, Territory, Population: Lectures at the Collège de France, 1977–78*. New York: Palgrave Macmillan.

———. 2008. *The Birth of Biopolitics: Lectures at the Collège de France, 1978–79*. New York: Palgrave Macmillan.

García, Raquel Ojeda, and Ángela Suárez Collado. 2015. "The Project of Advanced Regionalisation in Morocco: Analysis of a Lampedusian Reform." *British Journal of Middle Eastern Studies* 42, no. 1: 46–58.

Gause, F. Gregory. 2011. "Why Middle East Studies Missed the Arab Spring: The Myth of Authoritarian Stability." *Foreign Affairs* 90, no. 4: 81–90.

Ghalioun, Burhan. 2004. "The Persistence of Arab Authoritarianism." *Journal of Democracy* 15, no. 4: 126–32.

Ghannam, Fadoua, and Youssef Aït Akdim. 2009. "Révolution urbaine." *TelQuel*, no. 390: 41–49.

Gharbaoui, Hayat. 2014. "Golfe: Les pétrodollars sont de retour!" *TelQuel*, no. 620: 29–33.

Glasser, Bradley L. 1995. "External Capital and Political Liberalizations: A Typology of Middle Eastern Development in the 1980s and 1990s." *Journal of International Affairs* 49, no. 1: 45–73.

Graciet, Catherine, and Eric Laurent. 2012. *Le roi prédateur: Main basse sur le Maroc*. Paris: Editions du Seuil.

Guazzone, Laura, and Daniela Pioppi, eds. 2009a. *The Arab State and Neo-Liberal Globalization: The Restructuring of State Power in the Middle East*. Reading: Ithaca Press.

———. 2009b. "Interpreting Change in the Arab World." In *The Arab State and Neo-Liberal Globalization: The Restructuring of State Power in the Middle East*, edited by Laura Guazzone and Daniela Pioppi, 1–15. Reading: Ithaca Press.

Hackworth, Jason. 2007. *The Neoliberal City: Governance, Ideology, and Development in American Urbanism*. Ithaca, N.Y.: Cornell University Press.

Hackworth, Jason, and Neil Smith. 2001. "The Changing State of Gentrification." *Tijdschrift voor Economische en Sociale Geografie* 92, no. 4: 464–77.

Haddad, Bassam. 2012. "Syria's State Bourgeoisie: An Organic Backbone for the Regime." *Middle East Critique* 21, no. 3: 231–57.

Hamzawy, Amr. 2011. "Egypt: At a Crucial Moment, Road Map toward Democracy." Carnegie Endowment for International Peace, February 1. http://carnegieendowment.org/2011/02/01/egypt-at-crucial-moment-road-map-toward-democracy-pub-42456.

Handoussa, Heba, ed. 1997. *Economic Transition in the Middle East: Global Challenges and Adjustment Strategies*. Cairo: American University in Cairo Press.

Hanieh, Adam. 2011. *Capitalism and Class in the Gulf Arab States*. New York: Palgrave Macmillan.

———. 2013. *Lineages of Revolt: Issues of Contemporary Capitalism in the Middle East*. Chicago: Haymarket Books.

Hansen, Thomas Blom, and Finn Stepputat. 2001. "Introduction: States of Imagination." In *States of Imagination: Ethnographic Explorations of the Postcolonial*

State, edited by Thomas Blom Hansen and Finn Stepputat, 1–38. Durham, N.C.: Duke University Press.

Harb, Mona. 2017. "Why Space Matters in the Arab Uprisings (and Beyond)." *Jadaliyya*, February 16. http://www.jadaliyya.com/pages/index/25883/why -space-matters-in-the-arab-uprisings-%28and-beyon?mc_cid=93bc5cdb2c &mc_eid=9178256b29.

Harmak, Réda. 2013. "Danger sur le Fogarim, les impayés s'envolent." *La Vie éco*, February 11. http://www.lavieeco.com/news/economie/danger-sur-le -fogarim-les-impayes-senvolent-24597.html.

Harvey, David. 1989a. "From Managerialism to Entrepreneurialism: The Transformation in Urban Governance in Late Capitalism." *Geografiska Annaler B* 71, no. 1: 3–17.

———. 1989b. *The Urban Experience*. Baltimore: Johns Hopkins University Press.

———. 2003. *The New Imperialism*. New York: Oxford University Press.

———. 2006a. *The Limits to Capital*. London: Verso.

———. 2006b. *Spaces of Global Capitalism: Towards a Theory of Uneven Geographical Development*. London: Verso.

———. 2010a. *A Companion to Marx's Capital*. London: Verso.

———. 2010b. *The Enigma of Capital and the Crises of Capitalism*. London: Profile Books.

———. 2014. *Seventeen Contradictions and the End of Capitalism*. London: Profile Books.

Hawthorne, Amy. 2004. *Middle Eastern Democracy: Is Civil Society the Answer?* Carnegie Papers 44. Washington, D.C.: Carnegie Endowment for International Peace.

Hazbun, Waleed. 2012. "The Middle East through the Lens of Critical Geopolitics." In *Is There a Middle East? The Evolution of a Geopolitical Concept*, edited by Michael E. Bonine, Abbas Amanat, and Michael Ezekiel Gasper, 207–30. Stanford: Stanford University Press.

Henry, Clement M., and Robert Springborg. 2001. *Globalization and the Politics of Development in the Middle East*. Cambridge: Cambridge University Press.

Herb, Michael. 1999. *All in the Family: Absolutism, Revolution, and Democracy in the Middle Eastern Monarchies*. Albany: State University of New York Press.

Hermann, Christoph. 2007. "Neoliberalism in the European Union." *Studies in Political Economy* 79 (Spring): 61–90.

Hernández, Felipe, and Peter Kellett. 2010. "Introduction: Reimagining the Informal in Latin America." In *Rethinking the Informal City: Critical Perspectives from Latin America*, edited by Felipe Hernández, Peter Kellet, and Lea K. Allen, 1–20. Oxford: Berghahn Books.

Heydemann, Steven. 2004a. "Introduction: Networks of Privilege; Rethinking the Politics of Economic Reform in the Middle East." In *Networks of Privilege in the Middle East: The Politics of Economic Reform Revisited*, edited by Steven Heydemann, 1–34. New York: Palgrave Macmillan.

———, ed. 2004b. *Networks of Privilege in the Middle East: The Politics of Economic Reform Revisited*. New York: Palgrave Macmillan.

————. 2007. *Upgrading Authoritarianism in the Arab World.* Analysis Paper 13. Washington, D.C.: Brookings Institution.

————. 2013. "Syria and the Future of Authoritarianism." *Journal of Democracy* 24, no. 4: 59–73.

Heydemann, Steven, and Reinoud Leenders. 2011. "Authoritarian Learning and Authoritarian Resilience: Regime Responses to the 'Arab Awakening.'" *Globalizations* 8, no. 5: 647–53.

Hibou, Béatrice. 2004a. "Fiscal Trajectories in Morocco and Tunisia." In *Networks of Privilege in the Middle East: The Politics of Economic Reform Revisited,* edited by Steven Heydemann, 201–22. New York: Palgrave Macmillan.

————. 2004b. "From Privatising the Economy to Privatising the State: An Analysis of the Continual Formation of the State." In *Privatising the State,* 1–46. London: Hurst.

————. 2006. "Domination and Control in Tunisia: Economic Levers for the Exercise of Authoritarian Power." *Review of African Political Economy* 33, no. 108: 185–206.

Hibou, Béatrice, and Mohamed Tozy. 2002a. "De la friture sur la ligne des réformes: La libéralisation des télécommunications au Maroc." *Critique internationale,* no. 14: 91–118.

————. 2002b. "Une lecture d'anthropologie politique de la corruption au Maroc: Fondement historique d'une prise de liberté avec le droit." *Tiers-Monde* 41, no. 161: 23–47.

————. 2015. "Gouvernement personnel et gouvernement institutionnalisé de la charité: L'INDH au Maroc." In *L'Etat d'injustice au Maghreb: Maroc et Tunisie,* edited by Irene Bono, Béatrice Hibou, Hamza Meddeb, and Mohamed Tozy, 379–428. Paris: Karthala.

Hinti, Said. 2005. *Gouvernance économique et développement des territoires au Maroc.* Rabat: El Maarif Al Jadida.

Hirst, Paul. 2005. *Space and Power: Politics, War and Architecture.* Cambridge: Polity.

Hobsbawm, Eric. 1975. *The Age of Capital.* London: Phoenix Press.

Hourani, Najib. 2014. "Urbanism and Neoliberal Order: The Development and Redevelopment of Amman." *Journal of Urban Affairs* 36, no. 2: 634–49.

Huchzermeyer, M. 2008. "Slum Upgrading in Nairobi within the Housing and Basic Services Market: A Housing Rights Concern." *Journal of Asian and African Studies* 43, no. 1: 19–39.

Hughes Rinker, Cortney. 2014. "Creating Neoliberal Citizens in Morocco: Reproductive Health, Development Policy, and Popular Islamic Beliefs." *Medical Anthropology* 34, no. 3: 1–17.

Huntington, Samuel P. 1993a. "The Clash of Civilizations?" *Foreign Affairs* 72, no. 3: 22–49.

————. 1993b. *The Third Wave: Democratization in the Late Twentieth Century.* Norman: University of Oklahoma Press.

Ibrahim, Saad E. M. 1975. "Over-Urbanization and Under-Urbanism: The Case of the Arab World." *International Journal of Middle East Studies* 6, no. 1: 29–45.

Idmaj Sakan. 2006. *Société Idmaj Sakan: Plan d'action 2006*. Casablanca: Wilaya de la region du Grand Casablanca.

Iraki, Aziz. 2006a. "Elites locales et territoires: De l'élite coopté a l'élite de proximité au Maroc." In *Pouvoirs locaux et systèmes municipaux dans le monde arabe*, edited by Abdelghani Abouhani, 77–96. Rabat: Institute National d'Aménagement rt d'Urbanisme (INAU); San Domenico di Fiesole: Centre Robert Schuman pour les études avancées.

———. 2006b. "L'organisation des solidarités dans des territoires en construction: Quartiers restructurés au Maroc." *Espaces et Sociétés* 127, no. 4: 63–77.

———. 2010. "Chapitre III: Réformes institutionnelles, refonte des territoires et rapports de pouvoir dans la ville." *Les Cahiers d'EMAM*, no. 19: 79–87.

———. 2013. "L'initiative nationale de développement humain au Maroc: Formes de mobilisation collective et intermédiation sociale dans la gestion urbaine." In *Les mondes urbains: Le parcours engagé de Françoise Navez-Bouchanine*, edited by Agnès Deboulet and Michèle Jolé, 203–18. Paris: Karthala.

Iraki, Aziz, and Abderrahmane Rachik. 2005. "Quartiers non-réglementaires: Intermédiation, élite de proximité et restructuration urbaine." In *Intégration à la ville et services urbains au Maroc*, edited by Claude de Miras, 97–144. Rabat: Institut National d'Aménagement et d'Urbanisme.

Iraqi, F., and Mehdi Michbal. 2010. "Big Bang Royal." *TelQuel*, no. 418: 18–28.

Ismail, Salwa. 2006. *Political Life in Cairo's New Quarters: Encountering the Everyday State*. Minneapolis: University of Minnesota Press.

Jaidi, Larabi. 1992. "L'industrialisation de l'économie marocaine: Acquis réels et modalités d'une remise en cause." In *Le Maroc actuel: Une modernisation au miroir de la tradition?*, edited by Jean-Claude Santucci. Paris: Editions du Centre national de la recherche scientifique, 91–117.

Jenkins, Rob. 2002. "The Emergence of the Governance Agenda: Sovereignty, Neo-Liberal Bias and the Politics of International Development." In *The Companion to Development Studies*, edited by Vandana Desai and Robert B. Potter, 485–89. New York: Oxford University Press.

Jessop, Bob. 2007. "From Micro-Powers to Governmentality: Foucault's Work on Statehood, State Formation, Statecraft and State Power." *Political Geography* 26, no. 1: 34–40.

———. 2008. *State Power*. Cambridge: Polity.

Joffe, George. 1988. "Morocco: Monarchy, Legitimacy and Succession." *Third World Quarterly* 10, no. 1: 201–28.

Johnson, Katherine Marshall. 1972. *Urbanization in Morocco: An International Urbanization Survey Report to the Ford Foundation*. New York: International Urbanization Survey.

Jones, Branwen Gruffydd. 2012. "'Bankable Slums': The Global Politics of Slum Upgrading." *Third World Quarterly* 33, no. 5: 769–89.

Juiad, Issam. 2010. "Expropriation et protection des droits de propriété au Maroc: Cas dus projet d'aménagement et de mise en valeur de la vallée du Bouregreg." Master's thesis, Université Mohammed V.

Kably, Mouna. 2011. "Yassir Zenagui: Nous avons approché d'autres fonds souverains en Chine . . ." *Actuel*, no. 119 (December 2). http://www.actuel.ma/index.php?option=com_magazines&view=detail&id=826.

Kaioua, Abdelkader. 1996. *Casablanca, L'industrie et la ville*. Tours: Urbama.

Kamrava, Mehran, and Frank O. Mora. 1998. "Civil Society and Democratisation in Comparative Perspective: Latin America and the Middle East." *Third World Quarterly* 19, no. 5: 893–916.

Kanai, Miguel, and William Kutz. 2011. "Entrepreneurialism in the Globalising City-Region of Tangier, Morocco." *Tijdschrift voor economische en sociale geografie* 102, no. 3: 346–60.

Kandil, Hazem. 2012. "Why Did the Egyptian Middle Class March to Tahrir Square?" *Mediterranean Politics* 17, no. 2: 197–215.

Kanna, Ahmed. 2009. "Making Cadres of the 'City-Corporation': Cultural and Identity Politics in Neoliberal Dubai." *Review of Middle East Studies* 43, no. 2: 207–18.

———. 2011. *Dubai, the City Corporation*. Minneapolis: University of Minnesota Press.

———. 2012. "Urbanist Ideology and the Production of Space in the United Arab Emirates: An Anthropological Critique." In *Global Downtowns*, edited by Marina Peterson and Gary W. McDonogh, 90–109. Philadelphia: University of Pennsylvania Press.

———. 2014. "Speaking of the City: Establishing Urban Expertise in the Arab Gulf." *International Journal of Middle East Studies* 46, no. 1: 169–71.

Kapoor, Ilan. 2008. *The Postcolonial Politics of Development*. London: Routledge.

Karaman, Ozan. 2013. "Urban Renewal in Istanbul: Reconfigured Spaces, Robotic Lives." *International Journal of Urban and Regional Research* 37, no. 2: 715–33.

Karim, Douichi. 2006. "Taoufik Hjira: 'Le Fogarim vise 50.000 prêts par an.'" *Infos du Maroc*, October 5. http://www.infosdumaroc.com/economie/taoufik -hjira-le-fogarim-vise-50-000-prets-par-an/.

Khanna, Parag. 2011. "Getting on the Right Side of History." *Foreign Policy*, February 3. http://www.foreignpolicy.com/articles/2011/02/03/getting_on_ the_right_side_of_history#sthash.CW8dD9n5.dpbs.

Khosrowshahi, Cameron. 1997. "Privatization in Morocco: The Politics of Development." *Middle East Journal* 51, no. 2: 242–55.

Kienle, Eberhard. 2001. *A Grand Delusion: Democracy and Economic Reform in Egypt*. New York: I.B. Tauris.

Kohstall, Florian. 2010. "Morocco's Monarchical Legacy and Its Capacity to Implement Social Reforms." In *Contested Sovereignties: Government and Democracy in Middle Eastern and European Perspectives*, edited by Elisabeth Özdalga and Sune Persson, 197–208. Istanbul: Swedish Research Institute.

Krijnen, Marieke, and Christiaan De Beukelaer. 2015. "Capital, State and Conflict: The Various Drivers of Diverse Gentrification Processes in Beirut, Lebanon." In *Global Gentrifications: Uneven Development and Displacement*, edited by Loretta Lees, Hyun Bang Shin, and Ernesto López-Morales, 285–309. Bristol: Policy Press.

Krijnen, Marieke, and Mona Fawaz. 2010. "Exception as the Rule: High-End Developments in Neoliberal Beirut." *Built Environment* 36, no. 2: 245–59.

Lahzem, Abdellah. 1995. "Le système de la promotion foncière et immobilière non institutionnelle au Maroc: Cas de deux villes; Salé et Tétouan." In *L'Etat et les quartiers populaires au Maroc: De la marginalisation a l'emeute; Habitat spontané et mouvements sociaux*, edited by Abdelghani Abouhani, 29–55. Dakar: Council for the Development of Social Science Research in Africa.

Lakoff, Sanford. 2004. "The Reality of Muslim Exceptionalism." *Journal of Democracy* 15, no. 4: 133–39.

Laval, Alice, et al. 2010. "On Clandestine Housing: An Interview with Horia Serhane." In *Colonial Modern: Aesthetics of the Past, Rebellions for the Future*, edited by Tom Avermaete, Serhat Karakayali, and Marion von Osten, 207–9. London: Black Dog.

Le Bec, Christophe. 2014. "Les 50 qui font le Maroc: Miriem Bensalah Chaqroun." *Jeune Afrique*, January 16. http://www.jeuneafrique.com/134932/archives-thematique/les-50-qui-font-le-maroc-miriem-bensalah-chaqroun/.

Lefebvre, Henri. 1996. *Writings on Cities*. Edited by Eleonore Kofman and Elizabeth Lebas. Oxford: Blackwell.

———. 2003. *The Urban Revolution*. Minneapolis: University of Minnesota Press.

Lemke, Thomas. 2001. "'The Birth of Bio-Politics': Michel Foucault's Lecture at the Collège de France on Neo-Liberal Governmentality." *Economy and Society* 30, no. 2: 190–207.

———. 2002. "Foucault, Governmentality, and Critique." *Rethinking Marxism* 14, no. 3: 49–64.

———. 2007. "An Indigestible Meal? Foucault, Governmentality and State Theory." *Distinktion: Scandinavian Journal of Social Theory* 8, no. 2: 43–64.

Le Tellier, Julien. 2009a. "Accompagnement social, microcrédit logement et résorption des bidonvilles au Maroc: Une étude de cas; L'opération de recasement Karyan El Oued À Salé." *Les Cahiers d'EMAM*, no. 17: 55–70.

———. 2009b. "Programme villes sans Bidonvilles et ingénierie sociale urbaine au Maroc." In *Politiques d'habitat social au Maghreb et au Sénégal: Gouvernance urbaine et participation en questions*, edited by Julien Le Tellier and Aziz Iraki, 193–212. Paris: L'Harmattan.

Le Tellier, Julien, and Isabelle Guérin. 2009. "'Participation,' accompagnement social et microcrédit logement pour la résorption des bidonvilles au Maroc." *Revue d'Economie Régionale & Urbaine*, no. 4 (November): 657–82.

Leveau, Rémy. 1985. *Le fellah marocain: Défenseur du trône*. Paris: Presses de la Fondation Nationale des Science Politiques.

———. 1997. "Morocco at the Crossroads." *Mediterranean Politics* 2, no. 2: 95–113.

Lewis, Bernard. 2001. "The Roots of Muslim Rage." *Policy* 17, no. 4: 17–26.

Lockman, Zachary, ed. 1994. *Workers and Working Classes in the Middle East: Struggles, Histories, Historiographies*. Albany: State University of New York Press.

Lucas, Russell E. 2004. "Monarchical Authoritarianism: Survival and Political Liberalization in a Middle Eastern Regime Type." *International Journal of Middle East Studies* 36, no. 1: 103–99.

Luciani, Giacomo. 1990. "Allocations States vs. Production States." In *The Arab State*, edited by Giacomo Luciani, 65–84. London: Routledge.

Lust-Okar, Ellen. 2005. *Structuring Conflict in the Arab World: Incumbents, Opponents, and Institutions*. New York: Cambridge University Press.

Madani, Mohamed. 1995. "Les turbulances urbaines au Maroc." In *L'Etat et les quartiers populaires au Maroc: De la marginalisation à l'emeute; Habitat spontané et mouvements sociaux*, edited by Abdelghani Abouhani, 141–61. Dakar: Council for the Development of Social Science Research in Africa.

Maestri, Elena. 2012. "The Gulf in the Southern Mediterranean." In *Ideational and Material Power in the Mediterranean: The Role of Turkey and the Gulf Cooperation Council*, 1–9. Mediterranean Paper Series, German Marshall Fund of the United States. http://www.iai.it/sites/default/files/mediterra nean-paper_17.pdf.

Maghraoui, Abdeslam. 2002. "Depoliticization in Morocco." *Journal of Democracy* 13, no. 4: 24–32.

Makdisi, Saree. 1997. "Laying Claim to Beirut: Urban Narrative and Spatial Identity in the Age of Solidere." *Critical Inquiry* 23, no. 3: 661–705.

Malka, Haim, and Jon B. Alterman. 2006. "Arab Reform and Foreign Aid: Lessons from Morocco." *CSIS Press: Significant Issues Series* 28, no. 4: 1–95.

Mansion, Aurore, and Virginie Rachmuhl, eds. 2012. *Building Cities for All: Lessons from Four African Experiences*. Series 34. Nogent-sur-Mame: GLTN/ UN-Habitat and GRET.

Marsden, Richard. 1999. *The Nature of Capital: Marx after Foucault*. New York: Routledge.

Martín, Iván. 2006. "Morocco Wakes Up to Human Development." *Mediterranean Politics* 11, no. 3: 433–39.

Marx, Karl. 1992. *Capital: A Critique of Political Economy*. Vol. 1, *Capitalist Production*. Harmondsworth: Penguin Books.

Masoud, Tarek. 2015. "Has the Door Closed on Arab Democracy?" *Journal of Democracy* 26, no. 1: 74–87.

Massey, Doreen. 2005. *For Space*. London: SAGE.

———. 2010. *World City*. Cambridge: Polity.

Mayer, Margit, and Jenny Künkel. 2011. "Introduction: Neoliberal Urbanism and Its Contestations; Crossing Theoretical Boundaries." In *Neoliberal Urbanism and Its Contestations: Crossing Theoretical Boundaries*, edited by Jenny Künkel and Margit Mayer, 3–26. New York: Palgrave Macmillan.

Mbembe, Achille. 2003. "Necropolitics." *Public Culture* 15, no. 1: 11–40.

McFaul, Michael. 2004. "Democracy Promotion as a World Value." *Washington Quarterly* 28, no. 1: 147–63.

McGuinness, Justin. 2013. "L'évolution des médinas et la politique urbaine: Entretien avec Olivier Toutain (Kasbah Des Oudayas, Rabat, février 2011)." In *Médinas immuables*, edited by Elsa Colsado, Justin McGuinness, and Catherine Miller, 359–68. Rabat: Centre Jacques Berque.

McKinsey & Company. 2012. "Affordable Housing for All." World Bank Housing Finance Conference, Washington, D.C., May.

McMurray, David. 2014. "Center-Periphery Relations in Morocco." *MERIP Middle East Report* 44, no. 272: 22–27.

M'Hammedi, Mouna, and Khadija Karibi. 2012. "Des ambiances de la médina a la marina: La dimension sacrifiée des grands projets urbain au Maroc." In *Ambiances in Action/Ambiances en acte(s): Proceedings of the Second International Conference on Ambiances*, edited by Jean-Paul Thibaud and Daniel Siret, 353–58. Montreal: International Ambiances Network.

Michbal, Mehdi. 2014. "Tarik Senhaji: 'Le co-investissement est inscrit dans l'ADN de Wessal Capital.'" *Jeune Afrique*, May 15. http://www.jeuneafri que.com/10053/economie/tarik-senhaji-le-co-investissement-est-inscrit -dans-l-adn-de-wessal-capital/.

Milbert, Isabelle. 2006. "Slums, Slum Dwellers and Multilevel Governance." *European Journal of Development Research* 18, no. 2: 299–318.

Ministère de L'Economie et des Finances (MEF). 2014. "Tableau de bord FOGARIM—Aout 2014." Rabat. https://www.finances.gov.ma/Docs/2014/ DTFE/TB%20FOGARIM%20Aout%20%202014.pdf.

Ministère Délégué Chargé de l'Habitat et de L'Urbanisme (MHU). 2004. *Accompagnement social des opérations de lutte contre l'habitat insalubre: Guide méthodologique.* Rabat: Kingdom of Morocco.

———. 2012. *Résorption des bidonvilles: L'expérience marocaine; Rapport national.* http://www.abhatoo.net.ma/maalama-textuelle/developpement-econom ique-et-social/developpement-social/logement-et-habitat/programmes-d -habitat/resorption-des-bidonvilles-l-experience-marocaine-rapport-na tional. Rabat: Kingdom of Morocco.

Ministère de l'Equipement et des Transports (MET). 2011. "La stratégie portuaire nationale à l'horizon 2030." Royaume du Maroc, Rabat. http://www .anp.org.ma/Publications/Documents/Strategie_portuaire/StrategiePor tuaire_a_lhorizon_2030.pdf.

Ministère de l'Habitat de l'Urbanisme et de l'Aménagement de l'Espace (MHUAE). 2009. *Cadre d'orientation pour une stratégie nationale de développement urbain.* Rabat: Kingdom of Morocco.

Mitchell, Katharyne. 2006. "Neoliberal Governmentality in the European Union: Education, Training, and Technologies of Citizenship." *Environment and Planning D: Society and Space* 24, no. 3: 389–407.

Mitchell, Timothy. 2002. *Rule of Experts: Egypt, Techno-Politics, Modernity.* Berkeley: University of California Press.

———. 2004. "The Properties of Markets: Informal Housing and Capitalism's Mystery." Cultural Political Economy Working Paper Series, no. 2, Institute of Advanced Studies in Social Management Sciences, University of Lancaster. https://www.unc.edu/courses/2005fall/geog/160/001/GEC'05/2 mitchell.doc.

———. 2006. "Society, Economy, and the State Effect." In *The Anthropology of the State*, edited by Aradhana Sharma and Akhil Gupta, 169–86. Oxford: Blackwell.

———. 2011. *Carbon Democracy: Political Power in the Age of Oil.* London: Verso.

Moujid, Rahal. 1989. *L'Agence urbaine de Casablanca*. Casablanca: Afrique Orient.

Mouloudi, Hicham. 2015a. "La mobilisation des acteurs locaux en réaction aux projets d'aménagement des fronts d'eau de Rabat: Émergence de nouveaux acteurs et évolution des répertoires de l'action collective." *L'Année du Maghreb*, no. 12: 93–113.

———. 2015b. *Les ambitions d'une capitale: Les projets d'aménagement des fronts d'eau de Rabat*. Rabat: Centre Jacques Berque.

Nachoui, Mostafa. 1998. *Casablanca: Espace et société*. Vol. 1, *Genèse et mutations de l'espace urbain de Casablanca*. Casablanca: Najah El Jadida.

Naciri, Mohamed. 1984. "Politiques urbaine et 'politiques' de l'habitat au Maroc: Incertitudes d'une stratégie?" In *Politiques urbaines dans le monde arabe*, edited by J. Métral and G. Mutin, 71–98. Lyon: Maison de l'Orient Méditerranéen.

———. 1987. "L'aménagement des villes et ses enjeux." *Maghreb-Machrek*, no. 118: 46–70.

———. 1989. "L'aménagement des villes: Peut-Il prévenir leurs soubresauts?" In *Urban Crises and Social Movements in the Middle East*, edited by Kenneth L. Brown, 237–48. Paris: L'Harmattan.

———. 1999. "Territoire: Contrôler ou développer, le dilemme du pouvoir depuis un siècle." *Maghreb-Machrek*, no. 164: 9–35.

Najem, Tom. 2001. "Privatization and the State in Morocco: Nominal Objectives and Problematic Realities." *Mediterranean Politics* 6, no. 2: 51–67.

Navez-Bouchanine, Françoise. 1995. "Initiatives populaires et développement urbain au Maroc." In *L'Etat et les quartiers populaires au Maroc: De la marginalisation à l'emeute; Habitat spontané et mouvements sociaux*, edited by Abdelghani Abouhani, 99–120. Dakar: Council for the Development of Social Science Research in Africa.

———. 1997. *Habiter la ville marocaine*. Paris: L'Harmattan.

———. 2002a. "Evolution de la prise en compte de la dimension sociale dans les interventions en bidonville sous le gouvernement d'alternance." *Critique Economique*, no. 8: 285–301.

———. 2002b. "Fragmentation spatial et urbanité au Maghreb." In *La fragmentation en question: Des villes entre fragmentation spatiale et fragmentation sociale?*, edited by Françoise Navez-Bouchanine, 153–93. Paris: L'Harmattan.

———. 2002c. *Les interventions en bidonville au Maroc*. Rabat: Agence nationale de lutte contre l'habitat insalubre.

———. 2003. "Les chemins tortueux de l'expérience démocratique marocaine à travers les bidonvilles." *Espaces et Sociétés* 112, no. 1: 59–81.

———. 2004. "La maitrise d'ouvrage sociale (MOS) au Maroc: Une état des lieux." *Les Cahiers d'Al Omrane*, nos. 19–20 (September): 8–14.

———. 2005a. "L'habitat informel, ressource pour la fabrication de la ville?" In *Villes réelles, villes projetées: Villes maghrébines en fabrication*, edited by Nadir Boumaza, 547–59. Paris: Maisonneuve & Larose.

———. 2005b. "Organisation de la maitrise d'ouvrage social: Stratégies, objectives et taches." Rabat, February. http://www.ads.ma/fileadmin/AdsDocu theque/FrDocuments/ADS_organisation_.pdf.

———. 2007. "Le développement urbain durable: 'Best Practice' ou leurre méthodologique." *Espaces et Sociétés* 131, no. 4: 101–16.

———. 2009. "Evolution of Urban Policy and Slum Clearance in Morocco: Successes and Transformations of 'Social Contracting.'" *International Social Science Journal* 59, no. 193–94: 359–80.

———. 2010. "Public Space in Moroccan Cities." In *Colonial Modern: Aesthetics of the Past, Rebellions for the Future*, edited by Tom Avermaete, Serhat Karakayali, and Marion von Osten, 212–21. London: Black Dog.

Navez-Bouchanine, Françoise, and Isabelle Berry-Chikhaoui. 2005. "L'Entredeux des politiques urbaines et des dynamiques sociales dans les villes marocaines." In *Intégration à la ville et services urbains au Maroc*, edited by Claude de Miras, 43–96. Rabat: Institut National d'Aménagement et d'Urbanisme.

Nsehe, Mfonobong. 2013. "Why Morocco Is Attracting Foreign Manufacturers." *Forbes*, July 23. http://www.forbes.com/sites/mfonobongnsehe/2013/07/23/why-morocco-is-attracting-foreign-manufacturers/.

Ong, Aihwa. 2000. "Graduated Sovereignty in South-East Asia." *Theory, Culture & Society* 17, no. 4: 55–75.

———. 2006. *Neoliberalism as Exception: Mutations in Citizenship and Sovereignty*. Durham, N.C.: Duke University Press.

Ossman, Susan. 1994. *Picturing Casablanca. Portraits of Power in a Modern City*. Berkeley: University of California Press.

Ott, Jan C. 2009. "Good Governance and Happiness in Nations: Technical Quality Precedes Democracy and Quality Beats Size." *Journal of Happiness Studies* 11, no. 3: 353–68.

Ottaway, Marina, and Michele Dunne. 2007. *Incumbent Regimes and the 'King's Dilemma' in the Arab World: Promise and Threat of Managed Reform*. Carnegie Papers 88. Washington, D.C.: Carnegie Endowment for International Peace.

Oubenal, Mohamed, and Abdellatif Zeroual. 2017. "Gouverner par la gouvernance: Les nouvelles modalités de contrôle politique des élites économiques au Maroc." *Critique internationale* 74, no. 1: 9–32.

Owen, Roger. 2012. *The Rise and Fall of Presidents for Life*. Cambridge, Mass.: Harvard University Press.

Painter, Joe. 2006. "Prosaic Geographies of Stateness." *Political Geography* 25, no. 7: 752–74.

Panitch, Leo. 1998. "'The State in a Changing World': Social-Democratizing Global Capitalism?" *Monthly Review* 50, no. 5: 11–22.

Parker, Christopher. 2004. "Globalization and the Dialectics of Authoritarian Persistence: Complexes of Power and Contemporary Political Change in the Hashemite Kingdom of Jordan." PhD diss., Ghent University.

———. 2006. "From Forced Revolution to Failed Transition: The Nightmarish Agency of Revolutionary Neo-Liberalism in Iraq." *UNISCI Discussion Papers*, no. 12 (October): 81–101.

———. 2009. "Tunnel-Bypasses and Minarets of Capitalism: Amman as Neoliberal Assemblage." *Political Geography* 28, no. 2: 110–20.

Parker, Christopher, and Pascal Debruyne. 2012. "Reassembling the Political Life of Community: Naturalizing Neoliberalism in Amman." In *Neoliberal Urbanism and Its Contestations*, edited by Jenny Künkel and Margit Mayer, 155–72. New York: Palgrave Macmillan.

Paul, Darel E. 2004. "World Cities as Hegemonic Projects: The Politics of Global Imagineering in Montreal." *Political Geography* 23, no. 5: 571–96.

Peck, Jamie, and Adam Tickell. 2002. "Neoliberalizing Space." *Antipode* 34, no. 3: 380–404.

———. 2007. "Conceptualizing Neoliberalism, Thinking Thatcherism." In *Contesting Neoliberalism: Urban Frontiers*, edited by Helga Leitner, Jamie Peck, and Eric Sheppard, 26–50. New York: Guilford Press.

Pennell, C. R. 2000. *Morocco since 1830: A History*. London: Hurst.

Perrault, Gilles. 1990. *Notre ami le roi*. Paris: Gallimard.

Philifert, Pascale. 2011. "Les agencies urbaines au Maroc: Un tournant politique et professional?" In *L'action urbaine au Maghreb: Enjeux professionels et politiques*, edited by Lamia Zaki, 143–67. Tunis: Institut de Recherche sur le Maghreb Contemporain; Paris: Karthala.

———. 2014. "Morocco 2011/2012: Persistence of Past Urban Policies or a New Historical Sequence for Urban Action?" *Built Environment* 40, no. 1: 72–84.

———. 2016. "Urban Planning in Morocco: Historical Legacy, Approaches to Urban Policies, and Changes in Urban Planners' Roles and Practices, 1960–2010." In *Urban Planning in North Africa*, edited by Carlos Nunes Silva, 58–70. Farnham, Surrey: Ashgate.

Philifert, Pascale, and Michèle Jolé. 2005. "La décentralisation au Maroc: Une nouvelle dynamique pour les acteurs et les métiers de l'aménagement urbain?" In *Intégration à la ville et services urbains au Maroc*, edited by Claude de Miras, 363–99. Rabat: Institut National d'Aménagement et d'Urbanisme.

Pijl, Kees van der. 2012. *The Making of an Atlantic Ruling Class*. London: Verso.

Planel, Sabine. 2009. "Transformations de l'etat et politiques territoriales dans le Maroc contemporain." *L'Espace Politique*, no. 7: 1–14.

———. 2011. "Mobilisations et immobilisme dans l'arrière-pays de Tanger-Med: Effet des contradictions de la réforme de l'état." *Revue Tiers Monde*, hs (special issue), no. 5: 189–206.

Prahalad, C. K. 2005. *The Fortune at the Bottom of the Pyramid: Eradicating Poverty through Profits*. Upper Saddle River, N.J.: Wharton School Publishing.

Quandt, William B. 2004. "America and the Middle East: A Fifty-Year Overview." In *Diplomacy in the Middle East: The International Relations of Regional and Outside Powers*, edited by L. Carl Brown, 59–74. London: I.B. Tauris.

Rabinow, Paul. 1995. *French Modern: Norms and Forms of the Social Environment*. 2nd ed. Chicago: University of Chicago Press.

Rachik, Abderrahmane. 1995. *Ville et pouvoirs au Maroc*. Casablanca: Afrique-Orient.

———. 2002. *Casablanca: L'Urbanisme de l'urgence*. Casablanca: La Fondation Konrad Adenauer.

Rami, Mohammed. 2007. *Essai sur le déploiement du capital privé dans le secteur industriel au Maroc des origines a nos jours: Le modèle d'accumulation du capital en question.* Paris: Publibook.

Read, Jason. 2009. "A Genealogy of Homo-Economicus: Neoliberalism and the Production of Subjectivity." *Foucault Studies,* no. 6 (February): 25–36.

Ren, Xuefei, and Liza Weinstein. 2013. "Urban Governance, Mega-Projects and Scalar Transformations in China and India." In *Locating Right to the City in the Global South,* edited by Tony Roshan Samara, Shenjing He, and Guo Chen, 107–26. London: Routledge.

Resnick, Stephen, and Richard Wolff. 1987. *Knowledge and Class: A Marxian Critique of Political Economy.* Chicago: University of Chicago Press.

Rhazaoui, Ahmed. 1987. "Recent Economic Trends: Managing the Indebtedness." In *The Political Economy of Morocco,* edited by William I. Zartman, 141–58. New York: Praeger.

Richards, Alan, and John Waterbury. 2008. *A Political Economy of the Middle East.* 3rd ed. Boulder, Colo.: Westview Press.

Roberson, Jennifer. 2014. "The Changing Face of Morocco under King Hassan II." *Mediterranean Studies* 22, no. 1: 57–83.

Rose, Nikolas. 1999. *Powers of Freedom: Reframing Political Thought.* Cambridge: Cambridge University Press.

Rose-Redwood, Reuben S. 2006. "Governmentality, Geography, and the Geo-Coded World." *Progress in Human Geography* 30, no. 4: 469–86.

Rotenberg, Robert. 2001. "Metropolitanism and the Transformation of Urban Space in Nineteenth-Century Colonial Metropoles." *American Anthropologist* 103, no. 1: 7–15.

Rousset, Michel. 1992. "Politique administrative et contrôle social." In *Le Maroc actuel: Une modernisation au miroir de la tradition?,* edited by Jean-Claude Santucci, 151–69. Paris: Editions du Centre national de la recherche scientifique.

Roy, Ananya. 2005. "Urban Informality: Toward an Epistemology of Planning." *Journal of the American Planning Association* 71, no. 2: 147–58.

———. 2010. *Poverty Capital: Microfinance and the Making of Development.* New York: Routledge.

Royal Commission. 2003. *Parti d'aménagement global.* Rabat: Kingdom of Morocco. http://www.bouregreg.com/parti-damenagement-global-3/.

Ruccio, David. 2011. *Development and Globalization: A Marxian Class Analysis.* New York: Routledge.

Ruccio, David, Stephen Resnick, and Richard Wolff. 1990. "Class beyond the Nation-State." *Review of Radical Political Economics* 22, no. 1: 14–27.

Sarda, Pawan. 2014. "A New Generation of Real-Estate Developers Focusing on Low-Income Housing." *Private Sector & Development,* no. 19 (July): 5–8.

Sassen, Saskia. 1991. *The Global City: New York, London, Tokyo.* Princeton, N.J.: Princeton University Press.

Sater, James. 2002. "Civil Society, Political Change and the Private Sector in Morocco: The Case of the Employer's Federation Confédération Générale Des Entreprises Du Maroc (CGEM)." *Mediterranean Politics* 7, no. 2: 13–29.

———. 2010. *Morocco: Challenges to Tradition and Modernity.* New York: Routledge.

Schatan, Jacobo. 1987. *World Debt: Who Is to Pay?* London: Zed Books.

Schmitt, Carl. 2007. *The Concept of the Political.* Expanded Edition. Chicago: University of Chicago Press.

Schwedler, Jillian. 2012. "The Political Geography of Protest in Neoliberal Jordan." *Middle East Critique* 21, no. 3: 259–70.

Seddon, David. 1989. "Popular Protest and Political Opposition in Tunisia, Morocco and Sudan 1984–1985." In *Urban Crises and Social Movements in the Middle East*, edited by Kenneth Brown, 179–97. Paris: L'Harmattan.

Seddon, David, and Leo Zeilig. 2005. "Class & Protest in Africa: New Waves." *Review of African Political Economy* 32, no. 103: 9–27.

Sedjari, Ali. 2008. *Gouvernance, réforme et gestion du changement, ou quand le Maroc se modernisera . . .* Paris: L'Harmattan.

Sidaway, James D. 2007. "Spaces of Postdevelopment." *Progress in Human Geography* 31, no. 3: 345–61.

Singerman, Diane, and Paul Amar, eds. 2006a. *Cairo Cosmopolitan: Politics, Culture, and Urban Space in the New Globalized Middle East.* Cairo: American University in Cairo Press.

———. 2006b. "Contesting Myths, Critiquing Cosmopolitanism, and Creating the New Cairo School of Urban Studies." In *Cairo Cosmopolitan: Politics, Culture, and Urban Space in the New Globalized Middle East*, edited by Diane Singerman and Paul Amar, 3–43. Cairo: American University in Cairo Press.

Sklar, Richard L. 1979. "The Nature of Class Domination in Africa." *Journal of Modern African Studies* 17, no. 4: 531–52.

Smith, A. 2002. "Imagining Geographies of the 'New Europe': Geo-Economic Power and the New European Architecture of Integration." *Political Geography* 21, no. 5: 647–70.

Smith, Michael Peter. 1998. "Looking for the Global Spaces in Local Politics." *Political Geography* 17, no. 1: 35–40.

Smith, Neil. 2002. "New Globalism, New Urbanism: Gentrification as Global Urban Strategy." *Antipode* 34, no. 3: 427–50.

Soja, Edward W. 1980. "The Socio-Spatial Dialectic." *Annals of the Association of American Geographers* 70, no. 2: 207–25.

Springborg, Robert. 2011. "Game Over: The Chance for Democracy in Egypt Is Lost." *Foreign Policy*, February 2. http://foreignpolicy.com/2011/02/02/game-over-the-chance-for-democracy-in-egypt-is-lost/.

Stepan, Alfred, and Juan J. Linz. 2013. "Democratization Theory and the 'Arab Spring.'" *Journal of Democracy* 24, no. 2: 15–30.

Stiglitz, Joseph E. 2004. "The Post Washington Consensus Consensus." The Initiative for Policy Dialogue. http://policydialogue.org/files/events/Stiglitz_Post_Washington_Consensus_Paper.pdf.

Storm, Lise. 2007. *Democratization in Morocco: The Political Elite and Struggles for Power in the Post-Independence State.* London: Routledge.

Strange, Susan. 1996. *The Retreat of the State: The Diffusion of Power in the World Economy.* Cambridge: Cambridge University Press.

Swearingen, Will D. 1987. "Morocco's Agricultural Crisis." In *The Political Economy of Morocco*, edited by William I. Zartman. New York, 159–72: Praeger Publishers.

Swyngedouw, Erik, Frank Moulaert, and Arantxa Rodriguez. 2002. "Neoliberal Urbanization in Europe: Large-Scale Urban Development Projects and the New Urban Policy." *Antipode* 34, no. 3: 542–77.

Thiam, Bachir, and Faiçal Faquihi. 2013. "Fogarim: Les banques tirent la sonnette d'alarme." *L'Economiste*, no. 4070 (July 9). http://www.leconomiste .com/article/908701-fogarim-les-banques-tirent-la-sonnette-d-alarme.

Thomas, Frédéric. 2014. "Les syndicats du sud face au dérèglement néolibéral." *Alternatives Sud* 21, no. 4: 7–24.

Toutain, Olivier. 2008. "Bilan evaluation du dispositif d'accompagnement social dans les opérations de résorption de l'habitat insalubre: Rapport provisoire." Rabat: Al Omrane.

———. 2009a. "Bilan, enjeux et perspectives des dispositifs d'ingénierie sociale: Le programme villes sans bidonvilles au Maroc." In *Politiques d'habitat social au Maghreb et au Sénégal: Gouvernance urbaine et participation en questions*, edited by Julien Le Tellier and Aziz Iraki, 213–24. Paris: L'Harmattan.

———. 2009b. "Bilan evaluation du FOGARIM." Unpublished document in author's possession.

———. 2011. "Retour sur l'expérience d'accompagnement social des projets (ASP) de résorption de l'habitat insalubre au Maroc." In *L'action publique au Maghreb: Enjeux professionnels et politiques*, edited by Lamia Zaki, 169–82. Paris: Karthala.

———. 2014. "Involving Third-Party Partners to Finance the Rehousing of Morocco's Slum Dwellers." *Private Sector and Development*, no. 19 (July): 25–27.

Toutain, Olivier, and Virginie Rachmuhl. 2013. "Le programme 'Villes sans Bidonvilles' au Maroc: Un bilan social questionné dans un contexte urbain sous tension." In *Quartiers informels d'un monde arabe en transition: Réflexions et perspectives pour l'action urbaine*, edited by Pierre-Arnaud Barthel and Sylvy Jaglin, 91–108. Paris: Laboratoire Techniques, Territoires et Sociétés; Agence Française de Développement.

———. 2014. "Evaluation et impact du Programme d'appui à la résorption de l'habitat insalubre et des bidonvilles au Maroc." *Evaluation de l'AFD*, no. 55 (January). Paris.

Tozy, Mohamed. 2008. "Islamists, Technocrats, and the Palace." *Journal of Democracy* 19, no. 1: 34–41.

Tsing, Anna. 2000. "The Global Situation." *Cultural Anthropology* 15, no. 3: 327–60.

———. 2005. *Friction: An Ethnography of Global Connection*. Princeton, N.J.: Princeton University Press.

Tuquoi, Jean-Pierre. 2006. *"Majesté, je dois beaucoup à votre père . . .": France-Maroc, une affaire de famille*. Paris: Albin Michel.

Turner, John F. C. 1976. *Housing by People*. London: Marion Boyars.

United Nations Human Settlements Programme (UN-Habitat). 2003. *The Challenge of Slums: Global Report on Human Settlements*. London: Earthscan.

———. 2012. *The State of Arab Cities 2012: Challenges of Urban Transition*. Nairobi: United Nations.

———. 2013. *Evaluation du programme national "Villes Sans Bidonvilles": Propositions pour en accroître les performances*. Rabat: United Nations.

———. 2014. *The State of African Cities 2014: Re-Imagining Sustainable Urban Transitions*. Nairobi: United Nations.

United States Agency for International Development (USAID). 2007. "Projet de Gouvernance Locale—Maroc: Participation citoyenne à la résorption des bidonvilles; Management de la mission d'accompagnement social des opérations de résorption des bidonvilles au Maroc; Quelques repères méthodologiques."

Valbjørn, Morten. 2012. "Upgrading Post-Democratization Studies: Examining a Re-Politicized Arab World in a Transition to Somewhere." *Middle East Critique* 21, no. 1: 25–35.

Valbjørn, Morten, and André Bank. 2010. "Examining the 'Post' in Post-Democratization: The Future of Middle Eastern Political Rule through Lenses of the Past." *Middle East Critique* 19, no. 3: 183–200.

Valverde, Mariana. 2007. "Genealogies of European States: Foucauldian Reflections." *Economy and Society* 36, no. 1: 159–78.

Vanderelst, Vera. 2010. "Het stedelijke ontwikkelingsproject van de vallei van de Bouregreg: Een politiek-geografische kijk achter de schermen." Master's thesis, Ghent University.

Veltmeyer, Henry. 2011. "Unrest and Change: Dispatches from the Frontline of a Class War in Egypt." *Globalizations* 8, no. 5: 609–16.

Verdeil, Eric. 2006. "Marchés, lieux d'exercice et profils professionnels de l'urbanisme." In *Concevoir et gérer les villes: Milieux d'urbanistes du sud de la Méditerranée*, edited by Taoufik Souami and Eric Verdeil, 149–96. Paris: Economica.

Vermeren, Pierre. 2002. *Histoire du Maroc depuis l'indépendance*. Paris: La Découverte.

———. 2009. *Le Maroc de Mohammed VI: La transition inachevée*. Paris: La Découverte.

Volpi, Frédéric. 2004. "Pseudo democracy in the Muslim World." *Third World Quarterly* 25, no. 6: 1061–78.

Wallenstein, Sven-Olov. 2010. "Security and Freedom: Reflections on Foucault." In *Colonial Modern: Aesthetics of the Past, Rebellions for the Future*, edited by Tom Avermaete, Serhat Karakayali, and Marion von Osten, 188–205. London: Black Dog.

Walley, Simon. 2014. "Housing the World: Leveraging Private Sector Resources for the Public Good." *Private Sector & Development*, no. 19 (July): 2–4.

Walton, John. 1998. "Urban Conflict and Social Movements in Poor Countries: Theory and Evidence of Collective Action." *International Journal of Urban and Regional Research* 22, no. 3: 460–81.

Walton, John, and David Seddon. 1994. *Free Markets and Food Riots: The Politics of Global Adjustment*. Oxford: Blackwell.

Waterbury, John. 1970. *The Commander of the Faithful: The Moroccan Political Elite: A Study in Segment Politics.* New York: Columbia University Press.

———. 1991. "Twilight of the State Bourgeoisie?" *International Journal of Middle East Studies* 23, no. 1: 1–17.

Weber, Heloise. 2002. "The Imposition of a Global Development Architecture: The Example of Microcredit." *Review of International Studies* 28, no. 3: 537–55.

Weber, Rachel. 2002. "Extracting Value from the City: Neoliberalism and Urban Redevelopment." *Antipode* 34, no. 3: 519–40.

Werlin, Herbert. 1999. "The Slum Upgrading Myth." *Urban Studies* 36, no. 9: 1523–34.

White, Gregory. 2007. "The Maghreb's Subordinate Position in the World's Political Economy." *Middle East Policy* 14, no. 4: 42–54.

World Bank. 1981. *Morocco: Economic and Social Development Report.* Washington, D.C.: World Bank.

———. 1987. *Morocco CEM: Issues for a Medium-Term Structural Adjustment Program.* Washington, D.C.: World Bank.

———. 1990. *Kingdom of Morocco: Sustained Investment and Growth in the Nineties.* Vol. 1, *Main Report.* Washington, D.C.: World Bank.

———. 1997. *World Development Report 1997: The State in a Changing World.* Washington, D.C.: World Bank.

———. 2001a. *Kingdom of Morocco: Poverty Update.* Vol. 1, *Main Report.* Washington, D.C.: World Bank.

———. 2001b. *World Development Report 2000/2001: Attacking Poverty.* Washington, D.C.: World Bank.

———. 2002. *World Development Report 2002: Building Institutions for Markets.* Washington, D.C.: World Bank.

———. 2003. *Better Governance for Development in the Middle East and North Africa: Enhancing Inclusiveness and Accountability.* MENA Development Report. Washington, D.C.: World Bank.

———. 2006a. *Maroc programme villes sans bidonvilles: Rapport finale; Analyse d'impact social et sur la pauvreté.* Washington, D.C.: World Bank.

———. 2006b. *Project Appraisal Document on a Proposed Loan in the Amount of US$100 Million to the Kingdom of Morocco for a National Initiative for Human Development Support Project.* Washington, D.C.: World Bank.

———. 2011. *Poor Places, Thriving People: How the Middle East and North Africa Can Rise above Spatial Disparities.* MENA Development Report. Washington, D.C.: World Bank.

———. 2012. *Program Appraisal Document on a Proposed Loan in the Amount of Euro 227 Million (US$300 Million Equivalent) to the Kingdom of Morocco for a National Initiative for Human Development 2 Program.* Washington, D.C.: World Bank.

———. 2014. *Country Partnership Strategy (CPS) for the Kingdom of Morocco for the Period FY2014–2017.* Washington, D.C.: World Bank.

World Finance. 2014. "Capitalising on Casablanca." *World Finance*, October 27. http://www.worldfinance.com/home/news/wessal-casa-port.

Wright, Erik Olin. 2005. "Foundations of a Neo-Marxist Class Analysis." In *Approaches to Class Analysis*, edited by Erik Olin Wright, 4–30. Cambridge: Cambridge University Press.

———. 2009. "Understanding Class: Towards an Integrated Analytical Approach." *New Left Review*, no. 60: 101–16.

Wright, Gwendolyn. 1991. *The Politics of Design in French Colonial Urbanism.* Chicago: University of Chicago Press.

Wurzel, Ulrich G. 2009. "The Political Economy of Authoritarianism in Egypt: Insufficient Structural Reforms, Limited Outcomes and a Lack of New Actors." In *The Arab State and Neo-Liberal Globalization: The Restructuring of State Power in the Middle East*, edited by Laura Guazzone and Daniela Pioppi, 97–123. Reading: Ithaca Press.

Yom, Sean L., and F. Gregory Gause. 2012. "Resilient Royals: How Arab Monarchies Hang On." *Journal of Democracy* 23, no. 4: 74–88.

Zaki, Lamia. 2005. "Pratiques politques au bidonville, Casablanca (2000–2005)." PhD diss., Institut d'Etudes Politiques, Paris.

———. 2008. "Transforming the City from Below: Shantytown Dwellers and the Fight for Electricity in Casablanca." In *Subalterns and Social Protest: History from below in the Middle East and North Africa*, edited by Stephanie Cronin, 116–37. New York: Routledge.

———, ed. 2011a. *L'action urbaine au Maghreb: Enjeux professionnels et politiques.* Tunis: Institut de Recherche sur le Maghreb Contemporain; Paris: Karthala.

———. 2011b. "La féderation nationale des promoteurs immobiliers: la mobilisation corporatiste de nouveaux acteurs de la fabrication des villes au Maroc." In *L'action urbaine au Maghreb: Enjeux professionnels et politiques*, edited by Lamia Zaki, 255–85. Tunis: Institut de Recherche sur le Maghreb Contemporain; Paris: Karthala.

Zemni, Sami. 2013. "From Socio-Economic Protest to National Revolt: The Labor Origins of the Tunisian Revolution." In *The Making of the Tunisian Revolution: Contexts, Architects, Prospects*, 127–46. Edinburgh: Edinburgh University Press.

Zemni, Sami, and Koenraad Bogaert. 2006. "Morocco and the Mirages of Democracy and Good Governance." *UNISCI Discussion Papers*, no. 12 (October): 103–20.

———. 2009. "Trade, Security and Neoliberal Politics: Whither Arab Reform? Evidence from the Moroccan Case." *Journal of North African Studies* 14, no. 1: 91–107.

Zemni, Sami, Brecht De Smet, and Koenraad Bogaert. 2013. "Luxemburg on Tahrir Square: Reading the Arab Revolutions with Rosa Luxemburg's *The Mass Strike*." *Antipode* 45, no. 4: 888–907.

Zeroual, Abdellatif. 2014. "Modernisation néolibérale et transformation du profil des dirigeants des entreprises publiques au Maroc: Cas de La caisse de Dépôt et Du Gestion (CDG): 1959–2009." *Afrika Focus* 27, no. 2: 23–47.

Zriouli, M'hamed. 1998. "Urbanisation et gestion des crises urbaines: Stratégies d'intervention publique au Maroc." In *La problématique urbaine au Maroc: De la permanence aux ruptures*, edited by Mohamed M. Benlahcen Tlemçani, 229–49. Perpignan: Presses Universitaires de Perpignan.

INDEX

Aabar fund, 85
Abdali megaproject, 52
Abdeljalil, Omar, 262n7
Abrahamian, Ervand, 97, 99
absolute monarchy: Arab political
    change and, 38–40; national
    consensus ideology and,
    182–83
Abu Dhabi: investment in Morocco
    by, 137; Wessal Capital project
    and, 84–85
accompagnement social (AS), 217–18,
    221–24, 229–30, 236–39, 241–44,
    275n13
Accor, 107
accumulation: austerity and privati-
    zation as practices of, 104–7;
    biopower of capitalist expansion
    and, 177–81
Addoha company, 111
ad hoc urbanism: economy of
    appearances and, 147–48; uneven
    development and, 142–61, 251
administrative apparatus: anti-
    corruption campaign in Morocco
    and, 109–13; Bouregreg Valley
    project and, 131–36; Cities With-
    out Slums program, 214–17;
    deconcentration of state power
    and, 186–92, 201–3; depoliticiza-
    tion of socioeconomic problems

and, 235–39; executive agencies
    and, 192–95; governmental power
    and, 40–41; Moroccan reform of,
    56–57, 78–80; privatization in
    Morocco and, 74–76; ruling elite
    and, 101–3; social engineering
    mechanisms, 217–27; social policy
    programs and, 174–76; social
    unrest and, 67–70; of TMSA,
    149–50
advanced regionalization program: in
    Morocco, 188–92
Agamben, Giorgio, 266n11
Agence Nationale de Réglementation
    des Télécommunications (ANRT),
    106
Agence Nationale pour l'Habitat
    Insalubre (ANHI), 193–95, 207–9,
    214–15
Agence pour l'Aménagement de la
    Vallée du Bouregreg (AAVB), 17,
    19, 77, 91, 115; as autonomous
    agency, 131–33, 136–37; business
    model of, 144–46; establishment
    of, 124, 127–28; guiding principles
    of, 143–44, 249–51; as model for
    urban development, 149–50;
    powers of, 134–36; social impact
    of Bouregreg project and, 156–61;
    sovereignty issues and, 142; state
    relations with, 137–41

35–41; globalization and, 245–57; governmentality and, 181–83; Marxist analysis of, 117–19; media repression under, 261n3; neoliberal governmentality and, 167–76, 251–57; project-oriented neoliberalism and, 45–48; protection of capitalism and, 167; scholarship debates over persistence of, 34–35, 117–19, 260n1; slum securitization and, 23, 184–85; slum upgrading and, 23, 166–67, 243–44; social unrest and, 23, 56–57, 66–74, 167; urban control through, 185–86; urban development and, 20–23, 50–52, 91–92, 200–203

Axa, 107

Ba'ath parties, 61
Bab Al Bahr real estate project, 128–29, 140–41, 147–48
Bakkoury, Mustapha, 115–16
Bank, André, 31–33, 37
banking industry, 105–7
Banque de Paris et de Pays Bas, 63
Basri, Driss, 56, 273n24
Batatu, Hanna, 95, 97, 99
Bayat, Asef, 141
behavioral change: housing development and, 240–44
Beinin, Joel, 97, 99
Belfkih, Abdelaziz Meziane, 132
Benabdallah, Nabil, 212
Ben Ali, Driss, 99, 102–3
Ben Arka, Mehdi, 262n7, 262n9
Benhaddou, Ali, 99–100, 117, 264n2
Benhima, Driss, 60–61
Bergh, Sylvia, 174–75
Berriane, Yasmine, 173–74
Berry-Chikhaoui, Isabelle, 200–201
bidonvilles (oilcan cities): in Casablanca, 1–2; proliferation in Morocco of, 64–65, 209–12. *See also* slum upgrading
Biekart, Kees, 141
Bill, James, 96

biopolitics: capitalist expansion and, 176–81; governmentality and, 181–83, 270n13; neoliberal transformation and, 183–203; of slum upgrading, 227–44, 274n3; urban development and, 4, 11–12, 25, 167
Blair, Tony, 6
Bouabid, Abderrahim, 112
Boucetta, M'hamed, 112
Bouregreg Agency. *See* Agence pour l'Aménagement de la Vallée du Bouregreg
Bouregreg Valley project, 4, 16–18, 21–22, 52, 123–61; Al Saha Al Kabira phase of, 130–31; Bab Al Bahr/La Marina Morocco phase of, 128–29; class politics and, 249–51; economy of appearances in, 147–48; globalization and, 246–57; Gulf investment in, 137–41; imagineering in, 155–61; marginalization of traditional culture in, 152–61; political change due to, 141–42, 245–46; relational aspects of power and, 121; as roll-out neoliberalism, 58–61; royal influence in, 79, 132–33; segregation in, 155–61; state power and, 91, 126–42; as state within a state, 131–33; urbanism of projects and, 123–26; as urban spectacle, 150–51
Bouygues, 91, 107
bread riots of 1981 (Casablanca), 166–67, 184–86
Brenner, Neil, 134, 270n13
bureaucracy: anti-corruption campaign in Morocco and, 109–13; depoliticization of socioeconomic problems and, 235–39; *étatisme* and, 61; governmental power and, 40–41; Moroccan reform of, 56–57, 78–80; privatization in Morocco and, 74–76; ruling elite and, 101–3; social policy programs and, 174–76
Bush, Ray, 44–45

KOENRAAD BOGAERT is assistant professor in the Department of Conflict and Development Studies and member of the Middle East and North Africa Research Group (MENARG) at Ghent University.

www.ingramcontent.com/pod-product-compliance
Ingram Content Group UK Ltd.
Pitfield, Milton Keynes, MK11 3LW, UK
UKHW031130120325
456135UK00007B/213